ECONOMICS

Reality Through Theory

ECONOMICS

Reality Through Theory

WILLIAM C. BLANCHFIELD / JACOB OSER

Utica College of Syracuse University

HARCOURT BRACE JOVANOVICH, INC.

New York   Chicago   San Francisco   Atlanta

To

who endured the pangs of authorship.

ISBN: 0-15-518802-X

Library of Congress Catalog Card Number: 72-93332

Printed in the United States of America

ACKNOWLEDGMENT
For the illustration on page 21, adapted from GROSS NATIONAL PRODUCT: The Flow of Income and Expenditures in the United States, 1969. Copyright © 1970 by The Twentieth Century Fund, New York. Used by permission of The Twentieth Century Fund.

PICTURE CREDITS
Cover: John Zoiner. Page 10: top, Cities Service Company by Anthony Link; center left, Harbrace; center right, Standard Oil Co. (N.J.); bottom, Harbrace. Page 90: top, Harbrace by Jacques Jangoux; bottom, Harbrace. Page 174: top left, Daniel J. Ransohoff; top right, Harbrace by Jim Theologos; center, Harbrace; bottom, Grant Heilman.

PREFACE

Economics: Reality Through Theory is directed toward those students who wish to understand our economic system and how it causes or corrects poverty, economic discrimination, the deterioration of the cities, ecological imbalance, and other such problems.

The book is unusual in four important respects.

First, we relate theories to the students' own experiences and knowledge, whenever possible. Examples of this method can be seen in Chapter 3 in the discussion of consumption, saving, and investment; in Chapter 5 on the law of diminishing marginal utility; and in Chapter 7 on interpersonal comparisons of utility.

Second, we emphasize practical applications of the theories. To illustrate, in Chapter 5 we apply elasticity of demand to taxation, advertising, and government price supports in agriculture; in Chapter 6 we ask if pure competition really would produce lower prices than oligopoly or monopoly; in Chapter 8 we apply economic theories to the difficult problems of stabilizing the economy.

Third, we evaluate economic theories, analyzing their strengths and weaknesses. These evaluations are found throughout the book, and complete sections of evaluation appear at the end of Chapters 2 through 7.

Finally, we raise questions that are beyond the usual range of problems generally included in economics textbooks. In Chapter 2 we ask if military spending enriches or impoverishes us; in Chapter 4 we ask if consumer credit increases or decreases total consumption spending; in Chapter 9 we show how various levels of government permit or promote monopoly. We have not hesitated to be controversial. We do not claim to know the whole truth, nor do we expect agreement by all students and instructors on the positions we take. But we do hope that this book will stimulate lively discussions and a deep probing of theories and problems.

The book is designed for a one-semester course, although it may be used for two semesters, and it lends itself to a variety of teaching methods. The instructor could, for example, present the first seven chapters concerning theory and its evaluation and allow the students to present the nine problem chapters after the theory has been discussed. Or if the instructor prefers to present the whole course himself, he may follow the order of the book or reverse the order, with the problems presented first and the theory following. Outside current sources could be used to supplement the problems section. Indeed, each individual instructor may devise a method to suit his own requirements.

We have been helped along the way by several patient reviewers, especially William Baumol of Princeton University, who read the first seven chapters and suggested many improvements. Our wives read the entire manuscript and improved its style and readability. Marilyn Cooper of Harcourt Brace Jovanovich carefully edited the book and helped immensely throughout the entire process of publication from beginning to end. Susan Wladawsky of Harcourt Brace Jovanovich also contributed to whatever success the book may enjoy. We accept responsibility for any shortcomings that remain.

Finally we wish to thank our many students at Utica College. It is they who demanded that we provide them with answers to difficult problems or at least honest admissions of uncertainty.

WILLIAM C. BLANCHFIELD
JACOB OSER

CONTENTS

vii

 Microeconomics: The Individual
and the Firm   91

THREE Problems of the Nation's
Economy   175

ECONOMICS

Reality Through Theory

1

Introduction

If you took all the economists in the world and laid them end to end,
they still wouldn't reach a conclusion.
—*George Bernard Shaw*

Economics certainly is a controversial subject. Ask your friends what they
think of wage and price controls, unions, job discrimination, big business,
welfare programs, military spending, and foreign aid. You will get a variety of opinions and lively disagreements.

Why the disagreements? There are two basic reasons: first, a lack of
knowledge of how the economy works and what the effects are of different policies and programs; second, people have different, conflicting economic interests and social viewpoints.

In this book we address ourselves to both problems. We not only describe how the economy works, but also present the controversies that
involve different value judgments and social philosophies. We expect far
less agreement on the second type of issue than on the first.

Economics is one of the social sciences. It is social in the sense that it
deals with people living, working, and spending in a specific arrangement
called a society, and it is scientific in the sense that it has evolved reliable
methods for studying such people and such processes. While the methods of study in economics have reached a high level of sophistication,
there is still a great deal of disagreement among economists about what
to study.

With What Is Economics Concerned?

We might define economics as the study of the means and activities by
which people make a living. This study is applicable to all kinds of societies, including self-sufficient traditional systems exemplified by the Eskimos
and the American Indians a century or more ago, private enterprise societies such as ours, and socialist societies as in China or Soviet Russia. Our
interest in how people make a living is more concerned with social and (in
our type of society) financial relationships than with purely technological
questions. We are not concerned with the engineering problems of build-

3

ing an automobile assembly plant. Rather we are concerned with what determines whether an auto plant will require a great deal of capital and little labor or little capital and a great deal of labor. We want to know how the entrepreneur decides how much labor and capital to employ, how many automobiles to produce, and what price to charge. By analyzing such problems, we seek to discover how society allocates its productive resources to make the tens of thousands of different items that consumers wish to buy.

We might also say that economics is concerned with economizing. Economizing in the broad sense means using the available resources to the best advantage. But what is best? The answer to such a question involves opinions, value judgments, and decisions. Should we tighten our belts now, thereby accumulating wealth to invest in order that we may enjoy greater abundance in the future? Should we produce more books or more automobiles? Should we build luxury homes or modest apartments? Many such decisions are made through the working of a free, uncontrolled market; they can also be influenced by government. The tasks of the economist are not only to participate in deciding what goals we should strive toward, but also to determine the most efficient means of achieving those goals once they are decided on.

An economist, then, is an individual who studies the different ways to commit resources. These resources include land, labor, managerial skill, and capital goods. The decision to commit some resources implies a decision not to commit others; therefore, economics involves making choices to achieve some goals, such as maximum profit or maximum output, with any given effort.

While economists are in general accord as to the definition of economics, they disagree on what approach to take. Some economists prefer to study problems on a microeconomic, or small level, while others are more concerned with the problems of larger economic units, or macroeconomics.

THE MARGINALISTS AND JOHN MAYNARD KEYNES   The debate over economic stabilization (discussed further in Chapter 8) illustrates the differences between microeconomists and macroeconomists. In the midst of the Great Depression of the 1930's, Lionel Robbins, a distinguished British economist of the marginalist school, declared that "economics is a study of the allocation of scarce means among given ends." While few would question Robbins' definition, another distinguished British economist, John Maynard Keynes, formulated a theory on a macroeconomic level for dealing with the problems of the Depression.

Keynes studied the reasons why our economy was operating at less than full employment. In his famous book *The General Theory of Employment, Interest and Money,* Keynes took Robbins' definition a step further and investigated the allocation of resources for the nation as a whole. He extended the studies of the marginalist school to fit the severe problems that our economy was faced with during the depression years. Keynes was concerned with the problem of stagnation in the economy as a whole, and how such stagnation could be relieved in the short run.

The differences in views between microeconomists like Robbins and macroeconomists like Keynes occur because different problems are being studied. Microeconomists concentrated on the problems of the individual firm, such as determining what and how much to produce, how to produce it, and what price to charge in order to make the maximum profit. Macroeconomists are concerned with how the economy as a whole functions, why we sometimes suffer from unemployment, and how full employment and price stability can be achieved. These two views came into conflict with each other when the microeconomists concluded that the economy, if left alone, tended toward full employment, that government regulation should be at a minimum, and that wage rates should be free to move upward or downward to keep the economy adapted and adjusted to changing conditions. The macroeconomists came to different conclusions. They believed that the economy might suffer from chronic unemployment, that the government should play a larger role than in the past in promoting stability, and that changes in wage rates were not a good approach to achieve full employment.

These two viewpoints have been modified and reconciled to some extent over recent decades. Advocates of both approaches recognize each other's role and contributions and cooperate in the solution of problems. For example, the macroeconomist can tell us something about how to avoid a depression. A microeconomist can help an automobile manufacturer decide what price to charge for cars in order to make the maximum profit or, given the cost of labor and machinery, how much labor-saving machinery to use in a new plant.

EMERGING CAPITALISM AND KARL MARX   Capitalism is an economic system characterized by private ownership of the tools of production. In 1776 two significant events took place: James Watt invented the steam engine, thus beginning the industrial revolution; and Adam Smith published *The Wealth of Nations,* a study of the economic mechanism of a capitalist society. By the middle of the nineteenth century capitalism had been defended and praised at great length by the classical economists. But Karl Marx took a different view.

Unlike earlier socialist writers who had merely criticized capitalism, Marx asked a larger question—how does society change? Marx envisioned society evolving through slavery, feudalism, capitalism, socialism, and ending inevitably with communism. While the orthodox economists were building a base to explain capitalism, Marx was dissecting its parts and predicting its inevitable demise. "Bourgeois," or Establishment, economists were proclaiming a harmony of interests among all groups of people, continuing economic growth, and the justice of the existing distribution of income. Marx was emphasizing the class struggle, the idea that the private enterprise system was a barrier to further growth, and the unjust exploitation of workers by the capitalists.

Just as Keynes came into conflict with the marginalists, so Marx was in basic conflict with both the classical school of Adam Smith and the marginalist school that arose in the 1870's. Disagreement also arose between Thorstein Veblen and the marginalist economists.

THE MARGINALISTS AND THORSTEIN VEBLEN   Thorstein Veblen also dissented from the orthodoxy of the economic studies of his time. An unusual man of many social eccentricities, Veblen concealed a finely tuned mind behind an unconventional but reserved exterior. Armed with two doctoral degrees, one in philosophy from Yale and one in economics from Cornell, he undertook the study of the social and philosophical underpinnings of the society in which he lived. He was, along with Wesley C. Mitchell and John R. Commons, a member of the "institutionalist school" of American economic thought, which appeared at the turn of the century. While most economists of his day were studying the mechanisms of the marketplace, Veblen was asking fundamental questions such as, What are the social implications of the distribution of income? What are the inefficiencies that result when the goal of making money supersedes the goal of making goods? While the marginalists were refining the tools of economic analysis, Veblen was analyzing the motives behind economic decisions.

Some of the economists previously discussed have made contributions to the methods of analysis; others have asked broader questions of social significance. In order to more fully understand the conflicts that occurred between them, we must consider their different approaches more closely.

Types of Economic Analysis

MICROECONOMICS: RESOURCE ALLOCATION   Lionel Robbins, as we mentioned above, was a microeconomist. Microeconomists are mainly concerned with how a society allocates its resources to achieve a given goal. One of the ways that some societies allocate their resources is through a market system. A microeconomist studies the market system, particularly as to how the exchange of goods and services is made, the price that is arrived at, and the changes in price when underlying conditions change. The microeconomist also studies the individual and the firm to determine how much and why they wish to buy and sell and at what prices.

MACROECONOMICS: THE PROBLEMS OF A NATION   Both micro- and macroeconomics are concerned with scarce resources. The difference lies in how the resources are to be used. The microeconomist studies the individual in his quest for either maximum profit or maximum utility, whereas the macroeconomist studies the modern nation-state and its quest for a maximum or optimum national income. Thus it is the unit of study that distinguishes micro- from macroeconomics. In contrast to these two branches of economic analysis are the dissenting theories—institutionalism and radical economics.

INSTITUTIONALISM: SOCIAL ECONOMICS As the name implies, institutionalism is a study of the organizations that make a modern society work. It is premised on the fact that a complex organism cannot be understood merely by concentrating on one part. The institutionalists attempted to integrate the study of economic activities with the social and political reasons for such activities. The institutionalists were strongly influenced by the German historical school of economic thought. The chief proponent of institutional thought was Thorstein Veblen.

RADICAL ECONOMICS: THE ECONOMICS OF DISSENT Just as John Maynard Keynes and Karl Marx dissented from the orthodoxy of their time, so many economists have differed with their peers over present-day economic thought. Radical economists are upset with the ends for which economic reasoning has been used. They disagree that economic theory should be used primarily to increase production and not to better race relations, control pollution, and alleviate social unrest. One of the concerns of the radicals (and many other economists as well) is the unequal distribution of income, wealth, and power that occurs in many different societies. They are also concerned with what they call the misallocation of resources in both Western and non-Western societies, the discriminatory racial system in the United States, and the alleged inability of our society to protect the environment against pollution, urban decay, and unreasonable depletion of natural resources.

The radicals question the basic assumptions on which orthodox economic thought is based. In the following sections we shall see how these assumptions are formulated and what effect they have had on economic thought.

The Uses of Economic Analysis

Economists study the role of money and credit in our society and the role of taxes and spending and its influence on our national economy. Some study housing and its shortages or agricultural or urban problems. Most of them come prepared to study these problems with mathematical and statistical skills. The way they approach a problem, however, is distinctly different for each, depending on whether he is a normative or positive economist.

While both normative and positive economists may use the same analysis to arrive at solutions to a problem, they differ in the formulation of the solution. The normative economist sets out a list of policy directives to guide the makers of public policy, while a positive economist only states the alternative solutions and lets others decide what course to take. A normative economist is strongly oriented toward formulating policies and programs. He states what he thinks *should be*, whereas a positive economist states *what is*. Both may use the same body of evidence and the same analytical skills, and both the positive and the normative economists use a convenient and useful methodological tool—model building.

MODEL BUILDING—AN OLD TOOL IN A NEW FORM All the economists we have discussed used models in their analyses. A model is an abstraction of reality used to simplify a problem in order to better understand it. Some models are mathematical in form, that is, the relationships are cast in a series of equations. Others rely on words, that is, they describe a relationship without having precise quantitative weights for the variables.

All models stand or fall on their usefulness in describing reality. Some macroeconomic models have been very useful in describing the interrelationships between elements in our economy, such as saving and investing or government taxing and spending. In the following chapters we will be describing national income models, supply and demand models, models of international trade, and others.

ASSUMPTIONS All models in economics are begun with a discussion of the assumptions present in the analyses. One common assumption in economic relationships is "other things equal." The social scientist is not unlike his counterpart the natural scientist in his desire to formulate a rigid scientific analysis of the subject under study. The natural scientist may hold pressure and volume constant and vary the temperature in order to see its effect on the system. Similarly, the economist may hold such things as taste, income, and the prices of other goods equal as he analyzes the effect of a price change on the quantity consumed by an individual. Thus the economist makes the assumption of "other things equal" in order to isolate the effect of one variable on another.

Such shortcuts in economic analysis are not to be misconstrued as being easy ways to uncover difficult phenomena. The study of economic relationships implies that the system be held static while dynamic elements are changing. The implications of this will be more obvious when we begin studying supply and demand models.

Economics is heavily permeated with value judgments, with opinions about what is good and what is bad, what is better and what is worse. This is what the controversies have been about from 1776 to today. This helps make economics an interesting, challenging, and useful subject.

Summary

In Chapter 1 we have seen the unique role that controversy and disagreement have played in the development of economic theory. While some economists, called microeconomists, are concerned with small units of economic activity, others, called macroeconomists, prefer to deal with larger units. Still others have rejected these categories altogether and have concentrated on man's total activity, including noneconomic factors. These economists, particularly Thorstein Veblen, are called institutionalists. Their name is easy to remember—they studied man in relation to his economic and social institutions.

Other, more modern, dissenters are called radical economists. They believe that present-day economic theory is misdirected and does not deal with serious, contemporary problems.

Finally, there are a number of tools that economists use, which were mentioned briefly in Chapter 1. As you follow along through the analyses presented in later chapters, remember the discussion about model building and the role of assumptions in developing economic theory. Economics, like other disciplines, has its own accumulated logic and methodology, and beginning students, especially, have to be careful to understand the way the arguments are presented.

QUESTIONS AND PROBLEMS

1   Conflict makes economic decisions necessary; give an example of a present-day conflict in policy and explain what decision must be made to resolve the conflict.

2   Give an example of what you consider a misallocation of resources in our society today.

3   Explain the basic difference between microeconomics and macroeconomics. Which problem areas does each type of analysis concentrate on?

4   Do you agree or disagree with the assessment of American society made by the radical economists? Why or why not?

5   One's assumptions influence one's conclusions. What assumptions do you have about the economy of the United States?

6   What other disciplines use the assumption "other things equal" as a tool?

BIBLIOGRAPHY

BRONFENBRENNER, MARTIN, "Radical Economics in America: a 1970 Survey," *The Journal of Economic Literature*, Vol. VIII, No. 3, September 1970.

KEYNES, JOHN M., *The General Theory of Employment, Interest and Money*. New York: Harcourt Brace Jovanovich, 1936.

MANDEL, ERNEST, *Marxist Economic Theory*, 2 vols., trans. Brian Pearce. New York: Monthly Review Press, 1970.

PART

ONE

MACROECONOMICS:
THE NATION'S INCOME

A knowledge of macroeconomics can enable us to understand why the official record of economic growth is not a satisfactory measure of our increased level of living. We can learn about the causes of and the cures for depressions, such as the one we had in the early 1970's. Our personal decisions to spend more or less on consumption or to save more or less have an impact on the whole economy that will be examined in the following chapters. The mysteries of money, banking, and credit creation will be explored. Why do depositors no longer panic and make runs on the banks to get their money out as they used to? Are they living in a fools' paradise, or is their confidence in the stability of the banking system justified? Why have interest rates been pushed up to their highest level in several generations? How does the vast expansion of consumer credit since the Second World War affect the volume of consumer goods and services that we can buy? We shall answer these and other significant questions through our study of macroeconomics.

In order to understand our nation's income, it is first necessary to develop an accounting system to measure such income. Chapter 2 is devoted to this subject and includes discussion of the conceptual and measurement problems inherent in any accounting system.

Once the system is developed, we need to know how it changes. What forces, both on the product and monetary side, affect the nation's income? How do we change such forces to provide a smoother route for economic growth? What problems are there in the theory of national income? All these questions that are important in understanding national income are dealt with in Chapters 2, 3, and 4.

This macroeconomic approach (looking at the economy as a whole) is a useful type of analysis, but it is not the only type. In Part II we shall look at economic problems from the viewpoint of the individual, the firm, and the industry. That type of theory is called microeconomics, and it is useful for answering a different set of questions.

National
Income
Concepts

The whole history of civilization is strewn with creeds and institutions which were invaluable at first, and deadly afterwards.
                                                        —*Walter Bagehot*

The worldwide importance of national income accounting was indicated when the 1971 Nobel Prize in economics was awarded to Simon Kuznets, the major figure in the development of national income concepts. This branch of economics, which looks at the economy as a whole, is called macroeconomics. The national income accounts enable us to see how well the economy is doing, how rapidly it is growing, how the different parts of the economy fit together, how changes in income arise, and how consumers, investors, and the government can influence the nation's output and income.

The national income accounts are stated in terms of money. We cannot compute the output of apples and trucks and books and beer in any single, comprehensive, and meaningful figure except by adding up the price tags that all the items carry. The trouble with stating the nation's income in terms of money is this: if income increases, we are not sure without further investigation whether the increase is due to an actual growth in production or whether the higher income is due to higher prices without any expansion of production. The former case—an increase in output—is called a rise in real output and in real income. The latter case—rising income because of inflation, or rising prices without any increase in the quantity of production—we call a rise in money output and money income. As we shall see later in this chapter, it is possible to make an adjustment for rising prices; then "national income in constant dollars" can tell us by how much the actual output of goods and services has changed.

There are five major categories in national income accounting: gross national product, net national product, national income, personal income, and disposable income. We shall take a close look at each of these concepts in order to see how they are defined, how they are calculated, and

13

what they signify. This will prepare us in later chapters to analyze how national income reaches the level that it does, why it fluctuates, and how stability and growth can be achieved.

The Accounting System

GROSS NATIONAL PRODUCT   Production is the source of income; gross national product (GNP) measures the total market value of the goods and services produced by the nation's economy. The total output can be divided into three categories. First, consumers buy the largest portion of the output, recently a little less than two-thirds, for their own use; this includes both goods, like shoes and automobiles, and services, like those of doctors, teachers, and entertainers. The second largest component of GNP is government spending on goods and services, including federal, state, and local governments; this makes up a little less than a quarter of GNP. Government spending includes goods, like schools, post offices, typewriters, and guns, and services, like those of schoolteachers, senators, doctors in veterans' hospitals, and office workers. The third and smallest element of GNP is gross private investment, both domestic and foreign, which makes up about a seventh of GNP; this includes such things as office and factory buildings, machinery used in production, trucks, ships, and railroad cars. Table 2-1 shows how the gross national product has changed over the years and how it is divided into the three major categories.

When we defined GNP as the total market value of the output of goods and services, we had a major qualification in mind: we meant *final* goods and services, not intermediate products like steel, cotton, and leather. If we included all sales in GNP, we would be counting many items two or three times or more. If a loaf of bread is sold to a consumer for thirty-five cents, that sum is counted in GNP; but we do not count separately

TABLE 2-1   Gross National Product, Selected Years, 1929–1971
(in billions of dollars)

	Year					
Category	1929	1933	1941	1950	1960	1971
Consumption	77.2	45.8	80.6	191.0	328.9	662.1
Gross private investment	17.3	1.8	19.2	55.9	75.4	151.6
Government purchases of goods and services	8.5	8.0	24.8	37.9	100.1	233.0
Gross national product	103.1	55.6	124.5	284.8	504.4	1,046.7

Source: Federal Reserve Bulletin.

the price of the wheat that the farmer sells to the miller, the price of the flour that the miller sells to the baker, or the price that the baker receives for the bread sold to the grocer. All the above payments are included in the final price of the bread.

Adding up the prices of final goods and services gives us the same result we would get from totaling the value added at each stage of production. To derive the value added, we subtract from the selling price at each stage of production the payments made to other businesses that will report their receipts as part of GNP, such as the cost of raw materials, electric power, and freight transportation. Value added is shown in Table 2-2. We assume in the table that the farmer keeps the whole 5 cents for the labor, capital, land, and management that he uses in the production of wheat. We can see at each stage of production that the value added is the selling price of the goods minus the payments to other businesses.

TABLE 2-2   The Value-Added Approach to Gross National Product

Stage of production	Sales	−Payments to other businesses	=Value added
The farmer sells wheat to the miller	$.05	$.00	$.05
The miller sells flour to the baker	.10	.05	.05
The baker sells bread to the grocer	.25	.10	.15
The grocer sells bread to the consumer	.35	.25	.10
Total	$.75	$.40	$.35

NET NATIONAL PRODUCT   We can now proceed to the second category in the national accounts, net national product (NNP). NNP excludes something that is included in GNP—the value of the capital used up. Imagine that you operate a one-truck transport business. Your gross receipts for the year total $30,000, and your total out-of-pocket expenses amount to $20,000. You feel moderately satisfied, and you spend your $10,000 net receipts on personal consumption. What will happen? You may soon find yourself out of business. If your truck costs $21,000 and you expect it to last five years (after which it will be worth $1,000), then you have to earmark $4,000 per year of your receipts as a depreciation charge that will be used to replace your truck after it wears out. This $4,000 per year represents capital used up. Your net income is $6,000, not $10,000.

excludes capital [handwritten margin note]

In national income accounting, GNP minus capital consumed equals NNP. Capital consumption can be considered synonymous with depreciation of capital, although it actually includes a little more than that: ships lost at sea, trucks and railroad trains damaged or destroyed in accidents, assets wiped out in fires, floods, hurricanes, and earthquakes, and so on.

NATIONAL INCOME National income (NI) is the total earnings of labor and property from the production of goods and services. We subtract indirect business taxes from NNP to get NI. These are taxes that are passed on in higher market prices of goods and services. A sales tax, for example, is levied on the sales of the merchant, but he passes it on in the form of higher prices; it is the buyer who pays the tax. The excise taxes on whiskey and cigarets are paid by the manufacturers, but they in turn raise the prices of their products, and the final consumers pay the tax. Property taxes on business buildings and machinery are passed on in the form of higher prices for the products that capital helps produce. Even a tax on owner-occupied houses is indirect; it is passed on in the form of a higher estimated rental value of the house, which the resident of the house as a tenant pays to himself as the owner.

What kinds of taxes are direct taxes? Those which cannot be passed on to anybody else; the person who pays the tax bears the final burden. The national income accountants assume, whether correctly or not, that corporate and personal income taxes cannot be shoved onto someone else's back. Property taxes on household goods and land are direct taxes; so are taxes for license plates for automobiles not used in business.

Sales taxes and other indirect business taxes, therefore, tend to increase GNP and NNP by raising the prices of goods; but national income is not increased by such taxes, because they are subtracted from NNP to derive NI.

PERSONAL INCOME Personal income (PI) is the total income received by individuals from all sources. NI includes all items earned by and belonging to people, even though they may never see some of this income; such items must be subtracted from NI to get PI. But people also receive some income that they have not earned by contributing to production; these items, which do not appear in NI, must be added into PI. There are three major subtractions and one addition involved in computing PI from NI.

First, corporations pay income taxes to the government. The money they earn belongs to the stockholders, but the government soon takes a large chunk of it in taxes. This is part of NI but not PI. It has to be subtracted.

Second, corporations pay out part of their earnings after taxes to stockholders; the part they retain is called undistributed profits or retained earnings. These belong to the stockholders, but they cannot get their hands on it. It has to be subtracted from NI to get PI.

Third, social security taxes are subtracted from NI to get PI, because they never enter the wage and salary paychecks that employees receive.

Fourth, transfer payments are added to NI to get PI. Transfer payments are income payments to individuals that were not earned during the current accounting period. Veterans' benefits and old-age pensions are transfer payments. These people did earn the benefits they receive, but not during the current accounting year. Similarly, unemployment compensation and welfare receipts are transfer payments.

Interest on the national debt is also counted as a transfer payment to be added into PI. The people who developed this accounting system concluded that the government borrowed and spent the money in the past, most of it during the Second World War. (However, the growth of the federal debt since 1945 is about to exceed the growth during the Second World War.) Interest still has to be paid on that debt, but the money borrowed is not currently being used for production. New bonds are sold to repay old bonds that have matured. Therefore, interest on the federal debt is a transfer payment. Even if the government borrowed money to build low-rent houses or to hire doctors to serve those who cannot pay for such services, the interest would be a transfer payment. In contrast, interest on corporate bonds is a payment for money borrowed and put to productive use; it is not a transfer payment.

It is interesting to note that of all the government bonds outstanding, 42 percent are held by government agencies such as the social security system and the Federal Reserve banks; the rest are held by private investors. Therefore, almost half the interest paid by the federal government is really paid to itself.

Since 1965 interest paid by consumers has been treated as a transfer payment, as is interest paid by government; it is no longer regarded as reflecting current production. Interest paid by consumers is unlike interest paid by businessmen. In the latter case the money is invested to increase production. Consumer loans are made to increase consumption; although production will be increased, this is not the direct and immediate purpose of such loans. Interest paid on consumer loans is, therefore, excluded from personal consumption expenditure and is included in personal income as a transfer payment.

DISPOSABLE INCOME Personal income minus personal income taxes and personal property taxes leaves disposable income (DI), what people have left to spend on consumption or to pay interest on consumer debt or to save. Here one can raise an objection: social security taxes are not counted as personal income, because the individuals never receive the money; why, then, count personal income taxes as part of personal income when they are deducted in advance from the paychecks? There are two possible reasons why income taxes are included in PI. First, many people, including landlords, doctors, authors, self-employed craftsmen, unincorporated business owners, farmers, and receivers of dividends and interests, receive their income without any tax deductions. Second, this system of national income accounting was devised before the withholding tax went into effect in 1943. Prior to that date, employees received their pay with no income tax deductions, and in April they had to pay the previous year's taxes in a lump sum.

We spend most of our disposable income on consumption and interest payments, and what is left is called personal saving.

AN OVERVIEW OF NATIONAL INCOME ACCOUNTING   We shall now summarize the major categories of national income accounting and their interrelationships by presenting the statistics for 1971. Earlier we said that GNP is the total production of final goods and services valued at current prices. Table 2-3 shows the three major components of GNP: consumption spending, investment spending, and government spending.

TABLE 2-3   Gross National Product for 1971:
Spending on Final Goods and Services
(in billions of dollars)

Total consumption expenditures	662	
Durable consumer goods		100
Nondurable consumer goods		279
Consumer services		283
Total investment expenditures	152	
New construction		79
Producers' durable equipment		71
Changes in inventories		2
Net foreign investment		0
Total government expenditures on goods and services	233	
Federal		98
State and local		135
Gross National Product	1,047	

Source: Federal Reserve Bulletin.

Consumption is subdivided into three components. The first and smallest is durable consumer goods, such as automobiles, furniture, refrigerators, and other "hard" goods. The second component is nondurable consumer goods, such as food, clothing, shoes, fuel oil, gasoline, and other single-use or "soft" multiple-use goods. The third component is consumer services, which include such nonmaterial purchases as electricity, gas, telephone, transportation, rent, theater admissions, and repairs.

Investment expenditures in Table 2-3 are broken down into four components. New construction includes such items as factory buildings, barns, and dwellings. Producers' durable equipment includes all kinds of machinery, trucks, railroad cars, and so forth. Changes in inventories cover the changes in the goods held by businesses during the year. Net foreign investment is the part of GNP that was saved to be invested abroad.

Government expenditures in Table 2-3 include spending only on goods and services by all levels of government—federal, state, and local.

There is another way of computing GNP besides adding the total output of final goods and services. GNP also represents the earnings of the people and corporations who participate in production with their labor, their capital, and their land. We arrive at GNP by adding together all the incomes received by all employees, all unincorporated businesses, and all corporations, including the taxes they pay; we also add the value of the capital used up. We have to omit from the total any money received without producing anything, such as capital gains. If you buy a painting, a share of stock, a house, or land, and you sell this item later at a handsome profit, this profit is a capital gain—an increase in the price of the assets you hold. Nothing is produced in such transactions, and, therefore, capital gains are not a part of GNP. Similarly, inheriting wealth, finding money on the street, or receiving old-age, unemployment, or welfare payments from the government do not represent production and are not counted in GNP. Of course the receipt of money from these sources may induce you to go out and buy more goods, and your spending can cause production to increase, which means that GNP increases. But it is important to realize that it is not your receiving the money without producing anything that generated GNP; instead, it was spending your money on goods or services that increased GNP.

Table 2-4 summarizes this method of computing GNP by adding all

TABLE 2-4 Gross National Product for 1971: Factor Earnings and Other Costs of Production
(in billions of dollars)

Employees' compensation	642	
Unincorporated business income	68	
Farm operators' income		16
Nonfarm business and professional income		52
Profits of corporations	81	
Taxes on corporate profits		38
Dividends paid		25
Undistributed profits		18
Rental income of persons	24	
Interest income of persons	36	
National Income	851	
Indirect business taxes	101	
Net National Product	952	
Capital consumption allowances	95	
Gross National Product	1,047	

Source: Federal Reserve Bulletin.

the incomes earned in producing the output. Table 2-5 presents the five major categories of national income accounting for 1971. We have already discussed these concepts near the beginning of this chapter. Figure 2-1 is analogous to Table 2-5. The figure shows the circular flow of production and how it is disposed of. Each dollar of taxes and saving drains dollars away from the stream of income. But as these dollars are spent by government, investors, or consumers, the stream of national income is replenished and renewed.

TABLE 2-5   Gross National Product for 1971: Its Composition
(in billions of dollars)

Gross National Product (GNP)	1,047
Minus: Value of capital consumed	95
Net National Product (NNP)	952
Minus: Indirect business taxes	101
National Income (NI)	851
Minus: Undistributed corporate profits	
(corporate saving)	18
Corporation income taxes	38
Social security taxes	65
Plus: Transfer payments	127
Personal Income (PI)	857
Minus: Personal taxes	116
Disposable Income (DI)	741
Consumption expenditures	662
Interest paid by consumers	18
Personal saving	61

Source: Federal Reserve Bulletin.

In the left part of the figure, we see that GNP is fed by three streams of spending: the largest is personal consumption; then comes government spending on goods and services; and the smallest is gross private investment. We are left with NNP after subtracting the capital consumed from GNP. By subtracting indirect business taxes from NNP, we get NI, which is not influenced by rising prices caused by higher taxes. To compute PI from NI we have to subtract that part of the earned income that is not paid to people: taxes on corporate profits, corporate income after taxes that is not paid out as dividends (corporate saving), and social security taxes paid by both corporations and individuals. We add into PI the transfer payments made by government and the interest paid by consumers. After we deduct the taxes that people pay, we have reduced PI to disposable income: what people have left to spend on consumption, to pay interest on consumer debts, or to save.

FIGURE 2-1. *Gross National Product: The Flow of Income and Expenditures*

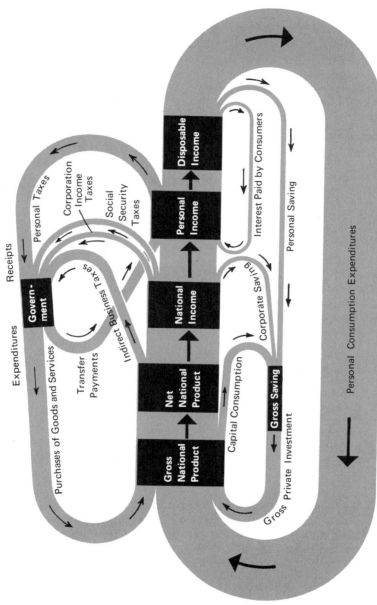

Source: The Twentieth Century Fund.

In the upper part of the figure, we see that the government (all levels of government) derives its funds from four different kinds of taxes: personal taxes, social security taxes, corporation income taxes, and indirect business taxes; these are in addition to any money the government might borrow by selling bonds and enlarging its debt. The money is spent on buying goods and services and on transfer payments, which include interest.

Immediately below GNP and NNP, we see the flow of saving and investment. Gross saving includes corporate and personal saving and funds earmarked to replace the capital consumed. These funds are used to finance gross private investment. The figure does not show the situation where saving may be used, not for private investment, but to buy government bonds to finance government spending beyond its income.

Now that we have reviewed the national income accounting system, we shall turn to the uses it can serve.

The Uses of National Income Accounting

ANALYZING THE FUNCTIONING AND GROWTH OF THE ECONOMY   National income accounting provides a barometer of the functioning and growth of the economy. Suppose we wish to analyze how well we did in 1970 compared with 1929. We find that in 1970 our GNP was $974 billion, while in 1929 it was $103 billion. In forty-one years our GNP increased $9\frac{1}{2}$ times. Does this imply that we were $9\frac{1}{2}$ times as well off in 1970 as in 1929? Not at all. We must make at least two corrections, allowing for changes in prices and in population.

To remove the effect of rising prices on GNP from 1929 to 1970, we have to know by how much prices have risen between these two years. The government's monthly publication *Survey of Current Business* tells us that if we look at the composite price index of the nation's total output, taking 1958 as 100, the price index was 50.6 in 1929 and 135.3 in 1970. Because we are comparing GNP for 1929 and 1970, we may take 1929 as our base year. The price indexes given above show that prices were 167.4 percent higher in 1970 than they were in 1929. Therefore, if we state the 1929 price index for GNP as 100, the 1970 index will be 267.4.

Now we can calculate the 1970 GNP in 1929 prices to compare the actual output of goods and services in the two years. We remove the effects of inflation by in effect tearing off all the price tags on the 1970 products and replacing them with 1929 price tags. By adding all the revised prices, we get a meaningful comparison of GNP in the two years.

We can eliminate the impact of rising or falling prices on GNP by using the following equation:

$$\frac{\text{GNP of year in question}}{\text{adjusted GNP}} = \frac{\text{price index of year in question}}{\text{price index of base year}}$$

The equation for the particular situation we are trying to analyze is:

$$\frac{1970 \text{ actual GNP}}{1970 \text{ adjusted GNP}} = \frac{1970 \text{ price index } (267.4)}{1929 \text{ price index } (100)}$$

We know that in 1970 GNP was $974 billion. The adjusted money GNP in terms of 1929 prices is what we are trying to find; we call that x. The price index for 1970 is 267.4, and the base year (1929) price index is 100. Our equation can now be solved:

$$\frac{974}{x} = \frac{267.4}{100}$$

$$x = 364$$

The real, or adjusted, GNP in 1970 in terms of actual goods and services produced was $364 billion, compared with $103 billion in 1929. Real GNP in 1970 was actually $3\frac{1}{2}$ times that of 1929 rather than $9\frac{1}{2}$ times, which was true of money GNP at current inflated prices.

Does this imply that in 1970 we were, on the average, $3\frac{1}{2}$ times as well off as we were in 1929? No. We said earlier that two major corrections had to be made, and we have not yet corrected for population changes. Population in the United States increased from 121.8 million in 1929 to 204.8 million in 1970. As the GNP in 1929 dollars was $103 billion in 1929 and $364 billion in 1970, the per capita income in 1929 dollars was $845 in 1929 and $1,777 in 1970. On the average, we were a little better than twice as well off.

Although national income accounting is useful in telling us in general how the national economy is doing, there are some things it cannot tell us. It says nothing, for example, about the distribution of income. Furthermore, it overlooks the changes in the quality of goods and services. A million dollars spent on medical care today probably produces much more health than the same sum spent in 1929. A record player that costs the same in 1929 dollars today as it did in the earlier year will give far greater satisfaction. These are the intangibles that are difficult or impossible to measure with national income accounting.

ANALYZING TRENDS OF VARIOUS SECTORS Besides providing a barometer of the functioning and growth of the economy as a whole, national income accounting helps us analyze the anatomy of the economy. If we had a laissez-faire society—a society in which there is a minimal role for the government in controlling the economic system—studying the performance of various sectors of our economic system would be of minor significance, because social and economic policies would not be used to influence the economy. If nothing is to be done to control economic activities, then a diagnosis of how the various parts function is of negligible practical importance. But we no longer have a predominantly laissez-faire society. The government, whether administered by Republicans or Democrats, is committed to influencing the economy to promote stability and growth. To achieve these goals, various trends have to be analyzed, and if these trends are unsatisfactory, they have to be neutralized or reversed as quickly as possible.

The national income accounts include such statistical series as industrial production, changes in inventories, consumer and wholesale prices, employment, average weekly hours worked, wage rates, personal income, consumer spending, residential construction, money supply and interest rates, federal government receipts and expenditures, exports and imports, and so on. By analyzing these statistics we can diagnose and even forecast the functioning of the economy and, if necessary, take corrective action. If, for example, investment spending is inadequate to maintain full employment and growth, the government can increase investment by offering tax concessions. If consumption is slackening, the government can lower income taxes or increase transfer payments. If consumption and investment spending are high enough to cause inflation or low enough to cause increased unemployment, the government can offset these effects by changing its own level of spending as well as by changing its rate of taxation. These matters will be explored further in Chapter 8. We shall now turn to consideration of the usefulness of the concepts we have explained in this chapter.

Is National Income Accounting Accurate?

ARE WE AS RICH AS WE THINK? Simon Kuznets, the 1971 Nobel Prize winner whom we mentioned at the beginning of this chapter, has criticized the present system of national income accounting, which he originated. National income, he says, is not a very good measure of our economic welfare. Its inadequacy is even greater if we use it to compare our economic welfare over the years and to compare our situation today with that of the less developed countries.

Nonmarket activities are excluded from national income, which makes our income appear to be lower than it really is. For example, housewives' services in the home are not included, nor are commodities produced by amateur gardeners, photographers, cabinet makers, and other people who practice such hobbies.

A second discrepancy has the reverse effect. The inclusion of what Kuznets calls "occupational expenses"—those that do not contribute to consumer satisfaction—inflates national income figures, thus making our income appear to be greater than it really is. We use cars to go to work, buy banking services because we are in a money economy, pay union dues, live in a city where rents are high. If we do not get personal satisfaction from these consumer expenditures, but rather have to incur them as a condition of earning our living, should these expenses be counted as a positive return from the economic system?

Kuznets concedes that the omission of nonmarket activities from national income and the inclusion of occupational expenses may partly offset each other. But over the years these two discrepancies both give an upward bias to national income. With urbanization, nonmarket activities shrink while occupational costs increase. Economic welfare over time, therefore, does not keep full pace with national income. If our real per capita national income doubles, it does not mean that our well-being has doubled. We simply count more production that used to be excluded from national income because people did it for themselves rather than for sale in a market, and our way of life becomes more expensive without increasing our satisfaction proportionally.

These same biases affect comparisons of national income between urban industrialized countries and agricultural underdeveloped countries. For example, there are a number of countries with average per capita GNP of less than $100 per year; among these are Burma, Nepal, Ethiopia, Tanzania, and Haiti. How do people survive at all with so little money? With such a low income in the United States, most of them would literally starve to death. While many do die of malnutrition and subsequent diseases, and most die earlier than they should because of deprivation, some people do survive. What is wrong with these international comparisons?

The answer lies in the fact that incomes are exaggerated in rich countries and understated in poor countries. Prices of the things poor people buy in underdeveloped countries are undoubtedly lower than in the United States, and money goes farther in poor economies. In addition, the value of things they produce for their own consumption is understated. The food they grow for themselves is unrecorded or underpriced. When a housewife in India bakes bread for her family, the value of the bread is excluded from India's national product. But the value of a loaf of bread purchased in a grocery store by a housewife in the United States is included in our national product. The clothing, housing, and recreation the people in low-income countries provide for themselves instead of buying in the market are not counted as part of their output. Part of the money they earn at odd jobs probably escapes the attention of the people who compile national income statistics, and payments in kind are even more difficult to discover and record. These views are not meant to deny that developed countries are much better off economically than those that are underdeveloped. But perhaps instead of being thirty or forty times better off on the average, as the per capita income statistics might indicate, they are only ten or fifteen times better off.

Government expenditures on goods and services are also a component of national income. The result of these expenditures, says Kuznets, has an even greater bearing than the items considered above on the question of whether national income is an accurate measure of welfare. How much government spending is an overhead cost of maintaining the social fabric —a precondition for net product, rather than the net product itself? To what extent does government activity represent the net final product? We classify all government activities that involve commodities and services (but not transfer payments) as yielding final products. Kuznets dissents from this view. He objects to treating the expenditure of a billion dollars on armament as equivalent in welfare results to a billion spent on food, clothing, and other direct means of providing for people's welfare. Even the costs of wars themselves, argues Kuznets, are related to the character of our social institutions. Thus an overwhelming proportion of government expenditures is an overhead cost of maintaining our social institutions, rather than a net return.

As a consequence, government activity gives an upward bias to estimates of economic progress if they are based on comparisons of annual figures for widely separated years. The same bias favors urban industrialized societies in comparisons with nonurban nonindustrialized countries.

Kuznets recommends instead that national income accounting should gauge the net positive contribution of the economy to certain ultimate social goals. He does not suggest that national income as a measure of economic welfare be discarded, but rather that national income concepts be developed further and handled more carefully and that the necessary data be collected.

ODDITIES THAT RAISE OUR NATIONAL INCOME If a woman divorces her husband and then works for him for wages, national income will rise. Payments within the family are excluded from NI, while payments for services rendered by people outside the family are included.

If I hire a neighbor to give my daughter piano lessons and she hires me to clean her house, income goes up by the payments we both receive; but if we exchange our services through barter without cash payments, we do not increase the nation's income.

If a steel mill pollutes the environment, no deduction is made from national income to offset part of the positive contribution to income that the mill generates. In fact, if the steel mill or the government installs a million dollars worth of equipment to curb pollution, the national income will rise by a million dollars.

Government subsidy payments to farmers are not called transfer payments; they are considered to be payments for the productive work that farmers do. Farmers get part of the compensation for their crops from the market and part from the government. Presumably, even when farmers get paid for not planting crops, they are being productive—perhaps by raising the prices of the crops that are planted. Government subsidies to farmers raised GNP and NI by $3.3 billion in 1970.

When banks render free services to checking account depositors, they are really paying a return on checking accounts in lieu of interest. The national income accountants therefore add to GNP and NI the "imputed interest" on deposits that the depositors do not receive in cash. In 1970 such "interest" amounted to $15 billion. This sum represents a cost of doing business in a money economy, and not any gain in economic welfare.

These oddities in national income accounting support Kuznets' contention that national income has certain deficiencies as a measure of economic well-being.

IS GROWTH OF NATIONAL INCOME NECESSARILY GOOD? One can argue that it is not necessarily true that a high and rising income means that people are well off and becoming better off. Growth is not always a good thing. Growth, with our methods of computing it, can come from calamities and catastrophes, from waste and destruction, from fire and flood and war fought on foreign soil. Does a hurricane destroy half a city or an earthquake shake California? As long as the economy is not fully employed, these events will have a favorable effect on GNP and NI through investment spending, and this growth in income will be only partially offset by the decline in the output of the productive facilities destroyed. Do rising numbers of people suffer greater agonies from cancer, emphysema, and automobile accidents? As long as there are unemployed people to fill the jobs of those who drop out of the labor force, these tragedies will enhance GNP and NI through greater consumption spending. Does the government spend over $500,000 to train a combat pilot and $20 billion to $30 billion a year to fight the war in Indochina? If those funds would not be spent in other ways, they increase GNP and NI. Income tends to rise with every breakdown of our automobiles and household goods, with every reusable bottle that is thrown away, with every road and street that deteriorates into potholes, with every frigid wind that increases the use of fuel. Only if our economy were fully employed without these wasteful expenditures would they add nothing to our income.

John M. Keynes, in his *General Theory of Employment, Interest and Money,* accepted wasteful spending as being preferable to unemployment, which it doubtless is:

> If the Treasury were to fill old bottles with banknotes, bury them at suitable depths in disused coal-mines which are then filled up to the surface with town rubbish, and leave it to private enterprise on well-tried principles of *laissez-faire* to dig the notes up again (the right to do so being obtained, of course, by tendering for leases of the note-bearing territory), there need be no more unemployment and, with the help of the repercussions, the real income of the community, and its capital wealth also, would probably become a good deal greater than it actually is. It would, indeed, be more sensible to build houses and the

like; but if there are political and practical difficulties in the way of this, the above would be better than nothing.

PRIVATE AND SOCIAL COSTS AND BENEFITS   Rising national income may also be bad if it leads to rising social costs. There is a branch of economics known as welfare economics that is concerned with, among other things, the discrepancies that arise among private and social costs and benefits. The private cost of a commodity or service is the expense the producer incurs in producing it; the social cost is the expense or damage to society as the consequence of its production. Private benefit is measured by the selling price of the product; social benefit is the total benefit society gets from its production.

These distinctions are significant, because in some cases social costs may be greater than social benefits, as with factories built in residential districts, child labor, pollution of the environment, excessive depletion of our natural resources, and the sale of dangerous drugs and medicines like heroin or thalidomide. There are opposite cases in which some benefits of private actions spill over to enrich society, while the person who renders the benefit is not compensated for it; then the social benefit exceeds the private benefit. For example, private investment in planting trees will benefit surrounding property owners. Preventing smoke from pouring out of factory chimneys will benefit the community at large much more than it will benefit the factory owner. Scientific research is frequently of greater value to society than to the researcher and inventor, although the patent laws aim at bringing private and social benefits closer together.

Industries whose private costs are low because they pass along some of the costs to society become too large. If they bore all the costs themselves, the prices of their products would have to rise, and they would sell less. Industries whose private profits are too small may remain smaller than is desirable for the public good. Thus we may have too much investment and employment in the industries producing automobiles, furs, advertising, and air conditioning, and too little in schools, hospitals, conservation, and pollution control. One conclusion which can be drawn is that the success of a business or the outcome of competition is not necessarily to the best advantage of society.

This type of analysis in terms of private and social costs and benefits can be applied to our vast military spending. The private cost is the sacrifices that members of the armed forces make in time and income and, indeed, in the loss of their lives. It also includes the corporations' expenditures in producing the military goods bought by the government. The private benefits are the military contracts handed out to businesses, the profits they provide, and the employment they make available. The social costs are the taxes we pay to finance military spending, the depletion of our resources, the diversion of funds from more useful projects, and the absorption of a large proportion of our brains and talents for basically useless activities. The Bureau of Labor Statistics of the United States Department of Labor calculated that in mid-1968 20 percent of the nation's engineers and 10 percent of its skilled and semiskilled workers were employed in military-related jobs. Defense and space projects occupied the talents of 59 percent of the nation's aeronautical engineers, 22 percent of its electrical engineers, 45 percent of its metallurgical, industrial, and chemical engineers, and 40 percent of its physicists. The social benefits of military spending are our security from attack, the establishment of more jobs than might have otherwise existed, and the spillover effects of people spending their income from defense contracts on consumer goods. The increased total spending is actually greater than the initial spending on military projects (this is the theory of the multiplier, which will be discussed in the next chapter).

On balance, do the social and private costs outweigh the social and private benefits of our military spending, or is it the other way around? To answer this question, let us consider only the economic, and not the political and military, effects of our military programs. We think the answers are clear and unequivocal: if the alternative to military spending is unemployment, military spending enriches us. But if the alternative to military spending is an equal amount of spending on useful things to meet our urgent needs, military spending impoverishes us.

We will return to further discussion of national income concepts later, after we have considered how national income fluctuates.

Summary

National income accounting measures the nation's total output or income. It enables us to compare the amount of growth between two years and the comparative state of development between different countries. While there are many pitfalls in such comparisons, they do have some usefulness.

This branch of economics is also concerned with the component parts of the nation's income. It can tell us what is happening to consumption, investment, and government spending. Any one of these sectors can expand too rapidly and cause inflation, or expand too slowly or actually shrink and cause depression. If such undesirable changes occur, something can be done about them. Therefore, underlying the concern with national income accounting is the conviction that the government can do something about stability and growth. If our government followed a laissez-faire policy, if we were convinced that nothing could or should be done to influence the economy, then national income accounting would lose much of its significance.

The nation's income is broken down into five major categories: gross national product, net national product, national income, personal income, and disposable income. This method of accounting enables us to trace what happens to total income or output and how much people receive and can spend on consumption, or save, or pay interest on their debts.

In this chapter we distinguished between money income and real income, and we saw how we can calculate real income. In our age of inflation, this is a significant correction to make in the raw national income figures as recorded in current prices.

Finally, our discussion of private and social costs and benefits raised questions that are becoming increasingly important as we become more concerned with the problems of our environment and its deterioration. The basic question is this: To what extent does a corporation's or a person's private economic activities help or harm society as a whole?

QUESTIONS AND PROBLEMS

1 Two identical products were produced in 1972. One is listed as consumption spending, the other as investment. Explain a possible reason for this. (There is more than one answer.)

2 Do you agree that all government spending on goods and services should be included as part of GNP and NI?

3 Some people have suggested that economic growth incurs more costs than benefits. Do you agree?

4 If you were given the task of revising our system of national income accounting, what changes would you suggest?

5 In Soviet Russia, the calculation of national income excludes the production of services, because that part of output is considered to be necessary but unproductive. This practice follows Marx, who agreed with the classical economists (including Adam Smith and David Ricardo) that the output of services is unproductive. What are the merits and demerits of excluding services from aggregate national income?

6 On page 28 the statement is made that "we may have too much investment and employment in the industries producing automobiles, furs, advertising, and air conditioning." What are the social costs of these industries?

7 Why does the government subsidize flood and erosion control?

8 What are the social costs and benefits of subsidized public housing?

9 How could we have a smaller national income and be better off? Or a larger national income and be worse off?

10 In 1958 GNP was $444 billion; in 1970 it was $974 billion. The GNP price level, taking 1958 as 100, was 135.3 in 1970. Calculate 1970 GNP in 1958 prices.

BIBLIOGRAPHY

CLARK, J. MAURICE, *Social Control of Business*, 2nd ed. New York: McGraw-Hill, 1939. (Originally published in 1926.)

KAPP, K. WILLIAM, *The Social Costs of Private Enterprise*. Cambridge, Mass.: Harvard University Press, 1950.

KUZNETS, SIMON, *Economic Change*. New York: Norton, 1953.

PIGOU, A. C., *The Economics of Welfare*, 4th ed. London: Macmillan, 1932. (Originally published in 1920.)

SHAPIRO, EDWARD, *Macroeconomic Analysis*, 2nd ed. New York: Harcourt Brace Jovanovich, 1970.

UNITED STATES DEPARTMENT OF COMMERCE, OFFICE OF BUSINESS ECONOMICS, *1969 Business Statistics, 17th Biennial Edition, A Supplement to the Survey of Current Business*, 1970.

UNITED STATES DEPARTMENT OF COMMERCE, OFFICE OF BUSINESS ECONOMICS, *Statistical Abstract of the United States, 1970*. Washington, D.C.: Government Printing Office, 1970.

UNITED STATES DEPARTMENT OF COMMERCE, OFFICE OF BUSINESS ECONOMICS, *Survey of Current Business* (Monthly publication).

How National
Income Changes:
The Product Market

Unemployment used to be concentrated among the less educated and less skilled workers. A few years ago a dramatic change occurred: unemployment appeared among professionally trained people. This reproduced on a modest scale some of the serious problems of the 1930's. What causes such fluctuations in our economy will be considered in this chapter. Fluctuations can be understood only if our theory is firmly grounded on the realities of our economic system.

Many of our current problems, such as pollution, poverty, and urban blight, are related to the same causes that produce fluctuations. In order to understand these problems, we must analyze how the economy changes.

These oscillations are more subdued than they were in the past. One reason for this improvement is that as we gain understanding, we can do something about improving the functioning of the system. While the current problems are serious enough, they are not of the magnitude of the 1930's. A basic tool for understanding the economy is the macroeconomic theory of how equilibrium income is determined and how it changes.

Income Determination and Income Changes

Every dollar spent on final goods and services becomes a dollar of income by bringing forth a dollar's worth of production. If you spend a dollar on beer, the production and sale of that beer generate income for the bartender, the owner of the tavern, the brewer and his employees, the truckdriver, the farmer who produces the raw materials, the railroad and its workers who transport the farm products, and so on. The total income will equal the total expenditures.

The total demand for goods and services is therefore crucial in determining total income. It is convenient to divide demand into three parts: consumption spending on goods and services to satsify people's wants; investment spending by businessmen and farmers who are in business to produce goods and services to sell at a profit; and government spending on goods and services.

CONSUMPTION AND SAVING   Most of the disposable income (income left over after taxes are paid) that people receive is spent on consumption. What they do not spend on consumption is considered saving; it is this saving, along with corporate saving (undistributed profits), that finances new investment.

Here we should pause to define saving carefully and thereby clear up a common misconception. If we define saving as disposable income not spent, we are wrong. The crucial characteristic of saving is that it is income not spent *on consumption*. It may be spent on investment goods.

Take, for example, a farmer who earns a disposable income of $10,000 during the year. He uses $6,000 of that money for living expenses and buys a tractor for $4,000. How much has he spent? $10,000. How much has he spent on consumption? $6,000. The $4,000 spent on the tractor is an investment and can also be considered as saving.

Of course you as an individual can save without buying investment goods. Suppose you receive $10,000 of income, you consume $6,000, and you save $4,000 which you deposit in your bank account. The banker will probably lend the $4,000 to a businessman, who will spend the money on investment; your saving, therefore, is spent, but not by you. In fact, most of personal saving is spent by people who did not do the saving. If the banker lends your $4,000 to people who spend it on consumption, then total saving is zero. What you have saved, the borrowers have spent on consumption.

Imagine income as a never ending stream. When we spend money on consumption, we feed the stream and maintain the flow. When we save, the stream shrinks, except that investment spending restores the volume of the flow. When total spending increases, the volume of flow in the stream increases; conversely, when total spending shrinks, the flow shrinks. Therefore, to analyze changes in the stream of national income, we must look at the major influences that determine consumption, investment, and government spending.

At different levels of income, people spend different percentages of their income on consumption. A hypothetical example is given in Table 3-1. Note that the lower the income of the imaginary family, the smaller the *amount* it spends on consumption, but the larger the *percentage* of income it spends on consumption; this often holds true in fact. A family with an income of $5,000 consumes $5,100; it "dissaves" $100 (spends $100 more than

TABLE 3-1   Hypothetical Consumption and Saving of a Family
at Different Levels of Income

Income	Consumption	Saving	Average propensity to consume	Average propensity to save
$5,000	$5,100	− $100	102%	− 2%
6,000	6,000	0	100	0
7,000	6,800	200	97	3
8,000	7,500	500	94	6
9,000	8,100	900	90	10
10,000	8,600	1,400	86	14

its income), perhaps by spending past saving or by going into debt. Thus this family spends 102 percent of its income. Conversely, the greater the income of the family, the more money it spends on consumption, but the smaller the percentage. Therefore, with such a consumption pattern, the larger a family's income, the more money it saves and the larger the percentage of its income that it saves.

The interrelationships among income, consumption, and saving can be illustrated in the following way. If

Y = income
C = consumption
S = saving
APC = average propensity to consume
APS = average propensity to save

then

$$Y = C + S$$

and

$$APC = \frac{C}{Y}$$

This means that the average propensity to consume is the fraction, or percentage, of total income spent on consumption. The average propensity to save is the fraction of income saved.

$$APS = \frac{S}{Y}$$

As the income we are considering is disposable income (income after taxes), consumption and saving account for all of it; therefore

$$APC + APS = 1 = 100\%$$

FIGURE 3-1.   Hypothetical Consumption Schedule of a Family
(in thousands of dollars)

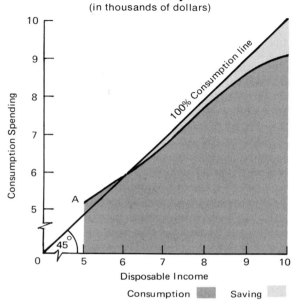

Source: Table 3-1.

A visual representation of the data in Table 3-1 is given in Figure 3-1. Point A in the figure indicates that at an income of $5,000, consumption will be $5,100, as the table indicates. If a family spends all its disposable income on consumption its consumption curve is on the forty-five-degree diagonal line in the figure. From Table 3-1 we see that the family with an income of $6,000 spends $6,000 on consumption. To show this in the figure we draw a vertical line upward from the horizontal axis at $6,000 and a horizontal line from the vertical axis to the right at $6,000. Both lines intersect on the forty-five-degree diagonal line, which shows 100 percent of income consumed. If at $8,000 a family spent all its income on consumption, the vertical and horizontal lines starting at $8,000 on both axes also would meet at the diagonal line.

In low-income families the consumption curve is above the diagonal line (as at point A), showing that the family then consumes more than 100 percent of its income. In higher-income families the consumption curve is below the diagonal, showing that some of the income is saved. As the consumption curve becomes less steep toward the right, it shows that the amount of consumption rises with higher incomes, but the percentage of income spent on consumption falls; both the amount and percentage of income saved rise with rising income.

How realistic is Figure 3-1? Is it true that the higher one's income, the larger the percentage saved? Figure 3-2 presents the actual statistics for 1960–61. We see that the consumption curve in Figure 3-2 is quite similar to our hypothetical consumption curve in Figure 3-1. We can accept the following propositions as being true:

$$
\text{As income rises}
\begin{cases}
\text{the percentage saved rises,} \\
\text{the percentage spent on consumption falls,} \\
\text{the amount saved rises,} \\
\text{the amount consumed rises.}
\end{cases}
$$

APC

In other words, as income rises, saving increases at a faster rate than consumption.

This principle describing the average propensity to consume with changing income once caused consternation among some American followers of Keynes. Known as the American Stagnationists, their gloom was understandable in the context of the late 1930's. Keynes, in his *The General Theory of Employment, Interest and Money*, wrote about the two afflictions of rich societies that ultimately stifle growth if the government does

FIGURE 3-2.   Consumption and Saving at Different Levels of Income, All Families, 1960–61
(in thousands of dollars)

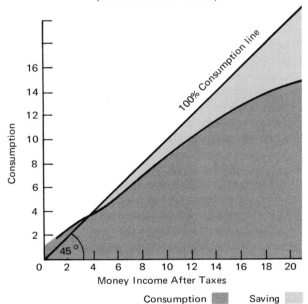

Source: *United States Department of Labor,* Handbook of Labor Statistics, 1969, *Bulletin No. 1630. Washington, D.C.: Government Printing Office, 1969, p. 331.*

not interfere and laissez faire prevails. First, the more capital we invest, the less profitable any new investment becomes; for example, a second railway from London to York, said Keynes, would not be as profitable as the first. Second, the richer we become, the lower the percentage of our income we spend on consumption. As our investment shrinks, we will pull out of the national income stream through saving more than we will put into it through investment and consumption spending. The growth in our wealth may therefore become self-terminating under a system of laissez faire. We have the Midas touch, said Keynes. The mythical King Midas of Greece was greedy (and foolish) enough to wish that all he touched would turn into gold. The wish was granted, and then his troubles began. His food and drink turned to gold, and he nearly starved to death. His little daughter came to console him, and when he stroked her head she became a lovely golden statue. The fate of Midas is indeed a dreadful prospect.

But Keynes and the stagnationists were wrong in at least one important respect: it is not true that as we as a society become richer over the years, we save a larger percentage of our disposable income. It is true in the short run that the richer an individual is, the higher his average propensity to save. But this is not true of our society as a whole viewed over a span of years. *As our real income has risen with the passage of time, the percentages consumed and saved have remained remarkably stable.*

Figure 3-3 represents the situation from 1946 through 1970. The horizontal axis shows our disposable per capita incomes in 1958 dollars. The vertical axis measures the per capita consumption spending in 1958 dollars. The forty-five-degree diagonal line represents the case where 100 percent of our income is spent on consumption. On the average, during the years 1946–70 we consumed 92 percent of our disposable income. Therefore, if a line is drawn below and to the right of the 100 percent consumption line, indicating the 92 percent level of consumption, the points representing consumption for each of the years between 1946 and 1970 fall on or near this line. We can see that although real per capita disposable income increased 62 percent from 1946 to 1970, the percentage consumed did not fall.

Why is it that at any one time rich people spend a smaller percentage of their disposable income on consumption than poor people, yet as we all become richer the percentage consumed does not fall? There are a number of reasons for this phenomenon. First, if the people around you spend $2,-000 a year on consumption, you stand out as an important and affluent person if you spend $4,000; but if at a later date everybody else spends $5,000 and you continue with a $4,000 outlay, you look like an impoverished failure. Consequently, you spend more. This is what Thorstein Veblen called "conspicuous consumption"—flaunting your wealth by trying to outspend your neighbors.

A second reason for the average propensity to consume remaining con-

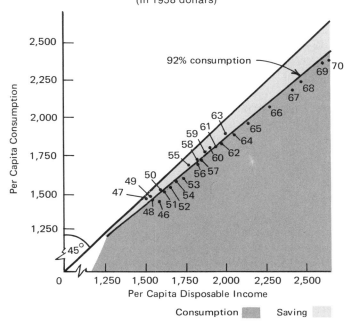

FIGURE 3-3.   *Per Capita Disposable Income and Consumption, 1946–70*
(in 1958 dollars)

Consumption ▓   Saving ▓

Source: Computed from Survey of Current Business, *Vol. 51, No. 7 (July 1971), p. 42.*

stant over the years is that more and more products are developed, and more and more advertising persuades us to buy them. It is much easier to spend large amounts on consumption now than it was in 1900.

Third, people used to be impelled to save more for a "rainy day" than they are now. With retirement benefits (modest as they are) built into the system, with government aid to higher education, with health insurance and unemployment compensation, we can increase our consumption without risking complete destitution later on.

Fourth, the expansion of consumer credit as our income rises enables us to raise our consumption proportionately with rising income. If we include interest payments as part of consumer spending (that is, disposable income that is not saved), then consumption spending rises with growing debt.

Yet the stagnationists had a valid basis for their pessimism. While the percentage saved remains constant as incomes rise, the amount saved rises. Therefore, ever larger investment is required to absorb the growing dollar volume of saving. If investment does not keep pace, we are likely to have unemployment, falling income, and reduced saving to match the limited investment. Massive government spending, along with other government measures to stimulate private consumption and investment, has been necessary to overcome tendencies toward stagnation.

SAVING AND INVESTMENT   When we speak of saving here, we are concerned with *actual* or *realized* saving and investment for any past period; in the next section we shall consider the saving and investment that people *plan* to achieve. We assume for the moment that there is no government and so no taxation or government spending. We should remember that by saving, we are pulling money out of the stream of income and causing that stream to shrink. By spending on investment goods, we replenish the income stream. We also assume that consumption is a stable proportion of income at each level, and if income is constant, so is consumption.

What do we do with the income we receive? We either spend it on consumption, or we save it. Therefore, if

$$Y = \text{income}$$
$$C = \text{consumption}$$
$$S = \text{saving}$$
$$I = \text{investment}$$

then

$$Y = C + S$$

How is income generated? By spending on final goods and services. Therefore,

$$C + I = Y$$

As a consequence,

$$C + S = C + I$$

or

$$S = I$$

This basic proposition asserts that (neglecting the role of government) *for any given period, saving and investment are equal.*

But of course this assertion seems implausible. One is tempted to try to refute such economic folly in this fashion:

> I receive $100 a week, and I customarily consume it all; the merchants lie in wait for me as I saunter down the street. But I am going to fool the merchants, the economists, the national income compilers, and the investors. I will withhold a $20 bill and keep it in my wallet. I won't deposit it in a bank, because if I did, the bank could lend it

out to an investor; then the economists can smugly proclaim that my increased saving is equal to someone else's increased investment. But if I keep the $20 in my wallet, where is the increased investment to maintain S = I?

The answer to that challenge is as follows. The merchants expected to sell you $100-worth of goods, and they built up their inventories in anticipation. When $20 of sales to you failed to materialize, their investment in inventory was $20 higher than they wished or expected. *Your $20 of saving are offset by an extra $20 of investment by the merchants.* They are not happy about this, because when sales are falling they are hardly eager to increase inventories. What can they do about this unplanned, undesired increase in investment? They can cut back on orders from the factories. Some people lose their jobs, some investors face reduced profits. As their incomes fall, their saving falls. Your $20 of increased saving are offset at first by an equal increase of investment and ultimately by reduced saving of others, because of lower incomes. This is known as "the paradox of thrift." If consumers seek to save a larger amount out of any given level of income, that attempt to save more *may* lead to an actual decrease in saving, because of falling income.

The paradox of thrift can be illustrated by this hypothetical example. Suppose this week our income is $10 billion, our consumption is $8 billion, and our saving and investment are $2 billion each. If next week we decide to spend $7 billion on consumption and save $3 billion, investors may cut their investment from $2 billion to $1 billion because the demand for their goods has shrunk. Total spending, and therefore total income, falls to $8 billion ($7 billion consumption and $1 billion investment). Since income is $8 billion and consumption spending is $7 billion, only $1 billion can be saved. Saving falls from the original $2 billion to $1 billion. Our attempt to save more has resulted in our saving less. This would not have happened, of course, if as we attempted to increase our saving to $3 billion, businessmen had increased their investment to $3 billion also. Thrift, which may be a virtue from the individual's point of view, may do harm to society if the consequence is falling income and reduced saving for others.

In the above example, the necessary equality between saving and investment can be seen from another view. *Anything the entrepreneur invests, society has to refrain from consuming.* Production generates income, but all of the capital goods that are produced are not consumed; investment is exactly that portion of income which society has saved.

If the banks expand credit when the economy is already at full employment, they generate inflation by creating additional purchasing power. From society's point of view, inflation will curtail consumption by people with fixed incomes; reduced consumption means increased saving, which will equal the increased investment. Any goods not purchased by consumers are considered to be investment in inventory. Who are the individuals who increase their saving as inflation develops? Those who gain from rising prices, such as debtors, farmers, and entrepreneurs. This is an example of "forced saving," of people unwillingly reducing their consumption because of inflation.

We will now introduce the government, thereby disturbing the equality between actual saving and investment. The following equations illustrate the interrelationships among income, consumption, saving, investment, government spending, and taxes.

We dispose of our income through consumption, saving, or paying taxes. Therefore, if

$$Y = \text{income}$$
$$C = \text{consumption}$$
$$S = \text{saving}$$
$$I = \text{investment}$$
$$G = \text{government spending}$$
$$T = \text{taxes}$$

then

$$Y = C + S + T$$

Income is generated by three kinds of spending: consumption, investment, and government. Therefore,

$$C + I + G = Y$$
$$C + S + T = C + I + G$$
$$S + T = I + G$$

Saving and taxes are what we pull out of the income stream; investment and government spending are what we pump back into it.

The last equation above can be written as

$$S = I + (G - T)$$

If government spending is larger than tax receipts, the budget is in deficit and $(G - T)$ is positive. Therefore,

$$S = I + \text{government deficit}$$

If government spending is smaller than tax receipts, the budget is in surplus and $(G - T)$ is negative. Then

$$S = I - \text{government surplus}$$

What do these equations mean? Suppose people save $2 billion. One billion is used for private investment and the other billion goes into government bonds to finance deficit spending.

S ($2 billion) = I ($1 billion) + government deficit ($1 billion)

But suppose the government runs a surplus of a billion dollars and pays off its bondholders; this sum can now be invested.

S($1 billion) = I ($2 billion) − government surplus ($1 billion)

Therefore, S = I only if there is no government or if the government budget is exactly balanced. Otherwise, saving plus taxes equal investment plus government spending.

EQUILIBRIUM NATIONAL INCOME   The word *equilibrium* means in balance. Equilibrium national income means that national income is neither falling nor rising. For example, excluding government, if saving exceeds investment, we are pulling more out of the economy than we are putting back in, and income falls. When income falls to the point where saving is at the same level as investment, equilibrium is reached. Conversely, if investment exceeds saving, we are pumping more into the economy than we are draining off, and income rises. As income goes up, saving goes up, and equilibrium is attained when S = I.

At this point you are probably muttering a protest. Didn't we just go to great lengths to show that actual saving and investment are always equal? Why do we suddenly admit that they may not be equal? The answer lies in the very important distinction between *actual* and *planned* saving and investment. As most planned saving and investment are done by different people, it would be a rare coincidence that they would be exactly equal. It is the inequality between planned saving and investment that results in those changes in income that produce the required equality between actual saving and investment.

These relationships and the movement toward equilibrium are illustrated in Table 3-2. We assume that all income up to $400 billion is spent on consumption. Of any income above that, 70 percent is spent on consumption and 30 percent is saved. We also assume that businessmen wish to invest $60 billion regardless of the level of income. If income were $400

TABLE 3-2   How Equilibrium Income Is Attained
(in billions of dollars)

Income	Planned consumption	Planned saving	Planned investment	New income C + I	Result
400	400	0	60	460	income rising
500	470	30	60	530	income rising
600	540	60	60	600	EQUILIBRIUM
700	610	90	60	670	income falling
800	680	120	60	740	income falling

billion, people would intend to consume it all and save nothing. Investors would plan to invest $60 billion. If consumption and investment total $460 billion, income cannot be maintained at $400 billion, and it must rise.

But if income were at $800 billion, planned consumption would be $680 billion, planned saving would be $120 billion, and planned investment would be $60 billion. As total consumption plus investment add up to $740 billion, income cannot be maintained at $800 billion, and it will fall.

In our example, $600 billion would be the equilibrium income. At that level planned saving and investment are equal, and total planned consumption plus investment spending equals income.

Figure 3-4 is a visual presentation of Table 3-2. Intersections with the forty-five-degree diagonal line represent points of equilibrium, because on the forty-five-degree line the vertical and horizontal coordinates are equal; this means that total spending on final goods and services equals total income.

FIGURE 3-4.   How Equilibrium Income Is Attained
(in billions of dollars)

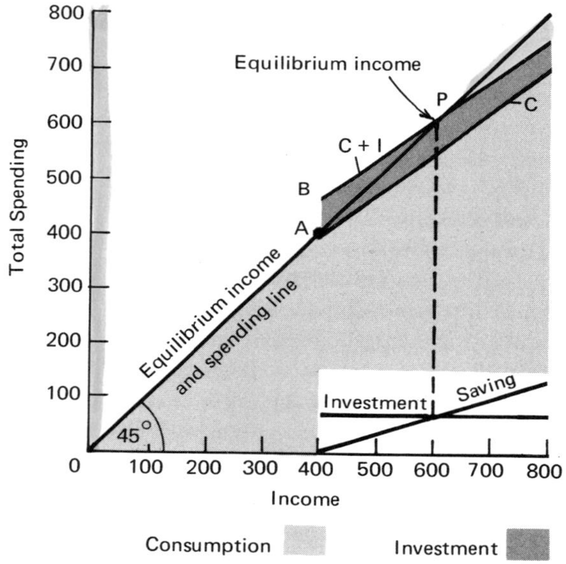

Source: Table 3-2.

Line C represents the consumption for different levels of income. At an income of $400 billion (point A), if there were no investment, line C would represent total demand, and income could not rise. With investment of $60 billion, line C + I represents total demand, and the equilibrium income is $600 billion (point P). At any income lower than the equilibrium level, planned consumption plus investment exceeds income. For example,

at an income of $400 billion, C+I is given by point B, which lies above in-
come level A; thus income must rise. At any income higher than the equilibrium level, C+I falls short of income, and income must fall. Thus point
P, the intersection between the total demand line (C+I) and the forty-
five-degree equilibrium income and spending line, represents the only sus-
tainable level of income. Starting from any other income level, the income
will either rise or fall in the direction of point P. That is the sense in which
P is described as the "equilibrium" point.

This is also confirmed by saving-investment analysis. Note that in the
lower right portion of the figure, planned saving and investment are equal
at $600 billion of income—the equilibrium income level.

Now we shall bring government into the models we are constructing.
Table 3-3 is based on Table 3-2 with some additional assumptions. We pos-
tulate that taxes are $70 billion at all levels of income, and they all come
out of consumption; therefore, the planned consumption column in Table
3-3 is exactly $70 billion less than the planned consumption column in
Table 3-2. Planned saving remains the same, and so does planned investment. We assume that government spending is $100 billion at all levels of
income.

TABLE 3-3   Equilibrium Income Including Government
(in billions of dollars)

In-come	Planned consump-tion	Taxes	Planned saving	S+T	Planned invest-ment	G	I+G	New income C+I+G	Result
400	330	70	0	70	60	100	160	490	income rising
500	400	70	30	100	60	100	160	560	income rising
600	470	70	60	130	60	100	160	630	income rising
700	540	70	90	160	60	100	160	700	EQUILIBRIUM
800	610	70	120	190	60	100	160	770	income falling

Source: Table 3-2.

If income were at $400 billion, planned consumption plus investment
plus government spending would add up to $490 billion, and income must
rise. In other words, at $400 billion income, what we try to pull out of the
economy (S+T=$70 billion) is less than what we wish to put into the
economy (I+G=$160 billion), and income will rise.

If income were at $800 billion, total planned spending (C+I+G)
would add up to $770 billion, and income would fall. At an income of $800
billion, S+T=$190 billion and I+G=$160 billion, and the stream of income must shrink.

At $700 billion income, equilibrium is reached. Saving plus taxes are equal to investment plus government spending, and consumption plus investment plus government spending are equal to income.

Figure 3-5 presents the data of Table 3-3 in visual form. It shows that equilibrium is reached where $S+T=I+G$, and where $C+I+G=$equilibrium income at \$700 billion.

FIGURE 3-5.   *Equilibrium Income Including Government*
(in billions of dollars)

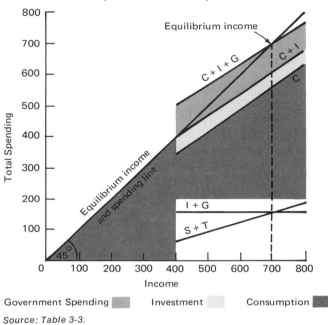

Source: Table 3-3.

THE THEORY OF THE MULTIPLIER   From the preceding discussion it is clear that the amount of private investment and government expenditure affects the equilibrium level of income. But by how much? The theory of the multiplier is designed to answer the question, If there is a change in investment or government spending, what will be the total effect on income? We will see that if spending changes, income is likely to change by a multiple of the initial change. Spending, and hence income, can, of course, move either upward or downward.

To analyze how the multiplier works, we shall introduce a new concept: the *marginal propensity to consume* (MPC). If there is an increase or decrease in income, consumption will change by a fraction of that change in income. If income increases by one dollar and consumption increases by 75 cents, the marginal propensity to consume is then defined as ¾, or 75 percent. If with an increased income of a dollar, consumption goes up 80 cents, MPC is ⁸⁄₁₀, or 80 percent. More generally,

$$MPC = \frac{\text{Change in consumption (C)}}{\text{Change in income (Y)}}$$

Similarly, the marginal propensity to save (MPS) is defined as the change in saving expressed as a fraction or percentage of any change in income. If income increases by one dollar and saving increases by 25 cents, MPS equals $\frac{1}{4}$, or 25 percent. If with an increased income of a dollar, saving goes up 20 cents, MPS equals $\frac{1}{5}$, or 20 percent.

Disposable income by definition can only be saved or consumed. That is, if income goes up by a dollar and 83 cents of it is spent on consumption, 17 cents must be added to saving. Thus it follows that

$$MPC + MPS = 100\%$$

To elucidate these concepts further, we utilize Table 3-4, which reproduces Table 3-1 with two columns added. We see that if income goes from $5,000 to $6,000, consumption goes from $5,100 to $6,000. This extra $900 of consumption resulting from an extra $1,000 of income means that MPC is $\frac{9}{10}$, or 90 percent. Since saving increases by $100 at the same time (going from minus $100 to zero), MPS is $\frac{1}{10}$, or 10 percent. If income goes from $6,000 to $7,000, consumption increases $800 and saving increases $200. Therefore MPC = 80 percent and MPS = 20 percent.

TABLE 3-4   Average and Marginal Propensity to Consume and Save

Income	Consumption	Saving	APC	APS	MPC	MPS
$5,000	$5,100	−$100	102%	−2%		
6,000	6,000	0	100	0	90%	10%
7,000	6,800	200	97	3	80	20
8,000	7,500	500	94	6	70	30
9,000	8,100	900	90	10	60	40
10,000	8,600	1,400	86	14	50	50

Now we have a clue as to why there is a multiplier, that is, why a given increase in expenditure produces a larger increase in income. If investment or government spending goes up by a dollar, income goes up by a dollar. If MPC is 75 percent, when income goes up by a dollar, consumption goes up by 75 cents; that raises income another 75 cents. By now the initial dollar of expenditure will have raised income by $1.75. And so it goes in successive rounds of increased income, increased consumption, and further increases of income, until the multiplier effect peters out due to increased saving.

Table 3-5 illustrates how the multiplier works. It is convenient to define a period that is a time interval during which income is received but not spent. We can call it a "day." That is, income received in period 1 cannot be spent that "day," but it can be spent in period 2.

TABLE 3-5   The Multiplier, Assuming MPC = 75%
(in dollars)

Period	1	2	3	4	5	6	7	After seven periods		
								Increased income	Increased consumption	Increased saving
1	$1.00	.75	.56	.42	.32	.24	.18	3.47	2.47	1.00
2		1.00	.75	.56	.42	.32	.24			
3			1.00	.75	.56	.42	.32			
4				1.00	.75	.56	.42			
5					1.00	.75	.56			
6						1.00	.75			
7							1.00			

7th period: Increased income 3.47
Increased consumption 2.47
Increased saving 1.00

Let us now consider the first line of Table 3-5. In period 1 investment or government spending increases by one dollar. As spending generates income, that increases income by one dollar. As a consequence, as MPC is 75 percent, consumption increases by 75 cents in period 2, and income goes up by that amount. MPS is 25 percent, and 25 cents is saved in period 2. The further effect of the increase of income in period 2 is that in period 3 consumption goes up by 75 percent of 75 cents, or 56 cents, and that represents the next increase in income. Twenty-five percent of 75 cents, or 19 cents, is saved. In each period, consumption rises by 75 percent of the increased income of the previous period, and saving rises by 25 percent.

At the end of seven periods, in the first line of the table, we see that income rose by $3.47, consumption rose by $2.47, and saving rose by $1.00. This result is obtained because we ended after the seventh period, and we counted the 18 cents of increased income as all saved. If we carried the table beyond seven periods, we would divide the 18 cents between 14 cents of consumption and 4 cents of saving, and so on. If we extended the table through about fifteen periods, we would find that the original dollar of increased spending would result in a total of 4 dollars of increased income, 3 dollars of increased consumption, and one dollar of increased saving. When the extra dollar injected into the income stream at the beginning period is pulled out in the form of saving, there are no further increases in income.

The multiplier measures the effect of an initial change in spending on total income. In the example given above, the multiplier is 4, because an increase of spending of one dollar resulted in increased income of 4 dollars. The higher the marginal propensity to consume (and therefore the lower the marginal propensity to save), the greater the multiplier. If the marginal propensity to consume is $9/10$, an increase in income of a dollar will result in 90 cents being spent on consumption in the next round of spending, and the multiplier will be 10. If the marginal propensity to consume is $1/2$, a dollar increase in income will result in an increase in consumption and income of 50 cents in the next round of spending, and the multiplier will be 2.

The size of the multiplier is equal to the reciprocal of the marginal propensity to save. If MPS is $1/10$, the multiplier is 10; if MPS is $1/2$, the multiplier is 2. If none of the increased income is spent on consumption, the marginal propensity to save is 100 percent or $1/1$. The reciprocal is 1, which is the size of the multiplier. This tells us that an extra dollar of spending results in one dollar of increased income, but as that dollar is pulled out of the income stream in the form of saving, there are no further effects on income.

Now we can go back to see the effect of the multiplier in Table 3-2 on page 43. We assumed that MPC was 70 percent or $7/10$. Therefore, MPS was $3/10$. The reciprocal of that is $3 1/3$. Therefore, every extra dollar of spending would increase income by $3.33, consumption by $2.33, and saving by $1.00. In the first line of Table 3-2 we can see that without investment, income could not rise above $400 billion, because at that level, income and consumption would be equal. As there is $60 billion of investment, income should rise by $3 1/3$ times that, or $200 billion. Consumption should rise by $2 1/3$ times that, or $140 billion. Saving should rise by an amount equal to investment, or $60 billion, the difference between increased income and increased consumption. These things do happen in Table 3-2. The third, or equilibrium, line shows that income settled at $600 billion, consumption at $540 billion, and saving at $60 billion.

How the multiplier works can be illustrated in Figure 3-4 on page 44. Suppose investment rises from $60 billion to $90 billion. Draw a new horizontal investment line 50 percent higher than the original line, opposite 90 on the vertical scale. The saving line and the new investment line intersect over the $700 billion income on the horizontal scale. This shows that an increase in investment of $30 billion caused income to rise $100 billion; the multiplier is $3 1/3$.

In Table 3-3 on page 45 we see the multiplier effect of a change in government spending. As taxes are $70 billion and government spending is $100 billion, the initial increase in spending is $30 billion. The multiplier is $3 1/3$, and income should rise by $100 billion, consumption by $70 billion, and saving by $30 billion. This is exactly what happens as the equilibrium position goes from the third to the fourth line in the table.

In Figure 3-5 on page 46, draw a new investment plus government spending line at 190, instead of its original 160. It will now intersect the saving plus taxes line at the 800 level of income; an increase of spending of $30 billion causes income to rise by $100 billion.

We can now look at the rest of Table 3-5 and see how useful the multiplier is in predicting the effects of changes in spending. Suppose we are suffering from a serious depression. The government can engage in deficit financing, selling bonds to the banks to finance its increased spending. If the increased expenditures total an extra $1 billion each period, and if MPC is 75 percent, after about fifteen periods the increased income will be $4 billion each period. The higher the multiplier, the more effective any extra spending in raising total incomes above the depressed level.

The trouble in the 1930's was, as Keynes pointed out, that the multiplier in the United States was not 4, but between 2 and 2½. This means that the marginal propensity to consume was 50 to 60 percent of disposable income. A billion dollars of extra spending each period would increase income by only $2 or $2½ billion.

We may well wonder why, in the midst of the worst depression we had ever experienced, MPC was only 50 to 60 percent, which is surprisingly low. One reason is that some of the government spending increases the incomes of wealthy people who have low marginal propensities to consume. Second, even poor people may use their increased income to pay off debts, which represents saving rather than consumption. Third, with an increased demand for goods, some businessmen may sell goods out of inventory without reordering; they thereby reduce investment, which offsets increased government spending. Fourth, some people may have higher incomes without increasing employment; dentists and doctors, for example, may work longer hours and have higher incomes because of government spending, but no additional people are employed. Fifth, rising prices of goods that result from rising demand may increase money income without increasing real income.

It is important to remember that the multiplier works on the downward side as well as the upward. If MPC is 75 percent and if investment or government spending declines by a billion dollars, income will fall by $4 billion. Also, if there is any independent or autonomous change in consumption spending, that also will have a multiplied effect on total income.

The upward movement of income through the action of the multiplier is useful and desirable if we have unemployment. If the economy is fully employed, however, any increased spending will have a multiplied effect on consumption and income, but only in monetary terms; thus inflation will occur. With full employment, then, the lower the multiplier, the lower the inflationary impact of any increase in spending.

Some of the applications of national income theory have already been discussed, because they cannot be easily separated from the theory itself. We shall now turn to a further examination of the applications of this type of theorizing.

Applications of National Income Theory

National income studies are of decisive importance in analyzing fluctuations of the economy, in forecasting future trends, and in controlling the economy to foster an acceptable employment level, steady prices, and a stable rate of growth. The investigation of business cycles has become important on the government level ever since we departed from the laissez-faire system in order to use government policies to try to overcome cyclical fluctuations in the economy. Forecasting is desirable both for public policies to curb fluctuations and for private profit-making, as in the stock market or in planning capital expansion.

National income investigation is also important in analyzing the nation's growth, including the determinants of growth, growth rates, and changing patterns of growth. The government, for example, issues a large number of pamphlets advising people about the prospects in different lines of work; this involves forecasting where employment opportunities will expand and where they will shrink. If it is determined that education is crucial to growth, and if the government wishes to foster growth, it will subsidize education. These are practical applications of the theories.

National income studies are far more important to giant corporations than they are to small businesses. The business cycle is of prime importance to the profitability of a big steel corporation; but to a small grocer, the business cycle is far less significant than the opening of a supermarket across the street. If a corporation is thinking of erecting another steel mill or automobile assembly plant, it has to forecast growth in population, growth in income, growth in demand for its product, population shifts within the country, prospects of exporting its product and of facing rival imports, and so on.

Business cycle analysts were looking at the aggregate economy (the macroeconomic approach) long before this methodology was given preeminence by Keynes in the 1930's. They had relied on two major concepts: first, that business cycles grow out of the laissez-faire capitalistic economy and are not thrust on us by forces outside the economy; and second, that prosperity and depression tend to be cumulative, feeding on themselves. Our analysis of business cycles will illustrate these ideas.

Many economists in the past resisted the idea that business cycles are inherent in a private enterprise laissez-faire system, as this view seemed to question the viability of capitalism. They therefore looked outside the economic system for the causes of the fluctuations. A hundred years ago W. Stanley Jevons, the world-renowned British economist, believed that business fluctuations are caused by the sunspot cycle. This cycle influences weather, which in turn affects the size of crops. Large crops occur when sunspots are at a minimum, and the resulting low prices of agricultural products stimulate the economy. The effects, Jevons asserted, may manifest themselves internationally; a large crop and cheap food in India will leave the wage-earner surplus income for clothing, thereby promoting prosperity for the cotton mills of Manchester, England.

Apparently business cycles are inherent in a free-enterprise capitalistic economy, and prosperity and depression feed on themselves. The significance of our description of fluctuations is, first, that if we understand them, we can invoke government stabilization policies to offset or overcome these tendencies toward instability. Second, if government is to act and if fluctuations are cumulative, then forecasting becomes of prime importance; the sooner we recognize an undesirable fluctuation, the sooner the trend can be stopped or reversed.

Let us begin with the cyclical phase of prosperity and expansion. Ultimately the expansion comes to an end because business firms encounter obstacles to further growth. Among these obstacles that build up during prosperity is the slow but sure increase in the costs of doing business. Capital goods and raw materials rise in price, and business loans are less available and carry higher interest rates than formerly because of the increased demand for loans. Wage costs rise because of labor shortages and the use of overtime labor, which is more expensive and less productive than normal labor; in addition, wage rates are rising because they are beginning to catch up with rising prices due to the strong bargaining position of some workers at full employment. Waste in production increases as businessmen grow careless and overoptimistic. Rising production costs encroach on profits, especially since the prices of finished goods cannot be easily raised in the later stages of prosperity. The expansion of productive capacity, which promoted the growth of prosperity during its earlier period, adds to the supply of goods and increases the difficulty of raising selling prices. Buyers ultimately resist rising prices because they cannot or will not continually pay more for goods. Consumers postpone the purchases of durable goods. Businessmen become more cautious and are likely to reduce their commitments for the future. They reduce their inventories, their new orders for machinery, and their contracts for commercial and industrial construction. Gloom spreads, unemployment grows, consumer income and expenditure decline, and the economy sinks into a depression. Growing pessimism pervades the economy and tends to worsen the downturn. Credit shrinks, and a widening wave of bankruptcies pulls down one business after another.

Given enough time, a depression generates within itself the forces that produce an upturn. Businessmen cut waste and costs to the bone. Labor costs fall because overtime is eliminated, inefficient workers are discharged, and employed workers are driven to greater efforts by the fear of unemployment. Capital goods wear out and grow obsolete and need to be replaced. Interest rates fall because of the reduced demand for loans. Inventories, which have been reduced to the barest minimum during depression, must be rebuilt as business begins to expand again. As prices begin to rise, the anticipation of further price increases stimulates additional orders for goods. Credit expands as business conditions improve. Consumers who have curtailed and postponed their purchases of durable goods find that they can no longer keep their old goods in satisfactory repair. As employment and income begin to rise, they increase their buying of durable goods. Optimism spreads, and the economy is once again on a cumulative upswing.

In order to take prompt action to offset undesirable fluctuations or to maximize profits or minimize losses that can result from fluctuations, good forecasting is desirable and necessary, but it is also difficult to achieve. One of the tools of forecasting is a set of lead indicators. These are statistical measures of activities that foreshadow turning points in the business cycle; they are signals of things to come. New orders for machinery and equipment, for example, expand and shrink before the expansion and contraction of the economy as a whole. The same is true for commercial and industrial construction contracts and private nonfarm housing starts. The incorporation of new businesses and aggregate liabilities of business failures are also lead indicators, as are changes in business inventories and changes in unfilled orders of the durable goods industries.

Declines in the lead indicators have frequently been followed by a decline in aggregate economic activity. But there is no historical basis for knowing precisely how long the time lag will be between the change in the lead indicators and the change in the whole economy. In addition, we do not know whether the decline in the lead indicators is signaling a lull, a minor setback, or a decline of sufficient depth and duration to be designated a recession. At most, such declines can be interpreted as signaling a decline in aggregate economic activity of unknown amplitude and duration. However, they may also give false signals signifying nothing.

Another approach to the study of business fluctuations is the econometric model approach, in which the gross national product and its components are forecasted mathematically on the basis of the historical relations between consumption, private investment, government, and the various components of these major aggregates.

Although national income theory arose in the Depression of the 1930's, it is fully as applicable during inflationary periods. By using the imaginary economy portrayed in Figure 3-6, we can demonstrate how national income theories can be applied to the problems of avoiding or overcoming inflation or depression. First, however, we must define what is meant by full employment. Full employment does not mean that everyone who wants a job has one. This did not even happen at the height of the Second World War in 1944, when unemployment reached a low point of 1.2 percent of

FIGURE 3-6.   *The Inflationary and Deflationary Gap*
(in billions of dollars)

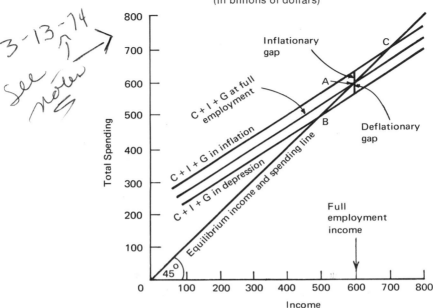

3-13-74
see note

the civilian labor force. At that time we had overfull employment, for the number of unfilled jobs exceeded by far the number of unemployed people. One consequence of this situation was strong inflationary pressures that were kept under control by government price and wage controls and the rationing of many consumer goods to keep the demand low enough to match the reduced supply.

Why was there unemployment in 1944 when there was such a great shortage of labor? First, there is less than perfect mobility of labor. If welders are unemployed in New England and there is a great shortage of welders on the West Coast, workers do not immediately move to the jobs. It takes time to make the move; the workers first must give up hope for jobs in the East, sell their homes, and so on. Second, there is considerable occupational immobility of labor. There may be a great shortage of machinists and a surplus of clothing workers, who cannot fill the vacant jobs. Third, a person can be unemployed while choosing among many job offers. If a college graduate in 1944 had fifteen job offers, he might take two weeks to look at the positions and decide which one he preferred; during those two weeks he would be genuinely unemployed.

Full employment has been defined as a situation in which the number of unemployed people is equal to the number of unfilled jobs. This typically may be the situation with 3 or 4 percent unemployment. In the economy portrayed in Figure 3-6, we assume that full employment exists when the nation's income is $600 billion (point A). If total consumption plus investment plus government spending were equal to $600 billion, we would be at full employment equilibrium, since the total spending line would intersect the forty-five-degree line at point A.

Suppose now that total spending falls. The lowered amount of spending could occur in any of the three components of spending or in a combination of all three. Perhaps investors, growing pessimistic about future business prospects, cut their investment. Government might reduce its spending, or consumers might cut their volume of consumption, perhaps because the government is taxing more without spending more. If the total of C+I+G falls, income will fall by a larger amount because of the multiplier. Suppose the marginal propensity to consume is $\frac{2}{3}$, the multiplier, then, is 3 (the reciprocal of the marginal propensity to save). If the initial reduction in spending is $33\frac{1}{3}$ billion, income will fall $100 billion, from $600 billion to $500 billion. The economy then reaches equilibrium at less than full employment (point B). The deflationary gap is a shortage of $33\frac{1}{3}$ billion of spending; if total spending could be raised by that amount, the multiplier would raise total income $100 billion, from $500 billion to $600 billion.

What can be done to raise total spending to the full employment level? The government can call forth greater consumption spending by reducing income taxes and other taxes or by making transfer payments to low-income people. If the government lowers business taxes or if interest rates fall, investment is very likely to increase. The government can also increase its own spending on goods and services without raising taxes.

Depression

When C+I+G is too great to maintain equilibrium at full employment, inflation develops, as total spending magnifies the initial increase in spending because of the multiplier. With an increase in spending of $33\frac{1}{3}$ billion, if MPC is $\frac{2}{3}$, equilibrium is then reached at $700 billion of income (point C). To curb inflation, the government might force a reduction in consumer spending by raising taxes or reducing transfer payments. Investors might limit their spending if taxes or interest rates rise. A reduction in government spending on goods and services while taxes are increased also will have an antiinflationary effect.

Inflation

One difficulty with these remedies for fluctuations is that they sometimes involve goals that are in conflict with each other. Suppose we want public agencies to take care of destitute people, and we want enough schools for our children, but an inflationary economy calls for reduced government spending; what shall we do? Suppose lower taxes are called for to counteract a depression, but local governments with poor credit ratings desperately need more revenue to meet urgent public needs and cannot reduce taxes. Suppose lower interest rates were desirable to stimulate private investment, but they cannot be pushed down low enough to bring us to full employment. A government can, if necessary, lend money at a zero rate of interest, but bankers cannot. These problems are not insoluble, but they involve making compromises and deciding the relative importance of conflicting goals and the most acceptable means to achieve them.

Evaluation of National Income Theory

The opinions offered here are not meant to deny the basic validity of national income analysis. The type of theory presented above is fundamental to the understanding of our economy and to attempts to improve its functioning. But the theory of the inflationary and deflationary gap given above has a faintly antiquated air about it. The analysis implies that we can control the economy to have full employment without inflation. If we experience rising prices, we can use a number of devices to curb that trend. If we have falling prices or incomes, or both, we can implement a different set of policies to overcome that tendency. But what can the theory tell us, and what can we do, if we have simultaneous inflation and unemployment, as we did during 1970–71? We need higher interest rates, heavier taxes, and less government spending to curb inflation, and at the same time lower interest rates, lighter taxes, and more government spending to increase employment.

This aspect of national income theory has lost some of its relevance because of the changes that have occurred in recent decades. Certain structural alterations in our economy have helped produce an inflationary tendency. The growth of large-scale enterprises with immense market power has given an upward push to prices. Powerful unions not only try to raise wages to make up for past increases in the cost of living, but try to anticipate and make up in advance for future price increases. Government supports for prices of farm products and payments for restriction of farm output prevent those prices from falling. The regulated public utilities, electric, telephone, and gas companies, raise prices frequently, but seldom lower them. All these forces give an upward push to prices that persists even when unemployment develops.

This problem of simultaneous unemployment and inflation is, of course, preferable to the massive unemployment and price reductions that we experienced in the 1930's. But we do need a continuing study of the changing structure and institutions of our economy; then we will better understand why old remedies to promote stability of prices and employment no longer work as well as they once did.

That our federal government has lost some faith in the old stabilization policies was indicated when a three-month wage and price freeze was imposed in August 1971, followed by modified controls on wages and prices starting in November of that year. Such controls were virtually unheard of in peacetime in the past. We can learn to live with such policies, and they may not reduce the viability of our economic system; but these controls certainly point toward a need for a new analysis of our economy.

The second question we should raise is how national income theory should be used. The theory is concerned with the *quantity* of consumption, investment, and government spending. Yet we see increasing concern for the *quality* of these three kinds of spending. The issues we raise here are, of course, political and social as well as economic.

Instead of considering all consumption spending as a lump sum, should we not be concerned with why and how we distribute our spending between cosmetics and health? Between champagne and milk? Between mink coats for dogs and shoes for children? Between Cadillacs and bus transportation? These questions involve value judgments about the distribution of income as well as the amount of income.

Investment, too, is added up without any value judgments as to whether it enhances the well-being of society and the quality of life to the maximum extent. Are we to be impartial on decisions between night clubs and housing? Between billboards and clothing factories? Between armament plants and canneries? Between clubs to kill seals and hammers to drive nails?

The outstanding example of wasteful and destructive spending is that engaged in by the federal government. In 1971 its total spending on goods and services (excluding transfer payments) was $98 billion. Of this, $71 billion was allocated for the military establishment. We began an analysis of military spending at the end of the last chapter. Now that national income theory has been discussed, we can carry it further.

In considering military spending we encounter an odd phenomenon that requires explaining. The New Deal, in trying to overcome the Depression, raised the federal debt from $21 billion at the end of 1932 to $49 billion at the end of 1941—an increase of $28 billion. At the time there was a great outcry against it, a denunciation of government waste and a warning of the impending threat of national bankruptcy. There was no outcry, however, when because of the Second World War the federal debt was raised from $49 billion to $259 billion at the end of 1945. Why the difference?

There are at least three possible reasons why the New Deal spending of the 1930's on social and welfare programs was condemned and the military spending starting in the 1940's was readily accepted. First, we may be more sophisticated about economics now. We have learned our Keynesian lessons, and we understand that government spending is preferable to depression and unemployment. Second, we are more willing to engage in deficit financing in times of desperation during wartime when the alternative might be to lose the war. Third and most important, we prefer military spending to spending for useful things because the people in power prefer it that way; they have brainwashed most of us to think as they do.

This is a serious charge, and we shall try to substantiate it. Orthodox economists generally assume that government spending adds to income, and through the multiplier effect the increase in income will be larger than the increase in government spending. What they sometimes ignore is the fact that if government spending scares off private spending of an equal amount, the increase in income is precisely zero. Therefore, government spending is generally aimed at pleasing rather than antagonizing the private investor. This constraint limits useful government expenditures and fosters useless ones.

From time to time there are proposals that federal, state, and local governments finance houses for low-income families. Even proposals specifying that the government is to subsidize only one-third the cost of the houses and to be paid back the other two-thirds are denounced as socialistic, a waste of public money, and subsidies to lazy, good-for-nothing people. But if military barracks are built completely with government money, this is accepted as all right. Why? Because the real estate interests, and especially the slum landlords, object to government competition in providing good housing at low rents. But nobody but the government builds barracks, and they would not be built unless public funds were available; therefore, because there is no competition they are accepted.

Military spending is well-suited to the people in power. It can be defended on the basis of patriotic necessity. It adds to, rather than competes with, private enterprise. The demand for weaponry is a bottomless pit. Armaments are rapidly consumed, and advanced weapons systems become obsolete as quickly as defense experts can think of "improvements" over existing systems. Thus many weapons systems have proved obsolete even before production on them was completed. Furthermore, a billion dollars spent on highly complex and sophisticated military hardware provides less employment for the nation as a whole and more income for the big military contractors than a billion dollars spent on labor, lumber, and other building materials for public civilian construction.

Firms producing for military contracts need not worry much over competition and economical production. There is virtually no market test for price and efficiency. If such firms were to produce for a civilian market, they might not be able to compete. Therefore they defend military spending regardless of whether it is needed or not for our national safety and security. The consequences of this sheltered market for the biggest firms are dramatic: Polaris submarines are produced for $12 per pound, while merchant ships must be produced at less than $1 per pound; air frames of military aircraft have been manufactured at a cost greater than their weight in gold, but these costs are inconceivable for commercial vehicles; electromechanical instruments about the size of an egg are constructed at $15,000 per unit. Military industry has lost the traditional American industrial capacity for offsetting high wages with high levels of productivity; it will defend military spending to the end. The electronics industry of Japan, free of military priorities, designs and produces excellent, low-cost electronics products for the world market. But in defense contracting, foreign firms are virtually excluded.

The inadequacy of social spending can be seen in the fact that with all the New Deal deficit financing, unemployment averaged 10 percent of the civilian labor force in 1941. The Second World War brought us to full employment. Unemployment exceeded 5 percent between 1948 and 1950; then the Korean War baled us out. In 1954, a year after that war ended, unemployment averaged more than 5 percent, a trend which recurred from 1958 to 1964, when the war in Vietnam moved us toward full employment again. Finally, in spite of the Vietnam war, unemployment exceeded 5 percent beginning in August 1970.

Why is $15 billion per year of public funds spent on highways and only $600 million of federal government funds on mass transit? Because the automobile manufacturers, the petroleum refiners, the steel makers, and others are interested in selling more automobiles. Mass transit may be rational, but it will not be as profitable.

Government spending for social benefit may upset the labor market. The New Deal aroused the fury of its critics when it hired unemployed people on labor-intensive projects at prevailing wage rates. Such policies curbed wage-cutting in the private sector, and they produced minimal benefits to the big corporations. Today, adequate welfare and unemployment payments would also upset the labor market, for people could resist working at the most miserable jobs paying the lowest wages. It is frequently pointed out that in some circumstances welfare payments exceed earnings on jobs, and people therefore may resist going to work. The usual conclusion is that welfare benefits are too high; one could just as readily conclude that wages in some fields are too low.

Summary

In this chapter we studied how the level of income is determined, and we examined the forces that generate changes in income. We saw that the total demand for goods and services results in an equilibrium level of income. Total demand can be broken down into the components of consumption, investment, and government spending.

People as a whole spend a very large part of their disposable income on consumption. The fraction, or percentage, of their total income that they spend on consumption is called the average propensity to consume. The proportion of any extra dollar of income that they spend on consumption is called the marginal propensity to consume. Alternatively, the marginal propensity to consume can be measured by assuming a reduction of a dollar of disposable income and seeing by what portion of a dollar consumption spending will fall.

The total amount spent on consumption depends on aggregate disposable income and the average propensity to consume.

Changes in income are influenced by the marginal propensity to consume. Since what is not consumed out of disposable income is saved, the marginal propensity to consume plus the marginal propensity to save (the fraction of extra income that is saved) equals one or 100 percent. Suppose the marginal propensity to consume and to save are one-half each. If income goes up by a dollar, perhaps because of increased investment or government spending, successive rounds of rising consumption and income would raise income by a total of two dollars. This is the working of the multiplier, which is the reciprocal of the marginal propensity to save. It tells us to what extent income will ultimately change, either upward or downward, as the result of an initial change in income.

Spending on investment depends on the expected rate of profit over the life of the contemplated investment. In terms of percentage fluctuations, investment is much more variable than consumption. Changes in the business outlook can cause great changes in the capital that businessmen commit in their enterprises. In the past, this has been one of the great initiating causes of business fluctuations, but in recent decades investment has become more stable.

Government spending is the third type of spending that influences income. Changes in government expenditures can help stabilize the economy by offsetting inflationary or deflationary trends arising from changes in consumption and investment spending. The government also influences consumption spending by altering disposable income through changes in taxes and transfer payments. Investment spending is also influenced by the rise or fall of government buying from businesses.

The equilibrium level of the nation's income is attained when the total income is equal to the total amount that consumers, investors, and government wish to spend. If the total they wish to spend is greater than their aggregate income, income will rise; if it is less, income will fall. For any past period, total income will equal total spending by the three groups.

The paradox of thrift is seen when consumers try to save more than in the past. This may cause falling incomes and, therefore, reduced saving. This illustrates the idea that the interests of the individual and of society may be inconsistent and incompatible.

QUESTIONS AND PROBLEMS

1   What do you think would happen in our economy if military spending were eliminated?

2   How can the government increase society's saving by its citizens? How can it increase their consumption?

3 Calculate GNP and NNP from the following data (hypothetical figures in billions of dollars).

Consumer spending on goods	200
Consumer spending on services	175
Payments of wages and salaries	400
Gross private domestic investment	100
Foreign investment	4
Depreciation of capital	50
Capital destroyed in floods and fires	5
Corporate profits after paying taxes and dividends	15
Federal government spending on goods and services	75
State and local government spending on goods and services	90
Government transfer payments	25
Interest on the federal debt	20
Government tax receipts	210

4 What would happen in our economy if we made automobiles, refrigerators, washing machines, and heating systems that could last fifty years?

5 Under what conditions are "guns and butter" alternative outputs? Under what conditions does their output rise and fall together?

6 Look up the volume and purposes of federal government spending in *Statistical Abstract of the United States* and compare it with state and local government spending, which you can find in the same source.

7 Suppose Y = 500, C = 350, I = 100, S = 100, G = 50, T = 50, and MPC = 50 percent. Assume that I rises to 110. Calculate the new Y, C, I, S, G, and T.

8 In problem 7, assume that I falls to 90. Calculate the new Y, C, I, S, G, and T.

9 In problem 7, assume that G rises from 50 to 70, and because of it I falls from 100 to 90. Calculate the new Y, C, I, S, G, and T.

BIBLIOGRAPHY

DERNBURG, THOMAS F., and McDOUGALL, DUNCAN M., *Macroeconomics,* 3rd ed. New York: McGraw-Hill, 1968.

KEYNES, JOHN MAYNARD, *The General Theory of Employment, Interest and Money.* New York: Harcourt Brace Jovanovich, 1936.

LEE, MAURICE W., *Macroeconomics: Fluctuations, Growth, and Stability,* 4th ed. Homewood, Ill.: Richard D. Irwin, 1967.

MELMAN, SEYMOUR, *Our Depleted Society.* New York: Holt, Rinehart and Winston, 1965.

MERMELSTEIN, DAVID, ed., *Economics: Mainstream Readings and Radical Critiques.* New York: Random House, 1970.

UNITED STATES DEPARTMENT OF COMMERCE, BUREAU OF THE CENSUS, *Business Conditions Digest* (Monthly publication).

How National
Income Changes:
The Money Market

There are three main causes that dispose men to madness:
love, ambition, and the study of currency problems.
— *Walter Leaf*

The use of money permeates our society. As with so many aspects of economics, the significance of money is controversial. In the past some economists thought that money was a veil that obscured the real workings of the economy—the production, distribution, and consumption of goods. Even today there is disagreement about how important money is in achieving a stable, sound, and growing economy. Is the control of money the key to improving the functioning of our economy? Or is it just one among many important factors that influence economic affairs?

Of this we can be certain: in our type of society, money is very convenient, for its use saves us much time and trouble. If we relied on a barter system as an alternative, making payments would be awkward and difficult. The convenience of using money will be noted as we examine the functions of money.

The Monetary System

THE FUNCTIONS OF MONEY If we used a barter system, in order to engage in trade we would have to find pairs of people who desired each other's goods. Suppose, for example, you were negotiating with a college for the payment of tuition. You are told that two hogs to be served up in the dining hall would be the payment for your semester's tuition. Unfortunately you do not have any hogs, but you do have a ton of wheat. You find a man with two hogs to sell, but he wants a wagon in exchange. Then you locate a man who is willing to part with his surplus wagon, but he wants to trade it for a horse. Finally you are successful: you find a man who will exchange his horse for your wheat. You trade your wheat for the horse, the

63

horse for the wagon, the wagon for the hogs, and you lead the hogs up the front walk to the slaughterhouse behind the dining hall. You have paid a semester's tuition. Obviously money makes such payments for goods and services much simpler and more efficient—if you have the money. This use of money as a medium of exchange is its first and most important function.

Second, money is a standard of value or a common measure of value or a common denominator of value. Money acts as a yardstick that measures the value of all kinds of goods and services. Imagine again that we are on a barter system and the following exchanges in the market occur:

10 pair of socks for 1 pair of shoes
20 cans of soup for 1 hat
1 cow for 1 horse
2 hogs for 1 semester's tuition
30 dozen eggs for 1 auto tire

How many dozen eggs, how many hats, will pay for a semester's tuition? We do not know. But if every commodity carried a price tag in dollars and cents, we could quickly find out how many hats or eggs we would have to sell to pay that college fee. Without the yardstick of money, there would be, in our complex society, a chaos of hundreds of thousands of barter equations with all kinds of discrepancies and inconsistencies among them.

Third, money serves as a standard of deferred payments. Contracts which involve payments in the future state these intended payments in terms of dollars. Wage and salary agreements, loans and repayments, construction contracts, commitments for future deliveries of goods—these and many other kinds of agreements are stated in dollar terms. The problem involved with using money as a standard of deferred payments is that its own value, measured by its purchasing power, keeps changing—mostly downward in recent decades. The value of money is the inverse of the price level: if prices rise 10 percent, the value of money falls 10 percent. As prices change, contracts for future payments hurt some people and benefit others.

Fourth, money is a store of value. Money represents general purchasing power, and you want to hold some if you can for your day-to-day expenses, for unforeseen emergencies that require extra expenditures, or for unexpected opportunities to buy bargains. These are short-term purposes and involve modest amounts. You probably would not wish to hold large sums of money for long periods of time for two reasons: you earn no interest on money held, and the value of money tends to melt away as prices rise. There are other ways to store value for the future: hold stocks, bonds, real estate, works of art, savings accounts, and so on. You might say, "I don't get much from a 5 percent government bond if prices are rising 6 percent per year and I have to pay income taxes on the interest that I get. I'm worse off at the end of the year than at the beginning." True, but you would be even worse off if you kept your money in your wallet or in a checking account.

We shall now offer a definition of money and take a closer look at our money supply.

OUR MONEY SUPPLY Money is anything that is generally accepted as a medium of exchange. This includes currency (coins and paper money) and checking accounts (demand deposits) in commercial banks. Late in 1971 we had $52 billion of currency in circulation and $175 billion of demand deposits.

The acceptability of money does not depend on law, but it is influenced by government. If you do not trust the money, you can refuse to sell your goods for cash. You can demand goods in exchange; you can say that you will sell a pair of socks for two dozen eggs. How does the government influence the acceptability of money? By not overissuing the amount of currency, as some governments have done in the past through printing more and more paper currency in larger and larger denominations. By not allowing the wild expansion of the dollar volume of checking accounts. By preventing runaway inflations. And by enforcing contracts and property rights, so that if you pay for goods by check, the seller is very confident (although not absolutely certain) that he will collect on that check sooner or later.

Now we can see why gold and silver were so important in our monetary system before 1933. There was some suspicion that our government might overissue paper money unless some controls were imposed. One of the controls was that part of our paper money supply should be redeemable in gold, dollar for dollar, and another part would be redeemable in silver. In addition, gold and silver coins were circulated.

In 1933 we went off the domestic gold standard. The government continued to buy all the gold produced in the country, and gold was used in international payments, but gold coins were recalled, and no paper money was redeemable in gold. The government did this in order to manage our monetary system, expanding our money supply in time of depression without worrying about how much gold the government had in its possession.

But we were not yet ready to divorce our money completely from gold. Most of our paper money is issued by the twelve Federal Reserve banks, which were created in 1914. These are central banks whose major purpose is to control the operation of our system of money and banking in order to facilitate stability and growth in our economy. We used to require that each dollar of currency issued by the Federal Reserve banks be backed by at least 25 cents in gold. This regulation was probably intended to curb the overissue of currency. If there were no controls over the amount of paper money the Federal Reserve banks issued, what would prevent them from printing such vast quantities that it would cause inflation? The Federal Reserve authorities, however, did not and would not permit the expansion of our supply of currency even up to the limits imposed by the gold reserve requirement. For example, by 1949 we had over $14 billion of surplus gold, and the Federal Reserve authorities could have issued $56 billion of additional paper currency if the gold reserve requirement were the only limiting factor. But they have other ways to carry out their responsibility to prevent the overissue of money.

Although we had a vast surplus of gold in 1949, beginning some time in 1965 we would have run short of gold if the 25 percent reserve requirement had been maintained, since we had exported more than half our 1949 gold supply to foreign countries (in Chapter 15 we shall discuss the reasons for this). The United States Congress therefore repealed the gold reserve requirement for Federal Reserve notes in 1968. (You may wonder why, if we would have run short of gold reserves after 1965, the gold reserve requirement for Federal Reserve notes was not dropped until 1968. As will be explained later, gold reserves also were required for deposits held at the Federal Reserve banks by the member banks. This gold reserve requirement was dropped by Congress early in 1965.)

Another reason for discontinuing the use of gold in our monetary system is the decline in gold production. Gold output has not kept pace with our expansion of income, population, and the use of money. Gold production in the United States had actually declined 64 percent from 1940 to 1969, for a very good reason: gold is probably the only commodity whose price has not changed at all from 1934 to 1971. At the official price of $35 per ounce, gold mining was much more profitable before the Second World War, when its cost of production was much lower, than it has been since then. (In 1971 the government stopped buying and selling gold and raised its price to $38 per ounce. This simply changed the exchange rate between the dollar and foreign currencies.)

Silver also has been eliminated from our monetary system. The government fixed the price at which it would buy silver at $1.293 per ounce. Until 1966 the market price was below that, and silver producers were eager to sell their output to the government. Silver coins and silver certificates (paper money redeemable in silver) were circulated. But after 1966 the market price of silver rose above the government price, and people demanded that their silver certificates be redeemed. The Federal Reserve banks stopped issuing silver certificates and the Treasury reduced the silver content of coins in order that the metal would not be worth more than the face value of the coins. It would no longer be profitable to melt coins and sell the metal.

Thus the economic facts of life have forced us to eliminate one phase of irrationality from our lives. To augment our money supply, we no longer have to take gold and silver out of the ground, process them, and then bury them in the ground again in some vault. We can issue money at a much lower cost than that. Issuing paper money under strict controls is much more economical than relying on gold and silver.

As we have seen, the government cannot force us to accept money, although it can protect its acceptability by restraining the expansion of its quantity. But the government can enact laws determining which part of the money supply will be legal tender. If money is legal tender, it must be accepted in payment of debts. If it is not legal tender, the creditor may refuse it. All our currency—coins and paper money—is legal tender in unlimited amounts; demand deposits are not. If you owe someone $1,000 and you offer him a personal check, he has the right to refuse it and demand cash. But if you offer him 100,000 pennies, he must accept them. If he refuses, the debt is not cancelled, but interest on the debt no longer accumulates. If he sues you, you may offer him the 680 pounds of pennies, and he has to take them if he wants to be paid.

But money that is legal tender may not be generally acceptable for goods; although it must be accepted in payment of debts. This is what happened to German currency in the wild inflation of the early 1920's. Obviously money does not have to be legal tender to be generally acceptable; demand deposits are generally accepted although they are not legal tender. Demand deposits make up 77 percent of our money supply. How are they created?

THE PROCESS OF CREDIT CREATION Only commercial banks—banks that accept demand deposits—create credit; savings banks do not. To illustrate the process of credit creation in its simplest form, imagine a single bank in an isolated, self-sufficient community. As shown in Figure 4-1, three people deposit $100 each in their checking accounts in the bank. Each person then

FIGURE 4-1. Credit Creation in One Isolated Bank

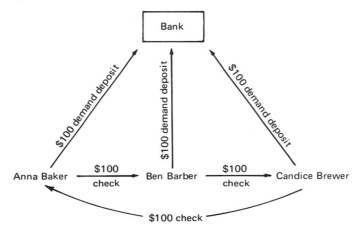

pays out and receives a $100 check in doing business with the others. What is the most remarkable thing about these transactions? It is that no money has left the bank!

Each person now goes to the banker and asks to borrow $900. The banker is willing to lend the money—at 8 percent interest. But how does he do it; where does he get the money to lend? He creates the money with pen and ink. You can play banker, and you can lend each person $900 in the following way: add a zero to each checking account, and each $100 now becomes $1,000. This is called credit creation. Now each person can add a zero to the check written. There has still been no money leaving the bank; what has occurred instead is an exchange of demand deposits. This means that each person can do ten times the volume of business he could do formerly.

Here you might object that such an oversimplified picture gives us a wild exaggeration. There is usually more than one bank in a community; what happens if someone writes a check and it is deposited in a second bank? The first bank must pay the second, and if it does not have enough money, it may go bankrupt. Bankers, too, may object to this description of credit creation, because they used to deny that they created any credit at all. They asserted, "We lend out other people's money, and we lend less than is deposited with us. Therefore we do not create credit."

It is true that when there are many banks, one bank cannot create credit out of line with the others. To illustrate this process, look at Figure 4-2, which shows four banks. Anna Baker deposited $100 of cash in Bank A. This did not change the total money supply, because currency in circulation has been reduced $100 while demand deposits have been increased by an equal amount. Let us assume that both the law and prudent practice require that 10 percent of demand deposits be kept on reserve. After all, every tenth or twentieth depositor may want to withdraw cash from his or her checking account. A demand deposit means that the bank has to pay on demand, and it is a good idea to hold some reserve funds.

FIGURE 4-2.   Credit Creation with Many Banks

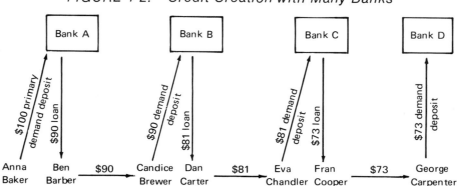

Bank A, having received $100 cash which is now credited to Anna Baker's checking account, keeps $10 on reserve and lends out $90 in cash. This is why the bankers claimed they did not create credit, but rather lent out less money than was deposited. But Bank A really did create credit. By lending $90, the money supply has increased by that amount. Anna Baker's $100 checking account is still part of the total money supply, and the bank has recirculated $90 of the cash she deposited.

Bank A lends the $90 to Ben Barber, who buys $90 worth of goods from Candice Brewer. She deposits the $90 in her checking account with Bank B. The bank keeps 10 percent, or $9, as a reserve, and it lends $81 to Dan Carter. He owes this much money to Eva Chandler and pays it to her. She deposits it in Bank C. The bank keeps 10 percent as a reserve and lends $73 to Fran Cooper, who uses it to pay George Carpenter for repairing her bicycle. He in turn deposits it in Bank D, which can lend 90 percent of that sum.

What are the sums we have so far? Total deposits in Figure 4-2 are $344. Total loans are $244. Total held on reserve is $27 plus the last $73 deposited in Bank D, none of which is lent out yet. What will the totals be when this process is completed with fifteen or twenty deposits and loans? Total deposits will be $1,000, total loans $900, and total reserves $100. When the original deposit of $100 is entirely earmarked as reserves, no further credit creation is possible until additional reserves are acquired. The final result is the same as that shown in the isolated bank in Figure 4-1, where, with reserves of $300 and a 10 percent reserve requirement, $3,000 of deposits and $2,700 of loans were possible.

We can now specify the size of the deposit expansion multiplier based on the fractional reserve requirement. If the required reserve is $1/10$, deposits will be 10 times reserves. If the required reserve is 20 percent, or $1/5$, deposits will be 5 times reserves.

Suppose the deposit expansion multiplier is 5, and a bank acquires additional reserves either from the owners' assets or through the Federal Reserve banks. Both deposits and loans can be 5 times the additional reserves. Suppose instead that the bank acquires additional reserves because someone made a cash deposit. Then total deposits will be 5 times the addition to reserves, but loans will be only 4 times the increase in reserves, since 20 percent of the cash deposit must be kept in reserve.

The amount of bank reserves does have an effect on national income. Suppose the marginal propensity to consume is 60 percent, giving us a national income multiplier of $2\frac{1}{2}$. Suppose also that the reserve requirement is 20 percent, making the deposit expansion multiplier 5. If we were in an inflationary situation, the Federal Reserve authorities could force a reduction of a billion dollars in bank reserves. This would force banks to reduce their demand deposits and loans by $5 billion. Investment and possibly consumption would be reduced immediately by that amount. The final effect of a $5 billion reduction in investment would be a total reduction of

$12½ billion of spending and income. The effect would be good counterinflation medicine.

Conversely, if we were in a depression, the Federal Reserve authorities could increase bank reserves by a billion dollars. The banks in turn could lend out an extra $5 billion, and ultimately, total spending and income would rise by $12½ billion. This does much to alleviate a depression, but it may not always work. If conditions are bad, why should business borrow more simply because the banks have acquired an increased ability to lend? The extra reserves may remain unused.

THE ORGANIZATION OF THE FEDERAL RESERVE SYSTEM   Our twelve Federal Reserve banks are central banks, or bankers' banks. They were established in 1914 under the Federal Reserve Act of 1913. We were among the last of the great economic powers to establish central banking. The Bank of Amsterdam was founded in 1609, the Bank of Sweden in 1656, the Bank of England in 1694, the Bank of France in 1800, and the Bank of Belgium in 1835.

Every national commercial bank must be a member of the Federal Reserve bank in its district. A national bank is a bank chartered by the federal government. State-chartered commercial banks may join the Federal Reserve system (Fed) but most have refused for several reasons. First, many of them cannot qualify for membership because they cannot meet the minimum-capital requirement. Second, members of the Fed must pay the face value of checks drawn by their depositors if the checks are presented by other banks for payment; some banks wish to deduct a service charge. Third, reserve requirements are lower under state laws. Fourth, there are other limitations imposed by the Fed on its members, and state laws are more lenient. Fifth, many services of the Fed, such as its help in clearing checks, are available to nonmember banks.

Yet the largest of the state-chartered banks have voluntarily joined the Fed. As of mid-1971, 1,138 state banks were members of the Federal Reserve system, and they had $107 billion of deposits. A total of 7,811 state banks were not members, and their total deposits were $100 billion.

Each Federal Reserve bank is owned by the member banks of its district. To become a member, a bank has to buy stock of its Federal Reserve bank in an amount equal to 3 percent of its own paid-up capital and surplus. Dividends on this stock may not exceed 6 percent, with the excess profits going to the United States Treasury. Lately the Fed has been paying $3½ billion per year to the government; it has no reason to worry about making a profit. Its major overall purposes are to promote stability in the economy and to smooth the operation of the monetary system. It will therefore do things that reduce its own profit while it helps the economy. But the Fed, as the ultimate source of credit creation, cannot help being profitable.

While the Federal Reserve banks are privately owned, they are controlled by the government. The Board of Governors is appointed by the President of the United States with the advice and consent of the Senate. Many laws regulate the Fed, but the laws do allow the Federal Reserve authorities some latitude in which to work to promote stability in their day-to-day activities.

In the following sections we will discuss the major purposes and functions of the Fed.

OPEN MARKET OPERATIONS Open market operations are the dealings the Federal Reserve banks have with the general public in buying and selling securities. Where do they get the money to buy? They manufacture it. Here is how this process of credit creation works: if the Federal Reserve bank buys a $1,000 government bond from you, it writes a $1,000 check and sends it to you; it does not need cash. You deposit the check in your checking account, and your bank sends it to the Fed for collection. The Federal Reserve bank now agrees with your bank that the latter has an extra $1,000 in its reserve account, and the banking system can now expand loans by perhaps $4,000.

Conversely, if you buy a $1,000 bond from the Fed, you send a check which the Federal Reserve bank deducts from your bank's reserve account. Your bank has lost $1,000 of reserves, and bank loans must shrink by a multiple of that sum.

Open market operations are useful in offsetting any undesirable changes in bank reserves. Suppose, for example, we draw a billion dollars out of our checking accounts as the Christmas season approaches. There is no immediate change in our money supply. We have decreased demand deposits by a billion dollars, and we have increased currency in circulation by a billion dollars. But the banks have a billion dollars less of reserves. This can be accounted for by either of two processes or by a combination of both. Banks can count the currency in their vaults as part of their legal reserves; thus, if they pay out currency, their reserves have fallen. Or if the banks run short of cash, they can draw cash from the Fed out of their reserve deposits, just as you can draw cash out of your checking account. If the banks get a billion dollars of currency from the Fed to replenish their holdings, they have lost a billion of reserves on deposit with the Fed. In either case, they must reduce their loans by perhaps $4 billion.

But the Christmas season is hardly the time to reduce loans. Business is booming, and it is a time for seasonal expansion of loans rather than contraction. To remedy this situation, the Fed can buy a billion dollars' worth of bonds in the open market and thereby replenish depleted bank reserves. After Christmas, as merchants deposit their cash receipts in the banks, reserves increase. If these added reserves might cause an inflationary expansion of bank credit, the Fed can sell bonds in the open market and thereby offset the augmented supply of reserves.

Federal Reserve open market operations have an additional purpose that is far more significant than taking care of our desire for more cash before Christmas. Their purpose is to promote a stable economy, to help offset both inflations and depressions. This will be discussed in Chapter 8.

RESERVE REQUIREMENTS   As of 1971, big-city banks that are members of the Fed must keep from 10 to 22 percent of their demand deposits as reserves. Within these limits the Fed determines the reserve requirements, and it has settled for 17 or 17½ percent, depending on the size of the bank. Small-city and rural banks by law must keep from 7 to 14 percent of their demand deposits on reserve, and the Fed requirement is 12½ or 13 percent, depending on the size of the bank. Savings deposits in all member banks by law must have reserves of 3 to 10 percent, and the Fed requirement is 3 percent.

As noted on page 66, until early 1965 the Fed had to hold 25 percent of gold as a reserve behind member bank reserve deposits. Presumably this requirement was designed to curb the power of the Fed to permit the runaway expansion of demand deposits. But in 1949 we had over $14 billion of surplus gold beyond what was required to back Federal Reserve notes and member bank deposits with the Fed. If the Fed had expanded bank reserves up to the limit permitted by the gold requirement, it could have created $56 billion of bank reserves. Assuming a deposit expansion multiplier of 5, demand deposits arising from bank loans and investments could have increased by $280 billion. Contrast this with the total demand deposits of all banks, members of the Fed and nonmembers, of $101 billion in 1949. We could have almost quadrupled our checking accounts! Obviously the Fed was not curbed by the gold reserve requirement, but rather by its own sensible judgments of how to stabilize the economy. The Fed certainly can make and has made mistakes, but it would not be so idiotic as to cause a terrible inflation just because we had enough gold to permit it according to the law. The gold reserve requirement was unnecessary and had no function after the establishment of the Fed.

DISCOUNTS AND ADVANCES   If the reserve account of a member bank is suddenly depleted, it can augment its reserves by discounting with the Fed the promissory notes it holds from business. Suppose a businessman wants to borrow $100 from a bank for three months at 8 percent interest. The bank "discounts" the note by deducting the interest first and lending the businessman $98. If the bank has to augment its reserves, perhaps because of adverse check clearings payable to other banks, the bank can rediscount the note at its Federal Reserve bank.

Commercial banks do not often discount short-term promissory notes with the Fed. They usually borrow from the Fed more directly by getting advances. When the Fed makes an advance to one of its member banks, it lends money with government securities or promissory notes from business as collateral. The Fed can also, if it wishes, make advances to member banks with other types of collateral, but in that case the rate of interest must be at least a half percent higher than for the other types of loans.

Fed interest rates are changed frequently. In May 1972 the rate of discount and normal advances was $4\frac{1}{2}$ percent; the rate on special advances not secured by government securities or promissory notes was 5 percent.

One benefit of discounts and advances is that the Fed can give its member banks great liquidity, that is, cash to pay off depositors if necessary. In times of panic this can be of crucial importance to the banking system. In the past many banks have failed, not because they did not have enough assets to cover their liabilities, but because their assets were not liquid enough. A demand deposit means that you can draw cash on demand; the banker cannot say, "I'm low on cash. Come back tomorrow." He may hold perfectly good promissory notes that will mature over the coming weeks and months. He may hold first mortgages that are as sound as can be but that will not be fully paid off for years. If there is a run of depositors who want to draw cash, the bank can go bankrupt because its assets cannot be sold for cash. The Fed can, however, advance cash to the member bank on its own signature backed by any sound collateral. Even the bank's building and furniture can serve as collateral to raise cash.

Marriner S. Eccles, once Chairman of the Board of Governors of the Fed, told how his bank in Utah was saved during a run by depositors in 1931. The rumor had spread that the bank could not pay off its depositors, and a line began to form early in the morning. Of course no bank ordinarily can pay off all its depositors unless it gets advances from the Fed. Eccles instructed his bank employees to smile, be pleasant, talk about the weather, show no signs of panic, and pay out very slowly in small bills. Every signature card had to be looked up even if the teller knew the depositor well. Meanwhile an armored car brought currency from the Federal Reserve bank in Salt Lake City, and the guards carried the bags of currency into the bank in front of frightened and worried people waiting in line. Of course Eccles' bank could only draw its excess reserves from the Fed plus one-fifth of any reduction in demand deposits, assuming a 20 percent reserve requirement. Obviously a bank cannot pay back all its depositors that way.

When the people in line saw that the bank was paying its depositors, and when the bags of additional currency were brought in, some of them left the line and went home. After all, they only wanted to withdraw their money because they were afraid the bank was about to go bankrupt; if the bank could pay, they did not want it. The bank was saved by paying out very slowly and by assuring its depositors that the supply of currency was adequate to pay everybody, which it was not.

Eccles could not help wondering if he and other bankers were not making matters worse. By trying to keep liquid, they were forcing the liquidation of loans and securities to meet the demands of the depositors. This drove prices down and made it increasingly difficult for debtors to pay back what they had borrowed from the banks. Monetary ease rather than credit stringency was required; but such a policy could be instituted only by the Fed, not by individual bankers. The Fed has now instituted such a policy.

Nowadays the Fed is the ultimate source of liquidity for the entire financial system. Another factor that promotes confidence and prevents runs on banks is the Federal Deposit Insurance Corporation, which will be discussed later in this chapter. It is still true, however, that if a bank makes bad investments and loans and if its liabilities exceed its assets, it can go bankrupt.

CLEARING CHECKS Before 1914 the process of clearing checks, or verifying the actual transfer of funds, was a laborious one, taking two weeks or more. Now the Fed has increased the speed so that it only takes a few days. Suppose you live in New York City and you send a $5 check to Edna Bookseller in San Francisco. How does this amount move from you to her? By a series of bookkeeping entries involving you and her, your bank (call it Manhattan National) and her bank (San Francisco National), the Federal Reserve banks of New York and San Francisco, and the Interdistrict Settlement Fund. This fund was established by the Board of Governors in Washington, D.C., with each Federal Reserve bank maintaining an account there.

Edna Bookseller deposits your $5 check in her account with San Francisco National, which increases that bank's liabilities by $5, because the bank owes $5 to Edna's account. The bank sends the check to the Fed of San Francisco for collection, which increases its reserve account, an asset, by $5. The Fed of San Francisco now has an extra liability of $5—the increased reserve of its member bank. But it also increases its assets by $5 when it collects that sum from the Fed of New York. This payment is made by reducing the Fed of New York account with the Interdistrict Settlement Fund by $5 and increasing the Fed of San Francisco account with the Fund by $5.

Your check is sent to the Fed of New York, which has reduced assets of $5 in its account with the Interdistrict Settlement Fund. Its liabilities also are reduced by $5 when the check clears against the reserve account of Manhattan National, which is reduced by that amount. Manhattan National's assets (its reserve account) are reduced by $5, but so are its liabilities, for it reduces your checking account by that amount. As you can see, payment has been made across the continent without any currency actually being shipped.

OTHER PURPOSES AND FUNCTIONS OF THE FED The Fed supervises and examines member banks. It issues and retires Federal Reserve notes (paper currency). It acts as fiscal agent for the government, handling its checking accounts, selling and redeeming its securities, buying and selling gold and foreign exchange on behalf of the Treasury whenever that is permitted by the government, and lending money to the Treasury. The Fed regulates stock market credit, and in the past it has regulated the terms and conditions of consumer installment credit and mortgage credit on homes.

Applications of Monetary Theory

BANK FAILURES AND DEPOSIT INSURANCE In the past there have been many bank failures in the United States. From 1921 through 1929 a total of 5,712 commercial banks were closed permanently or temporarily because of financial difficulties. From 1930 through 1933 another 9,100 commercial banks failed. This total of 14,812 banks failing in 13 years is a larger number than the commercial banks in existence in 1971, not counting branches. A temporary plan for the insurance of bank deposits was adopted in 1933, and the Federal Deposit Insurance Corporation (FDIC) was organized in 1935. During the period 1934–69 only 421 banks failed. Much of the credit for this success can be attributed to the FDIC.

However, a further investigation of the workings of the FDIC might shake your confidence. As of mid-1971, the total demand and time deposits (savings accounts) of insured banks amounted to $501 billion. As each account is only insured up to a maximum of $20,000, the insurance coverage would be less than $501 billion, but perhaps not very much less. And how much in the way of assets does the FDIC have to draw on to cover these potential liabilities? It has accumulated a reserve fund of something over $4 billion from the insurance premiums that it charges the banks. It is also authorized to draw up to $3 billion from the United States Treasury, a right that it has never used. That is all—$7 billion to cover liabilities that could possibly go as high as $400 billion. Just because the FDIC is a wholly government owned corporation, that does not mean the government must guarantee its obligations. Regardless of whether a corporation is owned privately or by government, the owners have limited liability and cannot be held responsible for the debts of the corporation. The government is not liable beyond its commitment to lend $3 billion to the FDIC.

But there really is nothing to worry about in this matter. If you suffer from excessive anxiety, you might be distressed over the fact that if all insured people died suddenly, the insurance companies would go bankrupt and could not pay off on all their policies; if all buildings burned, insurance payments would not be forthcoming for all claims. Such catastrophes seldom occur.

The FDIC is rather unique in that its very existence reduces the risk that it insures against. The existence of life insurance probably increases the risk of murder slightly. Fire insurance raises the risk of arson by a little. But deposit insurance reduces the risk of bank failures. With most deposits now insured, people no longer make runs on banks. With bank closings reduced to a minimum, waves of panic do not sweep across communities as they once did.

LIQUIDITY PREFERENCE AND THE RATE OF INTEREST   Interest is the price of money, and the equilibrium rate of interest can be shown in an ordinary supply-demand diagram such as Figure 4-3 below. The rate of interest is considered to be important in analyzing changes in national income. The level of interest can be determined by the supply of and the demand for money; but what we want to do is look at the underlying forces that influence supply and demand.

As we discussed earlier in this chapter and will discuss further in Chapter 8, the supply of money can be determined by the monetary authorities. We can therefore assume that the supply is fixed at any one time. The supply of money is represented by a vertical line in Figure 4-3. As national income rises, the supply of money is permitted to rise, and the line shifts to the right with the passage of time, but it remains vertical.

The concept of a demand for money may seem strange to you, for it means that there is a definite and limited amount of money that we want at each rate of interest. Take a poll among your friends. How much money do they want? A million dollars each? A hundred million? A billion? There seems to be no limit. But this is not so. What they really want is wealth that they will *not* keep tied up in cash. If we consider money only that which can be used as a medium of exchange—currency and checking accounts—you and your friends do not want very much money. If you were given a large amount of cash you would surely want to get rid of it in short order—by spending some of it on goods and services and investing much of the rest in assets producing interest, dividends, or other types of earning. Your satisfaction would diminish instead of increase if someone gave you a million dollars on condition that you keep it in the form of money for the rest of your life, never moving it from your checking account. You would earn nothing on it, you could not buy anything with it, your credit rating would not be improved, because nobody could seize any of it if you were to fail to pay your obligations. As you can see, we want only limited amounts of money to serve as a medium of exchange.

Our demand for money is really a demand for liquidity. Keynes argued that interest is not a reward for saving, because a person who hoards saving in the form of money earns no interest. Rather, interest is the reward for parting with liquidity.

There are three reasons for preferring *some* liquidity, that is, for wanting to hold some cash that is neither used to earn interest nor to buy goods. The first and most important is the transactions motive, the need to hold money temporarily until one comes to pay for goods and services used for both consumption and production. If you draw $100 pay each week, and by next payday it is all gone, on the average you wish to hold $50 for transactions.

The second reason for liquidity preference is the precautionary motive. This impels us to hold more money than we think we will use because there may be unexpected expenses or unforeseen failures of cash receipts to materialize. We may try to hold $100 in our checking accounts for just such emergencies.

The third and perhaps least important reason for liquidity preference is the speculative motive. This means we desire to hold money in anticipation that the price of investments will fall; then a quick purchase of stocks, bonds, commodities, or real estate can be made if money is on hand. This is a motive that would apply only to fairly wealthy people, and they would want to hold money for such speculative purposes only for short periods. For a longer period they would rather invest their money so that they could earn some interest on it. And with inflation going on continually, it is even less advantageous to hold idle money, since the money keeps losing purchasing power.

Interest is the price that brings into balance demand, the desire to hold wealth in the form of money, and supply, the available quantity of money. The higher the rate of interest, the more liquidity people are will-

FIGURE 4-3.   The Market Determination of the Rate of Interest

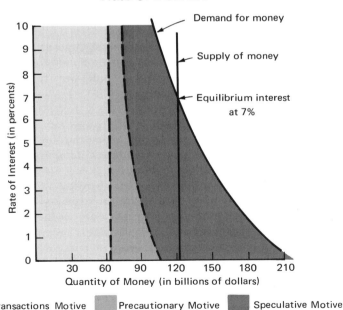

ing to give up, that is, the less willing they will be to demand money to hold idle. The lower the rate of interest, the less sacrifice is involved in holding idle money so the quantity desired will increase. These ideas are represented in Figure 4-3.

If the rate of interest were 9 percent in Figure 4-3, people would want to hold less money than the quantity in existence, and they would be ready to borrow less. Since the supply of money would be greater than the demand, the rate of interest would fall toward the point of equilibrium where the two lines cross. If the rate of interest were 5 percent, people would want to hold more money than is available. The demand would be greater than the supply, and the rate of interest would be forced upward. The equilibrium rate of interest for the supply of and demand for money shown in Figure 4-3 would settle at 7 percent.

Of course the higher our incomes, the greater the demand for money. If we are richer, we want to spend more on consumption and so hold more money for transactions. Suppose you receive $200 a week and spend $180 on consumption, when formerly you received and spent $100 weekly. Your money for transactions is $180 on payday and nothing at the end of the week, or an average of $90 instead of $50. You also want to hold more money for precautionary purposes. Therefore, as we grow richer, the demand-for-money curve shifts upward toward the right. If the supply of money remained fixed, the rate of interest would rise. Conversely, if we grow poorer, the demand-for-money curve will shift downward toward the left, and, with a fixed supply of money, the rate of interest would fall.

In Figure 4-3 we can also visualize what would happen if the monetary authorities increased the supply of money, say by lowering the percentage of reserves required to back up demand deposits. The vertical supply curve would shift to the right, and the rate of interest would fall. Conversely, a reduced quantity of money would shift the supply curve to the left, and the rate of interest would rise.

THE RATE OF INTEREST AND INVESTMENT We have seen in Chapter 3 how important the amount of investment is in determining national income. Now we shall examine how the rate of interest influences the quantity of investment.

Suppose businessmen are considering investing a million dollars in each of ten projects. They have to estimate the expected rate of profit over the life of each investment. We define profit here as the net return to the enterprise after deducting all costs of the business except interest costs on the money used. We do not count interest in our costs, because we are comparing rates of interest with rates of profit. Whether entrepreneurs invest their own money or borrow money, they are supposed to compare the going rate of interest with the expected rate of profit to decide if an investment is worth their while.

Figure 4-4 shows ten different million-dollar investments that are being contemplated and the expected return on each over the life of the investment. The prospective investments are arranged in descending order of return from left to right. A line connecting the expected rates of return represents the demand-for-capital curve. The rate of interest is assumed to be 7 percent, as shown in Figure 4-3. All the investments that are expected to yield a 7 percent or higher rate of return are made. Even the pet food plant in Omaha would be undertaken, because the owners expect to make the going rate of interest on their investment. Thus, $1 million is invested in each of the first four projects listed in Figure 4-4, making a total of $4 million invested. All those projects that are expected to yield less than the going rate of interest will not be undertaken. But if the rate of interest were to fall to 6 percent, the toy factory in Atlanta would become profit-

FIGURE 4-4. The Equilibrium Level of Investment

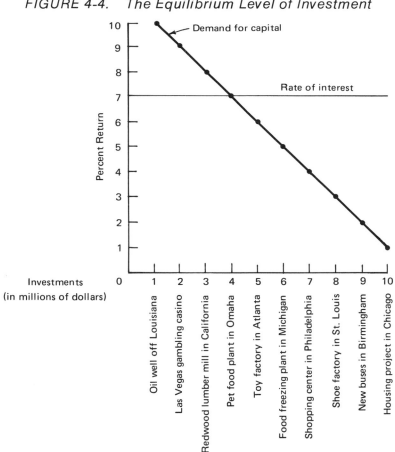

able, and another million dollars would be invested. At a 5 percent rate of interest, a food freezing plant would be built in Michigan, and a total of $6 million would have been invested.

If the expected profitability of industry increased, the whole demand curve would shift upward toward the right, and more capital would be invested than formerly at each level of interest. With a decrease of expected profitability, the demand curve would shift downward toward the left, and investment would fall.

According to this type of analysis, raising interest rates is effective against inflation because it cuts down investment. In depression, lowered interest rates will stimulate investment, thereby easing the depression.

THE EQUATION OF EXCHANGE AND THE QUANTITY THEORY OF MONEY The supply-and-demand analysis of money presented above allows an explanation of another phenomenon that has attracted attention over the last several centuries. Thoughtful observers noticed that as the quantity of money increased, prices tended to rise. This came to be known as the quantity theory of money, and it was popularized by Irving Fisher of Yale University in the early 1900's. His theory was based on the equation of exchange

$$MV = PT$$

Here M is the quantity of money, including both currency and demand deposits. V is the velocity of circulation of money, the number of times, on the average, a piece of money is spent during a certain period. P is the average level of prices. T is the total number of transactions involving intermediate as well as final goods and services. By definition, MV is the total amount of expenditure, or the work that money does. PT is the total receipts for the year for all goods and services sold; it is, therefore, much larger than GNP, which adds only *final* goods and services.

The equation of exchange is set up in such a way that it must be true. MV is what we pay for the goods and PT is what the total supply of goods costs. Of course the two quantities are equal.

No necessary cause-and-effect relationship is implied by the equation; it merely tells us something about the interrelationships that exist. If something happens to change one element of the equation, one or more of the remaining elements must also change. If, for example, the volume of business (T) increases, the quantity of money (M) or the velocity of circulation V) may increase; if not, prices (P) must fall. Alternatively, if P falls, M or V is likely to fall. If M rises, P or T is likely to rise, or V will fall.

The quantity theory of money makes use of the equation of exchange, but it goes on to introduce a cause-and-effect relationship among the four variables. Irving Fisher assumed that V remains fairly constant. T, the physical volume of business, remains constant in the short run because in his analysis the economy was always at full employment. Therefore, the only variables are M and P. If M is increased, P will rise, and if M is reduced, P will fall. Therefore, any desirable price level can be established by manipulating the quantity of money.

This theory is most useful when it is applied in periods of full employment or inflation. If the quantity of money is increased and prices soar, the velocity of circulation of money is then also likely to increase, as people try to spend their money quickly before its value shrinks further. Prices may rise more than the quantity of money rises. If the quantity of money is reduced, perhaps by repudiating the old inflated currency and limiting severely the issue of new currency, inflation may be brought under control.

The quantity theory of money is least likely to be valid under conditions of depression and unemployment. If M is increased during a depression, V may fall as people hoard money because they fear prolonged depression, or T may rise while P remains constant, until full employment is approached.

The modern version of the quantity theory of money has been developed and popularized by Milton Friedman of the University of Chicago. He and other "monetarists" emphasize that economic activity can be regulated by the manipulation of the money supply. They assume that the velocity of circulation is fairly stable and that the supply of money influences not only the price level, but also the level of output and employment. They argue for a laissez-faire policy in which the government should do as little as possible to try to direct or influence the economy. According to Friedman, the government need only be concerned with the supply of money. If the growth of real national income is to be maintained at 4 or 5 percent per year, then the government should allow the money supply to increase by the same percentage to maintain conditions for growth without inflation.

Friedman stated the following in testimony before a Congressional committee:

> If the stock of money can be kept growing at a relatively steady rate, without erratic fluctuations in short periods, it is highly unlikely if not impossible that we would experience either a sharp price rise—like that during World Wars I and II and after World War I—or a substantial price or output decline—like those experienced from 1920–21, 1929–33, 1937–38.

It certainly sounds easy to control fluctuations by this simple procedure. But as we shall argue in Chapter 8, there are many complicated causes of fluctuations, and no single simple cure is likely to produce stability.

Evaluation of Monetary Theory

IS THE ROLE OF INTEREST RATES EXAGGERATED?   There is little doubt that monetary policy, along with fiscal policy, can have a powerful effect on the economy. At the very least, monetary policy can influence the banks' ability to lend by controlling the volume of bank reserves. But is monetary theory always as reliable as it seems to be?

What we are questioning here is the extent of the role of the rate of interest in influencing the volume of investment as pictured in Figure 4-4 above. The geometric precision shown there is largely unrelated to the real world. The expected rate of profit on new investment over its life cannot be projected as a clean-cut line; it is rather a broad and wavy smudge, and the longer the expected life of the investment, the greater the uncertainty. If you are contemplating establishing a new toy factory that you expect to last for twenty-five years, how can you possibly tell what your profits will be over that length of time? What will happen to labor costs, costs of materials, taxes, and the selling price of toys? What will happen to national income, birth rates, and consumer tastes? Suppose that over the coming decades people spend less on toys and more on family camping? How will you fare in competition with other domestic toy makers and with imports? How soon will your machines grow obsolete as new and better ones are invented? These and other uncertainties make it almost impossible to project an expected rate of profit accurate enough to be used as a tool in the determination of monetary policy.

Businessmen must, of course, make choices about what line of business to invest in, how much to invest, what kinds of combinations of capital and labor to use, how much to spend on advertising, and so on. The expected rate of profit is an important factor that guides them in reaching decisions. But because it is far less precise than the charts indicate, many small and medium-sized businesses show small rates of profit, or they lose money and go bankrupt. Conversely, many small businesses may temporarily make large profits because potential rivals underestimated prospective profits.

Even an absolutely correct estimate of a situation can produce failure because of unplanned and uncoordinated decisions that conflict with the known reality. For example, suppose businessmen are absolutely correct when they predict that five new toy factories will produce a good rate of return. If each of ten entrepreneurs erects a toy factory, each hoping to capture 20 percent of the expanded market, they may all face trouble because together they exceeded the new investment that was justified by their own correct predictions—they have built ten new toy factories instead of five. The risks and the failures are therefore compounded by uncoordinated decisions under competitive conditions.

Another difficulty is that the demand-for-capital curve and the rate of interest line shown in Figure 4-4 may influence each other, and instead of producing equilibrium, they may produce cumulative change. Suppose there is an investment boom and the demand-for-capital curve shifts up and to the right. The increase in investment will increase incomes and consumption spending measured in current dollars. Therefore, the demand for money to be used for transactions increases; the demand-for-money curve in Figure 4-3 shifts up and to the right. By looking at Figure 4-3 we see that interest rates rise. Because of rising incomes and interest rates, people expect a higher level of prosperity and inflation; consumer spending thus increases, which, in turn, increases profits still more. More money is invested and the demand-for-capital curve in Figure 4-4 shifts still further upward and to the right. Instead of higher interest rates cutting down investment, they helped produce the climate that increases investment. This may well have been the process operating in the late 1960's.

Conversely, falling interest rates may help produce a climate of pessimism signaling that worse times are coming, and the demand for capital may therefore fall. This seems to have been a factor in the decline of the early 1970's.

Furthermore, we may question why the rate of interest is singled out as the key variable that determines investment. There are other costs, like those of labor, or materials, or taxes, that may be far more important. Surveys have shown that businessmen themselves believe that the rate of interest is not very significant in influencing their investment decisions. If they downgrade the role of interest, interest becomes less important. The "law" determining the amount of investment is not like the law of gravity. Isaac Newton's principle operates whether you understand it or not; you do not have to know physics to fall downward out of the tree. But if businessmen deny that the rate of interest has a significant influence on their investment decisions, then the whole analysis is of doubtful validity and relevance.

It is a gross oversimplification to assert that a contemplated investment will be made if the expected rate of profit is above the going rate of interest. This is most likely to be true under competitive conditions and least likely to be true under monopolistic conditions. Suppose we had a competitive auto industry with easy entry by new firms, and suppose that an entrepreneur could enter the industry by building a new plant whose anticipated profitability in the long run would be 12 percent, when the rate of interest was 6 percent. This would indeed be an attractive prospect. But the auto industry in reality is more monopolistic than competitive. If General Motors were considering building another plant, it would have to evaluate the effect of this new plant on the profitability of its existing plants. If a new plant would reduce GM's rate of return on all other investments by one-fourth of a percent because the price of cars would have to be lowered to sell more of them, the new investment will not be made. Under monopolistic conditions, therefore, profits are kept much higher than the average by restricting new investment and by restricting output from existing investments.

If maintaining a monopolistic position is more important than the rate of return on a new investment considered by itself, the whole decision-making process becomes clothed in uncertainty. If, in our example, the new investment yielding 12 percent would have been made under competition, but not where monopoly elements are present, we may conclude that even if Figure 4-4 shows a true system of equilibrium, it conceals the disservice shown to society when investment is curtailed to protect high profits. The implication of this type of theory is that the outcome of market equilibrium is both natural and beneficial. But it may be neither.

There is some truth in the idea that the rate of interest can influence investment. If you wish to buy a home, high interest rates may make the monthly payments too high for you to undertake; if you are willing to buy the home anyhow, the bank may turn down your request for credit. Investments that require huge capital expenditures that must be paid off over a long period of time may be undertaken or rejected because of the level of interest; hydroelectric power plants and apartment houses are examples. The point we are making here is that the rate of interest is probably less influential in making investment decisions than the theory leads us to believe.

Keynes focused his attention on the rate of interest not because it is the most powerful influence, but because it is the one most easily manipulated by government policy.

THE EFFECT OF CREDIT ON CONSUMPTION   In considering our system of credit, there is a widespread illusion that consumer credit necessarily increases consumption. (Keep in mind that mortgages on owner-occupied houses are not a part of consumer credit. As we saw in Chapter 2, houses represent investment.) If greater consumption is considered to be good, then it is believed that consumer credit is desirable. But it is more probable that consumer credit reduces consumption. We can illustrate this idea by making the following assumption, which we believe to be realistic: borrowers must pay their debts during their lifetimes or at death.

For example, let us compare two families. The Joneses pay cash for everything. The Smiths buy everything on credit because they are trying to keep up with and get ahead of the Joneses in spending. Both families have the same annual earnings and the breadwinners have worked exactly the same number of years. Who will have a higher level of consumption? The Joneses, of course, because they do not have to pay interest, and interest charges represent a deduction from consumption. Thus the abolition of consumer credit would probably increase consumption.

But you might ask, "How would the Smiths ever save up for a car if there were no credit? They'd spend their money on beer, books, and beauticians instead." This may be true, but economists are supposed to avoid value judgments. Who is to say that the auto is the wiser purchase? All we can say is that consumer credit may change the things people buy, and people can buy some things sooner than they otherwise would. Smith, buying on credit, will buy a car sooner than Jones, who has to save up for it, but Jones will consume more than Smith over a lifetime.

Consumer credit can increase total consumption if it grows each year by more than the interest payments; yet this is unlikely to happen in the long run. Total consumer debt rose from $6 billion at the end of 1945 to $127 billion at the end of 1970. The debt rose $4 billion during 1970 alone, and consumer interest payments totaled $17 billion. These payments clearly reduced total consumption.

VEBLEN'S CRITICISM OF THE CREDIT SYSTEM Thorstein Veblen, the great American economist and social critic, denied that credit contributes anything to production. He claimed that it merely enchances the possibilities for manipulation and profiteering. According to him, credit has a special role to play in modern business. Borrowing money can increase profits as long as the current rate of profit exceeds the rate of interest. Under competitive conditions, what is profitable for one businessman to undertake becomes compulsory for all competitors. Those who take advantage of the opportunities afforded by credit are in a position to undersell those who do not. Therefore, almost all businessmen rely on credit. The competitive earning capacity of an enterprise comes to rest on the basis of the initial capital plus such borrowed funds as this capital will support. As total earnings are only slightly larger than they might have been without credit, the rate of profit on the total amount invested tends to fall. The competitive use of credit in extending business operations gives a business concern a differential advantage against other competitors, but the expansion of credit has no collective effect on earnings or on total industrial output. In fact, total net profits from industry are reduced by the amount of interest that has to be paid to creditors outside the industrial process.

Credit created by banks, said Veblen, has little real wealth behind it; credit, therefore, has only a pecuniary (business) existence, and not a material (industrial) one. It represents merely fictitious industrial equipment. The extension of credit enables competing businessmen to bid up the prices of the material capital goods used in industry. As the dollar value of these goods increases, the goods serve as collateral for a further extension of credit. The extension of loans on collateral, such as shares of stock or real property, thus has a cumulative character. Credit expands even more with the organization of monopolies, for the costs of the reorganization and the promoters' profits are turned into capital by issuing securities. The expected increase in the profits of the monopolies and the imputed goodwill of the new corporations are also capitalized and used as collateral for further credit.

This cumulative extension of credit causes the expanding economy to rest on a shaky foundation. Sooner or later a discrepancy will arise between the actual money value of the collateral and the capitalized value of the collateral, which is computed on expected earnings. In other words, the rise in earnings does not keep pace with the inflation of the nominal capital (capital plus loans); the business is not worth the investment as recorded in its financial records. When this discrepancy becomes obvious, a period of liquidation begins. The industrial crisis caused by liquidation is accompanied by credit cancellations, high discount rates, falling prices, forced sales, shrinkage of capitalization, and reduced output. The creditors take over business properties, thereby further consolidating ownership and control into fewer hands because of bankruptcies. But Veblen's theories can also be criticized. In our private-enterprise economy, bank credit enables a businessman to mobilize a supply of labor from among those who are unemployed, underemployed, or self-employed (such as artisans, door-to-door salesmen, and farmers). The drawing of labor into large industrial establishments increases the total output of industry and therefore of the economy. Credit also permits the mobilization of raw materials and capital equipment and the expansion of their supply. It widens the markets and thereby stimulates greater production. Even if an economy is fully employed, the expansion of credit can increase saving and investment through the process of inflation. As prices rise, consumers must curtail their consumption if their incomes are fixed or if their incomes rise more slowly than prices. Credit, therefore, may have a significant effect on the economy.

It would be unfair to Veblen, however, to criticize the inadequacies of his theory in describing a private-enterprise economy. He did not accept that frame of reference, and he looked at our society as a detached observer. In his analysis of credit, he probably meant that credit is not essential to economic life. Primitive societies certainly functioned without it. A modern technological society could dispense with credit if it were organized as some sort of industrial republic run by engineers or as a socialist society. From this vantage point credit adds nothing to the functioning of an industrial society. In fact, credit detracts from it to the extent that it opens the way to financial manipulation, speculation, increased costs, and greater profit. Therefore, credit, in Veblen's gloomy view, added nothing to society.

Summary

Money is anything that is generally accepted in payment for goods and services. It includes currency and demand deposits. The most important functions of money are its use as a medium of exchange and as a common measure of the values of all kinds of things.

The government has passed legislation stating that all our currency is legal tender; this means it must be accepted in payment for debts. While demand deposits are not legal tender, they are just as acceptable as currency in making most payments.

In this chapter we described how the commercial banks create credit through their fractional reserve requirements. We saw how the Federal Reserve banks can regulate the flow of credit through open market buying and selling of the securities that the federal government issues, through altering the reserve requirements on the demand deposits of the commercial banks that belong to the Fed, and through discounting promissory notes held by member banks or lending money to the banks on their own promises to pay. The Fed also clears checks, issues most of our paper currency, regulates stock market credit, and acts as the fiscal agent for the federal government. The Federal Reserve System and the Federal Deposit Insurance Corporation have given great stability to the banking system by reducing bank failures to a minimum; this has helped stabilize the economy as a whole.

Interest is defined as the cost of borrowing money, and it depends on the supply of and demand for money. The demand for money is really a demand for liquidity, and interest is the price paid to those who give up liquidity. According to Keynesian theory, for interest rates above some minimum level, the lower the rate of interest, the greater the volume of investment, and vice versa. The rate of interest can be affected by manipulating the supply of money. The greater the supply of money, primarily bank credit, the lower the rate of interest, and vice versa. Therefore, the Fed, by loosening or tightening the controls over bank credit, can lower or raise the rate of interest; this influences investment spending and through it the nation's income and average level of prices. The equation of exchange, $MV = PT$, tells us that a rising money supply is likely to increase prices or the level of business, or both; a reduced money supply is likely to lower prices and economic activity.

Keynes and his followers believed that monetary policy is one significant method of controlling and stabilizing the economy; it should be supplemented by fiscal policy—government taxing, spending, and, for the more radical Keynesians, redistributing income from rich to poor if the average and marginal propensities to consume are to be raised. The modern "monetarists," however, prefer less government intervention in the economy. They believe that simply controlling the supply of money, letting it grow in pace with rising output of goods and services, will keep prices stable and the nation's income rising at a steady rate.

QUESTIONS AND PROBLEMS

1   Try to find out what things have been used as money in the past in different societies and discuss why they were used.

2   Why are savings accounts not considered to be money?

3   What would happen to the banking business if the reserve requirement on demand deposits were raised to 100 percent?

4   Compare your demand for money with that of your parents.

5   Suppose you buy a house with a twenty-five-year, $25,000 mortgage at 7 percent interest. You will pay interest plus $1,000 on the principal each year. When the mortgage is paid off, how much interest will you have paid? (Books on the mathematics of finance can help you answer this question.)

6   Suppose you obtain $500 of consumer credit, and you pay back $50 a month for a year. What is the rate of interest?

7   If a corporation retains and invests part of its own earnings, are its decisions influenced in any way by the rate of interest?

8   In the past many economists believed that interest is the reward for postponing consumption, which was regarded as a painful sacrifice. Evaluate this concept.

9   If the banking system as a whole borrows a billion dollars from the Fed, it can lend out an additional $6 billion or so. Therefore, what influence does the Fed's rate of discount have on bank lending, and what keeps the banks from heavy discounting in order to expand their loans?

10   Studies in the 1950's and 1960's showed that investment in college education gave a higher rate of return than capital investments. Yet bankers would not extend loans to college students without government guarantees or cosigners of the obligations. Why?

11   How could the expansion of credit increase both consumption and investment?

12   Bank credit enables a businessman to mobilize a supply of labor from among those who are unemployed. Can a society find any other way to employ the unemployed?

BIBLIOGRAPHY

BOARD OF GOVERNORS OF THE FEDERAL RESERVE SYSTEM, *Federal Reserve Bulletin* (Monthly publication).

BOARD OF GOVERNORS OF THE FEDERAL RESERVE SYSTEM, *The Federal Reserve System, Purposes and Functions*, 5th ed. Washington, D.C.: 1967.

CHANDLER, LESTER V., *The Economics of Money and Banking*, 5th ed. New York: Harper & Row, 1969.

ECCLES, MARRINER S., *Beckoning Frontiers, Public and Personal Recollections*. New York: Knopf, 1951.

KLEIN, JOHN J., *Money and the Economy*, 2nd ed. New York: Harcourt Brace Jovanovich, 1970.

VEBLEN, THORSTEIN, *The Theory of Business Enterprise*. New York: Scribner's, 1904.

PART

TWO

MICROECONOMICS:
THE INDIVIDUAL
AND THE FIRM

Until now we have looked at the functioning of the economy as a whole. In the next three chapters we shall study the roles of individuals and business firms.

The national economy is made up of many firms and individuals all making economic decisions in the marketplace. In order to understand the whole, we must know the anatomy of its parts. Individuals and firms generate the income that, added together, becomes the national income. Microeconomics is the basis on which macroeconomics has been erected.

Chapters 5 and 6 develop the theory of the firm in two different situations: perfect and imperfect competition. The economic motivations behind the myriad of decisions that firms make are studied in these important chapters.

This type of theory also is concerned with the distribution of income. Here again we see that micro- and macroeconomics overlap, illuminating the same problems from different perspectives. Microeconomics analyzes the distribution of income primarily in a free-market society. Macroeconomics can be used to study the distribution of income under various types of institutional arrangements, such as labor unionism and government measures to influence that distribution.

In this part of the book we shall look at the individual consumer to see how a person distributes his or her expenditures in order to get the maximum satisfaction from limited means. We shall see how the supplier decides what the most profitable output will be. Economic theory will be used as a tool to explore such questions as, What happens to our spending patterns if the price of a good rises? Who finally pays a tax on commodities? Does government restriction of output in agriculture really help farmers, and if so, why and how? What effect does advertising and the reduction of competition have on prices and profits? What is the effect of speculation in the commodity markets? What are the causes and effects of our economy becoming less competitive? What determines the level of rent, interest, wages, and profit? These and other matters can be analyzed on the basis of microeconomic theory and its applications, which are presented in this section.

5

Demand, Supply, and Competitive Market Price

Civilization and profits go hand in hand.
—*Calvin Coolidge*

In this chapter we analyze the theory of how prices are formed under conditions of perfect competition. Perfect competition is at the opposite end of the spectrum of market situations from pure monopoly. A perfectly competitive market has many buyers and sellers, so that no one buyer or seller exerts a noticeable influence on price. If extra profits earned in that type of business make it attractive, people can easily establish new businesses to compete with those already in existence; this is called free entry. The goods are perfectly homogeneous: one firm's product is not preferred over another firm's. As the commodities are identical, prices also are identical. There are no brand names, no advertising, and no considerations of friendship when buyers and sellers do business; market relationships are coldly calculating and impersonal.

As you can see, the conditions of perfect competition do not exist in manufacturing and retail trade. This market situation occurs in the markets for the basic agricultural commodities, for example, the wholesale wheat market. There are tens of thousands of sellers of wheat and thousands of buyers or potential buyers. Each kind and grade of wheat is highly standardized, so that no farmer advertises, "Buy my wheat; it's better than any other wheat." At any one moment, the latest price of wheat is known throughout the country and the world. If the price is $2.00 a bushel, no one will sell at $1.99, and no one will offer $2.01 a bushel. Buyers and sellers deal in an impersonal way with each other, generally never even meeting.

You may wonder why we should study a market situation that is rarely encountered outside agriculture. There are several important reasons that justify this type of analysis. First, wholesale agricultural markets do provide a significant illustration of perfect competition. Second, many urban markets approach the conditions of pure competition. This can be seen in downtown business districts when a dozen hawkers near each other sell identical leather belts, scarves, bags of peanuts, and shoelaces; or a dozen stores in the same area sell identical cameras, photographic film, records, and razor blades. Third, an analysis of perfect competition introduces us to a type of theory that will help us understand other market situations. We shall learn about demand and supply; fixed, variable, and marginal costs; elasticity of demand and supply; and how the decline of competition favors the sellers. This chapter, therefore, provides a foundation for the study of microeconomics.

The Theory of Demand

It has been said that a man taught his parrot to say "supply and demand," and the bird became an economist. You should be forewarned that at the end of this discussion we will conclude that supply and demand determine price. But the situation is rather more complex than this. We shall analyze basic questions that the parrot cannot answer: What influences supply? What influences demand?

We shall be considering market situations that range from perfect competition at one extreme to pure monopoly at the other. Monopoly means, of course, that there is only one seller of a particular commodity. In between these extreme and relatively rare situations, are found monopolistic competition and oligopoly, which will be discussed in the following chapter.

In monopolistic competition there are many sellers of a product, which indicates much competition; but each seller has a monopoly formed by his brand name, location, or circle of loyal customers. In other words, a small degree of monopoly exists. This market situation is not only characterized by the existence of brand names and advertising, but also by a downward-sloping demand curve for each firm's product. This curve tells us that the firm cannot sell all it wants to at the going market price, as the wheat farmer can.

Oligopoly means a few sellers of a single product, the situation in many manufacturing industries, such as steel, autos, farm machinery, and computers.

INDIVIDUAL DEMAND AND TOTAL MARKET DEMAND Let us see how individual demands are added to give us total market demand. Table 5-1 illustrates the demand for chicken by three people and the total demand. Eva Chandler is fairly affluent, and she prefers filet mignon or sirloin steak to chicken. She would increase her monthly purchases of chicken if the price fell, but not by much. Anna Baker has a large family to feed, and she has to be frugal. She will not buy any chicken at a high price, and at a low price she will increase her purchases considerably. Ben Barber is more af-

TABLE 5-1   Hypothetical Demand for Chicken
(in pounds per month)

Price per pound (in dollars)	Eva Chandler	Anna Baker	Ben Barber	Total
		Quantity		
1.00	1	0	4	5
.80	2	0	6	8
.60	3	5	8	16
.40	4	10	10	24
.20	5	20	12	37

fluent than Anna Baker, and he has a larger family to feed than Eva Chandler. He will buy more chicken at each price than Eva Chandler, but he will not be quite as bargain-conscious as Anna Baker. If we add all the quantities demanded by each person at each price, we get the total market demand for chicken by these three people.

Figure 5-1 is a graphic presentation of the data in Table 5-1. The distance AB shows the quantity of chicken Eva Chandler would buy at 60 cents per pound—3 pounds per month. AC shows the quantity Anna Baker would buy at that price—5 pounds. AD represents the 8 pounds that Ben Barber would buy. Adding the horizontal distances AB, AC, and AD gives

FIGURE 5-1.   Hypothetical Demand for Chicken
(in pounds per month)

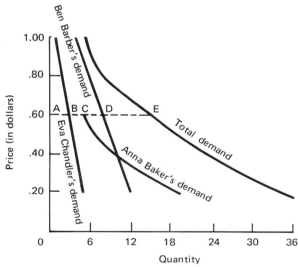

Source: Table 5-1.

us AE, which represents the total quantity of chicken that would be bought at 60 cents per pound—16 pounds per month.

Here we must make an important distinction. If the price of chicken were to fall from 60 cents per pound to 40 cents, the quantity of chicken sold would rise from 16 pounds per month to 24 pounds per month. This is not a change in demand; rather, it is a change in quantity demanded in response to a change in price. Demand refers to a series of alternative prices and quantities called a schedule. A change in demand refers to a shift of the demand curve, not to a movement along the curve. If we wanted twice as much chicken at each price as we formerly did, that would be an increase in demand, and the total demand curve would shift upward and to the right. If we wanted half as much chicken at each price as formerly, that would be a decrease in demand, and the curve would shift downward and to the left.

The reason this distinction is significant is that it helps us avoid the following false reasoning: "If price rises, demand decreases. If demand decreases, price falls. Therefore, price increases are self-defeating and cannot last." The correct statement is: If price rises, the quantity demanded decreases. Unless something else happens, the price will remain higher than it was.

The demand curve slopes down and to the right. This tells us that other things remaining unchanged, the lower the price, the greater the quantity we wish to buy; the higher the price, the less we wish to buy. Why is this so? There are two important reasons. First, the less expensive chicken is, the richer we are in real purchasing power and the more we can afford to buy; conversely, the higher the price of chicken, the less we can afford to buy. Second, the less expensive chicken is, the more we will use it as a substitute for other goods like red meat, fish, and other protein foods; but the more expensive chicken is, the more we will substitute other foods in its place. Underlying both these reasons is the law of diminishing marginal utility; this is a topic that is important enough to merit its own niche in the theory of demand.

THE LAW OF DIMINISHING MARGINAL UTILITY Utility refers to the satisfaction we get from the consumption of goods and services. If we ate chicken only once a month, we might look forward rather eagerly to the occasion; the utility would be high. If we had chicken twice a month, the second occasion would not be quite as joyous as the first. The total satisfaction of two chicken dinners is greater than of one, but the *extra* satisfaction of the second dinner would be less than that of the first. If we had thirty chicken dinners in a month, the total satisfaction would be greater than from two such dinners, but not fifteen times greater. The more units of a consumer good we acquire during any one period of time, the greater the *total* utility and the less the *extra* or *marginal* utility. It is conceivable that the marginal utility could fall to zero. If we had chicken so often that it began to nauseate us, the marginal utility might even be considered a negative quantity.

The marginal utility of the first chicken dinner per month is probably not extremely high, because there are other foods that are perfectly good substitutes. But with some goods there are no adequate substitutes. The first unit of such a good may have a very high marginal utility, and subsequent units then will have marginal utilities that decline rapidly. For example, the first pair of shoes you buy would have very high marginal utility, because the alternative might be to wrap your feet in burlap sacks or to go barefoot. Two pair of shoes are more satisfying than one, but not twice as satisfying. Three pair are more satisfying than two, but not much more so. Perhaps the sixth pair of shoes owned at any one time would have zero marginal utility. Then the maximum total utility would be at five pair of shoes, and a sixth pair would add nothing to our satisfaction.

The demand curve slopes down and to the right, because the more units of a good we acquire at any one time, the less useful each added unit is to us. Therefore, we will buy more units only if the price falls, to match the diminishing marginal utility of the good to us.

CONSUMER EQUILIBRIUM: THE BALANCING OF MARGINAL UTILITIES   We assume that consumers, with their limited buying power, distribute their consumption spending in a way that maximizes their total satisfaction. If they were to spend all their money on food, the principle of diminishing marginal utility would result in their getting less utility than they might if they purchased some other things.

Table 5-2 illustrates how consumers might distribute their spending, assuming they are totally rational and carefully calculating, in order to get maximum satisfaction from their limited resources. Suppose you are deposited in a city where you have never been before and you know nobody. You have four dollars in your pocket, and you may not call home collect for more money to be wired to you; you are on your own. How will you spend your four dollars to get maximum satisfaction?

Let us assume that your most urgent desire is for food, so you spend one dollar on a hamburger and french fries, as shown in the first line of the table. Now that you have temporarily subdued the worst of your hunger pangs, you begin to think of shelter; you rent floor space for the night for one dollar, as shown in line 2. As you are at least assured of being warm and dry for the night, the next most urgent desire is for more food, and so you spend your third dollar on cheesecake and coffee, as depicted in the third line. Finally, to celebrate your meeting your most basic and urgent requirements, you use your last dollar to meet a lower-order desire in your own scheme of priorities: you buy a bottle of wine.

Now the millionaire philanthropist you met in the bar, hearing of your

TABLE 5-2 The Balancing of Marginal Utilities

	Food	Clothing	Shelter	Wine
First four dollars	$1.00 [1]			
			$1.00 [2]	
	$1.00 [3]			
				$1.00 [4]
Second four dollars	$1.00 [5]			
			$1.00 [6]	
	$1.00 [7]			
			$1.00 [8]	
Third four dollars	$1.00 [9]			
		$1.00 [10]		
	$1.00 [11]			
				$1.00 [12]
Total	$6.00	1.00	3.00	2.00

predicament and wanting to stimulate your problem-solving mind, gives you another four dollars. You decide that the next most urgent priority is more food. Then you decide to spend an extra dollar on shelter so you can lie on a mattress. As you are still hungry, you spend another dollar on food, and then another dollar to get clean sheets on your mattress.

To round out your exciting day, you find four dollars on the street. Again you spend the first dollar on more food. Having taken care of most of your basic needs, your attention is turned toward that hole in your sock that is quite irritating; you spend a dollar on a new pair of socks. The third dollar you also spend on food, and the last on another bottle of wine.

What conclusions can we draw from this pattern of spending? Can you say that because you spend $6 on food, $1 on clothing, and $3 on shelter, that food is six times as useful to you as clothing, and shelter is three times as useful as clothing? Absolutely not! Food and shelter are matters of survival, while a new pair of socks was not all that crucial to you. What we can say is this: the last dollar spent on food was about as satisfying to you as the last dollar spent on clothing, shelter, and wine. _It is not the total spending in each category that measures total utility; rather, it is the last dollar spent in each category that should give about the same satisfaction as the last dollar spent in any other category_. If the last dollar spent on food gave you much more satisfaction than the last dollar spent on wine, you should have spent $7 on food instead of $6 and $1 on wine instead of $2. Each person determines his own pattern of spending to give him maximum total satisfaction from his limited means.

We can now explain the paradox that Adam Smith, the founder of modern economics, wrote about. He observed that water is much more useful than diamonds, but diamonds are much more expensive than water. His observation was correct as far as total utility is concerned. Rational people would much rather have water than diamonds if they had to choose one or the other, but an extra diamond is worth a great deal more than an extra gallon or even ton of water. The marginal utility of diamonds is much greater than that of water. Because water is abundant and cheap, we can satisfy our demand for it almost to the point of zero marginal utility. Because diamonds are scarce and expensive (and sold by a monopoly), the price and marginal utility remain high.

The Theory of Supply

We have completed our analysis of demand, which is one of the determinants of the market price of a good. We shall now take a close look at supply, which means what quantity sellers choose to offer at each price. This is the second factor that, along with demand, determines the market price.

THE ASSUMPTION OF MAXIMUM PROFIT It is convenient to assume that the businessman seeks to gain maximum profit (or minimum loss). He might, of course, have objectives other than profit maximization: his goal in life may be to have maximum sales or to give maximum employment to his fellow human beings. If he does not like dealing with labor and unions, he might wish to hire as few people as possible while still making a good living; therefore, he might charge such a high price that he receives less than maximum profit. But we shall assume that the businessman will select the level of production, prices, and sales that will be most profitable to him. In real life he may not be so precise, because he is not certain of the shape, slope, and location of the demand and supply curves; but in theory these can be located with great precision.

The first step in determining the most profitable price and quantity of production is to study the costs with which the entrepreneur is faced.

FIXED COST Fixed, or overhead, cost means those costs that remain the same regardless of the volume of output. These costs include property taxes, interest on bonds, fire insurance payments on buildings, rent on leased property, salaries of lawyers, accountants, and corporation executives, wages of night watchmen, and obsolescence of machinery. While total fixed cost remains constant at all levels of output, average fixed cost falls as production increases. The more you produce, the lower the fixed cost per unit of output, because you are dividing a fixed numerator by an increasing denominator. This is illustrated in Table 5-3 and Figure 5-2 on pages 101 and 102.

VARIABLE COST Variable costs are those costs that change with the changing level of output and can be eliminated by shutting down production. They include expenditures on electric power, raw materials, wages for production workers, wear and tear of machinery, freight charges, and containers. The greater the output, the larger the *total* variable costs is a safe generalization.

As seen in Table 5-3 and Figure 5-2, variable cost per unit of output (average variable cost) is high at low levels of output. It falls as output increases and then begins to rise again. Why is this so?

Imagine a factory with ten workers. There are twenty different machines, and each worker has to operate two machines. He loses time dashing about trying to do more than one man's job. Output is very low, the machines are idle half the time, and the wage cost per unit of output is high.

As more workers are added, the factory operates more efficiently. With twenty machines, the average variable cost may reach a minimum when twenty workers are hired. Beyond that point, if you employ additional workers, production will go up, but average variable cost will rise. Production does not expand in proportion to the expanding labor supply. This is called the *law of diminishing returns*, which we shall discuss again in Chapter 7. This principle states that if all factors of production are kept constant except one, sooner or later the output will increase at a slower rate than the increased variable factor. Thus, if diminishing returns have set in, increasing the labor used (while other means of production are held constant) will lower the average output per worker, even though total output increases.

TOTAL COST In price theory we define total cost in a very peculiar way. It includes a rate of profit that compensates the businessman for the risks he takes. Only those profits that are necessary to induce the entrepreneur to remain in business are included in cost. Besides the explicit fixed and variable costs, total cost includes some implicit costs. Implicit costs are such items as the businessman's salary for running his business, interest on his own money invested, and rent on the land he owns. These categories will be discussed further in Chapter 7.

The idea of the owner's salary being an implicit cost may sound quaint, but this figure should be included when calculating the total costs of a company with a sole proprietor. In the modern corporation, however, most owners (stockholders) have little or nothing to do with running the business. All corporation executives are paid, and their salaries are an explicit rather than an implicit cost.

As total cost includes profit, a businessman will be satisfied to sell goods at cost; he will then be making the necessary minimal profit to stay in business. He would, of course, like to make more than that if he can, but he will settle for cost price if necessary. If the businessman claimed his profit as a cost on his income tax return, he would go to jail; no one has yet gone to jail for developing economic theory in this fashion.

In Table 5-3 we can see that average total cost is the sum of average fixed cost and average variable cost. Average variable cost does not fall as output rises from 3,000 to 4,000 bushels, but average total cost does fall. Why? Because average fixed cost falls as the output increases. Beyond an output of 4,000 bushels, average fixed cost continues to fall, but it is overwhelmed by rising average variable cost, and average total cost begins to rise.

TABLE 5-3   Cost Schedules of the Wheat Farmer Under Perfect Competition

			Costs (in dollars)				
Quantity (in bushels)	Total fixed cost	Average fixed cost	Total variable cost	Average variable cost	Total cost	Average total cost	Marginal cost
1,000	1,500	1.50	2,000	2.00	3,500	3.50	2.00
2,000	1,500	.75	3,500	1.75	5,000	2.50	1.50
3,000	1,500	.50	4,500	1.50	6,000	2.00	1.00
4,000	1,500	.375	6,000	1.50	7,500	1.875	1.50
5,000	1,500	.30	8,750	1.75	10,250	2.05	2.75
6,000	1,500	.25	12,000	2.00	13,500	2.25	3.25

In Figure 5-2, based on Table 5-3, at any level of output, average fixed cost is indicated by the vertical distance from the horizontal axis to the average fixed cost curve. Average variable cost is indicated by the vertical distance from the horizontal axis to the average variable cost curve. Therefore, average total cost at any level of output is equal to the sum of the vertical distances to the average fixed cost curve and the average variable cost curve and is shown by the average total cost curve. In other words, at each level of output the vertical distance between the average variable cost

FIGURE 5-2.   *Cost Curves of the Wheat Farmer Under Perfect Competition*

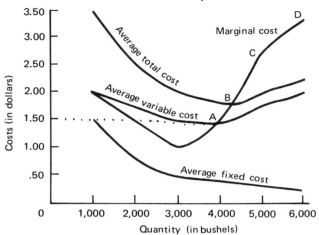

Source: Table 5-3.

and average total cost curves is equal to the distance from the horizontal axis to the average fixed cost curve.

MARGINAL COST   The concept of marginal cost is used in analyzing the decisions a businessman must arrive at in running his enterprise. If the entrepreneur is to receive the maximum profit, he must know whether to hire more or less labor, use more or less capital, utilize more or fewer managerial assistants. Capital and labor can be substituted for each other, and different kinds and qualities of capital and labor can be employed. The entrepreneur must decide what quantities of the different kinds of inputs he will use to obtain the maximum profit.

Marginal cost is the cost added to total cost as the result of producing one additional unit of output. Fixed cost does not change as output changes, so that marginal cost is not affected by fixed cost, but it is affected by variable cost.

In Table 5-3 total cost rises from $3,500 to $5,000 as output rises from 1,000 bushels to 2,000 bushels. Therefore, producing the extra 1,000 bushels adds $1,500 to total cost, or an average cost per bushel of $1.50; this is the marginal cost. As output rises from 2,000 bushels to 3,000 bushels, $1,000 is added to total cost; the marginal cost per bushel is therefore $1.00.

In Figure 5-2 we see that the marginal cost curve cuts the average variable cost curve at its lowest point. If marginal cost is below variable cost, it is pulling variable cost downward; if marginal cost is above variable cost, it is pulling variable cost upward. It is as if you had three exam grades that averaged out to 80 points. If on a fourth exam you received a grade of 70, that would pull your average down. If, alternatively, you received a marginal grade of 90 on your fourth exam, that would raise your average.

Therefore, marginal cost is equal to variable cost at the minimum variable cost. The same reasoning applies to average total cost, and marginal cost crosses the average total cost curve at its lowest point.

DERIVING A SUPPLY CURVE Suppose we wish to derive a supply curve for a single firm, in this case a wheat farmer. How much wheat will he produce? We see from Table 5-3 that his average total cost is at a minimum when he produces 4,000 bushels. Will he, then, produce just 4,000 bushels of wheat? Not necessarily, if he wishes to make the maximum possible profit. The quantity he will offer in the market depends on the price. The supply curve tells us how much he would offer *at each price*. The higher the price, the more he will offer, *for a high price justifies producing extra bushels* at *rising costs per bushel*.

In Table 5-3 and Figure 5-2 we can see that no wheat would be offered at a price below $1.50 per bushel. At those prices the farmer does not even get back his variable or out-of-pocket costs. If he stopped producing, he would lose his fixed costs—$1,500 per year. But if he continued producing wheat and sold it for less than $1.50, he would lose more than $1,500. He therefore shuts down.

If the price rises above $1.50, it pays the farmer to produce. At a price between points A and B in Figure 5-2, he is either losing money or making less than the average or expected rate of profit. But he loses less than he would if he shut down completely. At these prices he gets back all his variable costs (the height of A) plus something to cover part of his fixed costs.

If the price were at B, the farmer would be producing at his minimum average cost, and he would be making the average rate of profit. If, however, the price rose to $2.75 per bushel, he would produce the quantity indicated by point C even though his average cost per bushel is rising. If producing an extra bushel costs less than $2.75, it pays to produce it under perfect competition. If the added cost of producing another bushel is more than $2.75, it does not pay to produce that extra bushel. In other words, as long as the selling price is above marginal cost, it pays to increase production. Therefore, *maximum profit is made when production is expanded to the point where price equals marginal cost*.

Now we see why the marginal-cost concept is so necessary. If an extra bushel of wheat can be sold for $2.75, it will pay to produce and sell it as long as its cost of production is $2.00, $2.50, or $2.74. It will not pay to produce and sell that extra bushel if its cost is $2.76 or higher.

In the long run the price will be at B, the lowest point of the average total cost curve. If the price is below that, farmers will be receiving less than the cost of production, including the necessary profit to keep them in business. Some farmers will quit growing wheat and go into another line of production; others will reduce their output. As total wheat production declines, the price will rise toward B.

If the price is above B, farmers will be making extra profits, more than the minimum necessary to keep them producing wheat. Wheat farmers will expand their production; other farmers, lured by the high profits, will shift their output from their present crops to wheat. As the quantity of wheat offered in the market rises, the price will fall to B.

We have now derived one farmer's supply curve for wheat. We saw in Figure 5-2 that if the selling price of wheat were at the height of B, the farmer would offer to sell a quantity designated by a point vertically below B on the horizontal or quantity axis. If the price were at C, that would determine the quantity offered, which would be designated by the point vertically below C on the quantity axis. This is precisely the meaning of a supply curve: it tells us what quantity of goods will be offered at each price. The farmer's supply curve for wheat is that portion of the marginal cost curve that is above the average variable cost curve. At any point below the average variable cost curve, the farmer will not offer to sell any wheat at all, because he will not even get back his out-of-pocket costs incurred in producing the crop.

Analogously, with the total demand curve shown in Figure 5-1 on page 95, the total supply curve for wheat will be the horizontal sum of all the individual supply curves, with the quantities added together at each price. The total supply curve is arrived at by the same process that was used to calculate the total demand curve in Figure 5-1.

The Theory of Market Price

THE INTERACTION OF SUPPLY AND DEMAND   Now that we have seen how demand and supply curves are located, we can go on to show how the equilibrium market price is determined. In Table 5-4 and Figure 5-3, using the same example of wheat farmers in a situation of perfect competition, we see that at any price above $2.50, the quantity supplied exceeds the quantity demanded, and the price will be forced downward by the competitive pressures among sellers. At any price below $2.50, the quantity demanded exceeds the quantity supplied, and the price rises. At $2.50, when the quantities demanded and supplied are equal, equilibrium is attained. At any other price, the volume of sales will be lower than the 4 billion equilibrium, and some people who will want to do business at the going price will not be able to. At a price above $2.50, sellers wish to sell more than buyers wish to, but cannot, buy. At a price below $2.50, buyers wish to buy more than sellers wish to, but cannot, sell. At $2.50, all the people who wish to buy or sell can do so.

TABLE 5-4   Equilibrium Market Price Under Perfect Competition

Price per bushel (in dollars)	Quantity (in billions of bushels)		Consequence
	Demanded	Supplied	
1.50	6	2	Price rises
2.00	5	3	Price rises
2.50	4	4	EQUILIBRIUM
3.00	3	5	Price falls
3.50	2	6	Price falls

LONG-RUN EQUILIBRIUM   Until now we have been concerned with supply, demand, and market price in the short run. That is, we assumed that the number of plants, their size, and the type of machinery they had were fixed. If market conditions changed, the businessman could hire more or less labor, use more or less electric power, and buy more or less raw materials. But the time period was too short to build new plants or abandon old ones. That is why in the short run a firm might operate at a loss, because to go out of business might mean larger losses than staying in business. As long as the businessman can get some fixed costs back, he may lose less by staying in business than by closing down. Bankrupt railroads may volun-

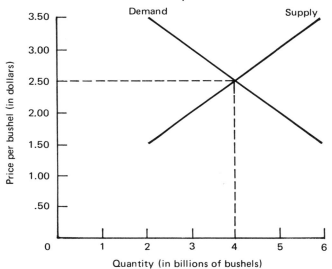

FIGURE 5-3.   Equilibrium Market Price Under Perfect Competition

Source: Table 5-4.

tarily remain in business for decades because the scrap value of a railroad line is relatively small. The company may lose less money by staying in business than by closing down, because it gets back at least part of its fixed investment. But when the rail line needs renovating, when more fixed investment is needed for it to continue operating, the company is likely to shut down unless its prospects improve.

In the long run there are no fixed costs. The businessman can eliminate costs by going out of business. He can increase costs by expanding the size of his plant or firm. In the long run all costs have to be covered, including the average or necessary rate of profit, or the business will fold. In the long run the businessman can expand existing plants, build new ones, or abandon obsolete ones. As more plants are built the total supply increases, with the curve shifting to the right. If plants are abandoned the supply curve shifts to the left. New technology also affects the supply curve.

The demand curve also shifts in the long run. As incomes rise, or as population grows, more will be demanded at each price than formerly. Changes in people's tastes, changes in the availability and prices of related goods, and changes in expectations of future prices also cause changes in demand.

Long-run market prices are shown in Figures 5-4, 5-5, and 5-6. Figure 5-4 shows a constant-cost industry, such as the razor blade industry. Regardless of the size of the industry and the volume of production, in the long run razor blades can be produced at an unchanging cost per unit.

FIGURE 5-4.   Changes in Price over Time in a Constant-Cost Industry

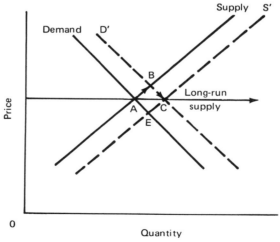

FIGURE 5-5.   Changes in Price over Time in an
                Increasing-Cost Industry

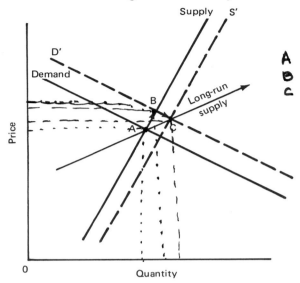

FIGURE 5-6.   Changes in Price over Time in a
                Decreasing-Cost Industry

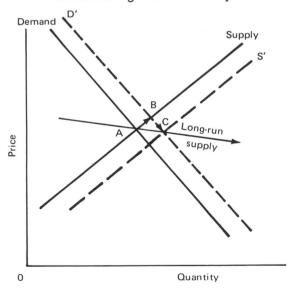

Equilibrium between supply and demand is shown at point A. With the growth of population, demand increases. That is, more razor blades are wanted at each price. The demand curve shifts upward and to the right, and the price rises to point B. Existing plants are pushed beyond lowest-cost production. This situation might correspond to that represented by point C in Figure 5-2, page 102. In the short run, extra workers may be hired, or workers might work overtime at time-and-a-half pay. But in the long run more plants can be built in order to produce a greater quantity at the same per-unit cost as formerly. More razor blades are available at each price, so the supply curve shifts to the right. The increased demand for steel and labor is small enough not to bid up the prices of these resources permanently. The long-run equilibrium price represented by point C in Figure 5-4 is the same as it was at point A. This is a constant-cost industry because, given enough time, increasing supplies will be forthcoming without a change in price.

This process works in the other direction also. Suppose the original demand and supply curves are represented by the dashed lines D' and S' in Figure 5-4. Now tastes change, and men grow beards. The demand for razor blades falls, and the demand curve shifts down to the left. The price falls to E along the dashed supply curve S'. Some firms do not get back all their fixed costs, and as their plants become obsolete, new ones are not built. Eventually supply falls and the supply curve shifts to the left. A new long-run equilibrium is attained at point A. The long-run price is unchanged.

Figure 5-5 represents the situation in an increasing-cost industry, such as wheat farming. If the demand for wheat increases, the demand curve shifts upward to the dashed demand curve D', and the price of wheat rises from point A to point B. Wheat land is worked more intensively, and the cost of producing extra wheat will be greater than formerly because of the law of diminishing returns. In addition, land is shifted from other uses to wheat production because of higher payments for wheat land; this also raises the cost of wheat. Assuming there is no improvement in the technology of growing wheat, the supply curve shifts to the right to the dashed supply curve S', and the long-run equilibrium price at point C is higher than the original price at point A.

Figure 5-6 illustrates the situation in decreasing-cost industries. It applies to those mass-production firms and industries that grow more efficient as they grow larger. In the short run, as demand increases, the price rises from point A to point B. In the long run, supply increases and since the per-unit cost is lower, the price falls to point C, which is lower than the original price. If these long-run falling costs result from the growth in the size of firms, this means the death of perfect competition. Small firms, whose costs are higher, will be unable to compete, and a few large firms will dominate the industry. This is what has happened in much of manufacturing, and to a lesser extent in retailing. Only in agriculture and in the stock and commodity markets do we have anything resembling the perfect competition of economic theory.

Applications of Competitive Pricing Analysis

ELASTICITY OF DEMAND AND SUPPLY   Elasticity of demand refers to the extent to which people will change the quantity of goods they demand in response to a change in price. In discussing elasticity of demand, we are considering movements along the demand curve rather than shifts of the curve itself. Five cases of elasticity will be considered: perfectly inelastic demand; relatively inelastic demand; the in-between case where elasticity equals one; relatively elastic demand; and perfectly elastic demand. These cases are presented visually in Figures 5-7 through 5-11.

The numerical value of elasticity of demand can be determined by the following equation:

$$\text{Elasticity of demand} = \frac{\text{Percent change in quantity demanded}}{\text{Percent change in price}}$$

If when the price changes 10 percent, the quantity demanded changes 20 percent, the elasticity of demand is two; this is relatively elastic. If when the price changes 10 percent the quantity demanded changes 5 percent, elasticity is one-half, which is relatively inelastic. The dividing line between elastic and inelastic is when the elasticity coefficient is one; for example, when the price and the quantity demanded both change 10 percent.

FIGURE 5-7.   Perfectly Inelastic Demand

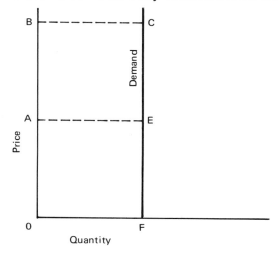

Figure 5-7 shows a perfectly inelastic demand. The quantity demanded remains the same regardless of price within the range shown. Even if the goods were free, we would not want more than a fixed quantity. Goods such as salt for table use or services such as appendectomies exhibit a perfectly inelastic demand curve. If the price were OA, we would spend OA times OF (the quantity) on the good or service; total expenditure is represented by the area OAEF. If the price were doubled to OB, we would spend OBCF, which is double the original expenditure, on the same quantity of goods. *With inelastic demand, the higher the price, the more we spend on a good or service; the lower the price, the less we spend.*

In Figure 5-8 any percentage change in price is accompanied by a smaller percentage change in quantity in the opposite direction. If prices rise, quantities demanded fall, but by a smaller percentage; if prices fall, quantities demanded rise by a smaller percentage. This type of demand might occur with meat or shoes or gasoline. *With relatively inelastic demand, the higher the price, the more we spend on a good or service, even though the quantity demanded is less; the lower the price, the less we spend, even though the quantity demanded is greater.*

FIGURE 5-8.   Relatively Inelastic Demand

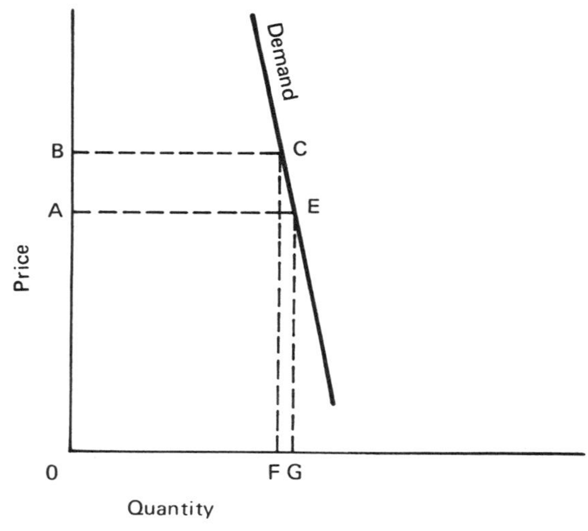

Inelastic demand is found under two conditions: if the expenditure on a good is small, or if there are no acceptable substitutes for a good. The demand for table salt illustrates both conditions. If the price of salt doubles, we in the United States do not have to economize on its use. In addition, there is no acceptable substitute for salt in food. Appendectomies are expensive, but the only substitutes are funerals, and they are not very satisfactory. There are substitutes for meat, shoes, and gasoline, but they are not very desirable.

Figure 5-9 shows a demand curve with an elasticity of demand of one. Every time the price changes, the quantity demanded changes by the same percentage in the opposite direction. The following hypothetical demand for motion picture tickets illustrates this elasticity. If the cost is $5.00 a ticket, you go once a month; if it is $2.50, you go twice a month; if it is $1.00, you go five times a month. *With an elasticity of demand of one, we spend the same amount on a good or service regardless of its price.*

FIGURE 5-9.   Elasticity of Demand of One

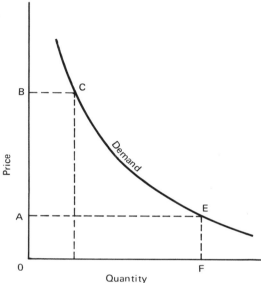

Figure 5-10 shows a relatively elastic demand. The demand for goods that have acceptable substitutes is relatively elastic. We have an inelastic demand for shoes because there are no acceptable substitutes, but the demand for Florsheim shoes is elastic because other brands of shoes are acceptable substitutes. The demand for meat is inelastic, but the demand for pork chops is elastic. As we can see in Figure 5-10, *with elastic demand, the lower the price, the more we spend on a good or service; the higher the price, the less we spend.*

Figure 5-11 shows a perfectly elastic demand curve. The demand for one farmer's wheat is perfectly elastic, although the total demand for wheat is inelastic, as shown in the graph at the right. Demand and supply interact in the total wheat market to set a price, shown here as OA per bushel. At that price each farmer can sell all he produces. If the market price is $2.00 per bushel, one farmer, whether he sells one thousand or ten thousand bushels, will have no noticeable impact on the price. If he charges $2.01 per bushel, he will not sell any wheat, because other farmers' wheat

FIGURE 5-10.   Relatively Elastic Demand

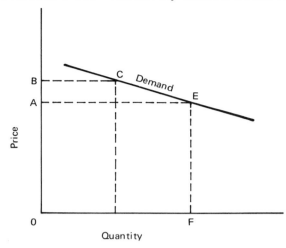

FIGURE 5-11.   Perfectly Elastic Demand

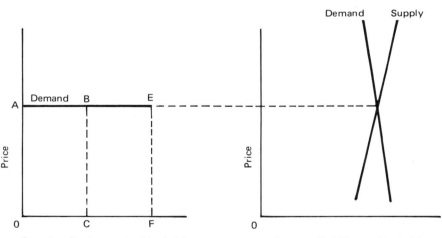

is a perfect substitute. He will not drop his price to $1.99, because he can sell all he has at $2.00. If he doubles his sales from OC bushels to OF bushels, he will double his gross receipts. *With perfectly elastic demand, the greater the quantity, the more we spend on a good or service; the lesser the quantity, the less we spend.*

The idea of elasticity of supply is similar to that of elasticity of demand, except that price and quantity change in the same direction instead of in opposite directions. The higher the price, the more will be offered for sale; the lower the price, the less will be offered. The equation for elasticity of supply is:

$$\text{Elasticity of supply} = \frac{\text{Percent change in quantity offered}}{\text{Percent change in price}}$$

If the elasticity of supply is 5, a percent increase in price will call forth a 5 percent increase in quantity offered, and a 1 percent decrease in price will cause a reduction of 5 percent in the quantity offered.

What is the significance of all this? In the next three sections we will see how these concepts of elasticity are applied in studying the economy.

GOVERNMENT TAXATION AND THE INCIDENCE OF TAXES Suppose you were advising the government on which commodities to tax, and the only requirement was that the excise taxes should disturb the pattern of production as little as possible; you were to ignore considerations of ethics or justice or welfare. Would you tax salt or crackers? Liquor or grapefruit juice? Matches or tomatoes? The answer is obvious: tax those things that have inelastic demands, those that have no acceptable substitutes. We will buy almost as much with the tax as without.

Now that we have decided what to tax, we should ask the question, Who finally pays a tax? Can it be passed on to someone else, or does the person who pays it bear the final burden? In the case of excise taxes on commodities, we can make a significant generalization: the taxes are paid by those people with the least power in the marketplace. And the people with the least power are those who have inelastic demand or supply; those with elastic demand or supply have the most power.

We shall consider the incidence of taxes in three situations: first, where there is an approximate equality of bargaining power between buyers and sellers; second, where the buyers have the upper hand because their demand is elastic while supply is inelastic; and third, where the sellers have the greatest advantage because their supply is elastic.

Figure 5-12 illustrates the situation where buyers and sellers have equal power. The original demand and supply (the solid lines) result in an equilibrium price of OB, and quantity OJ is sold. Now the government imposes a 25 percent tax on the commodity. At each quantity, the seller will now demand a price that is 25 percent higher than formerly at that quantity. The new supply curve S′ is therefore 25 percent higher than the old supply curve, measured vertically from the horizontal axis (for example, in Figure 5-12, the distance between points E and H is 25 percent greater than the distance between points G and H). The new equilibrium price is OC, but the sellers get to keep only the price indicated by OA. AC is the tax per unit. Total taxes are the tax per unit times the number of units, represented by the area ACEG. The price rose by less than the amount of the

FIGURE 5-12.   The Incidence of Taxes with Equal
Power Between Buyers and Sellers

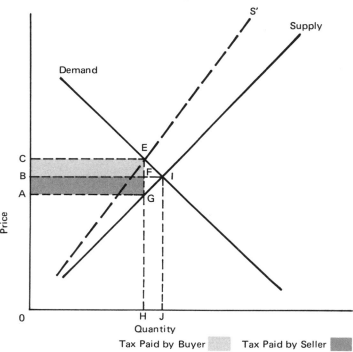

tax. Part of the tax is paid by the buyers, because the price rose from OB
to OC, but part of the tax is also borne by the sellers, who now get OA per
unit instead of OB. The sellers are willing to take a lower price than formerly for a smaller quantity of goods. With or without the tax, they would
have been willing to sell OH units at a price of OA.

We shall now consider what happens when a tax is imposed in a situation where demand is elastic and supply is inelastic. One example of such
a situation is the growing of coffee beans in Colombia. There are many
farmers producing coffee, and they have large investments in coffee trees
that bear crops for twenty or thirty years or more. The farmers will offer
their coffee for sale regardless of price, at least until the trees are old
enough to cut down; therefore, supply is inelastic. The demand for Colombian coffee is elastic. If the price goes up, coffee can be bought from
other countries. If the price of Colombian coffee goes down, buyers will
wish to buy much more. The situation is represented in Figure 5-13. If a 25
percent tax is imposed on coffee by the Colombian government, the sellers
pay the whole tax, because they lack market power; by withholding their
product, they would lose more money than by paying the tax. The market

FIGURE 5-13.   The Incidence of Taxes with Elastic
Demand and Inelastic Supply

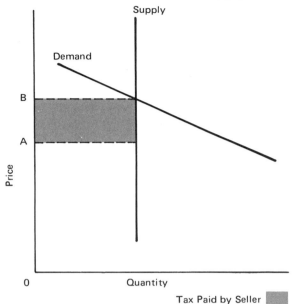

price remains unchanged, and the price the seller receives falls from
OB to OA.

Figure 5-14 illustrates the effect of a 25 percent excise tax in a situation where there is elastic supply and inelastic demand. This situation may
be typical in monopolistic pricing, as in the steel industry. The steel producers in effect say, "Our price is $100 per ton. Take it or leave it. What-
ever happens to your demand, we will not change our price." If the
government imposes a 25 percent tax, the steel producers will demand a
price that is 25 percent higher than formerly and the supply curve will
shift upward to S'. The sellers of steel get their price plus the tax, so that
the buyers are, in effect, paying the whole tax.

GOVERNMENT RESTRICTION OF OUTPUT IN AGRICULTURE   During the last
forty years the federal government has restricted the production and sale of
various farm products to increase the income of farmers. This policy works
best, from the point of view of the farmers, when the demand for their
products is inelastic. In that situation higher prices mean greater gross revenue. It is always more profitable to sell less goods for more money than it
is to sell more goods for less money.

In 1933 the government made a mistake in the farm program because
its advisers ignored elasticity of demand. To help the peach growers of

FIGURE 5-14.   The Incidence of Taxes with Inelastic
Demand and Elastic Supply

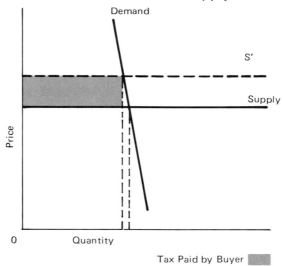

Tax Paid by Buyer

California, the Department of Agriculture restricted the canning of cling peaches in that state to 10 million cases. The rest of the peaches were left to rot in the orchards. In 1935 this program was abandoned; because of the increase in the price of canned peaches, people were buying canned pears instead. Because of the elastic demand for peaches, the farmers were worse off when output was restricted than before; they had smaller gross receipts because sales were reduced.

THE ROLE OF ADVERTISING AND THE REDUCTION OF COMPETITION Businessmen generally advertise their product in order to make more profit than they otherwise would. Advertising increases profits in two ways. First, because more people are made aware of the product, a greater quantity can be sold at each price than formerly; this is shown in Figure 5-15, with the new demand curve D′ moved out to the right from the old demand curve. Second, successful advertising makes the demand curve less elastic. If you are persuaded that no salt is as good as Morton's, no aspirin as good as Bayer's, or no shoes as good as Florsheim's, then you are willing to buy these products even if the prices are higher than those of competitive products. Reduced elasticity of demand allows an increase in sellers' profits.

It is interesting to note that as advertising results in a shift of the demand curve to the right, the shift itself reduces the elasticity of demand. In Figure 5-16, assume the price is OA. Without advertising, OH units would be sold, and the total revenue would be represented by the rectangle OAGH. If the price were raised to OB, total revenue would decrease to the

FIGURE 5-15.   Advertising and Elasticity of Demand

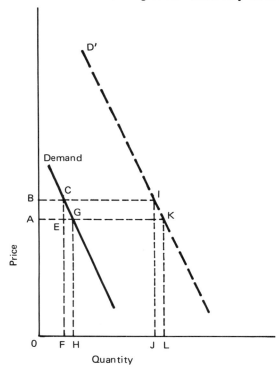

amount indicated by the rectangle OBCF. As the latter rectangle is smaller than the revenue rectangle at price OA, demand is elastic between C and G on the demand curve.

When the product is advertised, OL units are sold at price OA, and gross revenue is then OAKL. If the price were raised to OB, total revenue would increase to OBIJ. This shows an inelastic demand between I and K, and greater profits would be made by selling less goods for more money.

Attempts to reduce competition and promote a greater degree of monopoly are most profitable when demand is inelastic. It would hardly pay to try to monopolize the sale of canned peaches or mustache cups or plaid sport shirts, but it would be profitable to promote monopoly in antibiotics, salt, steel, automobiles, and medical services. The demand for large categories of goods for which there are unlikely to be acceptable substitutes is generally inelastic; the demand for one company's product is typically more elastic because other companies' products can be substituted.

PRICE FLOORS AND PRICE CEILINGS   Figure 5-16 shows what happens when the government tries to establish a price floor for agricultural products

FIGURE 5-16.   Price Floors for Agricultural Products

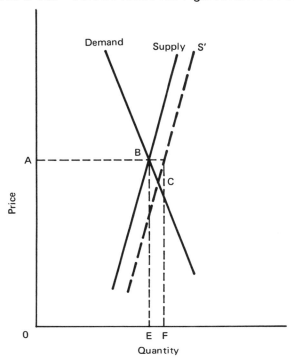

above the equilibrium price so that prices cannot fall below a certain level. Assume that the solid demand and supply curves represent the demand and supply that produce an equilibrium price at B. With the passage of time farmers learn to produce more efficiently, and they are willing to sell more at each price than formerly; the supply curve therefore shifts to S'. The new equilibrium price is at C. If the government tries to support the price at its original level, the sellers will offer the quantity OF, and the buyers will wish to buy OE. The unsold surplus, EF, will push prices downward unless the government buys up the surplus and stores or destroys it. The government may also try to force the farmers to produce less, forcing the supply curve back to its original position.

A problem created by price ceilings during the Second World War can be seen in Figure 5-17. The solid demand and supply curves show the prewar demand and supply, with the equilibrium price of OA per unit of output. As a result of the war, employment increased, incomes rose, and demand increased to D'. Supply was reduced to S', because some production had to be diverted to war supplies and because as costs rose, sellers were willing to offer less at each price than formerly. The new equilibrium price was OB. When the government imposed a price ceiling at prewar

FIGURE 5-17.   Price Ceilings During the Second World War

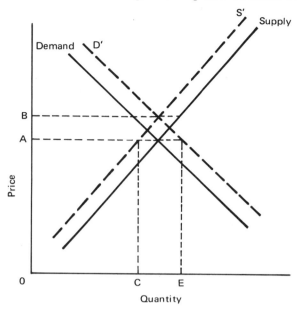

levels, so that prices were not allowed to rise above OA, demand and supply were no longer in equilibrium. At price OA, the quantity OE would be demanded, and only OC would be offered for sale; the shortage was the quantity CE. The government had to reduce the quantity demanded to OC by rationing goods. Rising prices act as a rationing device favorable to the rich; issuing rationing stamps to rich and poor alike was more favorable to the poor and to the wartime economy. If miners, for example, were to have the health and strength to do their work, they had to eat their share of meat instead of being priced out of that commodity.

HEDGING AND SPECULATION   The wholesale commodity markets, which deal in commodities such as wheat, lumber, and potatoes, provide us with our best examples of perfect competition. There are many actual or potential buyers and sellers. No one buyer or seller exerts a noticeable influence on price. Anybody can enter the market freely if he has the money to become a producer or a wholesale buyer or seller. Each commodity, like wheat, is homogeneous regardless of who produced it. There are no brand names, no advertising, and only impersonal relationships between buyers and sellers.

The wholesale commodity markets also provide opportunities for speculation in future price changes; but they also offer a means to avoid speculation, so that individuals can pass on the speculative risks to others.

Suppose a miller of flour needs 10,000 bushels of wheat each month. He can buy that quantity each month, making his normal profits on the products he turns out and sells. Or he may prefer to buy 120,000 bushels when the crop is harvested in July. That way he will not only have his year's requirement in his possession, but he will earn something on storing the grain instead of paying storage charges to other people. Buying wheat in advance, however, involves speculative risks that the miller may wish to avoid. Suppose the wheat he stored in July cost $2.00 per bushel, but by December the price falls to $1.80 a bushel. He will be selling products in competition with those millers who buy their supply every month; he will have to price his products as if the wheat cost him $1.80 a bushel. What the miller makes as a processor, he loses because the price of the wheat he held has fallen.

The miller can avoid this speculative loss by hedging. When he buys 120,000 bushels in July, he can simultaneously sell 10,000 bushels a month to be delivered in future months. But when the promised month of delivery arrives, the miller does not have to deliver the wheat; instead he makes or receives a cash payment depending on the rise or fall of wheat prices since the arrangement was made. These arrangements are called futures contracts. For example, in July the miller sells 10,000 bushels at $2.00 for delivery in December. By December the price of wheat has fallen to $1.80, and the miller has to pay only $1.80 a bushel for the 10,000 bushels he promised to deliver. He makes 20 cents per bushel profit. Thus, his gain in the futures market offsets his loss from holding wheat when the price falls.

Hedging eliminates speculative gains as well as losses. If in December the price of wheat rises to $2.20, the miller will raise the price of his products to reflect that price; he will make an extra 20 cents per bushel on the wheat he bought in July and processed in December. But he will lose 20 cents per bushel on his December-delivery contract; in July he sold 10,000 bushels at $2.00 a bushel, and in December he will have to pay 20 cents a bushel to settle the contract.

Speculators also even out prices throughout the year, and they help distribute our supplies so that they last throughout the year. Suppose all the wheat farmers, needing cash, throw their wheat on the market in July, and the price falls to $1.00. We may not eat much more bread at lower prices, but we may eat more cake; and we certainly will eat much more meat, eggs, and dairy products as their prices fall because of cheap wheat used as feed. Around March of the following year wheat is scarce because we used so much of it in the earlier months when prices were very low. Now wheat rises to $3.00 per bushel, and we have to tighten our belts as food prices rise.

The speculators, however, save us from these great fluctuations in prices and in the rate of consumption. If the price of wheat for future delivery is higher than the speculators think is justified, they offer to sell wheat for future delivery; that depresses the future price. If wheat is cheap in July, they will buy it in anticipation of rising prices. July wheat may therefore rise to $1.95, and March wheat may go in July for $2.05 to reflect storage and interest costs. Both the price of wheat and the rate of use throughout the year is much more even because of speculation.

This completes our discussion of applications of competitive pricing. We now turn to an evaluation of price theory. We shall begin with the problem we have been discussing—hedging and speculation.

Evaluation of Price Theory

You might think that hedging and speculation are not the best ways to allocate a wheat crop so that it lasts until the new crop is in. Why cannot society decide to use one-twelfth of its wheat crop each month? Or, if there are seasonal variations in wheat consumption, why cannot some sort of adjusted schedule of use be set up?

We do not do it this way because it would involve planning the allocation of commodities over time. Our economic system is based on decisions being made every day through the marketplace. Since nobody calculates at what rate we wish to use up our wheat supplies, fluctuating prices and speculation make that allocation for us.

What does it cost us to have this type of system? The Chicago Mercantile Exchange deals not only in the futures market for wheat, but also in pork bellies, orange juice, lumber, eggs, tomato paste, potatoes, tom turkeys, and other commodities. Less than 3 percent of the commodities traded on the futures market are delivered; the contracts are generally terminated by the losers paying the winners as prices change. Five hundred members of the Chicago Mercantile Exchange write about 4 million contracts a year that generate at least $168 million in commissions. The market value of their memberships is over $37 million. Thousands of people are employed as brokers, runners, board markers, pit clerks, secretaries, statisticians, telegraphers, and computer operators; they could be doing more useful things. In addition, the destruction of forests to produce the flood of paper they use could be reduced.

The Chicago Board of Trade is an even larger enterprise. (Some people might call it a larger gambling casino, but in pure gambling the risk is *created* in the act of wagering. The risks are *reduced* in commodity markets.) In 1970 the Chicago Board of Trade sold in the futures market twice as much wheat as was produced in the United States, two-and-a-half times as much corn, and nine times as much soybeans. In addition to the two Chicago markets for these grains, the Kansas City Board of Trade and the Minneapolis Grain Exchange also provide opportunities for trade and speculation. All of them swell the national income figures, but some people question their social usefulness.

Some economists regret the decline of competition that results from the growth of large-scale enterprises. They seem to regard perfect competition as the most desirable market situation. In such a market nobody has any market power, and therefore nobody can take advantage of others. With free entry into an industry, no excessive profits are made in the long run; each enterprise operates at lowest cost production, that is, at the minimum point of the average total cost curve (see Figure 5-2). If the selling price rises above cost (which you will recall includes the average or necessary rate of profit to keep the firm in business), new firms will be organized and with increased supply prices will fall again.

There are some doubts about the desirability of a market situation that approaches perfect competition, mainly when the comparative efficiency and welfare of the producers in small-scale and large-scale enterprises are considered. Agriculture, which operates in markets of perfect competition unless the government intervenes, has been in serious trouble for decades. Small retail business, which perhaps comes closer to perfect competition than any other area of economic activity outside of agriculture, is permeated with waste and inefficiency. Only three-fifths of the new firms survive their first year, and one-sixth reach the age of ten years. More than 10,000 businesses fail each year with liabilities of more than $1.2 billion. One can find three or four gasoline stations at one crossroad, but one would hardly expect to find three or four post offices in one place competing for business.

Finally we should note that elasticity of demand is perhaps less relevant in determining prices than it appears to be in economic theory. Large-scale enterprises that face inelastic demands for their products still may not raise prices for two reasons: first, they may fear antitrust prosecution, and second, they may fear that new firms will enter the industry and increase the competition.

Summary

The theory of competitive price is based on a market situation with many buyers and sellers who operate on so small a scale that no one has a significant influence over the quantity bought and sold and, therefore, no one can influence the price. Goods of different producers are identical in the minds of buyers and are perfect substitutes for each other. There are no restrictions on the entry of new firms or the exit of old ones from any line of business. There is no advertising, and the prices of the goods produced in an industry by many firms are identical.

The sum of all the individual market demands make up the total market demand, which means the total quantity of goods that buyers wish to purchase at each price. The demand curve slopes down and to the right because of the law of diminishing marginal utility, which states that the more units we acquire of a good at any one time, the greater the total satisfaction or utility we get, but the less the added utility from an extra unit compared to that from the previous units. A change in demand means a change in the quantity desired at each price and results in a shift of the whole demand curve.

A consumer gets the maximum utility by allocating his expenditures in such a way that the last dollar spent in any direction gives him the same satisfaction as the last dollar spent in any other direction.

We assume that the suppliers of goods seek to make maximum profits. Each supplier can sell all the goods he wants to at the going market price, but his output is limited by rising costs as he expands production. We analyzed four kinds of costs. First, fixed or overhead costs are those costs that remain the same regardless of the volume of output. Therefore, the greater the output, the lower the average fixed cost per unit produced. Second, variable costs are those costs that rise with the rising level of output. As output expands in a given plant from zero to some maximum, average variable cost is likely to fall at first and then rise. Third, total costs, the sum of variable and fixed costs, rise with increasing output, but average total cost per unit is likely to fall at first and then rise as output expands. Fourth, marginal cost is the addition to total cost when one additional unit is produced or the reduction in total cost when one unit less is produced.

Under perfect competition the businessman will expand production up to the point where marginal cost rises until it is equal to the price. The marginal cost curve above the average variable cost curve is, therefore, the supply curve of the firm; it tells us what quantity will be offered at each price.

The total market supply curve is the sum of all the individual firms' supply curves. At the intersection of the market demand and supply curves is an equilibrium market price. In long-run equilibrium the market price will be at the lowest point of the average total cost curve. At any lower price, some sellers would drop out of the industry because they would not be receiving the average expected rate of return. At any higher price, more firms would enter the industry and push prices downward as they increased the supply.

While individual firms under perfect competition face rising costs as they expand, industries may not. There are constant cost, increasing cost, and decreasing cost industries. An industry is classified on the basis of whether the cost per unit of output remains the same, rises, or falls as total production expands. An increased demand could leave prices unchanged in the long run or raise or lower them, depending on the type of industry we are looking at.

Elasticity of demand can be defined as the percentage change in the quantity demanded resulting from a 1 percent change in price. If demand is elastic, the higher the price the less we will spend on a good, and the lower the price the more we will spend. If demand is inelastic, more money is spent on the good at a high price even though the amount purchased is less, and less money is spent at a low price. With unitary elasticity of demand, the same amount is spent on the good regardless of the price.

The idea of elasticity of supply is similar to that of elasticity of demand, except that price and quantity change in the same direction instead of in opposite directions. It can be defined as the percentage change in quantity offered resulting from a 1 percent change in price. These concepts of elasticity have many practical applications, such as in determining who finally pays a tax on goods, whether the government should support agricultural prices, what the role of advertising should be, and whether competition should be reduced to maximize profits.

QUESTIONS AND PROBLEMS

1   How does the market situation differ when a farmer sells tomatoes to a cannery from where he sells tomatoes at his roadside stand?

2   If you had to, would you pay twice as much for table salt as you do? Why then does the price not go up much more than it has?

3   Can you imagine any cases where you might have constant or increasing marginal utility as you acquire more units of a good?

4   What happens to the demand for margarine as the price of margarine falls? What happens to the demand for butter as the price of margarine falls?

5   The producers of gasoline have from time to time criticized high taxes on gasoline. What does this tell you of their view of the elasticity of demand for gasoline?

6   Which are the fixed costs and which are the variable costs involved in driving a car an extra 1,000 miles? If someone wishes to share the costs with you on this 1,000-mile trip, which costs should he share?

7   The market system allocates our productive resources in a certain pattern. What are the shortcomings of this system? Can you think of ways to improve it?

8   Discuss the statement "There is pure competition in large areas of manufacturing and retailing because of the vigorous advertising that goes on."

9   Discuss the statement "If people did not work in and around the speculative commodity markets, there would be more unemployment."

10   What would automobile manufacturing be like if it operated under conditions approaching pure competition?

11 Your authors stated that the demand curve slopes down and to the right. Exceptions might be the demand curves for rich people's goods like expensive perfume or the demand curves for poor people's goods like bread to a late eighteenth-century British worker. Can you explain these unusual cases of the demand curves sloping up and to the right?

12 What happens if both supply and demand are elastic and the government imposes a 25 percent excise tax?

BIBLIOGRAPHY

BOBER, MANDELL M., *Intermediate Price and Income Theory*, 2nd ed., New York: Norton, 1962.

BOULDING, KENNETH E., *Economic Analysis*, Vol. 1, *Microeconomics*, 4th ed., New York: Harper & Row, 1966.

STIGLER, GEORGE J., *The Theory of Price*, 3rd ed., New York: Macmillan, 1966.

WATSON, DONALD S., *Price Theory and Its Uses*, 2nd ed., Boston: Houghton Mifflin, 1968.

Monopolistic Competition, Oligopoly, and Monopoly

What do I care about the law? Hain't I got the power?
—Cornelius Vanderbilt

The World of Imperfect Competition and Monopoly

Perfect competition, you will remember from the discussion in Chapter 5, is a theoretical concept used to explain pricing practices and the theory of the firm. Imperfect competition, as the name implies, is a deviation from the model of perfect competition in that some imperfection characterizes the number of sellers in the market. It is important to note that the distinction between imperfect and perfect competition lies entirely in the number or behavior of the *sellers* in the market. It has nothing to do with the number of buyers. (Where there is a monopoly on the buyer's side, we call it monopsony.) The number of sellers also distinguishes between the three types of imperfect competition that we will be discussing: monopolistic competition, oligopoly, and monopoly.

One further warning is necessary before we begin our study. Students often differentiate sellers who operate under conditions of imperfect competition from those who operate under conditions of perfect competition on the basis of motivation. That is, the perfect competitor is generally taken to be a man who keeps his prices low because he is sincerely interested in the well-being of his potential customers, while the monopolistic competitor greedily tries to extract every penny he can. This is not true. The only difference between perfect competitors and imperfect competitors, if such a term may be used, is in the number of sellers. Thus the term *imperfect competition* is not used in a pejorative sense. The perfect competitor is no less eager to make a monopoly-level profit than his counterparts in imperfect competition. The difference is that he cannot: he is compelled by the market and the number of competing sellers to sell his product at the lowest possible price. With this in mind we can go on to discuss the theory of imperfect competition.

MONOPOLISTIC COMPETITION Like many theories of economics, the theory of monopolistic competition was presented almost simultaneously by two different economists, Joan Robinson and Edward H. Chamberlin. If one imagines a spectrum of situations ranging from the least competitive (monopoly) to the most competitive (perfect competition), monopolistic competition will lie right next to perfect competition. That is, monopolistic competition is more competitive than monopoly or oligopoly but is less competitive than perfect competition. Why the name monopolistic competition?

The individual seller in a monopolistic competitive market is both a monopolist and a competitor. He has a monopoly of the brand that he sells, but he has competition from similar products with a different brand name. The products in a monopolistic competitive market are largely undifferentiated even though they may have different names. Gasoline stations are good examples.

Regardless of what gasoline he is selling, and unless he has a complete monopoly, the local gas station manager has a monopoly on the brand he sells within a given geographic area by virtue of a franchise. No one selling his gasoline can enter his area without consent from the parent company. But, and this is the competitive part, if his firm does well and shows a higher than normal return on profit, he can be certain that he will have competition in the form of a gas station selling another brand of gasoline either across the street or close by. Thus, as we mentioned before, he has both a monopoly on a brand and competition in the product.

One very important idea to remember in discussing the theory of monopolistic competition is that the difference between monopolistic competition, oligopoly, and monopoly lies in the demand curve. The supply curve depends entirely on the cost of the factors of production the producers employ in the production of their goods and services. The cost curves depend entirely on whether the individual firm is efficient (whether it keeps costs down, whether it has good engineers) and on other considerations distinct from the demand side of the picture.

Figure 6-1, based on the data presented in Table 6-1, shows the cost curves that the monopolistic competitor is faced with. Note that they are identical to those of the firm in perfect competition that we developed in Chapter 5. The U-shaped average total cost curve (ATC) is high in the beginning because the first few products absorb all of the fixed cost and the variable cost attributed to them (remember average

$$cost = \frac{total\ cost}{number\ of\ units\ produced}).$$ As the number of units produced increases, the total cost does not increase as much, and the average cost curve begins to decline. After a minimum point is reached, the average cost curve rises again, because the law of diminishing returns sets in; this means that the average output per unit of variable input is falling. The

TABLE 6-1 A Shoe Firm in Monopolistic Competition Maximizing Profit

| Quantity (in pairs per day) | Price (in dollars) | | | | | | |
	Selling price	Total revenue	Marginal revenue	Total cost	Average total cost	Marginal cost	Profit
1	50	50	50	50	50		0
2	45	90	40	80	40	30	10
3	40	120	30	99	33	19	21
4	35	140	20	119	29.75	20	21
5	30	150	10	150	30	31	0
6	25	150	0	204	34	54	−54

relevant part of the marginal cost curve (MC), as explained in Chapter 5, is upward sloping and intersects the average total cost curve at the minimum point. Thus, the shapes of the cost curves are identical for a firm in monopolistic competition to those for firms in the other relevant forms of competition that we will be studying.

The demand curve, however, is different. Table 6-1 and Figure 6-1 show the firm in monopolistic competition with the cost curves, the de-

FIGURE 6-1. A Shoe Firm in Monopolistic Competition Maximizing Profit

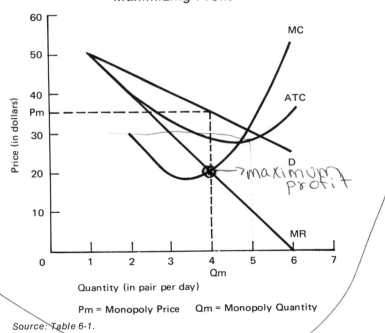

Pm = Monopoly Price   Qm = Monopoly Quantity

Source: Table 6-1.

mand curve, and the marginal revenue curve. In Figure 6-1, the demand curve (D) is the same as the average revenue curve. It tells us how much the consumers are willing to buy at each price. Also, and this is a distinguishing feature of the firm in imperfect competition, notice that the demand curve slopes down and to the right. This means that the firm, in order to sell more goods, must lower its price. The firm in monopolistic competition has some control over the price. Unlike the firm in perfect competition, which must take the price the market gives, the firm in imperfect competition may raise or lower the price and therefore change the amount its customers will buy.

You will also notice in Figure 6-1 the inclusion of the marginal revenue curve (MR). Marginal revenue is a new concept to you. It is defined as the addition to total revenue when an additional unit is sold. We can see how it is derived by referring to Table 6-1. If the businessman charges $50 for his product and sells one unit per day, his total or gross revenue is $50 per day. If he wishes to sell two units, he must drop his price to $45 per unit. His total revenue is then $90, and his added or marginal revenue in selling the second unit is $40. Or we can look at it this way: when the businessman sells two units per day, he charges $45 for the second unit, but since he had to drop the price of the first unit by $5, he only made $40 more than when he sold one unit per day; therefore, he adds $40 to his total receipts. That is why whenever the demand curve slopes down and to the right marginal revenue is less than average revenue or selling price. The relationship between the average revenue or demand curve and the marginal revenue curve is analogous to your average and marginal grades in college. If your average for three economics exams is 85 and your next grade (your marginal grade) is below 85, then your average will go down. If your marginal grade were above 85, your average would go up. If your grade were equal to 85, your average would remain the same. In our example, since the average revenue curve is going down, the marginal revenue must be *less* than the average revenue. Only under perfect competition, as when the wheat farmer can sell at the going price all the wheat he produced, is marginal revenue equal to average revenue or price.

Now let us determine how a firm in monopolistic competition makes a decision on what quantity to produce and what price to charge. Our shoe firm in monopolistic competition is trying to maximize profit. Thus, the firm will produce where marginal revenue equals marginal cost. Referring to Figure 6-1, locating the point where MR intersects MC gives us the quantity at which the firm will operate. Why should the intersection of MC and MR determine maximum profit? Remember a firm will produce an extra unit of output if the extra revenue (MR) is greater than the extra cost (MC). It will not produce beyond the intersection of MC and MR, because beyond that point MC is above MR, and it will not pay to produce beyond that point. This quantity is labeled Qm for the quantity of output that will give maximum profit. An output of four pair of shoes per day would be most profitable. We see from Table 6-1 that by producing the third unit, the firm adds $19 to its costs and $30 to its revenue; it therefore expands production. But if five units were produced, the firm would add $31 to cost and $10 to revenue; it therefore does not pay to produce the fifth unit.

In looking at Table 6-1, you may wonder why four pair per day is the most profitable output, and not three per day. Both outputs produce a profit of $21. Keep in mind that the profit shown in the table is that profit above the average necessary rate to keep the firm in business. With an output of four units, the firm makes a percentage of profit on a larger output in addition to the $21 of extra profit. In other words, if you are to make 8 percent profit on your total investment plus $21 of extra profit as shown in Table 6-1 above, it is better to make the 8 percent on a larger investment producing a larger output.

After the firm in monopolistic competition has decided on the output to produce, how does it decide on the price to charge? Obviously, any firm desires to charge the most profitable price it can get. How do we determine the most profitable price? The demand curve, an indication of the quantities that consumers will buy at given prices, tells us the maximum price that the firm may charge for four units is $35 a pair. This price is labeled Pm in Figure 6-1 for the price that will give maximum profit.

The monopolistic competitive firm is now maximizing profit with an output of four units and a price of $35. The profits that the firm is making are above a normal return. How do we know this? The average total cost curve includes the average necessary profit to keep the firm in business. Any profit above the average total cost curve is an extra return to the entrepeneur. Our hypothetical firm in Figure 6-1 is making a profit above that of the normal return.

As soon as the word is out that the firm is making above a normal return, other firms will enter the business of our monopolistic competitor. Since he has only a brand monopoly and not a product monopoly, he can expect that firms with other brands of the product will move in and try to take away some of his business. As firms move in and sell their products, our firm's demand and marginal revenue curves will shift to the left, as shown in Figure 6-2. Why does this happen? Remember that the demand curve tells us how much an individual will buy at a given price. The new firm cuts into the market of the old firm and so the old firm now sells less at the same price as before. In effect, his market has been cut.

One of the distinguishing features of monopolistic competition is that as long as an individual firm is making above the normal return in profits, new firms will enter the market and cause the individual demand curve to shift to the left. Let us return to our example of the corner gas station. It sells brand X to its customers; but as soon as a new gas station is built nearby, some customers are lost to brand Y, and as a result the demand curve shifts to the left.

How long does this process go on? Some firms enter, some firms exit,

FIGURE 6-2.   Long-Run Equilibrium
in Monopolistic Competition

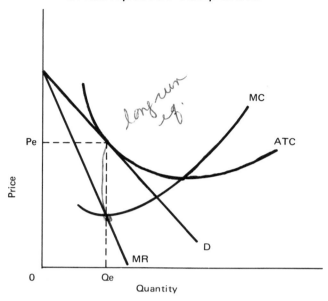

some firms make above a normal return, and some firms lose money. The
equilibrium point will be reached when a firm is making a normal return
for its investment, at which stage there will be no special incentive for
more firms to come in or leave the market. At the equilibrium point we are
left with too many gas stations, restaurants, and retail stores, all doing less
business than they might at a cost that is higher than their lowest possible
cost. This can be seen in Figure 6-2, where the price is higher and the
quantity smaller than they would be at the minimum point of the average
total cost curve.

Notice that the demand curve touches but does not cross the average
total cost curve. For the quantity indicated by the intersection of the marginal revenue curve and the marginal cost curve (the maximum profit
point), the price is the highest that it can be while still attaining a normal
return for the firm. In Figure 6-2 this quantity is labeled Qe for quantity at
equilibrium, and the price is labeled Pe, price at equilibrium. Since the
firm is only making a normal return, there is no incentive for other firms to
enter the market. This is the long-run equilibrium point for monopolistic
competition.

A firm in perfect competition has a horizontal demand curve, and the
long-run equilibrium point is tangent to the average total cost curve at the
minimum point of the average total cost curve. This is a geometric impossi-
bility in monopolistic competition since the demand curve slopes down-

ward. There is, however, a similarity in the fact that at both points of equilibrium the demand curves are tangent to the average total cost curves.

Thus, the monopolistic competitive equilibrium is almost as beneficial to the consumer as in the case of perfect competition, and the demand curve is tangent to the average total cost curve, resulting in no excess profits for the firm. Both firms are making no more than a normal return; however, the firm in perfect competition must charge a lower price, other things being equal, than the firm in monopolistic competition.

Now we will go on to analyze oligopoly in a similar way. Remember that the motivation of all firms, regardless of which situation they are in, is the same, that is, selling at a quantity and price that maximize profit.

OLIGOPOLY   In the spectrum of situations mentioned in our discussion of monopolistic competition, oligopoly would lie between monopolistic competition and monopoly. Oligopoly is the market situation that is characterized by very few sellers. Let us assume that very few sellers means a number small enough so that the market in an oligopoly situation is characterized by a price leader, rigid prices, and uncertainty in the pricing mechanism.

The price leader is the firm that either moves first on price changes or must ratify price changes if others proceed first. It is the dominant firm in the industry. Such is the case in the steel, auto, and chemical industries, to name a few.

The name of the game in oligopoly is uncertainty. The number of sellers is so small and the scale of industry is so big that any one seller is uncertain as to what his competitors will do. In perfect competition there is no uncertainty, because everyone knows what the equilibrium price is and every seller knows that he cannot sell at a higher price than the equilibrium price. Uncertainty is present in monopolistic competition, but the entrepeneur is at least assured of a brand monopoly in a certain geographic area. However, the firm in monopolistic competition is not assured that an individual will not locate close by him with a product of a different brand and cut into his market. Therefore, the uncertainty of monopolistic competition produces a situation where firms are willing to cut prices in order to preserve their share of the market. In oligopolistic markets, the uncertainty produces a rigid price, and weaker firms are dominated by price leaders.

Oligopoly characterizes much of American business today. Most of the large firms in terms of assets in the United States are in markets that are characterized by oligopolistic relationships. The question of how the oliogopoly evolved and what methods and mechanisms have promoted oligopoly will be left to a later discussion. In this chapter our purpose is to analyze, in a similar way that we analyzed perfect competition and monopolistic competition, the pricing and output decisions that an oligopolist makes. You will see from the analysis that an oligopolist has the same goals as does a businessman in monopolistic competition or perfect competition. The difference, again, is not in the motivation of the seller, but in the market structure that he is in.

Figure 6-3 shows the profit maximization behavior of a firm in an oligopolistic situation. The firm is behaving in a similar way to those we have mentioned before, that is, locating its quantity at the point where marginal revenue equals marginal cost and charging the highest price that it can get at that output as given by the demand curve. It is important to remember the sequence of steps that the entrepreneur goes through. First, he locates the point where marginal revenue equals marginal cost; this fixes the quantity that he can sell. Second, he proceeds up to the demand curve to determine the highest price that he can charge for that quantity. The profit maximization rule, then, produces a quantity, Qm, and a price, Pm, for the firm in an oligopolistic market.

What are the major differences between an oligopolistic firm and a firm in monopolistic competition? First, the oligopolistic firm is much larger; therefore, the quantities on the horizontal axis will be much larger in Figure 6-3 than in Figures 6-1 and 6-2. Second, the demand curve facing an oligopolist is steeper than the demand curve facing a producer in monopolistic competition; the reason is that with many firms there are many satisfactory substitutes for one firm's products, but with a few firms the al-

FIGURE 6-3.   A Firm in an Oligopolistic Market

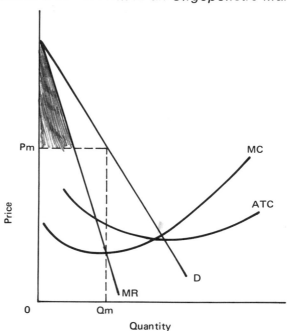

ternatives are fewer or, in other words, the demand is less elastic. Third, and most important, in monopolistic competition new firms can easily enter, and excess profits will soon disappear. But in an oligopoly, the situation shown in Figure 6-3 can persist; extra profits are made even in the long run.

Most oligopolistic markets are characterized by a price leader. Imagine that you are an executive of a firm with few rival sellers. You are compensated by a salary and a bonus that is contingent on your ability to maintain the sales level at a prescribed quota. How do you operate? Do you try to pick up all the marbles by constantly lowering or raising your prices and driving your competitors out of business? Could you, if you were an executive of the Ford Motor Company, for example, reasonably expect to put General Motors out of business? Quite the contrary. You would behave in a way that would insure that you stayed in business and within prescribed limits "competed" with the price leader in your particular industry.

In the case of automobiles, the price leader is General Motors. Other firms may initiate price increases but it remains for General Motors to ratify the particular price increase before the increase becomes standard in the industry. The reasons for such behavior are clear. No one at the Ford Motor Company or at General Motors really wants to start an all-out price war. Also, if all of General Motors' customers switched to Ford Motor Company, the company could not possibly make cars fast enough to satisfy them all. So firms act in a very narrow band of competitive behavior. In fact most competition in oligopoly is not characterized by price competition, but by model changes, advertising, or intangible differences between the products.

At least three times since the Second World War the following interesting phenomenon developed in the auto industry. First, Ford announced a price increase for the new models. Shortly afterward, General Motors announced a larger price increase. Then Ford increased its prices further to match those of General Motors. There are at least four significant conclusions that can be drawn from this pattern. First, General Motors, a giant of the industry, is the price leader in autos. The largest firm, however, may not always be the price leader. Second, there probably is no secret collusion between Ford and General Motors; if there were, and if the government found out about it, the companies would be hit with an antitrust suit. Third, price increases of both companies must be in line with each other, because each wants to retain its share of the market. Fourth, both companies will make more money with larger, rather than smaller, price increases. Each company faces a more elastic demand for its autos than the total industry demand, because the competitor's cars are a good substitute. But the total demand for cars is less elastic than the demand for a particular make of car; therefore, if both raise prices, their profits increase.

Oligopoly, then, is further away on the competitive scale from perfect competition and monopolistic competition. Its markets are characterized by rigid prices governed by a price leader. The consumer is at more of a disadvantage in an oligopolistic market than in perfect competition or a monopolistic competition market.

MONOPOLY We now turn to the least competitive market structure on our spectrum of competition. Monopoly means one seller. The market is thus characterized by a single seller, although there may be many buyers. A monopoly may be regional, local, or nationwide. The effects of a monopoly are not as clear-cut as the name implies. A monopolist, for example, may be producing a product that no one wants; he also may have such high costs that he is not making a profit. There are no guarantees that a monopolist will either make a profit or be flooded with customers.

If the monopolist is not guaranteed a profit, why then is there so much public concern over the extent of monopolistic elements in our economy? The key word is potential. A monopolist has the potential to raise prices to an exorbitant degree. A monopolist also may have erected barriers to entry that maintain and preserve his monopolistic position. Thus the danger is twofold: a monopolist may have no competition and may be able to make his pricing and output decisions without the threat of another firm undercutting him, and he may have erected such barriers to entry to preclude any further competition. In the perfectly competitive model described in Chapter 5, entry into the market was open, and if a firm made above a normal return, it could expect to have competition immediately. Monopoly is, therefore, the polar opposite of perfect competition. The monopolist is not only the sole producer of the product, but he has—either by patents, collusive agreements, or, in the case of natural monopolies like the telephone company, by government sanction—the exclusive rights to sell the particular product that he produces.

Figure 6-3 can apply to the monopolistic firm as well as to the oligopolistic firm. Maximum profits are realized at the output where marginal cost equals marginal revenue. These extra profits persist in the long run as long as the firm can maintain its monopolistic position.

We will consider monopolies and their public policy implications further in Chapter 9; here we will briefly describe the different types of monopolies. A natural monopoly, such as a public utility, is characterized by high fixed costs and by the fact that competition in the industry would be ruinous. A firm such as a telephone company is guaranteed a particular geographic monopoly in order to insure that it gets an adequate return on its investment and to insure that the consumer has adequate telephone service. Natural monopolies are also characterized by the efficiency that results from large-scale enterprises. As the size of the firm gets larger, the average cost of production gets lower; thus monopoly produces, in this case, a product at lower cost per unit than competition would have.

The other types of monopoly have been brought about by barriers to entry either resulting from such restrictions as a patent or from the firm's entrance into collusive or illegal arrangements to keep competition out. Such monopolies as The Aluminum Company of America and such giant trusts as the tobacco and cigaret trusts were brought about by a series of arrangements, activities, and mergers, the effects of which have kept out competition in these industries. Such monopolies are illegal in the United States as a consequence of the Sherman Anti-Trust Act of 1890.

Applications of the Theory of Imperfect Competition and Monopoly

WHICH PRODUCES LOWER PRICES? It seems logical that, in the abstract, most consumers would prefer competition rather than oligopoly or monopoly. They welcome the natural regulation by the market of the firm in perfect competition. Profits are minimal, and in the long run the average cost of production is at the lowest point of the average cost curve. Production is not restricted in order to raise prices.

Yet we cannot help but wonder if perfect competition is all that wonderful. Would we have more and cheaper automobiles if there were, say, 200 companies producing them? As John Kenneth Galbraith once pointed out, when people from other countries come to the United States to look at efficient companies, our State Department officials take them to those businesses that the Department of Justice has indicted most frequently for violating the antitrust laws.

In other words, perfect competition is preferable to oligopoly or monopoly enterprise only if we assume identical cost curves. But if large firms and plants are more efficient than small ones, then perfect competition would result in higher cost products and smaller output. Even if a firm under perfect competition produces at the lowest point of its ATC curve, that cost may be higher than the monopoly or oligopoly price charged by large firms. These relationships are illustrated in Figure 6-4. The competitive firm, shown in the upper part of the figure, in the long run produces at a price of OC and sells OE units. The giant firm, if it is more efficient, can sell at a price of OA, the lowest point on its average cost curve; it will still make average profits at that price. Instead, it charges the monopoly or oligopoly price OB, and it restricts output to OH in order to get that price. Nevertheless, it still sells its product cheaper than firms under perfect competition would. Its cost per unit is OA, and its excess profit per unit is AB. Total cost (including the necessary profit to keep the firm in business) is represented by the area OAGH. Total revenue is OBFH, and the oligopoly or monopoly profit is ABFG.

Thus, there are economic situations in which oligopoly or monopoly is

FIGURE 6-4.   Prices and Sales Under Perfect
Competition and Under Oligopoly or Monopoly

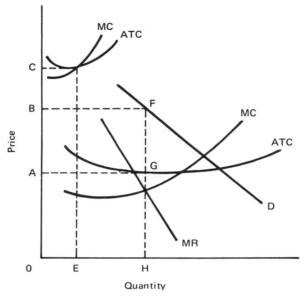

preferable to perfect competition. Another possible advantage of oligopoly or monopoly is that the pricing policies of imperfect competition are more flexible than those in perfect competition. One example is marginal-cost pricing.

MARGINAL COST IN RELATION TO PRICING   Suppose a businessman produces 100 refrigerators per day at an average cost (including the profit necessary to stay in business) of $200 per unit. He sells the refrigerators for $200 apiece, and his average profit is $10 each, or $1,000 per day.

Now suppose there is an offer from abroad from a buyer who wants 10 refrigerators per day if he can have them at $175 each. Should the manufacturer turn him down because his cost of production (excluding profit) is $190? Not necessarily, if he wants to maximize his profits.

Assume that the producer has enough capacity to turn out 110 refrigerators per day, and that the units he exports will not be sold back in the United States to undercut his regular sales and prices. Assume also that his actual fixed, or overhead, costs amount to $5,000 per day, or $50 per unit if the output is 100; variable costs for 100 units are $14,000, or $140 each. This gives an actual cost of $19,000 for 100 units, or $190 each, which with the $10 profit on each brings the price to $200.

If the entrepreneur is to produce another 10 refrigerators per day, his fixed costs will not increase at all. Even if his variable costs for the extra 10 units rise to $150 each, he will add $1,500 to his costs, but he will receive $1,750 from the sale of the extra 10 units, thereby increasing his profits $250 per day. *Even though he sells the extra 10 units below average cost, he increases his profit by selling them above marginal cost.*

As long as there is unused capacity to produce, it pays to sell some units at a lower price if prices on regular sales do not have to be lowered. This helps explain why some companies will sell goods abroad much cheaper than at home if they are not prevented by "antidumping duties." It also explains why in depressed times secret price cutting can occur.

MONOPOLY POWER TO RAISE PRICES WHEN LABOR COSTS RISE   Before analyzing the situation in the steel industry with respect to labor costs and increasing prices, it is necessary to introduce another term essential for our analysis—*productivity.* In the case of labor, productivity is measured by the amount per hour that labor produces. For the steel industry, the changes in productivity over the years could be measured through the comparison of statistics derived by dividing the amount of steel produced by the number of hours of labor it took to produce that steel. This productivity figure can be used to determine how much wages can be increased; if the productivity for an individual steel mill increases by 50 percent, then a 50 percent increase in wages will not result in any increase in labor cost. Increases in wages result in increases in labor cost only if they exceed the increase in productivity in the particular industry.

The steel industry has been faced with strong union pressures to increase wages. Between 1947 and 1958 the wage rate in the steel industry exceeded productivity increases by 58 percent (*Congressional Record,* June 30, 1959, p. 11164). Therefore, unit labor costs in the steel industry between 1947 and 1958 increased by 58 percent. The steel companies, however, increased their prices by 103 percent in the same time period. Even allowing for some marginal fringe benefits that would have increased the cost of labor, the steel industry more than doubled prices while the unit labor costs were increasing far less. How does the steel industry get its customers to accept such price increases?

As we saw above, the steel industry is in an oligopolistic position. The industry is characterized by a price leader, United States Steel, and has all the elements that characterize an oligopolistic market structure. As such, the industry leaders may raise the price above the price that would be set in a competitive market. Faced with increases in labor cost, it is only natural that they would take the opportunity to raise prices not only to cover labor costs, but also to increase their profit margins. The steel industry thus raises prices and blames the steel-workers' union for the increase.

Even if the steel industry had raised the price of steel to cover only the increased wage rates, this would have shown the power of an oligopoly. Raising prices is not a question of justice or ethics, but a question of *market power*. Suppose wage rates on wheat farms rise. Will the farmer raise the price of wheat to cover the increased costs? Certainly not; he cannot do that. Increased wage rates will reduce profit margins. Some farmers will stop growing wheat. Others will reduce their output. Eventually the supply curve will shift to the left, and a higher equilibrium price will be reached to cover the higher wage rates and still leave the necessary rate of profit for the farmer. The very fact that the steel companies are able to raise prices as soon as wages rise illustrates their market power.

We may well ask why the steel companies do not raise prices at will since they have so much market power. The answer is that there are some factors that limit their power. One is the fact that they do face a demand curve, and if they raise prices too high, their customers may switch to substitute products. Another limitation is their constant awareness of the possibility of government antitrust prosecution. Also, their effort to maximize profits requires them to select prices and outputs at which marginal cost equals marginal revenue; any deviation from this point involving a price rise *must reduce* profits.

ADVERTISING AND CONSPICUOUS CONSUMPTION   In Chapter 1 we discussed the allocation of resources among competing ends. The study of the market structure, of which oligopoly is one part, is essentially a study of how the resources of our economy are used. The public policy questions involved in whether our industry should or can adhere to the perfectly competitive model or to a less than competitive model will be settled only by a discussion of the goals of our economic society. One of these goals is efficiency.

In a modern industrial society the question of advertising and its cost and effect on the American consumer is an important consideration in the debate over efficiency. One must distinguish between two different types of advertising: one to inform us of the availability of products, and the other to create the desire for products of marginal usefulness or distinguishability. In a perfectly competitive model there would be no need for advertising. Since the products are homogeneous and since perfect knowledge of the products on the part of the consumers is assumed, none of the resources of an economy are expended on advertising. In a less than perfectly competitive society, which ours certainly is, advertising does play a part in informing potential customers of the product.

People who argue for advertising accept the fact that many of the advertising methods create an illusion in the mind of the consumer about the value of the product. But they go on to say that if the consumer thinks the product produces a certain effect, then this effect becomes a reality in the mind of the consumer. The question, from an economic point of view, is not whether advertising produces an illusory effect, but which would serve the consumer better—a dollar spent on advertising or a dollar reduction in the price of the product. As it stands, and this is a result of imperfectly competitive markets, the consumer has little choice as to the amount of advertising that goes into any product he buys. In some rare instances, when the considerations of health or national welfare are involved, such as in cigaret advertising on television, massive advertising campaigns may be banned. Certain other types of advertising, when determined to be false by the Federal Trade Commission, are also banned. But for the most part, the consumer, faced with a market structure that is characterized by few sellers, has little to say about the amount of advertising that the sellers buy. Since all the costs of a product are passed along to the consumer, advertising expenditures may raise prices. If advertising expenditures cause a huge increase in sales, and if the firm is large enough to achieve the increased efficiency of large-scale firms, the advertising expenditures may reduce the price of the product. In situations other than this, however, advertising expenditures do raise the price of the product.

If you had a choice, would you rather see a billion dollars spent on advertising or on research and development? From the point of view of the businessman, the returns from advertising are likely to be larger and more certain. That is why in 1969 business spent $19.6 billion on advertising and only $10.1 billion of its own funds on research and development. Furthermore, a great part of the latter expenditure is geared to selling efforts, such as market research, producing attractive packages, and developing other marketing gimmicks such as striped toothpaste—a great technological breakthrough!

Along with the growth of advertising and salesmanship, efforts are constantly being made to encourage the public to increase "conspicuous consumption." This phrase was coined and popularized by Thorstein Veblen in his first book, *The Theory of the Leisure Class* (1899). Veblen thought that the rich wish to consume in a way that displays their wealth, for a show of wealth indicates power, prestige, honor, and success in our pecuniary culture; and the poor try to emulate the rich. Since Veblen wrote this, we have seen how advertisers have tried to manipulate us to spend more and more conspicuously, even if it is wasteful.

Evaluation of the Theory of Imperfect Competition and Monopoly

IS THE COST CURVE REALLY U-SHAPED? We have been drawing the short-run average total cost curve as if it were U-shaped, that is, as if the average total cost decreased over a range, came to a bottom point, and then abruptly increased. In actual fact, economic research has indicated that the average total cost curve is more L-shaped, that is, it is flat at the bottom over quite a considerable range (see Conference on Price Research, Committee on Price Determination, *Cost Behavior and Price Poli-cy* [New York: National Bureau of Economic Research, 1943]; and John Johnston, *Statistical Cost Analysis* [New York: McGraw-Hill, 1960], Chapters 4 and 5). This is shown in Figure 6-5.

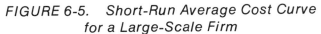

FIGURE 6-5. Short-Run Average Cost Curve
for a Large-Scale Firm

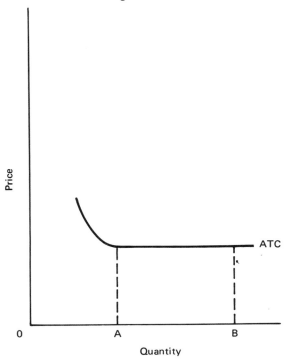

The implications of the L-shaped cost curve are that a firm, as shown in Figure 6-5, must be at least large enough to produce OA in order to produce efficiently the products that it sells. It also means that a large firm may be of a size as large as OB and still have constant costs. Thus, there are barriers of size to a firm's entry in an oligopoly market.

The fact that the actual ATC curve is L-shaped strengthens the argument that firms may be efficient over a wider range than is presumed by the standard analysis that postulates a U-shaped curve. If the bottom of the L-shaped curve occurs at a high level of production and extends out for large-scale production, then there is an economic justification for large firms in our economy.

DO FIRMS KNOW THE DEMAND CURVES IN THEIR MARKETS? The theory of the profit maximization behavior of firms that we have been describing in this chapter and in Chapter 5 has several underlying assumptions. Among them is the belief that the firm can determine its demand curve in addition to its cost schedule in order to make a rational decision on how much to produce and what price to charge. In fact, it is extremely difficult to determine the actual demand curve at any given time. There are several reasons for this.

One is the fact that the variables that are held constant in demand analysis (that is, the prices of other products, the taste of the consumer, and the income of the consumer) are not necessarily constant. Another reason is that the products that the firm is putting on the market are many and varied and are put out at many different times of the year; thus, the firm may not have an idea of the exact demand curve it faces that period. Even if it did have data on price outlays and on production and selling cost, it would take an extremely sophisticated mind to determine the profit maximization point for an individual firm.

The increasing use of advertising in recent years illustrates this point. Joan Robinson, the distinguished British economist, pointed out in 1953 in a now famous article (Joan Robinson, "Imperfect Competition Revisited," *Economic Journal*, Vol. LXIII, No. 251 [September 1953], pp. 579–93) that manufacturers find it difficult to foresee the consequences of advertising and that if advertisers knew the effects of advertising, there would be no necessity for the advertising industry to persuade them that the effect is greater than they think. She stated that the perceived demand curve is not a thin line or curve, but a smudge. By this she meant that at any given price for a given product in a given market, the businessman may only be able to estimate within a broad range how much he can sell.

So in spite of the elegance of the analysis in Chapters 5 and 6, the fact is that the individual producer may not have the knowledge necessary to make the profit-maximizing decisions. He may not have the fundamental data, as Joan Robinson says, to make the decision called for by the model, and he therefore proceeds on a hit or miss basis within a particular range. Not only is the individual entrepreneur oftentimes ignorant of the demand side of his market, but if he is in an oligopolistic situation, he may price his products not on his cost structure, but on his market power. Furthermore, maximizing profit may lead him into difficulties with either the government or his adversary, the labor unions.

Although economic theory may dictate that a businessman should use the marginal revenue and marginal cost to determine maximum profit, he may in fact not follow this reasoning. He may be unaware of marginal analysis or find it difficult to apply because of the problem of measuring marginal costs and revenues; or he may follow his intuition and use average costs and revenues to determine his output. In either case, the economic analysis may not conform to the real life decisions.

IS THE SUPPLY CURVE BASED ON COST?   The assumption in Chapter 5 was that the supply curve is based on the costs that the individual entrepreneur incurs in producing the product. In the case of perfect competition, the marginal cost curve is equal to the supply curve. The validity of this assumption, however, is questionable in oligopolistic markets. A good example of this is seen in the steel industry, where United States Steel is the price leader and prices its products above the increase in labor costs. The primary basis for pricing is one of market power and not necessarily of cost. In the short run, the oligopoly supply curve may be horizontal; that is, the individual firms in an oligopolistic market may be willing to vary their output but will not be willing to vary their price. The logic of this is sound if one considers, as we did above, the economics of an oligopolistic industry such as steel.

Each firm in the steel industry gets about the same share of the market that it could expect under competitive conditions but at a price that is higher than the market price would be under those conditions. The net effect of this is that contrary to what we have seen above, the supply and demand curves do not necessarily determine the market price, and the individual entrepreneur does not price his products (that is, determine his supply curve) based on his individual cost.

The way to test this is to determine what happens to the price of a product in an oligopolistic market when supply and demand change. Since the price leader in an oligopolistic market has the market power to continue his price at the same level or above, he would be unwilling to drop his price in a situation in which ordinary economic reasoning would dictate that his price should drop. In competitive conditions, for example, if the demand for a product dropped, one would expect that with a constant supply curve the price would drop. However, this has been shown not to be true in industries characterized by very few sellers.

Summary

You have now been through the world of perfect and imperfect competition; perfect competition was presented in Chapter 5 and imperfect competition in Chapter 6. Remember the differences. Wherever a firm has control over its price, that is, by lowering or raising its price it can affect its output, it is in imperfect competition.

Imperfect competition can range from monopoly, with a single seller, to monopolistic competition, where the seller has a brand monopoly with product competition. In between, and the source of much of the economic power in the United States, is oligopoly. Oligopoly means few sellers.

These few sellers, in order to insure their best interest, usually follow a price leader. The price leader sets the price or ratifies previous price increases. The other firms, unwilling to upset the balance of power, would not engage in individual price setting without the price leader's consent.

The effects of imperfect competition were also studied in Chapter 6. Oligopoly, when accompanied by a large-scale operation, in which costs decrease with increases in output, often produces lower prices than perfect competition. Most often, however, imperfect competition results in rigid prices even in a declining market and monopolistic market power to pass along increases in labor costs.

Finally we analyzed common contemporary developments: advertising and conspicuous consumption. The ability of large industries to create their own markets by advertising is superseding the ability of the consumer to decide which products he buys.

Price theory, of which this chapter describes but one part, tells us how our nation's resources are allocated. It gives us an analytical framework to help us understand why businessmen set the prices they do and why our nation's resources are distributed the way they are. In order to understand our economic system fully we must also study national income analysis. We will then have a better idea of how economic decisions are made, both by the individual and by the nation.

QUESTIONS AND PROBLEMS

1 One can tell whether a firm is in an imperfectly competitive market by examining the demand curve. Do you agree? Why or why not?

2 Give some examples of monopolies that you know of. Why has the Justice Department not taken action against regional monopolies?

3 Why does a firm not try to maximize total revenue?

4 Can you think of an instance where a firm would produce at less than maximum profit?

5 Most firms in the United States fall in the monopolistic competition category. Why, then, is there so much concern over oligopoly and monopoly?

6 If you were an executive in a firm faced with an oligopolistic market, how would you reduce the uncertainty in your pricing and output decisions?

7 Why is Ford Motor Company not the price leader in the automobile industry?

8 Does the concept of marginal decision-making have any relevance in your life? For example, suppose you were deciding, on an economic basis, whether to remain in college or leave at mid-semester. Would the marginal-cost concept assist you in your decision?

9 Give examples of the different types of advertising mentioned in this chapter. Do you think advertising is necessary for our economy?

BIBLIOGRAPHY

BLAIR, JOHN M., *Economic Concentration.* New York: Harcourt Brace Jovanovich, 1972.

CHAMBERLIN, EDWARD H., *The Theory of Monopolistic Competition,* 5th ed. Cambridge: Harvard University Press, 1946. (Originally published in 1933.)

JOHNSTON, JOHN, *Statistical Cost Analysis.* New York: McGraw-Hill, 1960.

NATIONAL BUREAU OF ECONOMIC RESEARCH, *Cost Behavior and Price Policy.* New York: National Bureau of Economic Research, 1943.

ROBINSON, JOAN, *The Economics of Imperfect Competition,* 2nd ed. New York: Macmillan, 1969. (Originally published in 1933.)

7

How National Income Is Distributed

Politics is the science of who gets what, when, and why.
—*Sidney Hillman*

The productive forces or factors that cooperate in generating output are land, labor, capital, and entrepreneurship. The rewards to the owners of these factors are rent, wages, interest, and profit. According to price theory, the distribution of income depends on the supply of and the demand for these factors of production. In this chapter we shall present the marginal productivity theory of distribution and look at the forces that influence supply and demand. This will provide the theoretical basis for looking at the actual distribution of income in the United States. In Chapter 11 we shall examine the realities of income distribution and the problems of poverty.

Rent

The theory of rent offers one of the first examples in history of the use of marginal analysis; it was developed by David Ricardo, Thomas R. Malthus, and others in 1815.

We define land as any free gift of nature. It includes not only actual land, but also minerals in the ground, fish in the rivers and oceans, waterfalls, climate, and so on. Some free gifts of nature are superabundant and cannot be appropriated into private ownership; they are free to the user, like sunshine. Other free gifts of nature are scarce, like land and minerals in the ground; they have been taken into private ownership and command a price even though they cost society nothing. Economic rent is the payment for the use of these scarce free gifts of nature, or natural resources.

To clarify the concept of rent as a payment for natural resources, we shall assume that farmers and businessmen are tenants, renting the land they use. If a farmer or a sole proprietor of a business owns his own land, does his own work, and invests his own capital, he is receiving the four types of factor incomes. He may lump them all together as profit or income, but conceptually his income can be divided into rent, wages, interest, and profit; the principles we shall develop still apply.

RENT ARISING FROM EXTENSIVE CULTIVATION   There are different grades and qualities of land that have inherently different productivities. If you treat them alike, you get different yields. This is the basis for rent being measured from the extensive margin of cultivation, as shown in Table 7-1. The extensive margin of cultivation refers to the worst land that is profitable for farmers to till. At first, when population is sparse and there is ample excellent land, only the best soil will be worked. But as population increases and the demand for farm products rises, it becomes profitable to work poorer land. At any time, under a given set of conditions, the marginal land is that which is barely profitable to bring into cultivation.

TABLE 7-1   Rent Arising from Extensive Cultivation
(in dollars)

| | | | Price | | | | | | | | | | | |
| | | | $.50 | | $.75 | | $1.00 | | $1.50 | | $3.00 | |
Grades of land	Cost of production	Yield, in bushels	Total revenue	Rent	Total revenue	Rent	Total revenue	Rent	Total revenue	Rent	Total revenue	Rent
A	15	30	15	0	22.50	7.50	30	15	45	30	90	75
B	15	20			15	0	20	5	30	15	60	45
C	15	15					15	0	22.50	7.50	45	30
D	15	10							15	0	30	15
E	15	5									15	0

In Table 7-1, A represents the best land and E the worst. Assume that you invest $15 on each acre of the different qualities of land, using the same amount of labor, fertilizer, seed, machinery, and other inputs. We define cost of production here in the economic sense, including the profit necessary to keep the tenant farmer in farming; if the cost of production is $15 per acre, the farmer will be satisfied if he gets $15 per acre in return. We assume no change in technology or cost of production. The yields of wheat on the different grades of land range from thirty bushels to five bushels.

Imagine a sparsely settled country with an abundance of grade A land. Assume also that nobody—neither government nor large private land-grabbers—has monopolized the land to withhold it from the public. Land is free, and with the costs and yields shown in Table 7-1, wheat would sell for 50 cents per bushel, because 50 cents times 30 bushels brings in the $15 we have assumed the farmer expects to earn. If the price were lower, farmers would be making less than a satisfactory return, output would fall, and the price would rise to 50 cents. If the price rose above 50 cents, more farmers would occupy more of the abundant and idle grade A land, the output would rise, and the price would fall to 50 cents. But as long as there is an abundance of grade A land, there is no rent paid and no price on land.

With the passage of time and the growth of population, all the grade A land is taken up and put to use. As the quantity of wheat supplied at 50 cents falls short of the quantity demanded, the price rises to 75 cents. Now that the price of wheat has risen to 75 cents per bushel, grade B land can be worked, but it produces no rent. It is the marginal land that just barely pays all costs of production, including an acceptable return for the tenant farmer. But the wheat from grade A land also sells for 75 cents per bushel, producing an extra revenue of $7.50 above all costs of production. Tenant farmers are eager to rent grade A land, and they offer $7.50 per acre for the right to use it. If the rent were higher, tenant farmers would be earning less than the necessary rate of return to stay in farming, so they would refuse to pay a rent higher than $7.50. If the rent were lower, tenants could make extra profit working the land, and they would compete with each other to get the land. As the rent rises to $7.50, the return to the tenant farmers would be the same on both grade A and grade B land, for they receive an average identical rate of return.

As population grows and the demand for wheat increases, all the grade B land is put to use. The price of wheat then rises to $1, and grade C land is farmed; it now becomes the marginal no-rent land. The rent on grade A land now rises to $15, and on grade B land rent is $5 per acre. And so on for the rest of the table. In each case rent arises from the extra productivity of the better than marginal land in use. In each case the tenant farmer gets the average rate of return, and the landlord gets the benefit of the extra value produced on the better land.

THE LAW OF DIMINISHING RETURNS AND INTENSIVE CULTIVATION   Rent can also arise on grade A land if it is worked more and more intensively, because of the law of diminishing returns. The law states that if the quantity of land is held constant, doubling the labor and capital input will increase the output, but the output will rise by a lower percentage than the percentage rise in the variable inputs. Therefore, the average output per unit of variable input will fall.

If there were no law of diminishing returns we could grow food for all the world on an acre of land. Suppose we invest ten hours of work and 100 pounds of fertilizer on an acre of land and get twenty bushels of wheat. If we invested 100 hours of work and 1,000 pounds of fertilizer on the acre, we would get 200 bushels. If we invested a million hours of labor and 10 million pounds of fertilizer, we would get 2 million bushels. What a wonderful world that would be! But unfortunately the law of diminishing returns prevents this possibility.

The law of diminishing returns assumes that technology remains constant. If technology improves, a doubling of inputs can even yield, say, a tripled output. Suppose this year we invest $15 on an acre of grade A land, and we harvest thirty bushels of wheat. Next year we plant a greatly improved variety of wheat, and a $30 investment produces ninety bushels. The law of diminishing returns still operates, because it must be considered within the framework of constant technology. If this year, with the current technology, we invested $15 we would get thirty bushels, and if we invested $30, we might get fifty bushels. Next year, with the much more productive variety of wheat, if we invested $15 in an acre of wheat, we might get fifty bushels, and if we invested an extra $15, we might get an extra forty bushels.

TABLE 7-2 Rent Arising from Intensive Cultivation
(in dollars)

Successive inputs of labor and capital	Total yield in bushels	Marginal yield in bushels	Price									
			$.50		$.75		$1.00		$1.50		$3.00	
			Marginal revenue	Rent	Marginal revenue	Rent	Marginal revenue	Rent	Marginal revenue	Rent	Marginal revenue	Rent
15	30	30	15	0	22.50	7.50	30	15	45	30	90	75
15	50	20			15	0	20	5	30	15	60	45
15	65	15					15	0	22.50	7.50	45	30
15	75	10							15	0	30	15
15	80	5									15	0
Total Rent Per Acre:				0		7.50		20		52.50		165

Table 7-2 shows how rent arises if grade A land is worked more and more intensively. Before all the best land is taken up, wheat will sell for 50 cents per bushel, $15 will be invested per acre, and there will be no rent. When the demand for wheat increases and the price rises to 75 cents, it pays to invest a second $15 in labor, capital, and entrepreneurship per acre. The second $15 just barely pays for itself, but the thirty bushels produced by the first $15 investment now produces a rent of $7.50. If the price of wheat rises to $1, the rent is $20 per acre: $15 from the extra productivity of the first $15 invested, and $5 from the second $15 invested.

Production expands simultaneously at the extensive and intensive margins of cultivation. If the demand for wheat increases and therefore the price rises, it will pay to work poorer land. It will also pay to make additional investments of labor and capital on the better land already being worked; this will be true even though the additional investment gives fewer bushels of wheat than the earlier investments did. The higher price of wheat justifies the additional inputs in spite of the law of diminishing returns.

One significant conclusion from the theory of rent is this: *it is not true that prices are high because rents are high. The reverse is true: high prices cause high rents.* As the price of wheat rises, more intensive and extensive cultivation are undertaken. The difference between the marginal production and the better than marginal output rises, and rent rises.

URBAN RENT   Urban land used for business purposes generates rent in a way similar to that in agriculture. Urban rent also depends on the value productivity of the land, that is, the revenue the land brings in, but it is based on the location of the land, rather than on its inherent fertility.

Assume perfect competition in the market for land. Macy's and Gimbel's department stores, located in the heart of Manhattan, generate large incomes because of the large number of people who shop in that area. A department store in a small town generates far less income. Businessmen offer large sums for the right to use land in Manhattan to build a store, and the extra profitability of that store goes to the landlord. Theoretically, the rate of profit left to the entrepreneur would be the same in Manhattan as in the small town. In fact, prices in Macy's and Gimbel's are no higher than in the small-town store, in spite of the high rents. If the owner of a store also owns the land, then part of his income is really rent rather than all of it being profit. Of course, we are excluding the rental value of buildings and other man-made goods. Economic rent refers only to the natural resources that cost society nothing.

THE PRICE OF LAND   The price of land is determined by two factors: the economic rent and the expected rate of return on investment in land. Suppose a piece of land produces an economic rent of $100 a year and is expected to do so forever. Suppose also that 10 percent is considered to be a reasonable rate of return. The land would then be worth $1,000, because $1,000 invested at 10 percent yields $100 per year. Anyone interested in buying land simply would not be willing to pay more for it, because he would not be getting what he considers to be an adequate return. He could invest his money more advantageously elsewhere.

If rates of profit and interest fall, and 5 percent were considered a good rate of return, land yielding $100 rent per year would now be worth $2,000. But suppose the land were located in Chile, and you thought the government might nationalize it. It would become a risky investment, and you would then expect a 20 percent annual return as a sort of insurance premium. If the rent were $100 per year, the land would be worth $500.

If rent rises to $200 per year and 10 percent is considered to be a reasonable return, the price of land would rise from $1,000 to $2,000. Then if the government suddenly imposed a $100 property tax where formerly there was none, the price of land would decline to $1,000.

These are our conclusions: rents are differential returns to different properties. The prices of different tracts of land depend on the rents they yield and on prevailing interest rates.

Wages

MARGINAL REVENUE PRODUCTIVITY—THE DEMAND FOR LABOR We have seen how the value of a natural resource may vary; now we turn our attention to the demand for labor.

The demand for any factor of production is a derived demand; the factor of production is purchased because it is used to produce a product. Consumers demand final products because of their utility to them. Thus, the demand for the factor of production is derived from the demand for the output it produces. Businessmen demand factors of production like land, labor, and capital to produce final products that consumers want, and in the process they make a profit.

The demand for labor depends on how much revenue labor adds to the earnings of the firm. If labor's value productivity is high, that is, if the extra output the worker produces has a high value, the entrepreneur is willing to offer a high wage; if it is low, only a low wage is justified to the employer. It is important to remember that we assume in this theory that the workers are of equal ability.

As more and more workers are hired by a firm, the average output per worker measured in physical units must sooner or later begin to fall, even though the workers are of equal ability. This is because the law of diminishing returns also applies to labor. Keeping other factors constant, adding workers may at first increase the average output per worker, because there will be a greater division of labor within the plant, but eventually diminishing returns will set in.

In Table 7-3 we imagine a shirt factory in which diminishing returns set in from the very beginning of the expansion of the labor force. As the employment of workers increases from one to six, total output of shirts rises from six to twenty-one. The marginal, or extra, output per worker falls from six to one; these figures are derived from the second column.

Assuming that this firm is operating in a perfectly competitive market, it can sell all the shirts it produces at $5 each. Total revenue is total output times $5.

In the next column we consider the cost of raw materials, a matter that is generally ignored in presenting this kind of theory. The assumption is usually made that you add labor without adding any other productive factors, so that the total extra output can be attributed to labor. But this is

TABLE 7-3   Marginal Revenue Productivity
of Labor Under Perfect Competition

Workers hired	Total output (shirts per day)	Marginal output (shirts per day)	Selling price	Total revenue	Cost of raw materials	Total revenue productivity of labor	Marginal revenue productivity
1	6	6	$5	$30	$6	$24	$24
2	11	5	5	55	11	44	20
3	15	4	5	75	15	60	16
4	18	3	5	90	18	72	12
5	20	2	5	100	20	80	8
6	21	1	5	105	21	84	4

impossible. We shall assume that as shirts are produced, $1 must be spent on raw materials for each shirt. The cost of raw materials is subtracted from total revenue to give the total revenue productivity added by labor.

In the last column we find the key we have been looking for. It is the demand schedule for labor, based on labor's marginal revenue productivity. It shows how much revenue each worker adds to the firm, not counting the extra cost of raw materials, but not deducting the wages paid, either. Marginal revenue productivity is derived from total revenue productivity. If one worker adds $24 to the revenue of the firm, and two workers add $44, the marginal revenue productivity of the second worker is $20.

If the wage rate were $16 per day, the demand curve for labor tells us that three workers would be hired. If the wage were higher, fewer workers would be hired; if lower, more. If the revenue produced by an extra worker is greater than his wage, it pays to hire him. If the revenue is lower than the wage, it does not pay to hire him. Equilibrium is attained at that level of employment where the marginal revenue of labor is equal to the wage.

In Figure 7-1, line A is plotted from the last column of Table 7-3. It is the demand curve for labor under perfect competition in the product market, and it slopes down and to the right because of the law of diminishing returns.

Table 7-4 illustrates the marginal revenue productivity of labor, or the demand schedule for labor, when the products are sold in a market of imperfect competition. The key difference between this situation and the one of perfect competition is that here the demand curve for the seller's product slopes down and to the right instead of being horizontal; in order to sell more shirts, he has to lower his price. Thus, in Table 7-4 you will note the selling price declining.

Notice how the situation has changed. We have shown that in perfect competition, at a wage of $16, three workers would be hired with shirts

FIGURE 7-1.   *Marginal Revenue Productivity of Labor Under Perfect and Imperfect Competition*

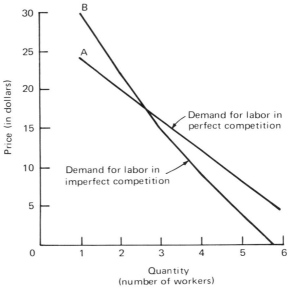

Source: *Tables 7-3 and 7-4.*

selling at $5 each. In this situation of imperfect competition, three workers would not be hired at $16 per day even though the shirts would sell for $5.50. By hiring the third worker, the firm adds $16 to its labor cost but only $15.25 to its net revenue. Therefore, it does not pay to hire the third worker.

The last column in Table 7-4 again shows how much revenue each additional worker adds to the firm. This is the demand for labor, and it is

TABLE 7-4   **Marginal Revenue Productivity
of Labor Under Imperfect Competition**

Workers hired	Total output (shirts per day)	Marginal output (shirts per day)	Selling price	Total revenue	Cost of raw materials	Total revenue productivity of labor	Marginal revenue productivity
1	6	6	$6.00	$36.00	$ 6	$30.00	$30.00
2	11	5	5.75	63.25	11	52.25	22.25
3	15	4	5.50	82.50	15	67.50	15.25
4	18	3	5.25	94.50	18	76.50	9.00
5	20	2	5.00	100.00	20	80.00	3.50
6	21	1	4.75	99.75	21	78.75	−1.25

shown as line B in Figure 7-1. It slopes down and to the right for two reasons: first, the law of diminishing returns; second, to sell more, the seller
has to drop the price. The second reason explains why line B is steeper
than line A.

Whenever we talk about the demand for labor, we shall be talking
about the marginal revenue productivity of labor, and we shall always
show it as a line sloping down and to the right.

THE SUPPLY OF LABOR AND THE EQUILIBRIUM WAGE   We have described the
demand side of the labor market, but we still have not explained completely the wage rate. As we know from previous chapters, both demand
and supply determine price. We have to explain the supply side of the
equation to explain wage rates fully.

Determining the supply of labor is complicated by human motivations
and attitudes toward work. These clearly affect the amount of labor a person will offer as the wage rate changes. We shall consider four different
supply curves in our analysis of the supply of labor. They differ because
they hold for different situations and different reactions of workers to wage
changes.

The first supply curve assumes that a fixed percentage of the population wants to work for wages. Suppose of every 100 people, 40 enter the
labor force and work for whatever wages they can get. The supply curve
would be a vertical line that moves slowly to the right over time as population grows. This is not a very realistic picture of the supply of labor, because the participation rate of the population in the labor force can vary
considerably. It depends, among other factors, on how many young people
go to school for how many years, to what extent wives seek gainful employment, and how many people of retirement age choose to stay working.

A second supply curve would be the labor force available to a small
firm. Suppose the going wage rate is $4 per hour, and at that wage an em-
ployer can hire any number of workers he is likely to want, say from one to
200. The supply curve of labor for that employer would be a horizontal
line at a height of $4 on the vertical, or price, axis.

A third supply curve slopes down and to the right, and it may be applicable to the total labor force in the country in the long run. Such a supply curve tells us that if wages are low and are expected to remain low, we
will have more people offering to work more hours in order to try to maintain a reasonable level of living. But if real wage rates rise and are
expected to remain high, more young people can afford to withdraw from
the labor force to get more education, and workers will desire more leisure
—a shorter working week, longer vacations, and earlier retirement. Therefore, less labor will be offered at a high wage than at a low wage.

The fourth possible supply curve, and the one we will use in Figure
7-2, slopes up and to the right. This tells us that at a high wage, more

FIGURE 7-2. The Equilibrium Rate of Wages

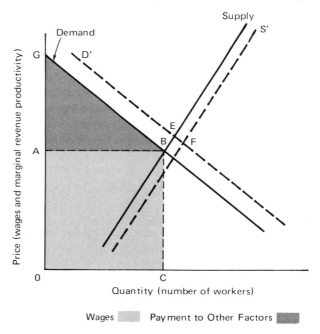

labor will be offered, and at a low wage, less. This may apply to the whole population in the short run. If wage rates are cut drastically, in the short run we may become angry and work less; we will go on strike and hold out for better pay. As long as we think the wage cuts are temporary, we will resist, although in the long run hunger may compel us to work more even if wages are low. If wage rates rise and we think the higher rates will not last, most of us will be eager to take advantage of the high wage by working longer hours. If there were a temporary opportunity to earn $20 an hour, your whole economics class, including your instructor, might rush out to fill the jobs.

The supply curve that slopes up and to the right may also apply to a large firm and to a city, state, or region. If wage rates rise, more people will seek employment with that firm or in that area; people can move from other firms or areas. If wage rates fall, fewer workers will remain with that firm or in that area.

Figure 7-2 shows the equilibrium rate of wages. The demand curve for labor is based on its marginal revenue productivity. The equilibrium wage rate is OA, and OC workers are hired. Total wages are represented by the area OABC. As total revenue produced is OGBC, the surplus above wages goes to the other factors of production; this is represented by the area AGB.

If output per man-hour increases because of improved technology, more and better capital, and a better educated and trained labor force, the marginal revenue productivity of labor increases. This is shown by the shift of the demand curve for labor to D'; wage rates then rise to E, and more workers are employed. If the supply of labor increases with the growth of population, the supply curve shifts to S', and a new equilibrium wage is reached at F.

Interest

Interest is the price paid for the use of loanable funds. The rate of interest depends on the demand for and supply of money.

The demand for money as a demand for liquidity was discussed in Chapter 4 (see pages 76–78). The demand for money for investment was depicted in Figure 4-4 on page 79. It shows a series of possible investments with the expected rate of return on each. The demand curve for money would slope down and to the right if we were to line up the investments from the most profitable to the least. Loanable funds are also demanded by households and by government. The supply of money depends on the rate of saving of individuals and businesses and on the money created by commercial bank lending as discussed in Chapter 4.

FIGURE 7-3.   The Equilibrium Rate of Interest

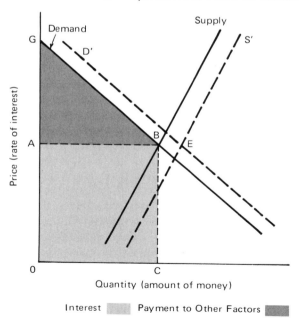

The demand and supply curves for money intersect to determine an equilibrium rate of interest as shown in Figure 7-3. OA is the rate of interest, OC is the quantity of money lent out, and OABC is the total interest paid. The area AGB represents payments to other factors of production.

In the long run new inventions are made, the size of the market grows, and new business opportunities arise. These increase the marginal revenue productivity of capital, and the demand for money or loanable funds shifts to D'. At the same time income rises, saving increases, and commercial banks expand credit. The supply therefore shifts to S'. Interest rates in the long run go from B to E. In this case they are shown as remaining at the same level as formerly, but this need not necessarily be so.

There is, of course, no such thing as a single rate of interest; there are many rates. The basic rate we are talking about might be the rate on government or high-grade corporate bonds. There is virtually no risk of default on such bonds, although there is a risk that the dollars paid back when the bonds mature will be worth less than the dollars used to buy the bonds.

Rates of interest can be higher than the basic rate if the lenders have more economic power than the borrowers, if the risks of default are high, or if the loan is small and the cost of making and collecting the loan is higher per dollar lent than with large loans. Interest also varies with the length of the loan, typically being higher with longer-term loans.

Profit

Profit is the residual income of a business after all explicit and implicit wages, interest, and rent have been met. As an illustration, suppose a man owns and operates a business. After meeting all expenses, including depreciation on his buildings and machinery, he has a net income of $20,000. He is likely to call this his profit for the year. But this is not what we mean by profit, because his total income includes implicit factor returns. Suppose this entrepreneur could get a job paying $10,000 a year; that sum is a labor income rather than profit. Suppose he has $100,000 of his own money invested in the business and he could have lent out that money at 6 percent interest; implicit interest is, therefore, $6,000 for the year. Assume that his business is located on land he owns and the rental value of the land is $1,000 per year; that is another implicit factor return. When all these implicit factor returns are subtracted from his net income, we see that his profit is $3,000, not $20,000.

There are many sources of profit, and we shall discuss five of them.

First, profit may be a reward for risk taking. The riskier the business, the higher the expected rate of return has to be to induce investment in it. An expansion of telephone or electric power facilities is fairly safe, and an expected rate of profit of 1 or 2 percent above the going rate of interest may be enough to bring in capital. But prospecting for oil is rather risky, and an expectation of a 15 percent rate of profit may be necessary to attract capital. Perhaps this is why in 1970 the telephone and telegraph companies had a 9.5 percent return on the net investment of the stockholders, and coal mining had a 14.5 percent return. Actually, the return on the total investment in telephone and telegraph was lower than 9.5 percent. Stockholders can increase the return on their investment by also investing money borrowed at a rate of interest that is lower than the rate of return on the invested capital. Here is an example: suppose the total investment in the telephone business gives a 7 percent return. Assume that you can borrow money at 6 percent interest. For every $100 of your own money that you invest, you invest $400 of borrowed money. The total investment of $500 yields a return of $35. You pay out $24 in interest on the $400, and you are left with an $11 return, or 11 percent on your $100 investment. These transactions are called leverage or trading on the equity.

Second, profit may result as a reward for innovation. The firm that introduced ball-point pens sold them for as high as $5 apiece and more. When more and more competitors entered the field, the price dropped to as low as 10 cents. Similarly, the invention of the camera that develops pictures immediately produced tremendous profits. Profits from innovation tend to disappear as imitators rush in to compete for business, but such profits can be perpetuated if protected by patents or other monopoly methods or by further refinement and improvement, that is, by further innovation.

A third source of profit is luck. A man who invested in a business in 1929 may have gone broke in the Great Depression, but the man of equal ability who invested in 1932 may have made a success of it. Take the case of two men of equal ability who want to open a restaurant in the same area. One has more money than the other, and he succeeds in going into business. He builds a restaurant for $200,000 of which he pays $100,000 of his own money and borrows $100,000 on a five-year loan at 10 percent interest. His first year's payment on his loan is $30,000; he cannot meet the payment and he goes bankrupt. The creditors take over the restaurant and sell it to the second man for $100,000. He has $50,000 of his own to invest, and he borrows $50,000, also on a five-year loan at 10 percent interest. His first year's payment on the loan is only $15,000 for principal and interest; he can easily meet this payment and he makes a success of the business. His success depended on the investment and failure of his predecessor, because bankruptcy can restore the profitability of enterprise by wiping out some of the capital values and, therefore, the fixed, or overhead, costs. And whether a business goes bankrupt or not may well be a matter of luck—either bad or good.

A fourth source of profit is monopolistic or oligopolistic power. The power of a monoploy or oligopoly can be seen in the fact that the industry producing drugs and medicines had a return of 19.1 percent on the net worth of the stockholders in 1971, while textile products had a 6.2 percent return. This power also explains why in 1971 General Motors had a return of 17.9 percent on the capital owned by the stockholders, and IBM had a 16.2 percent return, while the average for all manufacturing was 10.8 percent.

A fifth source of profit may be the extraordinary ability of the entrepreneur. His extra income, however, could be considered as a labor income to pay for his exceptional ability. He could get a job with someone else for a higher than average salary, in which case, part of his apparent profit would not really be profit at all.

The expectations of profit guide investment. Capital, seeking the maximum rate of return, flows to those areas where the outlook is best. Production expands where the profits or expected profits are highest, and production declines where profits are low.

Applications of the Theory of Distribution

HENRY GEORGE'S SINGLE TAX Henry George (1839–97) moved from Philadelphia to California as a young man and observed the speculative land craze there after the Civil War. As people poured into California, land prices rose phenomenally while many people remained impoverished. In 1879 George published his famous book *Progress and Poverty,* which sold millions of copies and continues to sell to this day.

George believed that all the gains of the growing efficiency of production go to the landowners. He believed that there should be a 100 percent tax on the economic rent of land. As land is a free gift of nature, no one should seize for himself the natural resources that should benefit everyone. In effect, George's scheme would nationalize land without compensation to the present owners. Land would then not be kept idle for speculative purposes; if the owner chose to retain title to the land, he would still owe the government its annual rental value whether the land was put to use or not.

George called this tax the "single tax" because he thought no other taxes would be necessary. Why tax man-made improvements or incomes when such taxes discourage capital investment and the earning of income through greater efforts? Taxing the land would still leave us with the same land available for productive use.

As economic rent rises, land prices rise proportionally. An extreme case of a high price for land is the land under Number One Wall Street in New York City; it has sold for $700 a square foot, which comes to $30.5 million an acre. The value of all land excluding minerals in the United States rose from $31 billion in 1900 to $715 billion in 1968.

In view of the trend toward ever-rising urban and mineral land values

—and to a lesser extent agricultural land values—Henry George will continue to have disciples. Nonetheless, it is clear that a single tax on economic rent would fall far short of the close to $300 billion raised in taxes each year by all levels of government.

UNIONS, WAGE RATES, AND EMPLOYMENT   Do unions cause unemployment by raising wages above the equilibrium level? Pre-Keynesian economists who were concerned with microeconomic distribution theory generally thought they did. Their reasoning can be seen by looking at the solid demand and supply curves for labor in Figure 7-2 on page 156. If unions raise wages above OA, the quantity of labor supplied will exceed the quantity demanded and unemployment will result. Similarly, in a depression the demand for labor will shift down toward the left, and it will intersect the supply schedule at a lower wage rate. The pre-Keynesian economists argued that if only workers accepted wage cuts, we would get out of the depression and back to full employment again.

This faulty economic theorizing is an example of "the fallacy of composition." It is fallacious to say that what is true of a part is necessarily true of the whole, or what is true in one case is true in all cases. Here are two examples: if you drive to college at 7 A.M., you will find plenty of parking spaces; but if everybody comes that early, they may not all find a parking space. If bad times are feared, you may be better off by saving more of your income; but if everybody reduces his consumption spending, everybody will be worse off by creating or worsening the depression that each person feared.

Wage cutting to maintain or restore full employment as a general rule is a fallacy of composition. Wage cutting may be correct for one industry but not for the whole economy. It has been recommended on the assumption that it would not affect the demand for goods or the marginal revenue productivity of labor. Suppose, for example, the auto workers in the United States took a 50 percent cut in wages, and the price of cars fell 25 percent. Would employment increase? Yes, very much. The auto workers would not be able to buy as many cars as they used to, but they do not loom large in the total car market. The rest of us would buy more cars, fewer cars would be imported, and more would be exported. And more workers would be needed to assemble these extra cars.

But what would happen if all workers in the country had a 50 percent cut in wages and prices fell 25 percent? We would buy far fewer cars and many other things, and employment would decrease. In Figure 7-2 the demand for labor would fall down and to the left. In other words, wages are not only a cost of production, they are also a source of demand for goods. Wage cuts in the whole economy would not restore full employment.

Even in a single industry, the marginal revenue productivity of labor will increase as wage rates rise. Suppose farm wage earners got a significant increase in their miserably low wages. Through the working of competitive market forces, provided that the capital involved remained constant, the price of farm products would rise, and, therefore, the revenue produced by each worker would rise. The demand curve for labor would shift up and to the right. In other words, as there is an inelastic demand for farm products, higher prices based on higher wages would not reduce employment much. In fact, it probably would not reduce employment at all, because the trend of rising incomes for the whole population and growing numbers of people would offset the higher prices in affecting the quantity of farm products demanded.

If unions raise money wages, and if all of the wage increase is passed on in higher prices, are workers better off? The answer is yes. If, for example, the auto workers get a pay increase, it is paid by everybody who pays the higher prices for cars. But what happens if all workers get wage increases and prices are raised by an equal amount of money? The workers will still be better off, as the following example illustrates. Suppose total output is equal to 100 measured in current dollars, and wages are 60. Now wages rise 10 percent to 66, and the aggregate prices of the output is raised to 106. This means that the total amount of wage increase was passed on as a price increase. Workers are now better off, because formerly they could buy 60 percent of total output and now they can buy 62.3 percent. They are better off because other groups, by buying their share of total output, help pay the wage increases.

Of course, if wages go up 10 percent and then prices are raised 10 percent, workers are no better off. This is usually what happens as we have more and more oligopoly pricing in our economy.

MONOPSONY IN THE LABOR MARKET   If there is one seller of a product, he is called a monopolist. If there is one buyer, he is called a monopsonist. Suppose there is monopsony in the labor market, which means there is only one employer in the area. The situation is shown in Table 7-5.

TABLE 7-5   Monopsony in the Labor Market

Number of workers	Wage rate	Total cost of labor	Marginal cost of labor	Marginal net revenue productivity of labor
1	$20	$20	$20	$44
2	22	44	24	40
3	24	72	28	36
4	26	104	32	32
5	28	140	36	28
6	30	180	40	24

We assume that the supply curve of labor slopes up and to the right. At a wage of $20, only one worker would offer to work; at $22, two workers, and so on. The total cost of labor is found by multiplying the number of workers by the wage rate. The fourth column gives the marginal cost of labor to the monopsony firm. One worker would cost the firm $20 per day, but adding a second worker adds $24 to the firm's cost. In other words, if the firm wants to hire two workers, not only will the second worker get a $22 wage, but the first worker also has to get $2 extra (we assume a uniform wage rate because all workers are of equal ability). To hire a third worker, the wage rate has to rise to $24. But $28 are added to the wage bill because the first and second workers get $2 per day more each when the third worker is hired. The monopsony, by hiring more workers, bids up the wage rate against itself; it will, therefore, be interested in restricting the amount of labor it hires, just as the monopolist is interested in restricting sales to raise prices.

The marginal net revenue productivity of labor is obtained by calculating the extra revenue that the firm receives as a result of the extra product the worker produces.

If the situation in Table 7-5 were one of perfect competition, the firm would have no control over wage rates. All it could do would be to decide how many workers to hire. The firm would hire five workers, because at that level the wage rate in the whole labor market would be equal to the marginal revenue productivity of labor—$28.

The monopsony, however, finds that if it hires the fifth worker, it adds $36 to its labor costs but only $28 to its revenue. It therefore cuts employment to four workers, where the marginal cost of labor and its marginal revenue productivity are equal at $32. The monopsony forces the wage rate down from the competitive level of $28 to the monopsony level of $26.

If a union is organized and insists that the wage rate be $28 a day regardless of the number employed, the supply curve of labor is now horizontal rather than upward-sloping. If the monopsony has to pay $28 to each worker hired, the marginal cost of labor is the same as the wage rate —$28. Consequently, the monopsony will hire five workers. The union has increased employment while it raised wages.

The situation shown in Table 7-5 appears also in Figure 7-4. Under competition, the supply and demand curves for labor intersect at point E, which determines the wage rate and the number of workers employed. With monopsony, the supply curve of labor is the marginal cost curve, which intersects the demand curve at A. The wage rate is CB, and the monopsony profit per worker is BA. If the union raises the wage rate to FE, the marginal cost of labor is now a horizontal line, and the firm hires five workers. If the union raises wages above the competitive equilibrium level to CA, employment declines to four, where it was before the union appeared, but monopsony profit has disappeared.

FIGURE 7-4. Monopsony in the Labor Market

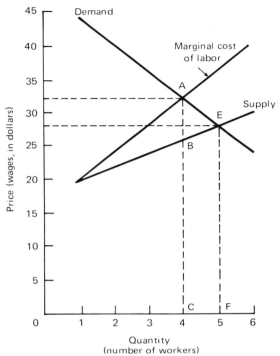

Source: Table 7-5.

An example of a monopsony firm hiring labor is the hiring of players of professional sports. When an athlete graduates from college, he may be drafted by one of the professional teams in his particular sport. Except for professional basketball and ice hockey, which at this point have two distinct leagues competing for players, all other sports are monopsony arrangements; that is, they are characterized by a single buyer. Thus, an individual who is drafted by a professional sports team in, say football, must play for that team or not play professionally in the United States. Under these conditions the laborer, in this case the college athlete, is stuck with a particular buyer of his services. He has no choice of buyers. This has resulted in a less than competitive wage for the athlete.

GAMBLING, INSURANCE, AND THE DISTRIBUTION OF INCOME In Chapter 5 we discussed the law of diminishing marginal utility in analyzing the demand for consumer goods and services. If it is true that the more units of a good you acquire in any period of time, the less satisfaction is derived from each added unit, the same is true of money. The more money you have, the greater its total utility but the less the utility of an extra dollar. The reverse is also true: the less money you have, the less its total utility but the greater the utility of an extra dollar.

This theory of the diminishing marginal utility of money can tell us something about the advisability of both gambling and buying insurance. Assuming that you do not get any pleasure from gambling itself, but only from winning, gambling does not pay. Suppose you bet your whole weekly paycheck, double or nothing, on the flip of a coin. If you lose, you lose dollars that are precious to you; without them you cannot buy that new tire or get milk for the kids or pay the rent. But if you win, the extra dollars have less utility than your week's earnings. Therefore, in gambling you stand to lose much more utility than you might gain.

The same reasoning leads to the conclusion that insurance does pay. Suppose you pay $25 per year for insurance on your personal possessions and some time during your lifetime you have a $1,500 fire that exactly equals the premiums you paid. Have you gained anything? Yes. The $25 you slice off the top of your income each year to pay for the insurance has low marginal utility. But the $1,500 you would lose at one time because of the fire would dig into your year's income and deprive you of dollars that have higher marginal utility.

One disturbing conclusion of the theory of the diminishing marginal utility of money to orthodox economists has been the following: if the more money you have, the lower its marginal utility, then total utility will be increased if wealth is transferred from the rich to the poor. The dollars the rich give up represent a smaller loss in satisfaction than the gain in satisfaction of the poor who receive those dollars.

There have been two major criticisms of the idea that the redistribution of income would increase total utility. First, we cannot compare utilities among different people; the rich may be more efficient "pleasure machines" than the poor. Second, if we go too far in redistributing incomes, incentives to work and to invest might be impaired, and the size of the national income pie might shrink, leaving everyone worse off.

On the first point, although experimentation is difficult in economics, we may be able to run an experiment testing whether money has a higher utility for the poor than for the rich. Suppose we lie in wait for Governor Nelson Rockefeller, and as he emerges from his office building onto the street, we release a $10 bill in the breeze and call out to him, "Go get it— it's yours!" Suppose we do the same for a man who is unemployed and destitute. The reactions we can expect from the two men will tell us something about the marginal utility of money to each.

On the second point: does the redistribution of income reduce the incentives to work and to invest? We were frightened with this tale over the centuries, but with productivity what it is today, the distribution of income in the United States is without doubt a more important issue than the growth of income. In fact, more growth will mean more pollution and more depletion of our natural resources. In addition, it is not at all certain that high taxes thwart incentives; they may cause an individual to work harder in order to maintain his customary standard of living.

Evaluation of Distribution Theory

Distribution theory appears to be very precise on paper. We know exactly how much each worker adds to output and how much revenue the extra output adds to the firm. But businessmen have only very vague notions of the marginal productivity of extra inputs and the marginal revenue derived from extra sales. In fact, surveys show that they think more in terms of average output per worker, average price per unit sold, and average profit. Once having determined the selling price for their product, they will buy productive factors up to the point where they produce all that can be sold at the going price. They are generally not guided by marginal considerations.

In considering the questions of marginal revenue productivity, diminishing returns to labor, and wage rates, let us look at the following typical case: in 1971 a migrant farm worker in central New York drove a farm tractor for $1.70 per hour with no pay on rainy days and no sick pay. The diesel tractor he drove cost $13,000, and the machine it pulled varied from a $2,100 disc harrow to an $18,000 bean picker. His fringe benefits were a one-way, $62 bus ticket from Florida for himself (but not for his wife and children), a free hovel to live in, and a small truck for his personal use. What determined his wage? What was his marginal revenue productivity? If the farmer hired another worker, what would his marginal revenue have been? In this case, these questions are irrelevant. This worker's wage had little to do with marginal revenue productivity; it had much more to do with unequal bargaining power, based on the large supply of labor.

The mythology of price theory has also been used to explain the length of the working day. Imagine a boy picking and eating berries. The more he eats, the lower the marginal utility of the extra berries. The longer he works, the greater the irksomeness or disutility of his labor. The marginal utility curve of berries slopes down and to the right, for it is a demand curve. The disutility curve of labor slopes up and to the right, for it is analogous to a supply curve. The point of intersection of the two curves determines the quantity of labor that will be performed in picking berries. This case is supposed to apply to the real world around us. We will work each day until the utility of the last hour's earnings is equal to the disutility of the last hour of work. At that point of equilibrium we will get maximum satisfaction.

Imagine you are negotiating for a job, and after you get it, you tell your employer, "Oh, by the way, I reach equilibrium after six hours of work, so I won't work the usual eight-hour shift." You know what will happen to you, don't you? In fact there have been labor arbitration cases in which Seventh Day Adventists refused to work overtime on Saturdays and in which truck drivers refused to work overtime at all; both the Seventh Day Adventists and the truck drivers were fired, and they stayed fired after arbitration.

The length of the working day depends on custom, law, and the outcome of centuries of conflict. Compare microeconomic theory with what Karl Marx had to say about the length of the working day:

> The capitalist maintains his rights as a purchaser when he tries to make the working day as long as possible, and to make, whenever possible, two working days out of one. On the other hand, the peculiar nature of the commodity sold implies a limit to its consumption by the purchaser, and the labourer maintains his right as a seller when he wishes to reduce the working day to one of definite normal duration. There is here, therefore, an antinomy, right against right, both equally bearing the seal of the law of exchanges. Between equal rights force decides. Hence is it that in the history of capitalist production, the determination of what is a working day, presents itself as the result of a struggle, a struggle between collective capital, *i.e.*, the class of capitalists, and collective labour, *i.e.*, the working class. (Karl Marx, *Capital*, Vol. 1, translated by Samuel Moore and Edward Aveling [Chicago: Charles H. Kerr, 1906], p. 259. [Originally published in German in 1867.]

The American economist John Bates Clark (1847–1938) was a leading figure in the development of distribution theory. He not only invented the term *marginal productivity,* but he presented the clearest and best analysis up to his time of the marginal productivity theory of distribution. His overall conclusion was that the division of income was based on natural law and that it was just and equitable. Society is not at liberty to violate the "fixed laws of distribution." If every man receives all he creates, the different classes of men who combine their forces in industry have no grievances against one another. Private property is ethically justified because it is based on an ethical distribution of income under laissez faire.

This theory ignores the power—or lack of it—that influences the distribution of income. It obscures the underlying realities of the economy. You probably have heard, for example, that the inflation of the late 1960's and the early 1970's was caused by labor's excessive wage demands. Let us look at the United States Department of Labor statistics. Comparing the figures for 1965, before the inflation began, with those for the first three months of 1972, we find that the consumer price index rose 30.9 percent, gross hourly earnings of production and nonsupervisory workers on private nonagricultural payrolls rose 44.9 percent to $3.55 per hour, and productivity (ouput per hour) rose 15.0 percent. Workers should have gotten increased wages to cover both the increased cost of living and increased productivity, but they fell 1.0 percent short of that. Except in special cases, labor has not gained excessive wage increases. (See Chapter 8 for a more complete discussion of the causes of inflation.)

You may wonder at our assumption that labor should get wages that reflect average increased productivity. You should be aware that if productivity goes up 10 percent over a period of time and wages go up 10 percent, this does not mean that labor gets the total benefit of the increased efficiency. This is illustrated in Table 7-6. Even without price increases, when productivity goes up 10 percent, everybody can get a 10 percent increase in revenue.

TABLE 7-6　Hypothetical Distribution of Income
with Increased Productivity

	Before increase in productivity	After increase in productivity
Real income	100	110
Wages	60	66
Rent	5	5.5
Interest	5	5.5
Profit	10	11
Taxes	20	22
Total	100	110

Not all sectors of the economy, however, increase their productivity by the same percentage. We expressed a value judgment in saying above that all workers should get an increase in real wages that reflects increased *average* productivity in the economy. A free market will, to a considerable extent, enforce this value judgment. Suppose since 1900 the productivity of steel workers increased 500 percent and the productivity of teachers did not increase at all. If each group of workers expected to get increased wages based on its own productivity, the real wages in steel mills should have gone up 500 percent since 1900, and the wages of teachers should not have gone up at all. But in this situation more and more people would try to work in the steel mills, pushing wages down; fewer people would become teachers, raising their wages. This illustrates the tendency for wages to go up by the average increase in productivity in the economy. If productivity in steel rises more than the average, steel prices fall; if productivity in education rises less than the average, prices of educational services rise. This is one of the reasons for the very large increases in the cost of education.

We referred above to the average hourly earnings of production and nonsupervisory workers on private nonagricultural payrolls of $3.55 during the first three months of 1972. Assuming a working year of 2,000 hours, this comes to $7,100 per year. The United States Department of Labor states that a modest but adequate budget for an urban family of four would have been $11,190 during the first three months of 1972. Actual earnings of wage earners, therefore, fell far short of this intermediate budget.

Are we rich enough so that everybody could have an adequate level of living? Net national product during the first three months of 1972 was at an annual rate of $1,002 billion; with 208 million people, this comes to $19,270 for every four people. Every four people could have had $11,190 of income and there would still be $420 billion left for higher incomes for some, for government spending, and for other purposes.

TABLE 7-7   Labor's Share of Value Added by Manufacturing, 1849–1967

Year	Wages of production workers (in millions of dollars)	Value added by manufacturing (in millions of dollars)	Wages as a percentage of value added
1849	236.8	464.0	51.0
1869	620.5	1,395.1	44.5
1889	1,820.9	4,102.3	44.4
1909	3,205.2	8,160.1	39.3
1929	10,884.9	30,591.4	35.6
1949	30,254.0	75,366.5	40.1
1969	93,331	305,908	30.5

Source: Computed from United States Bureau of the Census, Historical Statistics of the United States, Colonial Times to 1957. Washington, D.C.: Government Printing Office, 1960, p. 409; also Continuation to 1962 and Revisions, 1965, p. 134. Statistical Abstract of the United States, 1971, p. 685.

For more than a century, the wages of production workers in manufacturing as a percentage of value added has tended to fall as shown in Table 7-7. This reflects rising costs of financing and marketing the output, high profits, high salaries for company executives, and high taxes. In 1970 the chairman of the board of Johnson & Johnson received $509,793 in salary and other payments, and the head of International Telephone and Telegraph received $766,755. These payments would tend to lower both wages and the apparent profits of the company. We cannot help wondering how these officials' marginal productivity is measured. Or are they among the insiders who vote themselves large salaries whether they earn them or not? It is interesting to note that Ford company officials voted themselves large bonuses in the year the Edsel failed after a loss of over a quarter billion dollars.

If marginal productivity explains the distribution of income, the salaries of corporation executives show many bizarre relationships that do not fit the theory. The head of Pan American World Airways, for example, received a 51 percent increase in compensation in 1970 compared with the previous year, while the company was losing $48 million. The foundering Lockheed Aircraft Corporation gave its chairman $150,000 in 1970, the same salary that the chairman of the Xerox Corporation received. Henry Ford II must be twice as productive as the head of General Motors, because the former received $500,000 and the latter $250,000 in 1970. The head of Westinghouse is more productive than the head of General Electric, $308,748 to $243,761.

Our conclusion is that the theory of the distribution of income, however consistent, does not explain the actual distribution of income. Those people who are rich will pass on advantages to their children and their children's children; those who are poor will leave handicaps and disadvantages as their unwilling bequests to their descendants. It is as though after every race the runners were permitted to start again from the positions in which they found themselves at the end of the previous race. Unequal wealth supports unequal power, and those with greater wealth and power are in a better position to obtain additional wealth and power. The market system tends not only to protect inequality, but to enhance it.

Summary

In this chapter we looked at the marginal productivity theory of distribution. The nation's income can be divided into the major categories of rent, which is received by the owners of natural resources; wages, which go to labor; interest, which is paid for the use of loanable funds; and profit, which goes to the entrepreneurs as a reward for being enterprising and taking risks.

Historically the law of diminishing returns was applied first to labor and capital used in the intensive cultivation of the soil. If technology and the land area are held constant, adding labor and capital to a fixed area of land will increase total output; but beyond some point, the average output per unit of input must fall. As the last unit of labor and capital must receive the average or typical compensation, the extra return of the other inputs goes to the landowner in the form of rent.

The law of diminishing returns applies, of course, to all factors of production. Keeping technology and at least one factor of production constant, adding other factors of production will yield diminishing returns to the variable factors.

The marginal revenue productivity of labor is the receipts an extra worker adds to the firm's gross income after the extra cost of raw materials is deducted; this is the firm's demand schedule for labor. It pays to hire additional workers until the marginal revenue productivity of labor falls to a level that is equal to the wage rate. The supply of labor depends on the size of the population, the percentage of the population that is in the labor force, and how much labor people are willing to sell at different wage rates. The intersection of the demand and supply curves determines the price of labor, or the wage rate, for a particular kind of labor.

Interest is the price paid for the use of loanable funds. It depends on the demand for and supply of money. Loanable funds are demanded by businesses, householders, and government. The supply depends on the rate of saving of individuals and businesses, and on the money created by commercial bank lending.

Profit is what is left to the owner of a business after all explicit and implicit rent, wages, and interest have been met. It can arise as a reward for risk taking and innovation, or it can be based on luck, monopolistic power, or the extraordinary ability of the entrepreneur.

There have been many controversies over whether or how the distribution of income should be changed. Henry George proposed that there should be a 100 percent tax on economic rent and no other taxes. Others have advocated unionism, but opponents argue that higher wages will cause unemployment. We have seen that this involves "the fallacy of composition," which arises when we say that what is true of a part is necessarily true of the whole. If one firm raises wages, it will hire fewer workers, but if all firms raise wages, employment probably will not go down; this is because wages are both a cost of production and a source of demand for goods.

We have seen that when there is only one employer in a labor market (monopsony), the firm is likely to restrict employment because it wishes to avoid bidding up the rate of wages against itself. But if a union fixes a standard rate of wages, the supply curve of labor becomes horizontal instead of sloping upward. In such a situation, the monopsony employer is likely to increase the number of workers hired.

QUESTIONS AND PROBLEMS

1   If all marginal and submarginal land disappeared, rent would rise. Can you explain why?

2   Discuss the ethics and the desirability of Henry George's proposal to confiscate the land without compensation.

3   In recent years there has been increasing support for equality in incomes. Discuss how this could be achieved, and what the consequences might be.

4   Look up rates of profit for industries or companies in *Statistical Abstract of the United States*, *Fortune* magazine, or the *Monthly Economic Letter* of the

First National City Bank of New York. Why do rates of profit differ so widely among industries and even more so among companies?

5   Can you think of some examples of the "fallacy of composition" in addition to those given in this chapter?

6   Suppose you owned and operated a grocery store; what would be the implicit and explicit costs? When a large chain store corporation operates a supermarket, what are its implicit and explicit costs?

7   What would happen if, as you added more and more workers to a factory of a given size, the average output per worker remained constant?

8   How do you explain lower wages in agriculture than in industry? In retail trade than in manufacturing?

9   In colonial America, an abundance of excellent land was available. How, therefore, could a labor force be mobilized to work for others?

10   Many economists from different schools of thought believed that with the passage of time the rate of profit would tend to fall. On what basis could they come to this conclusion?

11   On page 151 it is stated that "theoretically, the rate of profit left to the entrepreneur would be the same in Manhattan as in the small town." Why may this not work out in practice?

12   What does your own personal supply curve of labor look like?

BIBLIOGRAPHY

BARKER, CHARLES A., *Henry George*. New York: Oxford University Press, 1955.

DUE, JOHN F., and Clower, Robert W., *Intermediate Economic Analysis*, 5th ed. Homewood, Ill.: Richard D. Irwin, 1966.

FREEDMAN, ROBERT, ed., *Marx on Economics*. New York: Harcourt Brace Jovanovich, 1961.

GEORGE, HENRY, *Progress and Poverty*. New York: Robert Schalkenbach Foundation, 1971. (Originally published in 1879.)

LEFTWICH, RICHARD H., *The Price System and Resource Allocation*, 3rd ed. New York: Holt, 1966.

OSER, JACOB, *Henry George*. New York: Twayne, 1973.

ROBINSON, JOAN, *The Economics of Imperfect Competition*. London: Macmillan, 1933.

STONIER, ALFRED W., and Hague, Douglas C., *A Textbook of Economic Theory*. London: Longmans, Green, 1953.

UNITED STATES DEPARTMENT OF LABOR, BUREAU OF LABOR STATISTICS, *Monthly Labor Review*.

PART

THREE

PROBLEMS OF THE NATION'S ECONOMY

In the nine chapters of this section we shall consider nine major economic problems of our time. The theories we have presented in Parts I and II will be applied in Part III. For example, microeconomics is relevant in the chapter on agriculture when we consider supply, demand, and the price-support program. Macroeconomics is of major importance in analyzing stabilization policies, international trade, and economic development.

While economic theory explains a great deal, many problems do not fit exactly into the framework of the theory. Thus we have to understand something about the political system in order to evaluate stabilization and regulation of business in Chapters 8 and 9. Human motivations and power relationships characterize much of the debate in the population, labor union, and income distribution chapters.

In Part III we shall study inflation and how it hurts some people while it benefits others. Government taxing, spending, and the redistribution of income also affect us all while at the same time they influence aggregate income. Can the federal government go bankrupt if it keeps on spending more than it receives and the national debt grows larger? How does the government permit monopolies to develop or actually promote them? How successful has the regulation of public utilities been? How can pollution be controlled? What is the role of labor unions, and what have they done or failed to do about the problems of black and women workers? What are the causes of and the cures for poverty? Are we faced with the threat of overpopulation and starvation? Why cannot farmers solve their own problems without the aid of government, and how do government programs for agriculture affect the rest of us who are not farmers? Can we become impoverished if we permit imports to come into our country without restrictions? Why are most of the countries of the world poor, and how can they overcome their poverty? These are the kinds of questions we shall try to answer in the following chapters.

Surely there are other issues of importance besides those discussed here. What you have learned in Parts I and II will be helpful in probing a wide range of topics that are or may become of major concern to you. Economic theories are tools that should illuminate the economic questions of our time. The following chapters illustrate how these tools may be used.

Stabilization Policies

There are plenty of good five-cent cigars in the country.
The trouble is they cost a quarter. What the country really
needs is a good five-cent nickel.
—*Franklin Pierce Adams*

Our nation's economy has been characterized by a great deal of instability, which has produced adverse economic, social, and psychological effects on people. The recent inflation and recession is an example of this instability and the unrest and dissatisfaction it can breed. The science of economics has made rapid strides in stabilizing the economy in the last forty years. Two methods of stabilizing the economy, monetary, and fiscal policies, will be analyzed in this chapter. A third policy, wage and price control, which cuts through both monetary and fiscal policies, will also be considered. As in previous chapters, the weaknesses and strengths of the various policies and their effects on individuals will be discussed.

The Impact Of Fluctuations

THE PROBLEM OF STABILIZATION In our discussion in Chapter 2 we described the national accounting system that is used in the United States to determine how well our economy is functioning. We must now make a transition from the world of the accounting statistics to the problems that the statistics reflect, that is, the effects of an increase or decrease in gross national product on individuals' employment, income, and expectations. Why study instability in our economy? Because periodic recessions, depressions, and inflations have caused tremendous economic and social problems in the United States. Not only has there been a loss of output as a result of each recession and a loss of real income due to inflation, but the individual's confidence in his own ability to support himself and his family has been seriously undermined. Thus the problem of economic stability becomes not only an academic discussion of why an economy goes up and down, but also a human drama concerned with the ability of a nation to support itself.

The instability of our economy is shown graphically in Table 8-1. No-

TABLE 8-1   Economic Instability in the United States, 1929–70
(in billions of dollars)

Selected years	Personal consumption expenses	Gross private domestic investment	Government purchases of goods and services	GNP *
1929	77.2	16.2	8.5	103.1
1930	69.9	10.3	9.2	90.4
1931	60.5	5.6	9.2	75.8
1932	48.6	1.0	8.1	58.0
1933	45.8	1.4	8.0	55.6
1934	51.3	3.3	9.8	65.1
1935	55.7	6.4	10.0	72.2
1940	70.8	13.1	14.0	99.7
1945	119.7	10.6	82.3	212.0
1950	191.0	54.1	37.9	248.8
1960	325.2	74.8	99.6	503.8
1970	616.8	135.8	220.5	976.5

* For purposes of simplicity the net export figure is not listed although it is included in GNP.

Source: Survey of Current Business, various issues.

tice that GNP for 1929 was $103.1 billion. By 1931 it had slipped to $75.8 billion; it went down even further in 1933 to $55.6 billion. Even while remembering all the warnings that were given in Chapter 2 concerning the analysis and use of GNP figures, it is significant to note that GNP decreased by some 50 percent in four years. Notice also that personal consumption expenditures in the same time period decreased from $77.2 billion to $45.8 billion. This means that individuals were spending less, by necessity, on personal items such as food, clothing, automobiles, and so forth. During the same time period, gross business investments went from $16.2 billion to $1.4 billion, a catastrophic drop. Net investment actually declined because the depreciation of capital goods was greater than new (replacement) investment. The only component of GNP that remained relatively constant was government expenditures, which were $8.5 billion in 1929 and $8.0 billion in 1933. By 1940 the GNP was almost back to where it was in 1929. By the end of the Second World War in 1945, GNP was more than double the figure for 1940.

These figures reflect the fact that there is, and was, a tremendous degree of instability in our economy. Even though there may not be a precise relationship between GNP and the welfare of the nation, it is a rough indicator of the economic health of the country. But leaving the GNP figures aside, what does economic stability mean in terms of employment and consumption expenditures for an individual?

The precise connection between GNP and employment is difficult to ascertain, but there is a rough relationship. In the 1930's, for example, while the GNP was decreasing, the unemployment rate was increasing, and it reached a high of 25 percent in 1933. This 25 percent figure understated the dimensions of the problem. There were many more people who were unemployed than were indicated in the unemployment figures, especially if part-time workers are considered. Not only were people out of work, but those who were working were working for less income.

Another indication of the economic situation in the 1930's was that gross private domestic investment, which includes residential home construction, dropped to almost nothing. Thus, we took a ten-year vacation in the United States from solving one of the pressing domestic problems— housing.

The figures for the 1930's indicate the down side of the economic picture. In recent years we have been faced with another problem, that is, rising prices. How do we measure inflation? There are many common *Price* indicators, all involving the construction of what is called a price index. A *Index* consumer price index is merely a weighted average of the prices of products that a typical consumer could be expected to buy. If an individual in our economy can be expected to spend money on food, clothing, shelter, education, recreation, health, hobbies, and transportation, a simplified price index may be constructed. Such a price index is shown in Table 8-2.

In Table 8-2 we wish to show the increased cost of living from some base year to the current year. Take, for example, the increased cost of food.

TABLE 8-2 Construction of a Simplified Price Index

Items	Base year prices	Present prices	Relative price changes	Weights	Weighted relative price changes
Food	$25	$35.00	140	18%	25.20
Clothing	10	10.20	102	5	5.10
Shelter	30	39.00	130	20	26.00
Education	8	9.76	122	15	18.30
Recreation	7	7.42	106	10	10.60
Health	4	7.00	175	12	21.00
Hobbies	3	3.09	103	5	5.15
Transportation	6	7.20	120	15	18.00
Total			998	100%	129.35

Unweighted average price index $\frac{998}{8}=124.7$

Weighted average price index $=129.35$

We take identical baskets of food, and we find that it would have cost $25 in the base year and $35 currently. We wish to find the current cost of food taking the base-year cost as 100. We do it with the following formula:

$$\frac{\text{Price in base year}}{\text{Price in current year}} = \frac{100}{X}$$

Inserting the price figures we get

$$\frac{\$25}{\$35} = \frac{100}{X}$$

And solving for X,

$$25X = 3,500$$

$$X = 140$$

we find that food costs rose 40 percent.

Now we have to weight each item in the budget according to its importance in the total pattern of spending. In the table we assume that we spend 20 percent of our income on shelter and only 5 percent on clothing. We should not, therefore, give the prices of shelter and clothing equal weight in the index: shelter should carry four times as much weight as clothing. We multiply the relative price change of each item by its percentage weight in the total pattern of spending; this gives us the weighted relative price changes. Adding them all up gives a weighted price index. The table shows that the cost of living rose 29.3 percent from the base year.

Now that we have measured inflation, let us discuss the effects of inflation on various groups within our economy.

WHO GAINS AND WHO LOSES IN INFLATION?   Obviously, if one is in a good bargaining position, such as a strong labor union or a managerial position that has built in increases tied to the price level, one could balance off the increases in prices with increases in wages. For example, if the increases in prices were 4.5 percent in a given year and you received a 4.5 percent increase in salary, then you would just about be keeping even with the increases in prices. There is a time lag, however; you paid the 4.5 percent increase in prices last year while your 4.5 percent increase in wages will begin next year.

Those on fixed incomes, such as Social Security recipients who get a fixed yearly amount, suffer the most from inflation. Since their incomes are fixed, if prices increase, then their real income falls behind, and they are left with less purchasing power to buy the things they need. For older people the problem is compounded by a greater need for certain services, such as medical care. And since medical care has had one of the most rapidly rising price indices of all the services, elderly people are caught in a double bind.

People who lend money in an inflationary period also fall behind. For example, if you lend $100 in 1970, the amount of money you are paid in 1975, even including the interest at a rate commensurate with the risk of default, may be worth less than the $100 you lent in 1970 because of price increases. The recent inflationary trends have, therefore, hurt people who invest their money in assets that have fixed dollar values. These include government and corporate bonds and savings accounts, all of which represent the lending of money.

Are banks, as lenders, hurt by inflation? Not really. They are simultaneous borrowers as well as lenders, for they borrow when they receive deposits. In other words, they lend out mostly other people's money, not their own, or else they create credit, as was shown in Chapter 4. As they do not lend their own money, they are not hurt by inflation. In fact, they benefit because inflation causes interest rates to rise.

Workers who are in a weak bargaining position tend to lose during inflation. There is a time lag between rising prices and their rising wages, and this reduces their real income. Those workers who are in a strong bargaining position can win wage increases in anticipation of rising prices.

Not all is bleak in inflation, however. Some groups benefit materially by increases in the price index. If you are in the fortunate situation of having a strong bargaining unit, you will be able to keep up with increases in prices in our economy. If you borrow money, you will be ahead in an inflationary situation as we saw in the example above. Thus it is wise for a student planning to attend college to borrow the money needed to complete his college program. If he can extend the payments over the course of his working lifetime, so that he is in fact repaying the debt with cheaper money, he benefits materially. Often the methods of financing college education, such as the Yale plan, which allows students to pay back to the college the cost of their education at a later time period, take into account the fact that inflation will benefit those who have borrowed. Thus students may also benefit from inflation. The old adage Neither a borrower nor a lender be should be amended to, Be a borrower or a lender depending on your estimation of the change in prices.

Businessmen and farmers typically gain during inflation. Some of their costs are "sticky" and do not rise as soon or as rapidly as the increase in the prices of the goods they sell. These include property taxes, depreciation of machinery and buildings, fees of lawyers and accountants, telephone and electric rates, railroad freight charges, some wage rates, and other costs. If prices rise sooner and to a greater extent than costs do, profit margins increase. In addition, there is a time lag between the purchase and sale of goods. If businesses carry large inventories of goods from the raw materials stage to finished pieces, every price rise gives them an extra margin of profit.

UNEMPLOYMENT OR INFLATION? Historically there has been an inverse relationship between unemployment and inflation. That is, when price increases were above average, unemployment figures were low, and the economy, fueled in part by the inflationary increases, was employing almost all of its resources. In periods of high unemployment, price indices have been on the whole relatively stable or downward moving. This inverse relationship between unemployment and price increases has been described by A. W. Phillips, a British economist, as a curve. The Phillips curve is based on a statistical analysis of unemployment and the rate of increases of prices in Great Britain from 1861 to 1957. His work has been extended to the United States economy in the same fashion. What it shows is that on the average, as unemployment increases, price indices decrease; likewise, as the price index rises, unemployment figures fall. As in many statistical studies, the larger question that evolves from the analysis is the causal relationship between the variables. Because there is an inverse relationship between unemployment figures and price indices, does it follow that an increase in price level will cause employment to pick up? Or is the increase in prices a concomitant but not a causal factor in the lessening of unemployment? Leaving aside the question of causality, the fact remains that in a broad sense, when the economy is operating at levels below full employment, the price level does not show any rapid increases for the most part, and when the economy is running at full employment of its resources, there is a tendency for the price level to increase.

Thus, there is a rough trade-off between price increases and unemployment. In other words there is a choice, although certainly not an exact one, between running the risk of price inflation and the risk of unemployment. This is a reasonable assumption about our economy when one considers that when the economy is running at full employment, it does not take much to tip the balance and cause a rash of price increases. And when resources are not fully employed, there is a great deal of slack to take up before the price inflation can take place. If the supply sector is fully employed, an increase in demand will not bring forth new goods but merely bid up the prices on existing goods. If the supply sector is not fully employed, an increase in demand will bring forth new goods to meet the demand.

This imprecise trade-off is important in considering what a government can do to correct economic imbalances.

The disturbing situation in our 1970–71 recession was that we had growing unemployment and simultaneous inflation. This is a very serious and difficult problem, because the remedies that might be expected to cure inflation are different from the remedies that might help to offset unemployment. Apparently our economy has changed since the Second World War toward profound and perpetual inflationary tendencies. This is the result of oligopolistic pricing to a greater extent than ever, strong unionism, and massive government spending.

The following sections will contain specific references to policy measures that the government may take at various times depending on the state of the economy. They are called fiscal and monetary policies. They do different things at different times and for different problems of the economy.

Fiscal Policy

Before discussing the weapons of fiscal policy, we must define the goals that fiscal policy attempts to achieve. The two main goals involved in both fiscal and monetary policies are economic stability and economic growth. In order to achieve these goals, governmental fiscal policy is employed. Fiscal policy is a conscious attempt to bring about stability and growth using the weapons of government taxing, spending, borrowing, lending, buying, and selling. These weapons differ both qualitatively and quantitatively. The effects on our social structure and on the amount of income that is transferred from individuals to the government and from government to individuals is different with different policies. The two main measures of governmental fiscal policy are government taxing and government spending. We shall discuss the taxing process first.

THE TAXING PROCESS Taxes are a little bit like the weather; everyone talks about them but no one seems to be able to do anything about them. Certainly no one likes to pay taxes, but since they are necessary it is important to devise the best tax. A good tax, for example, treats everyone the same, is easy to collect, difficult to avoid, and produces revenue adequate for the governmental agency. A bad tax, or a tax that has little to recommend it, would be one that treats people unequally, is easy to avoid, and produces little revenue for the governmental agency that collects it. What do we mean by treating people equally? Everyone has his own definition of equal treatment for people.

Some, for example, argue that a proportional tax provides equal treatment for different individuals. A proportional tax levies the same percentage of taxes on everyone. Thus an individual with $1 million in income would pay 20 percent of his income in taxes while a person who made $2,000 would also pay 20 percent. Others argue that a tax that treats equals equally and unequals unequally is a fair tax. This means that an individual who has a higher income is expected to pay a higher percentage of his income in taxes than an individual with a lower income. This is commonly called a progressive tax. A progressive tax has an incremental rise in rate. An individual who makes $15,000 may pay 20 percent on the first $5,000, 30 percent on the second $5,000, and 40 percent on the third $5,000. A progressive tax also attempts, in a rough and ready way, to equalize the disutility of taxation of individuals in different income brackets. Thus, it is assumed that an individual who makes $1 million can pay a substantial tax without suffering more than an individual who makes $5,000 and is taxed very little.

The proportional tax and the progressive tax both have their advocates, each arguing that his preferred taxes are fair. Hardly anyone openly favors regressiveness in taxation, that is, taxation that requires the poor to pay a higher percentage than the rich, though regressive taxes such as sales taxes on "necessities" continue to be imposed, presumably for other reasons.

Another consideration in determining a good tax is whether it is easy to collect and difficult to avoid. In our system the income tax for most wage earners is collected at the time the wages are paid. Thus, an individual takes home only a percentage of his gross income, the remainder being deducted as withholding taxes. On April 15 of every year he has to settle his account with the government and either pay more or receive some money back, depending on the amount of his withholding and the amount of his total tax. The federal income tax thus fulfills one of the criteria, that is, it is easy to collect. The federal income tax is also difficult to avoid.

Even though there are numerous stories and examples of individuals illegally avoiding taxes, the fact is that the United States has one of the most difficult tax systems to avoid of any of the industrial nations. This does not mean that there are not large-scale loopholes built into the law, but illegal avoidance of taxes is difficult for most people. Because the income tax is collected at the time wages are paid, it is a very difficult tax to escape.

The cost of collection is also an important criterion in determining the tax structure. Obviously, if an individual tax costs 25 percent of the revenue to administer, then the recipient governmental agency is receiving only 75 percent of the total amount that the tax generates. This would not fulfill our criterion of a tax that is easy and cheap to collect. Figures show, again, that the federal income tax is very cheap to collect, the cost of collection being less than 1 percent of the revenues that it generates.

Keeping in mind the criteria we have outlined above, let us consider various taxes, their equity in terms of the amount that they collect, and the overall effect on stability and economic growth.

INCOME TAXES   The term *income taxes* is actually a bit misleading, since all taxes must be paid in one way or another out of income. The term, however, does not refer to the source of your taxes, but on what your taxes are based. An income tax is a tax based on the amount of income that you make. In the United States it is a progressive tax. Income taxes are the primary source of revenue for the federal government.

There are numerous advantages to the income tax. For one, as we have mentioned above, it is easy to collect, difficult to avoid, and as it is progressive, it satisfies the criterion of equity. The income tax has another advantage in that the amount of tax revenue grows as the national income grows. As the nation matures and its national income and the requirement for services become greater, the income tax generates increasing revenue to meet the needs of the expanding country. One disadvantage of our income tax structure is that the rates are set so that people may be taxed even though they are below the officially defined poverty level.

PROPERTY TAXES   Local governments (cities, townships, villages) use property as the base on which their tax revenues are generated. Property includes land, houses, and businesses built on land. Thus, an individual living in the city has to pay to the city and county and school district in which he lives a tax based on the value of his property as determined by an assessment and with a rate that is set by the legislatures of the three governmental districts. How is the tax paid? It is, of course, paid out of income, but the rate is based on the value of the property that is owned. There are numerous problems with the property tax.

One serious deficiency of the property tax is that the value of the property is difficult to determine. How does one determine the value of a house? Does one use market value, and how is that judged? Is it the cost of replacement or some value determined by a disinterested third party? This difficulty means that taxes on high-priced property may be avoided.

Another criticism of the property tax is that it is not necessarily based either on the owner's investment in the property or on his income. Suppose two people each own $30,000 houses. One owns it free and clear, while the other has a $25,000 mortgage; they both pay the same taxes. Or suppose one owner just lost his job, while the other is a doctor who uses his house in his work; both will still pay the same tax.

Property taxes do not keep pace with the growing needs of local government. While income taxes rise with rising national income, property taxes lag behind. In addition, in many states the amount of property taxes that a local government can collect is legally set by law. Thus, the cities end up in a dilemma of trying to provide more services with less revenue. In order to ease this problem some cities and counties, and most states, have introduced sales taxes.

SALES TAXES   A sales tax is a tax levied on a percentage of the value of an item sold. In most cases it is a proportionate rate, like a flat 4 percent for all sales within the governmental district. A sales tax, since it has a single percentage for all taxable items and since lower-income people spend proportionally more of their income on consumption items than upper-income people, tends to discriminate against lower income-people. In this respect the sales tax is usually regressive. It takes a larger percentage out of low incomes than out of high incomes. There are other disadvantages to the sales tax as well.

Even though the sales tax may be administered by a higher governmental unit, that is, a state may administer the tax for a city, there are hidden administrative costs that are present in the collection process involving the sales tax. Every individual merchant has to keep records of the amount of sales tax revenue that he receives and remit such revenue to the governmental unit doing the taxing. Thus, even though the governmental unit does not show a large administrative cost for a sales tax, there are nonetheless societal costs that are carried by the merchants. Even though the sales tax is cheap to collect, the hidden costs involved in the administration of the sales tax make it a very cumbersome tax indeed. A variation of the common proportional sales tax is a value-added tax.

VALUE-ADDED TAX   A value-added tax is a sales tax in a different form. Instead of being a flat proportional rate for all sales, the amount that is taxed is the value added, or the increment that each particular producer adds on to the value of the product. Remember in Chapter 2 when national income statistics were discussed, the problem of double counting was solved by adding into gross national product figures only the value added by each particular producer. For example, the sale of bread would only involve the extra increment of value that the baker put into the bread and not the value of the wheat, flour, and so forth that earlier production units had supplied.

The value-added tax is very common in countries other than the United States. France was the first country to put a value-added tax into operation. Table 8-3 shows when the value-added tax was adopted by countries in western Europe and the basic percentage rate of the tax.

TAX LOOPHOLES   The complexity of the tax system, with many types and values of taxes, only serves to provide extraordinary loopholes enabling citizens to legally avoid paying taxes. A loophole means the legal avoidance of taxes. The middle income taxpayer is often quite familiar with the advantages of buying and selling property as compared with receiving the same income in the form of wages. Consider, for example, an individual earning $15,000 per year. Suppose that he has the choice of making an additional $500 in wages or the same $500 in capital gains. Leaving aside the question of how hard he has to work to achieve the $500, which would he choose strictly on the basis of tax considerations? The $500 in wages would be added on the $15,000 income and would be taxed at an incremental rate

TABLE 8-3   Timetable of Value-Added Tax Adoption and Basic Rate

Country	Year adopted	Percentage rate *
France	1955	23 †
Denmark	1967	12.50
Germany, Federal Republic of	1968	11
Netherlands	1969	12
Sweden	1969	11.11
Luxembourg	1970	8
Norway	1970	20
Belgium	1971	20
Italy	1972	‡

* Based on price excluding tax.
† As of January 1, 1970.
‡ Rate not available.
Source: Finance and Development, Vol. 7, No. 1, (March, 1970), p. 40.

of 25 percent (based on the 1970 tax rate for a married taxpayer filing a joint return). Thus, of the $500 in wages our hypothetical taxpayer would keep $375.

Let us consider the same taxpayer receiving the same $500 as a long-term capital gain. A long-term capital gain only applies when the property is held over six months. Suppose our hypothetical taxpayer bought this particular piece of property (real estate or common stock, for example), held it for over six months, and sold it at a profit of $500. In making out his taxes he would immediately take 50 percent of the $500 gain and subtract it from the original $500 gain; only $250 of the $500 would be eligible for taxation. The $250 would be taxed at the rate equal to 25 percent, that is, at the same rate as the income for an individual in that tax bracket. Our hypothetical taxpayer would pay a total of 25 percent of $250 or $62.50 in taxes instead of the $125 tax he would pay on an additional $500 in wages.

The above example illustrates the discrimination between taxation based on wages and taxation based on sale or exchange of property. The rationale given for the inequitable treatment is that the lower rate on the sale or exchange of property encourages people to take risks and thus provides new venture capital for up-and-coming businesses. When, however, the property, in the form of common stock, has been resold many times, one is not providing new capital for the business by buying such stock. Thus, what the capital gains arrangement amounts to is a private risk taken by an individual. If he wins, he pays less tax on the same amount of money than if he earned it in wages. There are other loopholes and inequities in the tax system.

The most flagrant loopholes are the tax-free interest on municipal bonds and the mineral depletion allowances. By refraining from taxing interest on municipal bonds, the government makes it cheaper for a municipality to borrow money. If, for example, a city had to raise money by selling bonds at the competitive market interest rate, it would have to pay quite sizeable sums in interest payments per year. If, however, there is no tax on the interest on municipal bonds, taxpayers, especially those in high income brackets, will accept a lower interest rate for the bonds. Thus, the municipalities end up paying less interest charges to the individual bondholder. Who buys municipal bonds? It is easy to see that the advantages of municipal bond buying are directly proportional to a person's tax bracket. Thus, the tax break goes to those with higher incomes.

The mineral depletion allowances permit extractive companies to write off a percentage of gross income before calculating the tax. This is in addition to deducting all other expenses, including depreciation of capital equipment. The percentage deduction varies with the mineral; with oil it is 22 percent. Thus, only 78 percent of an oil company's income is subject to taxation.

Why does the government allow extractive industries to do this? The rationale is that the extractive company is depleting the source of its capital by mining its particular mineral. In order to provide incentives for individuals to embark on this risky business, they are given a tax break.

The net effect of these various loopholes is to reduce the revenue that the governmental agency has, so that the rest of the taxpayers have to make up the difference. The loopholes also disrupt the equity of the tax system. One can make a moral case for taxing higher-income people at a higher percentage than lower-income people. What is hard to justify is the fact that higher-income people, through the advantage of municipal bonds, capital gains, depletion allowances, and other devices often end up paying less taxes for the same incremental income as individuals in lower income brackets.

The other side of fiscal policy is the spending process. In the case of state and local governments, the spending depends on the amount of taxes that they raise, and in some cases it depends on the amount of need. How a governmental unit spends, what it spends on, and how it makes the decision to spend on one project or another will all be considered next.

THE SPENDING PROCESS   The first step for any governmental unit involved in spending is to formulate a budget. A budget is a fiscal plan designed to show exactly how much a governmental body is going to raise in revenue and how much it will spend on various projects. Since a budget is a fiscal plan, it is always formulated before the actual spending. The formulation of a budget is a complicated affair for all units of government. In a budget there are two distinct parts: a current budget and a capital budget. A current budget is one that reflects payments for labor, supplies, and on-going projects. A capital budget reflects payments for buildings and large-scale equipment and projects that will be paid for over a period of years. The capital budget has been committed in a previous time period, that is, it has been mortgaged in the same way an individual mortgages his house. Thus, an individual legislator cannot do much with a capital budget, since in many cases the spending has actually been committed before he was elected.

The current side of the budget, however, reflects the payments that may be increased or reduced for that particular period. The formulation of a budget implies that one has the revenues to meet such commitments. Do governmental units ever spend more than they take in taxes? We all know from our experience that they do.

DEFICITS AND SURPLUSES   On a federal level it is not surprising that spending and tax revenues are not equal. Since the spending is projected approximately a year in advance and the expected revenues are projected for the same time period, the changes that take place in the economy during the year may in fact bring about less or more revenue or spending, throwing the balance of revenue and spending off. For example, if the gross national product increased more than was expected, this will show up in greater tax returns, and the revenues that the government has will be greater than anticipated. If spending remained constant, the increased revenues would produce a surplus. If, in contrast, the economy took a nose dive and the federal government spent more money than was expected, the combination of the greater money spent and the less revenue taken in would produce a deficit. These deficits and surpluses are unexpected and may be subject merely to changes in the economy. There may, however, be planned deficits or surpluses.

In times of inflation in order to lessen aggregate demand it is wise for a federal government to take in more tax revenue than it spends, thus generating a budget surplus. In a recession in order to increase demand it is wise for a government to apply the opposite remedy, that is, to spend more than it takes in. In the case of a deficit, the difference between the amount of revenue taken in and the amount spent is made up in borrowing. This borrowing is commonly called the government debt.

The size of the government debt and its relation to national income in American history is shown in Table 8-4.

Notice how the magnitude of the debt has increased from $58 billion in 1941 to $424 billion in 1971. A large part of the increase between these two years was a result of expenditures in the Second World War.

Is the size of the debt a problem? Could the United States pay it back if she had to? Should we be in debt as much as we are? These questions can only be answered by a careful analysis of the figures. We shall see later in the section on monetary policy (pp. 193–96) that the primary problem with the debt is the management of it, that is, the spacing of the

TABLE 8-4   Federal Debt and Its Relation to GNP,
Selected Years 1869–1971

Year	Federal debt (in billions of dollars)	Debt as a percentage of GNP
1869	2.5	37
1919	25	31
1932	20	34
1941	58	46
1950	257	90
1960	286	56
1971	424	40

maturity of the bonds so that the treasury does not get caught in a cash squeeze, with many bonds being due and little cash to pay them off. The absolute magnitude of the debt is deceptive since much of it is owned by agencies within the United States government. For example, of the $424 billion of debt at the end of 1971, $176 billion was owned by government agencies including Federal Reserve banks. Forty percent was held by government agencies, and the remaining 60 percent was held by private investors. Only $47 billion of the $424 billion in 1971 was held by foreign and international investors. Since so much of the debt is internally held it may be considered that the people owe money to themselves. The debt, therefore, is to be considered as an accounting liability to ourselves, with the bonds appearing as assets held by the public.

Another way to evaluate the size of the national debt is to consider it as a percentage of gross national product. Suppose one of your friends reported to you that he was in debt to the tune of $1,000. Is this alarming? Would the $1,000 debt indicate fiscal irresponsibility on his part? Not necessarily. Obviously, the next bit of information that you would like to know is the total capacity that he had for paying off the $1,000 debt. You would want to know something about his income, his other liabilities, and his overall ability to repay the debt when due. The same reasoning applies to the government. The gross national product, although certainly not all available for taxes, does give some idea of the productive capability of the nation. Thus, the national debt should be constructed as a percentage of GNP. These percentages are shown in Table 8-4.

THE ANALOGY OF FAMILY BUDGETS   Should one consider the national debt in the same way that individuals consider their family debts? In other words, is it unwise for a nation to borrow such a large percentage of its national income and effectively mortgage its future? The analogy between family budgets and the national budget is not suitable for several reasons. One is the fact that income in most families is limited. It may grow through increments year by year, but the opportunities to increase family income are limited. The national government, however, does not have the restraints that a family has. The federal government could raise taxes at any time to pay off a great deal of the national debt, although the wisdom of such a course would be open to question. It would be unwise to take so much of the private sector's purchasing power and redistribute it from individuals paying taxes to owners of the national debt. However, such a course could be taken if an emergency situation existed. It is important to note also that large corporations, especially public utility corporations whose income is more assured than most risky corporations, borrow a great deal to finance their operations. It is wise for an individual, as we considered earlier, to borrow if he expects that inflation will increase, assuming, of course, that he can maintain his present rate of income. Thus, many corporations, like the government, raise much of their working capital by borrowing.

All these reasons are important in considering the management and effect of a large national debt. This is not to imply that the debt is not an important matter. It most assuredly is. Any liability to the tune of $424 billion must be considered an important aspect of a nation's financial picture. However, it is not an indication of impending bankruptcy, and even though it is a difficult liability to manage, it is not an impossible situation.

As we have discussed above, fiscal policy implies changing taxes or spending to alter the course of economic activity. If an economy appears to be slowing down, an appropriate remedy would be either to cut taxes or raise the level of government spending. Has this remedy ever been tried? Has there been an attempt to influence the course of economic activity by altering the tax rates? The 1964 tax cut was the first fiscal experiment designed exclusively to perk up the economy.

A FISCAL EXPERIMENT—THE TAX CUT OF 1964   The tax cut of 1964 has been acclaimed as the first major test of the Keynesian remedy for a lagging economy, that is, decreasing taxes in order to spur consumer spending to bring the economy upward. What was so remarkable about this prescription? Why was a general reduction in the tax level considered to be a major innovative tool? The answer lies in the fact that the tax reduction came at the end of two years of federal budget deficits amounting to $6 billion yearly. For a nation that had been told for many years that a balanced budget was the key to economic stability and growth, the idea of purposely unbalancing the budget by reducing taxes when one had incurred budget deficits in previous years was a remarkable theory. What was the result? The tax cut produced the desired effect by stimulating consumer spending to the point where the upswing in business activity produced more tax revenues for the government than was expected, and, in fact, the anticipated budget deficit of $11 billion as a result of the tax cut did not materialize.

Cutting taxes, which on paper would amount to a reduction in revenues to the government, stimulated the economy to the point where the tax revenues were greater than anticipated. Thus, the stimulus produced the double effect of speeding economic activity and obtaining greater revenues for the government.

In spite of the success of the 1964 tax cut in spurring a lagging economy, there were some political problems on which the tax cut was contingent. Since tax cuts must be passed by Congress and approved by the president, the implementation of the tax cut becomes a political as well as an economic problem. Indeed, when a president refuses to increase taxes when necessary to fight inflation, as President Johnson did in 1965 and 1966, the problem becomes 100 percent political. Fiscal policy is not as automatic as it seems, nor does it produce the desired effect in all cases. The following section will detail some of the difficulties and problems encountered in trying to stabilize the nation's economy through fiscal policy.

WEAKNESSES OF FISCAL POLICY   In any governmental program to reduce or increase taxes or to raise or lower government spending, the chief problem comes in the time period allowed and the political problems in the implementation of the program. In the example of the 1964 tax cut given above, it took a full eighteen months before the tax cut wound its way through the halls of Congress and was finally signed into law. Most bills, with rare exceptions, take a great deal of time to pass Congress. Tax bills are especially difficult. The notion that an economy can be fine-tuned to the point that one need only press the prescribed button to produce the desired result is, therefore, not valid as long as Congress refuses to give rubber-stamp approval to tax measures. Changes in spending, unless they are a major departure from the present system, are easier to effect than a reduction or increase in taxes.

The second problem involved is a qualitative one. It is one thing to say we will reduce taxes and increase or decrease government spending, and it is another thing to say who gets the reduction or increase in taxes and who does the spending. How the tax bill is designed and what groups of individuals suffer or benefit as a result of it may make all the difference in the world to its success. For example, if tax revenues are increased by increasing taxes on people in low-income groups, then the effect on equity of such a measure is difficult to justify.

The same is true of government spending: the type and complexion of the spending is as important as the amount. While most people can agree that spending should be increased or decreased, there is much disagreement on how to spend. In recent years the military bills have had the greatest success in getting through Congress, and, therefore, spending to spur the economy has often been in the form of increased payments for military goods and services or salaries to individuals engaged in military service. Education bills, bills to relieve transportation difficulties, and aid for cities and other localities have had less success.

A third problem is the difference in spending between federal and local governments. While there seems to be much discussion about the economic problems of the country and a great deal of debate on whether the federal government should spend or not spend on certain projects, there is little debate on the state and local level as to whether government should spend to stimulate the economy or reduce spending to slow it down. Most of the evidence has shown that state and local governments do not spend in a countercyclical manner, but spend according to what needs they have and what they can afford. Thus, while the federal government may be engaged in spending programs in order to stimulate the economy, the state and local governments could be withholding from spending because of lack of revenue, high interest rates, or a lack of pressure from individuals for their particular projects. If state and local spending is not coordinated with federal government spending, then one may be doing quite the opposite from the other, and the effect of the fiscal policy may be dampened.

Monetary Policy

In addition to government fiscal policy, monetary policy can also be used to promote stability in the economy. We saw in Chapter 4 how the Federal Reserve authorities can engage in open market operations and in changing the discount rate and the reserve requirements.

During an inflation the Fed should sell bonds to offset the inflation. But what if nobody decides to buy? The price of bonds will fall, and at some price the public will buy them. This has a dual effect on counteracting inflation. First, if you buy a bond from the Fed, your check clears against your bank's reserve account with the Fed. Bank reserves fall by the dollar amount of bonds bought by the public, and banks must restrict their lending by a multiple of their loss of reserves. Second, as bond prices fall, interest rates rise. Indeed, the two statements really mean the same thing. A 4 percent bond that costs $100 will yield a 4 percent rate of interest. But if the price of the bond falls to $99 and will be paid off at $104 in a year, the yield is 5 percent. Therefore, open-market selling of bonds raises interest rates, which helps curb inflation.

In a depression the Fed would buy bonds in the open market. Bond prices would tend to rise, interest rates would fall, and bank reserves and their lending power would rise.

The Fed can change the discount rate to help stabilize the economy. By raising the rate, it requires banks to pay more when they borrow from the Fed; the banks then have to charge a higher rate of interest to their customers, and the effect is to counter inflation. If the Fed lowers the discount rate, banks can lower their interest rates, and this works to offset depression. The flaw in this remedy is that there is a tradition in the United States against banks borrowing regularly from the Fed. They do so only in special situations, as when adverse clearing of checks or heavy cash withdrawals by depositors causes a bank to run low on its legally required reserves. In April 1971, banks that were members of the Fed had $29.9 billion of reserves, of which they had only borrowed $147 million from the Fed. We must conclude that when the Fed changes its discount rate, it does not *force* a change in interest rates by the banks because they do not borrow much from the Fed, but it does *induce* them to change their interest rates in the same direction and degree. The Fed provides leadership to the banking system in determining interest rates with the objective being stability in the economy.

The Fed can also raise reserve requirements during inflation to curb the banks' ability to lend. It can lower them during depression to ease bank lending.

How have the Federal Reserve operations worked? Have they been successful in combatting inflation or recession? Have they worked in combination with or in opposition to fiscal policy? Economic stabilization requires that the economy be stimulated when it is lagging and slowed up when it is expanding too rapidly and outstripping the productive resources of the country. What role does monetary policy have in slowing down the price increases? It can have a substantial role if the price increases are of the type called demand pull. A demand pull inflation means that there is an excess of purchasing power within the country and the excess is pulling the prices of productive resources and goods up. Efforts by the Federal Reserve under these conditions have more chance of success than would be the case if the inflation were of a different type. If the inflation is what is called the cost push, in which the pressure for increasing prices comes largely as a result of the high cost of the resources that a producer has to employ, then the efforts by the Federal Reserve system to decrease the money supply and increase interest rates will in many cases have the opposite effect. The tightening of money in a cost push inflation will only drive the price of the productive resources up even further and thus exacerbate the prevailing inflation. A cost push inflation can be remedied by an increase in the supply of money, which in turn decreases the cost of borrowed money.

All the successes or failures of the Federal Reserve system manipulations depend largely on the combination of fiscal and monetary policy. If, for example, the monetary policy is attempting to reduce inflation and fiscal policy is working in the opposite direction by lowering taxes or increasing government expenditures, then the effect of monetary policy will, of course, not be felt within the economy. But if fiscal policy is remaining neutral or is operating in the same direction as monetary policy, then the combination of the two can have a great effect toward slowing down the economy in an inflationary period.

Another problem that has an effect on the actual power that the Federal Reserve Board has is the structure of American industry, the number of monopolistic and oligopolistic elements within the economy. If the economy is characterized by a large degree of economic power concentrated in the hands of a very few businesses, then any effort the Federal Reserve makes to decrease the amount of spending by raising interest rates will be wasted. The large businesses in the United States, General Motors for example, generate such huge amounts of internal funds by retained earnings that they can effectively finance their own spending by their own reserves. They do not have to go to the banking system to borrow money to increase either their investment or their scale of operations. For this reason Federal Reserve operations would have little impact in an economy that is characterized by large and pervasive oligopolistic or monopolistic elements.

On the other side, can the Federal Reserve Board stimulate the level of economic activity? The Federal Reserve has been thought to be less successful in stimulating the economy than in slowing it down. The reason for this is that in extreme cases, such as the Depression of the 1930's, any increase in the amount of money available and the subsequent decrease of interest rates will not stimulate businessmen to borrow for new plants and equipment if they have unused capacity to begin with. If a businessman is faced with a lagging demand for his products and he anticipates unused capacity in the future, he certainly is not going to expand his operations in the face of such a pessimistic outlook. Thus, in the extreme case of a depression economy, monetary policy has not been effective. In other than extreme cases, however, monetary policy may, in fact, provide some impetus for a lagging economy. If the amount of unproductive resources is small, that is, the slow-down in economic activity is a moderate one, then a decrease in the interest rate may provide the resources for producers to invest in marginal projects and thus stimulate the economy toward full employment.

There have been over the years other proposals for monetary policy. One of the more important proposals was made in 1948, by Marriner Eccles, who was at that time chairman of the Federal Reserve Board. His proposal, in order to provide more effective means of restraining inflationary pressures, asked that Congress pass legislation granting the system's Federal Open Market Committee temporary authority to require that all commercial banks hold a special reserve in addition to reserves required under existing laws. The unusual facet of this proposal was that the additional reserves could be in government securities. A bank normally has to liquidate its bonds to increase its reserves. That is why the scheme was named the "Security Reserve Proposal." This measure would accomplish two conflicting objectives. The price of government bonds would be supported because banks would wish to hold rather than sell them; therefore, interest on the government debt would be kept down. At the same time, bank lending would be restricted because of the increased reserve requirement. The bankers, of course, did not appreciate this proposal. They would much rather combat inflation through higher interest rates, at greater profit to themselves. Their opposition not only killed the proposal, but it got Eccles removed from the chairmanship of the Board of Governors and ultimately from the Federal Reserve Board itself.

Eccles' proposal only highlights the dilemma in which the Federal Reserve system finds itself. Even though it may know the prescribed remedy to correct the prevailing economic situation, it finds itself in many cases in opposition to political and fiscal forces that may have in mind another remedy or a modification of existing remedies. The problem of economic stabilization depends in large part on the willingness of the federal, state, and local governments to coordinate the prescribed actions as they see fit. Even if they all agree on what the prescribed course of action should be, it is a very difficult job indeed to get everyone to see the danger, to take effective means against it, and to proceed to stabilize the economy.

It is the fundamental nature of our economy that individuals often act in opposition to society's best interests. For example, if one foresees inflation remaining over a long period of time, one would buy goods now in order to avoid higher prices in the future. Such action would of course aggravate the inflation and cause it to continue later than otherwise might have been the case. In other words, people cannot be relied on to act in the interests of the community, for the penalties for such altruism are often formidable. Thus, it is up to the government to reverse the rewards and penalties, inducing individuals either by fiscal or monetary measures to take actions that help to stabilize the economy.

The dilemma of the Federal Reserve Board and the fiscal authorities is exemplified by the inflation in which the United States now finds itself. Since 1965 prices have been increasing at a rate that can be considered unusually high for our economy. The causes and the weapons that have been used to combat this inflation provide a good case study for the effectiveness of fiscal and monetary policy.

Inflation Since 1965

Since 1965 price increases have been proceeding at a rapid rate, yet a slowdown in economic activity occurred. How has this happened? Do not the two forces offset one another? Should not the slowdown in economic activity result in an easing of inflation? Answers to these questions must be sought in the complex structure of the United States economy.

The reason inflation and recession have occurred simultaneously is that there are so many monopolistic elements within the economy. The simple cure for a price inflation, a decrease in government spending or an increase in taxes and interest rates, has met with massive resistance. The presence of monopolistic and oligopolistic elements means that an individual firm with an oligopolistic position may not be willing to reduce prices when the sales of its product decrease. As we have seen in earlier chapters, the oligopolistic elements in the economy do not reduce prices when the economy slows down, but rather keep their products at the same high levels of prices in order to make maximum profits. The same argument holds for large unions. They are also unwilling to reduce the price of labor in a downswing in the economy. This illustration shows one of the major weak points of monetary policy. Prices no longer respond to stabilization policy.

There are other problems involved in the application of monetary policy to cure both inflation and depression. Even when the Fed moves rapidly to increase or decrease the money supply, it still takes time for the increases or decreases to be felt in the economy. But the single greatest weakness of monetary policy is that even with the application of tight or loose money policy, a resultant cure may not in fact take place. That is, even with higher or lower interest rates the businessman may or may not respond by decreasing or increasing the amount of investment. In the early part of the 1930's, the banks had billions of dollars of excess reserves. Those banks that were solvent had plenty of money to lend but no one willing to borrow, even though interest rates were very low. No producer who has excess capacity would want to borrow money and invest it for expanding his plant. This is especially true when his expectations for the future are pessimistic. Thus, the monetary policy works only when the expectation for the future is clear, when the businessman knows exactly where he wants to go; then he will borrow or restrict his investment in response to monetary policy.

Is there a clear division between those economists who advocate primarily fiscal policy and those who advocate mainly monetary policy as cures for our economy? No simple distinction exists. Most economists believe that the proper remedy for an economy in a given state of inflation or recession is a mixture of proper monetary and fiscal policy in order to lessen the uncertainties of the economy.

The last method of controlling the economy to be considered lies somewhere between monetary and fiscal policy. It requires direct action by the government, but it works within the established business structure. This method is called wage and price controls.

WAGE AND PRICE CONTROLS   Wage and price controls are not new. They were administered during the Second World War under the Office of Price Administration. Wage and price controls merely prohibit labor unions and businesses from receiving or granting increased prices or wages beyond a certain level. The level is determined largely by a study of the productivity increases in the economy. If our economy were running at a 3 percent increase in productivity per year, the government would prohibit unions from getting wage increases greater than the established 3 percent that year.

The problem in wage and price controls is one of administration and equity. Administrative problems come about in the attempts to police price controls. It is a monumental job, as we learned during the Second World War, to insure that businesses comply with the established procedures. It is also a very difficult job to determine an equitable level so as to treat all businesses and workers fairly. If a business was charging excessive mark-ups before controls went into effect, should it be permitted to do so afterward? If the wages of a group of workers are excessively low, should they be required to remain low?

As we know from our study of the economic system in earlier chapters, profits are supposedly a result and a reward for the risk incurred in establishing and running a business. To put a ceiling on price increases and thus affect the profit levels in our economy is to interfere with the workings of the private sector mechanism. However, in extreme cases, and one could argue that in the situation since 1965 the inflation is an extreme case it may be necessary to impose statutory controls on the economy. When this is done, it should be price and wage controls on everyone; no industry or labor union should escape the overall controls by the government. All elements—including wages, profits, interest, and rent—should be kept at a maximum level of increases in the given time period. No one likes price controls; the problems associated with them are enormous and the philosophy on which they draw is antithetical to the ideas that pervade the ideology of American business. If, however, there is an inflation in our economy, which has so many monopolistic and oligopolistic elements, it may be essential to impose in the short run some price and wage controls.

This is exactly what President Nixon did in his economic controls of 1971 and 1972. Realizing that the standard economic remedies, fiscal and monetary policies, were not reducing inflation, he declared a wage-price freeze for ninety days and then in Phase II instituted a system whereby the large firms and unions had to receive prior permission to raise prices and wages. The administration of the Phase II system was in the hands of two councils: a wage council and a price council. The wage-price freeze and its moderation in Phase II were drastic measures taken only when the conventional remedies did not work.

One further topic must be dealt with in our discussion of stabilization of the nation's economy. The monetary and fiscal controls and the wage and price controls are all dependent on specific actions by agencies within the government. There is, however, another set of stabilizers working within the economy that work more or less automatically and thus do not require any policy decisions by a governmental agency to put them into effect. These are called automatic stabilizers.

AUTOMATIC STABILIZERS As the name implies, automatic stabilizers work without direct human intervention, always influencing the economy to move in the opposite direction from which it is going. The common automatic stabilizers are unemployment insurance and other transfer payments, such as welfare benefits and the progressive income tax. If the economy is heading downward—corporate profits are down, wages are down, and people are put out of work—then unemployment insurance provides some wherewithal to the individuals affected by loss of jobs. Thus, instead of personal incomes declining to a low level, the unemployment insurance guarantees that the economy will level out or will not decrease to the level it would have if the insurance program were not in existence.

The progressive income tax is another automatic stabilizer. In a progressive tax system, the more money one makes the higher the marginal rate; as inflationary pressures develop, money incomes and the tax rate on the incremental amount increase. As national income gets larger and larger, the percentage that accrues to the government in the form of taxes grows even more; this has an automatic stabilizing effect operating against inflation.

The automatic stabilization process of the income tax system works in reverse also. If the economy is slowing down or is in a recession, the marginal tax rates on lower income are less, insuring that individuals have a greater percentage to spend.

Automatic stabilizers can be built into the government's fiscal system. The progressive income tax and the system of unemployment compensation are examples. Discretionary fiscal policy could change the tax rates by law, or alter the size and scope of transfer payments. Automatic stabilizers work quite well in the short run to smooth out minor ebbs and flows in our economy. But they cannot achieve stability by themselves. They do add one more device to the bag of tools that a modern economist works with in trying to stabilize the economy. Both deliberate and automatic controls are necessary.

Summary

After reviewing Chapter 8 you can understand how delicate the balance between unemployment and inflation is. The problem of stabilization is indeed a difficult one: to maintain steady growth with full employment and small price increases.

The federal government has many tools at hand to maintain steady growth. Fiscal policy—the control of taxation and spending—is one such tool. Equally common and important is monetary policy—the control of the nation's money supply. Fiscal policy, while more directly effective, has the disadvantage of being entangled in the political process. Thus, the delays in tax and spending bills may weaken the effects of such measures.

Monetary policy, while easier to implement, is less effective. It is based on increasing or decreasing the money supply, which in turn may or may not lead to more or less private investment. Indeed, the connection is sometimes a tenuous one.

Finally, we discussed the current inflation since 1965. It is unusual in that it is persistent and unyielding and accompanied by unemployment higher than desired or expected. The current inflation is due to a unique series of events beginning with the buildup for the Vietnam war in 1965. Since our economy is characterized by so many monopolistic elements, it is difficult to adjust the economy to full employment and price stability. Market forces become ineffective when industries have so much power over prices.

The use of wage and price controls is an admission by the government that in some situations normal fiscal and monetary policies do not work. They are the last economic resort to control persistent inflation.

QUESTIONS AND PROBLEMS

1   There are some very definite political reasons for preferring monetary controls over fiscal policy. What are these?

2   Fiscal policy has some definite drawbacks in the implementation phase. What are these?

3   Would a positive economist as contrasted with a normative economist prefer fiscal or monetary policy? Why?

4   The Federal Reserve system has controls that it may use to smooth out the economy. What are these, and which are most frequently used?

5   Of the four components of gross national product (consumption, investment, government spending, and exports-imports) which is the most unstable? Why?

6   What is a price index? How is it constructed?

7   If you could foresee a great deal of price inflation in the years ahead, what individual actions would you take to protect your assets from such erosion? What effect would your actions have on the inflation?

8   Are price inflation and unemployment mutually exclusive? Could they exist side by side?

BIBLIOGRAPHY

BOARD OF GOVERNORS, THE FEDERAL RESERVE SYSTEM, *Federal Reserve Bulletin* (Monthly publication).

BUCHANAN, JAMES M., *The Public Finances*, 3rd ed. Homewood, Ill.: Richard D. Irwin, 1970.

NATIONAL INDUSTRIAL CONFERENCE BOARD, *The Federal Budget, Its Impact on the Economy*. New York, 1970.

PECHMAN, JOSEPH A., *Federal Tax Policy*, 2nd. ed. Washington, D.C.: The Brookings Institution, 1970.

Government Regulation
of Business

Government is emphatically a machine: to the
discontented, a "taxing machine," to the
contented a "machine for securing property."
—*Thomas Carlyle*

You will remember from previous chapters the theory that accounts for market imperfections, specifically oligopoly and monopoly. What should the government do about such imperfections? Is the consumer to be left to the good will of the producer? Most consumers hope not.

The federal government should play an active role in curbing the abuses of an imperfect market. While many accept this principle, few, except for Ralph Nader and other citizens' groups, actively push for regulation to protect the consumer. Indeed, Nader's fight with General Motors illustrates why more citizens do not fight private businesses. Nader, in his effort to get the government to force General Motors to adopt antipollution and other safety devices, was personally threatened, and efforts were made to impugn his character.

Not all efforts at government regulation are so threatening, but there are great difficulties involved along with some reluctance to insure that consumers are guaranteed both good products at fair prices and an environment free of noise and pollutants.

Increased Government Participation
in Economic Affairs

There is no doubt that the government's role in economic affairs has increased significantly since the turn of the century. The increased complexity of our economy calls forth more and more regulation and control: pure food and drug laws protect consumers against hazardous food additives and other dangers; false advertising and false labeling are prohibited; labor relations are regulated; and social legislation such as minimum wage laws, compulsory unemployment compensation, and old age

203

pensions have been enacted. Beginning in the 1930's, federal stabilization policies were adopted. Farmers and others were helped by government programs. The regulation of public utilities has become necessary with the growth of the industries providing electricity, telephones, and natural gas. Antimonopoly laws became necessary as the size of firms grew phenomenally. The rise of radio and television required the orderly allocation of broadcasting bands. These are some of the reasons for increased government activity since 1900.

GOVERNMENT EMPLOYMENT On the federal level, the total number of government civilian employees has increased from 579,354 in 1929 to 2,928,000 in 1970. Certainly much of this increase can be accounted for by the increase in population in the United States, which required larger government to accomplish the same tasks as were accomplished in 1929. But a large part of the increase is accounted for by new and increased roles that the federal government has undertaken.

The state and local governments have also increased their direct employment of people. In 1929, state and local governments employed 2,-532,000 people. By 1970 this number had increased to 10,147,000. Since state and local governments are actively engaging in providing schools, in road and highway maintenance, and in general government activities, the increase is not surprising. All levels of government combined employed one worker out of every six in the labor force in 1970. In line with the increase in employment has come an increase in taxation and spending by all levels of government—federal, state, and local.

TAXATION AND SPENDING The federal government took in $2.9 billion in taxes in 1929. By 1970 the tax total had increased to $195 billion. Since the primary tax the federal government levies is the corporate and personal income tax, the increase is due partially to the increase in the size of the economy. As incomes grow, so do taxes, and by a more than proportional amount since the tax is progressive.

The largest amount of the increased tax revenues has been used to finance our growing commitment in defense and health, education, and welfare. In recent years expenditures on health, education, and welfare have grown at an increasing rate, necessitating additional revenues to finance them.

State and local governments have also increased their taxation, from a 1927 total of $9.4 billion to a 1969 total of $76.7 billion. Most of the increase in state and local revenue has been due to the property tax. Although the income tax is available to some states and a few cities, the property tax remains the main revenue source.

In line with the increased taxation has been an increase in expenditures. The federal government spent a total of $3.1 billion in 1929. By 1970 the figure had increased to $196.5 billion. State and local governments experienced an increase from $7.8 billion in 1927 to $131.6 billion in 1969.

The following tables will give some idea of the magnitude and the composition of governmental operations at all levels. The personal income tax accounted for 45 percent of the total revenue to the federal government. At the state and local levels the property tax supplied 23.2 percent of the total. Another big source of revenue for state and local governments is aid from the federal government. National defense accounts for the biggest expenditure on the federal level, while education is the largest category of state and local expenditures. The figures reflect the trend toward government regulation that has existed in our economy for the past seventy years.

TABLE 9-1 Federal Receipts and Expenditures for Fiscal 1971

Sources of Funds

Tax	Total receipts (in millions of dollars)	Percent of total
Personal income tax	86,164	45
Corporate income tax	26,806	14
Social insurance taxes and contributions	57,559	30
Excise taxes	16,629	8.7
Miscellaneous receipts	3,847	2.2
Total	191,005	100

Uses of Funds

Use	Total expenditures (in millions of dollars)	Percent of total
Defense and national security	77,621	36.8
International affairs and finance	2,994	1.5
Space research and technology	3,382	1.6
Agriculture and rural development	5,283	2.6
Natural resources	2,681	1.4
Commerce and transportation	11,364	5.5
Community development and housing	3,383	1.6
Education and manpower	8,639	4.3
Health	14,480	6.9
Income security	55,713	26.6
Interest	19,660	9.3
General government	3,964	1.9
Total	211,574	100

Source: U.S. Treasury Bulletin, September 1971.

TABLE 9-2   State and Local Receipts and Expenditures Fiscal 1969

Sources of Funds		
Source	Total receipts (in millions of dollars)	Percent of total
Federal government	19,153	14.5
Property taxes	30,673	23.2
Sales and gross receipts taxes	26,519	20.1
Individual income taxes	8,908	6.7
Corporation income taxes	3,180	2.4
Other taxes and charges	26,118	19.7
Utility and liquor stores revenues	7,840	5.9
Insurance trust revenue	9,764	7.4
Total	132,155	100.0

Uses of Funds		
Use	Total expenditures (in millions of dollars)	Percent of total
Education	47,238	35.9
Highways	15,417	11.7
Public welfare	12,110	9.2
Health and hospitals	8,520	6.4
Police and fire protection	5,694	4.4
Natural resources	2,552	1.9
Sanitation and sewerage	2,969	2.3
Utility and liquor store expenditure	8,820	6.7
Insurance trust expenditure	6,053	4.6
Miscellaneous	22,227	16.9
Total	131,600	100.0

Source: U.S. Department of Commerce, Statistical Abstract, 1971. Washington, D.C.: Government Printing Office, 1971, p. 403.

While government has grown, so has the size and scale of business. We call this increase *industry concentration.*

Industry Concentration and Antitrust Policies

The assumptions of the perfect competition model, particularly that of free entry and exit of firms, and that no one firm is large enough to dominate the industry, theoretically preclude an industry concentration from taking place. Adam Smith said years ago, "People of the same trade seldom meet together, even for merriment and diversion, but the conversation ends in a conspiracy against the public, or in some contrivance to raise prices." Smith obviously did not trust businessmen to do voluntarily what was best for the public. But he relied on the powerful forces of competition to curb their avarice. He said that while businessmen seek only to serve themselves, they are guided by an unseen hand to serve society. Competition would force them to make quality products and to sell them as cheaply as possible if they wished to stay in business and attract customers.

Is the perfect competition model, however, relevant to our study of American business? One does not have to look in a textbook to know that American business is characterized by large imperfections in the market. Where has the system gone wrong? Are giant firms inevitable? What can the government do about such firms? In order to study these questions and to gain a historical perspective on the nature of the antitrust problem, we will be discussing initially the dimensions of the problem.

THE PROBLEM OF BIGNESS Standard economic theory, which we have developed in earlier chapters, states that a firm tries to maximize its profits. Such a firm, if it is in a perfectly competitive market, is one of many small firms in an industry, no one of which is large enough to affect the market price. This arrangement precludes any monopolistic elements. If, for example, a firm has a temporary monopoly due to the invention of a new product, it is not long before other firms catch on to the production technique of such a product and inevitably start chipping away at the monopoly firm. Thus, there is a built-in mechanism for regulation according to standard economic theory.

Familiarity with American economic history shows that giant firms have been the rule rather than the exception in American business. During the latter part of the nineteenth century, business was characterized by a collective movement to stifle competition in many areas, including railroads, steel, tobacco, and aluminum. Giant firms forced out competitors in order to remain the only or the major producer in a given market. Such was the case when Judge Gary merged fourteen steel companies into what is now known as United States Steel.

The beginning student of economics, looking at the world around him, may venture a guess that large firms were successful as a result of their efficiency, superior products, and the general willingness of the public to buy such products at a reasonable price. These firms were thought to have grown large because of natural, competitive forces. This was not the case with most giant firms, and most especially not with United States Steel.

The situation in steel was not unusual. Mergers have produced most of the large-scale businesses that are in existence in the United States today. They have not been produced by purely competitive means; that is, their bigness is not attributed to the fact that they have outsold or outmarketed their competitors. The fact is that all the larger firms have grown large and stayed large because of practices that limit competition in their industry.

This discussion is not to be construed as an argument against bigness per se. To be sure, a firm must be large enough to achieve the economies of scale that only a large firm can produce. The important questions are: How large must a firm be in order to achieve maximum efficiency? And if it is large enough, does it pass along such efficiencies to the consumer in terms of lower prices?

THE DIMENSIONS OF THE PROBLEM OF BIGNESS   Most studies of industrial organization classify businesses by industry. At first glance, such a classification seems to be an elementary step in deciding whether there is competition. It is not such an easy task, though, to decide just what an industry is. For example, one would not think that automobile manufacturers and airplane manufacturers would be classified as being in the same industry. However, they are both modes of transportation, and in this expanded context an automobile manufacturer could indeed be seen as a member of the same industry as an airplane manufacturer.

The economic definition of an industry was proposed by Joan Robinson. She stated that one could classify products as being in the same industry if a price change of one product affected the sales of another product, that is, if there were a significant amount of cross-elasticity between the products. Cross-elasticity of demand means that a price change in one product will produce a significant change in the quantity demanded of another product. For example, if the price of coffee increases 20 percent and consequently the quantity demanded of tea increases 15 percent, then coffee and tea may be said to be substitute products, or products in the same industry.

To return to our above example, if an increase in the price of automobiles increases the sale of airline tickets and therefore airplanes, then manufacturers of automobiles and airplanes would be considered to be in the same industry. This definition of an industry, although logical from an economic point of view, makes the job of the courts difficult in deciding whether firms are in the same industry or not. As we already know, in order for an elasticity coefficient to be meaningful, other factors—taste, income, prices of substitute products other than the ones under consideration —all must remain constant. This is essential in order to isolate the relevant variables, in this case the price of one product and the quantity demanded of another. Such an elegant solution as cross-elasticity is obviously not practical in legal terms, as was clearly illustrated by the United States suit against the Du Pont Company in 1956 for monopolizing the cellophane industry.

The government attempted to show in its suit that Du Pont was guilty of excessive market power in the cellophane industry. During the period relevant to the case, Du Pont produced almost 75 percent of the cellophane sold in the United States, but this percentage constituted less than 20 percent of the sales of all flexible packaging materials. Obviously, if the government could establish the fact that the relevant market was cellophane, then the 75 percent figure would be enough to convict Du Pont of excessive market power under the Sherman Antitrust Act. Du Pont naturally argued that the relevant market was that of flexible packaging materials, which also included such items as aluminum foil, plastic wrap, and polyethylene foam. Since Du Pont's share of the latter market was only 20 percent, if the court accepted Du Pont's definition of the market, there could be no doubt that the outcome would be favorable for Du Pont.

The District Court judge held that the relevant market was flexible packaging materials. Competition from other flexible wrapping materials was found to have prevented Du Pont from possessing monopoly power over the market for cellophane. The Supreme Court upheld the District Court's opinion.

Although the industries that we will be concerned with in this chapter are less complicated in definition than the cellophane industry, it is still a difficult job sometimes to determine which industry a particular product is in. There are three general ways to evaluate the competitive aspects of a given industry. One can evaluate the percentage of the market that the firm has; this is called the structure of the industry. One can also evaluate either the performance of the firm or the conduct of the firm. Since a more precise definition of each term is needed, we shall proceed with some examples of how these different criteria have been used by economists and by legal experts in assessing American industry.

STRUCTURE, CONDUCT, AND PERFORMANCE   Of the three general ways to evaluate a given industry, by far the easiest is the study of the structure of the industry. Structure of the industry involves a number of elements: (1) the concentration ratios within the industry, (2) barriers to entry in the industry, (3) the growth of market demand over time within the industry, (4) the price elasticity of the products, and (5) the ratio of fixed to variable costs in the short run. What exactly are these elements, and how are they used to define the structure of an industry?

The concentration ratio in a given industry is merely the percentage of the total products produced by a predetermined number of firms. As we shall see in Table 9-3, the percentage of the products produced by the eight largest selling firms varies tremendously from industry to industry. Before examining the actual concentration ratios for various industries, remember that the concentration ratio provides a figure with which to evaluate and compare different industries. The amount of competition within industries can then be compared.

Table 9-3 shows the concentration ratios of the eight largest firms in

TABLE 9-3   Concentration Ratios in Selected Industries (1967)

Industry	Number of companies	Total receipts (in millions of dollars)	Percent by top eight companies
Cigarets	8	3,045	100
Motor vehicles	107	27,296	98
Tires and inner tubes	119	3,734	88
Metal cans	96	2,891	84
Photographic equipment and supplies	505	3,665	81
Aluminum rolling and drawing	155	2,959	79
Soap and other detergents	599	2,593	78
Radio and TV receiving sets	303	3,846	69
Motor vehicles parts	1,424	11,624	68
Copper rolling and drawing	86	2,391	65
Malt liquors	125	2,930	59
Petroleum refining	276	20,934	57
Farm machinery	1,526	4,300	56
Nonferrous wire drawing	206	3,591	55
Toilet preparations	628	2,516	52
Wood furniture	2,934	2,439	18
Sawmills	10,016	3,506	15
Ready mixed concrete	4,032	2,684	9
Women's dresses	5,008	3,086	9
Commercial printing	11,955	3,256	8

Source: U.S. Department of Commerce, Statistical Abstract of the United States, 1971. Washington, D.C.: Government Printing Office, 1971, pp. 699–700.

each industry. It also gives the total number of firms in the industry. Those industries shown range from a concentration ratio for the top eight firms of 100 percent in cigarets to 8 percent in commercial printing. What do these figures mean? What do they indicate in terms of the market power of the individual firms within the industry?

The concentrated industries, besides affording the consumer very little choice for his purchase, show a great deal of rigidity in pricing, or if prices are flexible, they are only so in an upward direction. The evils of oligopolistic markets that we have mentioned earlier all show up in the very concentrated industries.

Barriers to entry are also found in heavily concentrated industries. There may be financial barriers; the size and scale of the enterprise may be such that only sophisticated techniques requiring very large capital investments can produce the product. Or it may be a marketing barrier, which means the scope of advertising must be very large in order to effectively market the product. In chemicals, steel, and other heavy manufacturing industries, the barrier to entry is clearly the high cost of entry. The single biggest barrier to entry in the cigaret market is the tremendous advertising expense that a firm has to incur in order to break into the nationwide market.

The growth of demand over the years also has something to do with the concentration within the industry. Fast-growing industries generally are more likely to be competitive than industries with products that have had a stable demand over a number of years. Thus, the software industry in the computer business, unlike the computer hardware industry, is generally found to have numerous producers, whereas the steel and automobile industries are likely to be less competitive.

Another criterion in the structure of industry is the elasticity of demand. Generally the more elastic the demand for the product, the more competitive the market situation. Elasticity of demand may indicate one of two things: that there are a number of competitive products the consumer may switch to if he is dissatisfied with his present brand, or that he may do without the product entirely if its price becomes prohibitive.

Finally, the ratio of fixed to variable costs may indicate the structure of the industry. Industries with high fixed costs tend to be less competitive than those that have primarily variable costs. Once committed, fixed costs provide an investment that businesses like to protect by excluding competition if possible. Large fixed costs also provide a substantial barrier to entry, as we have seen.

All the quantitative factors mentioned above define the structure of an industry. Determining the conduct and performance of firms within each industry requires a qualitative evaluation of how the firms have been performing in relationship to each other. Qualitative criteria have been used in a number of court cases, particularly those involved in early enforcement of the Sherman Antitrust Act.

The market conduct involves the behavior of firms in the following areas: (1) their pricing practices, (2) their outputs, and (3) their product characteristics. All the areas that comprise market conduct criteria are important, but those involving prices and output are especially significant.

Standard economic theory tells us that the firms try to maximize profit and thus produce where the marginal revenue equals marginal cost. The concentrated industries listed in Table 9-3, however, do not operate that way. Their conduct in pricing is generally a "cost plus" arrangement.

Cost plus pricing means that the firms price their products not according to the competitive situation in their markets, but rather according to a formula that compensates them for their total costs plus a fixed return on their investment. Instead of taking the price as given to them, they set the price to achieve a fixed rate of profit. This does not mean that they may charge exorbitant prices, because strong pressure from the Justice Department and labor unions dictate that they be discreet in their pricing. Even with these pressures, however, they still do not conform to the model of the competitive firm. United States Steel, for example, uses a pricing method called full cost stable margin. It includes standard cost plus a stable margin of return that covers the risk plus a sizeable profit for the steel company.

Whether these practices are legal or not depends on whether a firm uses its pricing practices to force rivals out of business. A vertical squeeze, discussed below, is an example of such a practice.

Output decisions likewise exert a powerful influence on the rate of profit of large firms. Large firms try to achieve efficiencies of scale through a large volume of production and sales. Yet they are quick to reduce output in order to avoid cutting prices if market demand falls off.

The product characteristics are important in assessing whether a firm has been coercive in eliminating rivals. In many large, concentrated industries such as steel, undifferentiated products necessitate a type of advertising that tries to improve the institutional image of all producers. Thus you do not see on your television set a description of the differences between steel produced by United States Steel and Bethlehem Steel, but rather an emphasis on the value of steel as compared to other similar products. The steel companies wish to promote steel as a product rather than to differentiate between the companies that produce it. Other tactics include price-cutting in the tobacco industry and the vertical squeeze that takes place in vertically integrated industries.

Price-cutting in the tobacco industry led to the formation of the tobacco trust, which was dissolved after the passage of the Sherman Antitrust Act in 1890. When a vertically integrated industry—that is, one that owns both the raw material producer and the finished product manufacturer—puts the squeeze on a competitor it lowers the price of the final product and raises the price of the input of the product that a competing firm has to buy from the firm. For example, if a vertically integrated steel company produces the final steel product and owns the iron ore that goes into competing steel mills, it lowers the price of the final product of steel and raises the price of the iron ore; this imposes a double squeeze on a competitor. Such policies as price-cutting and squeezing potential competitors have been used over the years in order to eliminate or hold down potential rivals. Market conduct, then, involves the policies of the firm in pricing and producing their products in a particular market.

The performance criterion involves the determination of whether the industry and firms in the industry have produced a reasonable return on investment or have introduced new products. The performance criterion has been used as a defense by industries charged with violations of the antitrust laws.

The difficulty with evaluating industries by the conduct criterion is that the allegations have been difficult to prove. It is not easy to prove that price-cutting was done to coerce a rival out of existence. Moreover, price-cutting and price competition in general are thought to be proof of the viability of the competitive system. Because of these problems, in recent years the courts have leaned toward a quantitative evaluation of industry concentration; that is, they have favored the structure criterion over the conduct and performance criteria.

The conduct criterion was used in the court's decision to absolve United States Steel of antitrust violations in 1920. Using the "Rule of Reason" as their primary argument, the defense attorneys convinced the court that since United States Steel had not acted "unreasonably" toward its competitors, it had not violated the Sherman Antitrust Act. The Rule of Reason prevailed until 1945, when the Aluminum Company of America (ALCOA) was convicted of monopolizing the aluminum industry simply on the fact that it controlled over 90 percent of the market for virgin aluminum. Its conduct was not considered germane to the contention of the prosecution that it had monopolized its market.

HOW GOVERNMENT PROMOTES OR PERMITS MONOPOLY The idea is widespread that our federal government is a vigilant guardian of the competitive system. Like an embattled David, the government is pictured as continually fighting the Goliath of monopoly. It is more correct to say that to the extent the government does fight monopoly, it does so by first deliberately tying one hand behind its back. It permits monopoly more than it opposes it. This is true of local and state governments as well as federal; it is also true of all branches of government—executive, legislative, and judicial. There are numerous examples of how all levels and branches of government allow monopolistic enterprises to grow and thrive at the expense of smaller competitive businesses. If some arm of government does try to thwart monopolies, other branches of government sabotage the effort. Only three examples out of many will be cited here.

One of the most powerful devices for promoting monopoly is the holding company. By intercorporate stockholding, vast empires of productive wealth can be controlled with minimal investments by the controlling interests, sometimes as little as 1 or 2 percent ownership. The holding company works as follows. Suppose you build a steel mill for $100 million. To gain absolute control you have to invest $50 million in order to buy 50 percent of the common stock plus one additional share. But in actual practice you can control the company with a smaller investment. Instead of owning $50 million work of stock in the steel mill, you set up a holding company that issues $50 million of its own stock, and with the $50 million it receives, buys that amount of steel stock. Now you can control the holding company by buying half of its stock for $25 million. But why stop there? Call it Holding Company A, and organize Holding Company B, which will invest $25 million in Holding Company A. You invest $12.5 million in Holding Company B. If you organize Holding Company C, your investment of $6.25 million in its stock will give you absolute control of the steel mill. If a small investment can control such a large enterprise, you can then afford to buy up a controlling interest in many steel mills and thereby establish monopolistic control of the industry.

This is the way the Van Sweringen brothers of Cleveland controlled vast railroad properties in the 1920's with at least five layers of holding companies and an investment of less than 1 percent in the empire they controlled. This is also the way the Standard Oil Company of New Jersey controls over 200 companies under it with an aggregate investment of over $18 billion.

Under state laws, corporations once lacked the right to own stock in one another. This principle was abandoned first by New Jersey in 1889, and the new permissive approach facilitated the growth of monopoly. As a consequence of this change in state government policy, the federal government has to spend large amounts of time, energy, money, and brains to fight the monopolization that results from intercorporate stockholding. An army of lawyers, economists, judges, court stenographers, printers, and others are busy with the rivers of paper that flow from the tasks of prosecuting, defending, and analyzing holding companies.

Yet the federal corporate income tax structure could destroy, immediately and effectively, the holding company. An operating company has to pay taxes at a rate of 48 percent on its income above $25,000. If it passes dividends along to a holding company and that company's income were taxed at the same rate, some of the advantages of the holding company would be lost. If there were a second and third layer of holding companies, as there frequently are, the profits would soon be eaten away by taxes. But the legislative branch of the federal government has seemed to feel that this is an unsportsmanlike way to attack monopoly; so the law says that if a corporation's income is from dividends on stock held in other corporations, there will be an 85 percent tax forgiveness. As 15 percent of the dividends are taxed at a 48 percent rate, it comes to a 7.2 percent tax. This makes the holding company and monopolistic control possible and feasible. The 85 percent tax forgiveness on holding company income has existed since 1936. In 1935 it was 90 percent. From the time the income tax law was enacted through 1934, the corporate deduction on dividend income was 100 percent. This, then, is the reform that has been achieved in sixty years: where there was no taxation of dividends received by corporations there is now a tax on 15 percent of dividends.

A second example of government promotion of monopoly is the awarding of government contracts, especially for military goods, mostly to the giant corporations. In 1953 Charles E. Wilson, head of General Motors, left that position to become Secretary of Defense. When reporters asked Wilson why so many large contracts went to General Motors, he gave a reply that will live on as one of the more humorous statements of the decade: "What is good for the country is good for General Motors; and what is good for General Motors is good for the country."

The government granted General Motors a contact in 1953 to manufacture military tanks because its bid was 10 percent lower than Chrysler's. But it turned out that the government's specifications made it necessary for Chrysler to buy certain components from General Motors if Chrysler was to get the tank contract. General Motors quoted a higher price for these components to Chrysler than it did to its own subsidiaries. General Motors' successful bid for the contract was not based on greater efficiency and lower cost, but on monopolistic power that was further enhanced by the government. In fact, by awarding the contract to General Motors the government was in effect condoning or participating in a possible violation of the antitrust laws that prohibit price discrimination when the effect is to promote monopoly.

A third example of government promotion of monopoly is the quota system on petroleum imports imposed by the federal government. This raises the price of petroleum products, with the consumers paying an extra $5.2 billion per year. Furthermore, the oil companies, because of the oil depletion allowances discussed in Chapter 8, pay only 8 percent of their income in federal corporate income taxes compared with 40 percent for all corporations. This helps to explain why in 1968, twelve oil companies received $\frac{1}{5}$ of the after-tax profits of the 2,250 largest companies in the United States.

LEGAL PROBLEMS IN ANTITRUST   Laws are passed when public sentiment demands them. The Sherman Antitrust Act of 1890 was passed in response to a groundswell of opinion against giant trusts. The Act forbade "every contract, combination in the form of trust or otherwise, or conspiracy, in restraint of trade or commerce" and also specified that "every person who shall monopolize or attempt to monopolize, or combine or conspire with any other person or persons, to monopolize . . . shall be deemed guilty of a misdemeanor." Under the terms of the Sherman Act the tobacco and sugar trusts were prosecuted as being in restraint of trade. This was a good beginning, but the law had some serious loopholes.

Notice that the Sherman Act forbade *monopolizing,* that is, the act of forming a monopoly. However, it did not specify what *monopolizing* meant. The courts were left to formulate a definition and arrived at the "Rule of Reason," which we discussed on page 213.

The passage of the Clayton Act and the Federal Trade Commission Act, both in 1914, did close some of the loopholes present in the Sherman Antitrust Act. Both acts forbade specific business practices such as price discrimination, tying agreements, and exclusive dealer arrangements. Price discrimination is the charging of different prices for different customers in order to put rivals out of business. Both tying agreements and exclusive dealer arrangements require a customer to buy a complete line of goods if he wants to receive one item. Tying agreements are also called full-line forcing. For example, in the past, if you bought an A. B. Dick mimeograph machine you were obligated to use A. B. Dick stencils and ink and no other on that machine.

The Federal Trade Commission was set up to investigate "the organization, business conduct, practices, and management of companies engaged in interstate commerce." Thus, an official arm of the government was given investigative powers to determine whether unfair business practices existed. In recent years the Federal Trade Commission has surveyed the effects of mergers on the competitive aspects of American business. The Commission is empowered to issue "cease and desist" orders to block mergers that it feels will injure the competitive fabric in the particular industry in which the merger is taking place. The companies involved in the merger are free to contest such an order if they wish, and the courts then decide the case.

No significant laws have been passed since 1914. The attitude of the government has been one of vigilance but not action. There have been no great efforts to increase competition in the United States; rather, the attitude has been not to let a bad situation get much worse. One reason for the relative inactivity of the government has been the lack of resources allocated to the Justice Department to fight antitrust cases. While the laws prohibit antitrust offenses, the Antitrust Division must bring suit on the offenders. The long and costly court cases necessitate that the Division only prosecute a limited number of cases—those that they feel will be examples to the business community.

While unfair business practices have been weakly regulated, the same is not true for public utilities. Public utilities have been under government scrutiny in order to insure fair pricing for the consumer.

The Regulation of Public Utilities

Why are public utilities called natural monopolies? Natural monopolies are regional monopolies in which competition (more than one firm) would be injurious to the consumer. They are characterized by economies of scale, which means that they must be of sufficient size to bring down the average cost per unit of output. More than one firm in a given area would divide up the output so that the economies of scale would not be achieved by the two firms. Natural monopolies are also characterized by high fixed costs in relationship to their variable costs. For example, a producer of electric power must have a tremendous investment in generators, transmission lines, and sophisticated engineering equipment before he can produce any output. This equipment is all in the category of fixed costs. The variable cost would be the extra units of labor or fuel that increase with the level of output. Industries characterized by high fixed costs generally are subject to price-cutting. As we have seen in earlier chapters, it pays a producer to cut his price as long as he can cover the variable cost of extra sales. An example of this is a reduction in rates for long-distance telephone calls on weekends and late at night. The reduction in rates is to encourage people to use the telephone lines when they would otherwise not have much use. Since there are high fixed costs in telephone transmission and since the variable cost is more than covered by the reduced rate, it pays the telephone companies to offer reductions at certain times.

If an industry has high fixed costs, rival firms are likely to cut prices in order to achieve a greater share of the market. In order to prevent such rampant price-cutting, which would drive out or discourage potential or actual producers of the product, the government grants a license to one firm to operate in a given geographic region. Thus, the monopoly is granted and protected by the government.

The granting of a license to operate in a given geographic area by the government does not insure, however, that the firm will achieve exorbitant profits. Since the government grants a license to the monopoly, it also regulates the rates that the monopoly may charge its customers. The economic justification for this is easy to see. Since there is no competition and thus no natural regulator for the firm, the government must insure that the the interest of the consumers is protected. It does this by setting up a commission to regulate the pricing and output of the firm. There are also state regulating commissions in the field of public utilities.

Federal regulating agencies that control natural monopolies are the Federal Power Commission and the Interstate Commerce Commission. They have the power to set the rates that the natural monopolies will charge the consumers. The question of what rate is charged, how often it is adjusted, and on what it is based is a topic that evokes much disagreement among the monopolies themselves, the consumers, and other interested people.

PROBLEMS IN UTILITY REGULATION   It appears that regulating public utilities should be a simple matter. In return for the exclusive rights to operate within a given geographic region, the public utility agrees to be regulated by the relevant commission and to have its prices and return on investment decided by that commission. It is a simple concept, yet very difficult to administer.

The problem of regulating public utilities revolves around the definitions of cost and return on investment. The total cost, as we have seen in earlier chapters, includes the direct costs of producing a product and the indirect or implicit costs of the return for the risk taken. The direct costs are overhead, materials, labor, and other inputs. But it can be difficult to define what actual costs the public utility incurs. For example, suppose an executive of a large public utility corporation decided to include in costs enormous bonuses and salaries for the executives of the corporation. Would this be justifiable as costs? Should we, as consumers, pay for such costs? The definition of costs and of cost control is of crucial importance in determining a fair return for the public utility corporation.

Just as the Internal Revenue Service polices small businesses and their estimation of costs, so the Federal Power Commission establishes guidelines to determine the limits of costs, particularly bonuses and salaries, that public utilities incur. The most difficult part of cost control is the determination of how many people to put on a particular job and whether the job is in fact overinflated, with greater numbers of people hired than are required. We are all familiar with examples of industries that are overstocked with labor, such as the United States Army, in which the people are put to "work" watching other people working. Although this is not a common case in public utility operations, it could be a difficulty if the costs are not carefully evaluated and policed.

Another economic problem involved in regulating public utilities is determining a fair return. Return on investment is the percentage of profit that a firm makes using the total investment as a base. Total investment is the amount spent on tools of production, buildings, and other assets minus depreciation, and also the working capital required to pay wages, buy materials, and so on. In public utility regulation there is a controversy over whether the investment should be calculated on original cost minus depreciation or replacement cost minus depreciation. Obviously, replacement cost will be larger than original cost because of inflation; therefore, if one opts for replacement cost as the basis for return on investment, then the return will have to be larger than if the calculation were based on original cost.

Most commissions use original cost as a base on which to figure the amount of return the public utility is allowed to receive. Even with agreement on the concept of return on investment and with agreement on the things that should appear in the cost picture, where should a public utility price its products? Figure 9-1 shows how the optimum price that a public utility will charge is determined.

Unlike a firm in a competitive situation, the optimum price from the point of view of the consumer for a public utility firm is where the demand curve intersects the average total cost curve (point B). By receiving a price that is equal to the average total cost, the firm is having its cost met with a fair return, however calculated, on its investment. Thus, society receives the quantity of goods at a price that guarantees a normal return for the risk and investment involved for the particular firm. Without regulation and with an inelastic demand for the product, the public utility monopoly could charge a much higher price (point A) and make exorbitant profits, as shown in Figure 9-1.

With all of the problems mentioned above, what has been the record

FIGURE 9-1.   The Optimum Price for a Public Utility

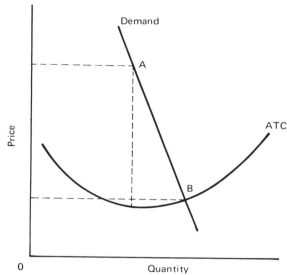

of the utility corporations and the commissions regulating them? Has the consumer had a product at a fair price and quantity? Has the public interest, indeed, been protected by the commissions? Public utility commissions have been in existence since 1907 when the states began regulating the pricing practices and profit rates of the utilities. The economic reason for regulation was, as we have mentioned, to insure that a satisfactory level of output would be obtained by the consumer at a fair price. In the absence of competition, the regulating commissions were to provide the protective element for the consumer. Unfortunately, the system has not worked as well as it should have.

The utilities have had profit rates that suggest that they are still using their position as local monopolies. Indeed, a comparison of the performance of public utilities in states with regulatory commissions and the performance in states without regulatory commissions indicates, in many cases, very little difference. It is not that the commissions have not devoted considerable time to establishing rates; the problem has been that they have perceived their job not as protecting the public interest so much as assuring "normal" profit for the regulated company. In addition, the firms' operating expenses have not been subjected to a very close examination, and the pressures of the regulating commissions have not succeeded in making the public utilities more efficient.

Part of the difficulty has been that public sentiment has usually caused the commission's birth, but the wane in public interest in further regulating public utilities has usually meant that the regulating commissions have been less than diligent in protecting the consumer. The second problem has been the action of the courts. The due process of law clause in the Fourteenth Amendment forbids the states from taking property from private corporations or individuals without full compensation. This clause has been perceived by the regulating commissions as preventing them from insuring that the public utilities get a limited but fair return.

Despite the problems mentioned above and the fact that the regulating commissions have not been overly zealous in their attempts to police the utility companies, the fact remains that the situation in public utilities is the best of a poor lot. Certainly, more diligence on the part of the regulating commissions would help immensely in providing more efficient service for the consumers. Unquestionably, more prodding by the general public and the commissions would make the utility companies more efficient. But in no way could the market revert to competitive conditions. The economic situation within the industry dicates that strong public control of the public utilities is necessary to protect the consumers.

In the United States we have leaned toward indirect control of businesses, rather than nationalization. In spite of the occasional furor over government interference with business, it is more often the case that business interferes with government. Although in recent years we have seen a regulation of pricing to hold down inflation, this is a rare occurrence. Rarely does the government nationalize industry. Unlike other countries where nationalization of crucial industries has taken place, the United States has taken the middle road; it has not permitted a strictly laissez-faire arrangement, but has opted for regulation of private ownership. The future will, no doubt, bring more of the same.

Problems of Pollution Control

In recent years there has been increasing awareness of the problems of pollution control. One need not be an economist or an ecology expert to realize that the environment is in serious condition in the United States. Daily air pollution reports tell us of how little free air there is. A favorite story of economics teachers a decade ago was that there was no economics of air, since air was so plentiful as not to need economizing. This statement is obviously no longer true. Economizing air, water, and natural resources is a prime concern to everyone today.

Why has pollution been just recently recognized as a problem? What does standard economic theory say about pollution control? We have had a massive pollution problem since the beginning of the industrialized world. Even before the industrial revolution, there were some problems in sanitary removal of waste and garbage. The reason why the pollution of air, water, and other natural resources has become such a problem in recent years is the fact that the concentration of people per square mile in most of the industrialized countries has increased at such a rate that the margin of error—that is, the ability of the environment to cleanse itself of the waste products—is becoming increasingly smaller. Fifty years ago, a town dumping waste into a stream was no particular problem if the next town along the stream was far enough away for the body of water to cleanse itself. However, as municipalities grew so close together that the waste products of one town ended up in the water supply of another town, the problem became serious. Such is also the case in air pollution.

When given a chance, the atmosphere will take away and discharge waste products dumped into it. However, the density of population in our major cities, particularly New York, Chicago, and Los Angeles, has created such an enormous amount of air pollution that the atmosphere cannot discharge the pollutants. At a busy intersection of either downtown New York or Los Angeles the pollutants, particularly carbon monoxide and nitrogen products, are sometimes in excess of the safe limits for humans.

It is a common mistake for people in the middle economic class to fix the entire blame for pollution on either businesses or people in the lower economic classes. In fact, consumption patterns of the middle-income class contribute a great deal to the amount of pollutants in the environment. Automobiles, waste products including tin cans, nonreturnable bottles, plastic products, and so forth, all contribute to the waste that our society is accumulating. Nonreturnable bottles, aluminum and tin cans, and plastics present particular problems because they do not decompose easily and, consequently, are not recycled back into the ecological system.

DIMENSIONS OF THE PROBLEM   The chief contaminants in air pollution are oxides of sulphur, carbon monoxide, and nitrogen oxide. The major cities of the United States, particularly Los Angeles, have the greatest problem in air pollution. The pollutants are primarily the result of the incomplete combustion of products in the internal combustion engine and in the case of oxides of sulfur from industry. A simple solution is to exclude automobiles from the cities unless they have effective controls to limit the amount of pollutants that they discharge into the air. Estimates by the automobile companies are that pollution control devices would add approximately $225 to the cost of the automobile. Of course, given the present oligopolistic structure of the automobile industry, such a cost would be passed along entirely to the consumer.

Water pollution may be caused by the waste of an urban, populated area, by industrial wastes, or it may be caused by animal waste. In recent years there has been an increasing problem of pollution by radioactive wastes from nuclear power plants. In addition, there is thermal pollution, which is the elevation of the temperature in the water to such a degree that the oxygen supply is seriously reduced: the result is death to many of the plants and animals living in that water. Thermal pollution is a result of dumping hot water from either an industrial or a power plant into a body of water. Because of the tremendous amounts of energy they generate, nuclear power plants have a particular problem with thermal pollution.

The problem of water pollution is more a public than a private problem. Cities along bodies of water are not constructing filtration plants to reduce the pollutants that enter the streams. The engineering problems connected with water pollution are not difficult. We have known for many years how to effectively treat wastes and waste products so that they enter the streams in a chemical form that allows the stream to purify it. The problem arises in paying for such treatment.

Since it is not clear exactly who should pay the entire cost of eliminating water pollution, the division of the cost becomes a political problem. For example, a city that dumps waste into the Hudson River affects all the downstream governmental units along the Hudson; everyone along the river is hurt by the action of a single municipality.

More than one governmental unit and more than one state may have to become involved in sharing the cost of the pollution control devices. Unlike air pollution, whereby the individual owner of an automobile would be assessed a certain cost to pay for his pollution control device, the economic problems of eliminating water pollution are more difficult. Cooperation between governmental units, however, has existed in the past, and no doubt some form of cross-governmental agency will be developed to provide the resources and control for effective water pollution devices.

The waste products of consumer living, as we have mentioned, also present a problem. The problem may be approached in two ways: either people must consume less or have fewer children. If we continue our present rate of population growth, then by necessity we must reduce our level of consumption. The only way we can continue along our present level of consumption is to reduce the rate of increase of our population. Most economists and environmentalists say that both remedies should be used.

Those who advocate a reduction in the population increase discuss it in terms of zero population growth. This means that every two people replace themselves by having an average of no more than 2.2 children, to allow for those people who never have children. When this is achieved the population would then level off to a point of stability. That is, the births would be roughly balanced by deaths.

DEFICIENCIES OF ECONOMIC THEORY We have developed the basics of economic theory in previous chapters. Briefly stated, the theory provides a rationale for the operation of the firm, explains its costs, and explains the theory of why consumers buy products at a given schedule of prices. On a larger scale, macroeconomic theory deals with the problems of a nation's economy. Stabilizing the economy, keeping it on an even growth keel, and preventing widespread inflations and recessions are the major topics of macroeconomic theory. One part of microeconomic theory can be interpreted as applying to pollution and its problems. The terms usually applied to such problems are *externalities* and *social costs*.

Externalities are, as the name implies, things that are outside the control of the firm. They may be positive or negative. For example, a firm receives positive externalities when it locates near transportation systems, a university that provides training for its workers, and a municipality that provides recreational services and other things that the firm would have to purchase to keep its employees happy. In contrast, if a firm is located downstream from a polluter and has to use the polluted waters in its operation, it is faced with negative externalities.

Social costs are a different way of stating positive and negative externalities. Social costs are costs that society has to pay for in addition to the direct outlay for goods and services. For example, suppose an industrial firm is polluting the atmosphere. In order to make a careful economic evaluation of the costs and benefits of the firm to the community, it would be necessary to list as costs the increased amount that people in the area of the plant have to pay in order to clean up their clothing, paint their houses more often, treat increased diseases either aggravated by or attributable to the air pollution, and, in general, compensate for the action of the pollutants. These extra costs are called social costs. The social benefits of the firm include the employment it provides and the goods it makes available to consumers.

Thus, in standard microeconomic theory there is some discussion of the problems of the environment that are facing us today. But standard theory does not adequately explain the problems, the reason they came about, and the possible solutions. It is important to remember that the problem in environmental studies is the nonquantifiable elements that enter the picture. While one can put a dollar sign on business costs, one cannot adequately assign a dollar value to the effect of overcrowding, anxiety about health care, and psychological disorders as a result of too many people in too small an area. The standard, customary equilibrium analysis used in economics is useless in determining how a system should operate to best suit its people.

The ecological problems we are faced with today are not merely a result of market failure. They also represent an inadequacy of the economic theory itself to properly explain the nonquantifiable elements that a modern society is faced with. In earlier parts of this chapter we confidently ascribed the problem of antitrust and monopolistic elements to the failure of the market system; we cannot do so with the problems that are currently facing us in the environment.

One of the reasons why economic theory has not been adequate to deal with such problems is the fact that the assumptions that economic theory are based on are those of a closed, narrow economic system with only minor effects on man's natural and social environment. It is not surprising that Alfred Marshall, who invented the concept of externalities, thought of economics as a separate sphere. In the late 1800's and early 1900's, the social sciences were viewed as existing in narrow bands isolated from and unrelated to each other. The unexplainable elements in economic theory were attributed to the irrationality of people. In recent years, however, we have lost the luxury of assigning economic problems only to the economic sphere. Today, there are few economic problems that do not have political or social overtones. As important as the study of the firm is, it is really an exercise in logic and deductive reasoning. The important policy decisions do not depend on whether the firm is maximizing profit, but on whether the resources of the firm are depleted or enriched and whether the products of the firm are truly needed or not.

To adequately meet the needs of our present-day economy, economic theory has to come to grips with problems on both a microeconomic and a macroeconomic basis. A microeconomic theorist must find a solution for the problem of autonomous consumer behavior. It has long been assumed that the consumer purchases products based on his balancing of the extra utility and the price of each product. He chooses product X over product Y if he gets more marginal utility per dollar spent on X than on Y. This analysis assumes that the consumer makes the choice of a particular product in a vacuum. As John Kenneth Galbraith has pointed out in numerous books, the consumer is really at the mercy of the producer; he does not have the autonomous sovereignty that we envision in microeconomic theory. Therefore, microeconomic theory has to be revised to include the interactions of producers, consumers, and the environment. A similar problem exists on a macroeconomic level.

We examined national income statistics in Chapters 2 and 3. The difficulty with these concepts and data is that while they measure income and production over a particular time period, they say nothing about the effects of production on the assets and liabilities of the whole economy. We need to develop figures and statistics that reflect the effect of production on the environmental balance and the depletion of our assets. Thus, one could expect to see beside the figures for steel production a measure of the social costs that the steel industry has incurred.

What is also needed for the nation is some measure of the quality of life. We must improve the areas of health care, housing, leisure time, economic security for the aged, and other psychological and economic facets in order to make life more livable. The national income statistics, reflecting only production and income, hide the effects of such production and income on the quality of life. We may in the future be faced with a reversal of economic thinking; that is, we may have to learn how to cut down on production rather than increase production. As Galbraith has pointed out, we have largely solved our production problems; the problems that remain concern distribution and the production and distribution of public goods such as education, medical care, and transportation.

We cannot, however, wait for economic theory to catch up with environmental problems. What is needed is a case by case study of how to implement effective pollution control devices. We must learn how we can prevent, either by punishment or reward, a company, a municipality, or an individual from polluting the environment.

OUTLOOK FOR THE FUTURE Air and water pollution and waste disposal are easier problems to tackle than those of population increases. There are two general ways to induce companies to control air and water pollution. One is to force them by means of punishment, such as a fine to comply with regulations set forth by governmental agencies. The second solution is to grant them tax incentives or a positive motivation to institute such pollution control devices. A third way is through some combination of the two methods. The engineering problems in air and water purification and garbage disposal are not enormous. The difficulty is in determining who should pay for such pollution control devices. As it stands now, due to the monopolistic and oligopolistic elements in our economy, one can expect that the consumer will have to pay the full costs for pollution control devices. Accepting that as given, then the consumer should have some say in what devices are instituted and should, through a governmental agency, have some effective say in the policing of such regulations. Since the consumer interest is at stake, businesses will no doubt have to resign themselves to the inevitability of effective pollution control.

Municipalities may be granted long-term loans from a higher governmental agency to control water pollution. Another possibility is, of course, to create an effective federal agency, with the costs of water pollution control being shared by people throughout the country. Whether on a regional or a national basis, the costs should be shared. It is certainly unfair to expect that a small municipality should bear the entire load of large-scale pollution control.

If the engineering solutions to air and water pollution are well-known, why has the problem not been solved earlier? Part of the answer lies in the fact that in a country like the United States with a heterogeneous population, advances in social welfare move rather slowly. The second reason is that businesses, like other institutions, do not move unless pushed. This is not to absolve individuals outside businesses from their responsibilities, but it is true, as *Consumer Reports* has pointed out, that in 1969 businesses spent $1 billion advertising their efforts in pollution control, which was ten times more than those companies spent for pollution control in the same period. This is, of course, one of the disturbing elements in the American economy: the willingness to create an image of change rather than the actuality of change.

But part of the unwillingness to control pollution has had justifiable economic roots. Without question, unless some tax incentive or other economic incentive is arranged, it is very costly for marginal firms with small profit margins to institute effective pollution control. Given a consumer choice in an area hard-hit by unemployment, the consumers would no doubt choose to keep the factory going and provide employment rather than to have cleaner air and no jobs. What is unfortunate about this situation is that only these two choices exist. There should be, of course, effective means of transferring people and assets into other forms of employment. However, in times of economic uncertainty, as we have had in recent years, businesses can encourage a certain resistance to any such costly programs that would put a marginal enterprise out of business.

Of course the question for society is not whether the marginal business stays or goes, but whether society really needs a business that cannot afford to curb pollution effectively. The same arguments were advanced when the minimum wage laws were passed. The reply to the argument that many businesses would be terminated because of increased labor costs was that if the businesses could not exist if they paid the legal minimum wages, then perhaps the resources should be used elsewhere. Choosing between what is good for society and what is good for one individual, however, is difficult. Thus, politicians and workers often opt for employment rather than pollution control.

A further problem has been a lack of vision by economic and political leaders in solving the pollution problem. We have long viewed the United States as providing an endless stream of resources in an open system. It is only recently that we are beginning to feel the effect of shortages of resources, particularly air and water, that we considered largely unlimited before. If we understand this as a necessary restraint on our way of life, we may be able to effect a change in the attitudes of individuals and politicians. It has been said that nothing is as powerful as an idea whose time has come. The same applies to effective pollution control: the time is coming, the means are there; the question is a reordering of priorities and economic theory to fit a new perception of the world.

Summary

Chapter 6 outlined the economic theory behind concentrations of economic power. Chapter 9 completed the system by analyzing the increasing role of the government in regulating business.

We have seen that government regulation is not new; indeed, it has been increasing rapidly since the turn of the century. The major effort by the government has been in antitrust activity—the breaking up of monopolies and the prohibition of unfair pricing and marketing policies. Antitrust policy rests on a theory that has evolved from an emphasis on business conduct to a more recent structural analysis of the percentage of market share by the top firms. It has never been a clear and consistent policy and has even worked sometimes to promote monopoly.

Public utility regulation is one clear example of effective government monopoly regulation. Recognizing early that competition would be injurious, the government moved to control the pricing and output of such firms.

While utility regulation has been effective, pollution control remains a problem. Economic theory does not provide a framework for effective action, and the conflicts between consumers and businesses seem to rest on their different definitions of economic freedom. No doubt there will be a solution; but when and who will pay for it remain questionable.

QUESTIONS AND PROBLEMS

1   How would you explain the growth in the size and scale of American businesses?

2   Why is the structure of industry preferred as a criterion for the determination of monopolies over conduct and performance?

3   Do you feel that the "Rule of Reason" provides a workable guideline for antitrust policy?

4   Review your understanding of fixed and variable costs. Why are high fixed costs associated with concentrated industries?

5   What was the purpose of the Clayton Act? What implications for labor were present in the Clayton Act?

6   Why are public utilities so heavily regulated?

7   Why is the optimum price of public utility products for consumers at the intersection of the ATC curve and the demand curve?

8   Why has pollution control become a problem in recent years? Has it always been a problem?

9   Why has economic theory not adequately accounted for pollution control?

BIBLIOGRAPHY

ADAMS, WALTER, and GRAY, HORACE M., *Monopoly in America: The Government as Promoter.* New York: Macmillan, 1955.

CAVES, RICHARD, *American Industry: Structure, Conduct, Performance,* 2nd ed. Englewood Cliffs: Prentice-Hall, 1967.

LOVE, GLEN A., and LOVE, RHODA M., eds., *Ecological Crisis.* New York: Harcourt Brace Jovanovich, 1970.

MINTZ, MORTON, and COHEN, JERRY S., *America, Inc. Who Owns and Operates the United States?* New York: The Dial Press, 1971.

SINGER, EUGENE M., *Antitrust Economics: Selected Legal Cases and Economic Models.* Englewood Cliffs: Prentice-Hall, 1968.

WEISS, LEONARD W., *Case Studies in American Industry,* 2nd ed. New York: Wiley, 1971.

10

Labor and Unions

Don't mourn for me. Organize.
—Last message of Joe Hill, executed 1915

Labor unions are familiar organizations. Most of us have heard of, formed opinions of, or perhaps belonged to a union. But many of us do not realize that unions have their roots in the same type of social protest that we see in the 1970's. For old time union members the fight against a harsh and insecure economic system was identical in fervor and commitment to the protest of our time.

While unorganized workers were frequently intimidated by employers, collectively they had power. Today the principle of collective bargaining is accepted by both employers and workers. But many struggles and much violence preceded the acceptance of labor's bargaining position.

In this chapter we shall be discussing unions from three different vantage points: first, from the viewpoint of the organized workers; second, from the viewpoint of management; and third, from the viewpoint of individuals outside unions.

Unions, Wages, and Full Employment

In order to determine the effect of union bargaining power on wage rates and employment levels, we must first define what a union is. We must also look at the union in a historical and social context; that is, we must see how the union has changed from earlier times to the present. We will also examine the social and political effects of such organizations.

Unions, like other institutions, are subject to various interpretations depending on the vantage point from which one looks at them. Unions may be viewed in three separate contexts. First, unions are organizations to settle conflicts. The conflicts that they are engaged in arise over the exercise of the power to determine the prices for their labor services and the rate of output that they are required to produce. Unions have always been engaged in such conflict.

Second, from the union members' point of view, unions are communities in which workers gain an identity. This is especially important in our age when massive technological changes and the mobility of people have uprooted so many individuals in the United States and around the world. Capitalistic production has alienated the worker from his work. As the production worker becomes a mere cog in a vast and complex organization, he can no longer point with pride to his craftsmanship, his product, his achievement. In addition, the worker as an isolated individual is virtually helpless in a confrontation with the vast corporate power. The union gives the worker self-esteem and bargaining power. In combination with other workers, he can meet the employer on a more equal basis. Through the union he can "tell the boss off." The mighty corporation cannot dispense with all its workers as easily as it can with any one worker.

Third, unions are thought by some to be exclusive groups that limit the supply of labor in order to keep prices, and therefore wages, up. Unions can contribute to higher prices; the question is whether it is their only role. As we know from earlier chapters on supply and demand, one way to keep prices up is to limit the supply in a market. Craft unions are especially interested in restricting the labor supply and thereby raising wages. Craft unions are those unions that combine all workers with similar skills. When the plumbers get together in their own union, that is a craft union; the same is true of the carpenters, the electricians, the bricklayers, and so on. A craft union tries to get employers to hire only union members. If there are not enough jobs for all the actual or potential members, the union closes its membership rolls and refuses to admit new members. Such restrictions of the labor supply tend to raise wage rates.

Industrial unions, in contrast, aim to include in the same union all employees of an industry below the level of foreman. For example, an industrial union in the auto industry would include carpenters, masons, bricklayers, tool and die makers, plumbers, and electricians, as well as auto assembly workers. With industrial unionism, there will be one union in a plant and/or industry instead of several. Industrial unions are more likely to remain open to new members than are craft unions.

The American Federation of Labor, founded in 1886, relied primarily on craft unionism. The Congress of Industrial Organizations, organized in 1935, proclaimed industrial unionization as a major principle. Which type of organization serves the workers better? If industrial unionism is preferable to craft organization from the point of view of the workers, why did the A.F. of L. cling so tenaciously for so many decades to craft unionism?

There are two basic reasons for the popularity of craft unionism before the merger of the A.F. of L. and the C.I.O. in 1955. The first and less important reason was that many union officials would lose their good jobs and their importance if small craft unions merged into large industrial unions. The second and more important reason was that highly skilled workers could serve their own interests better by bargaining only for themselves, excluding the mass of unskilled and semiskilled workers. A hypothetical example illustrates this point. Suppose a firm employs 10,000 workers, of whom 500 are highly skilled craftsmen and the rest are unskilled or semiskilled. If a union representing only the 500 skilled workers demands an increase of $10 per week, the employer may grant it rather readily in order to avoid shutting down his plant. But if an industrial union demands the same increase for all 10,000 employees, the employer may think this is worth resisting, and a strike ensues. Industrial unions serve more workers than the limited numbers in the craft unions. Craft unionism, however, serves the skilled workers better if the other workers are neglected and excluded from the benefits of unionism. Craft unionism created an aristocracy of labor, an elite group that benefited from the large gap between their own wage rates and those of the unorganized workers.

At the inception of the American Federation of Labor, Samuel Gompers, its founder, set down these six positions that he felt the American labor movement should follow.

1. The American labor movement, unlike its European counterparts, should accept private enterprise. Unions should not try to change private ownership of industry to state ownership.

2. The American labor movement should strive to obtain short-run gains, primarily in economic security and higher wages. [Gompers opted for achieving a series of small year-to-year gains, rather than trying to negotiate large long-run contracts.]

3. The labor movement should engage in direct negotiation with the employers. The negotiations should be conducted between employers and employees, and government action should be minimized or eliminated. [This preference for a hands-off policy by government resulted from the antilabor attitude of government, which was generally dominated by big business. Strike breaking by state and federal authorities was very common.]

4. If negotiations do not succeed, then the labor movement should threaten to strike.

5. Unions in the United States should be organized by trade or craft.

6. The labor unions should be political without affiliating with any political party. They should back candidates friendly to labor and oppose antagonistic candidates. No political labor party should be organized in the United States as was done by the British unions. [Certainly the American labor movement has supported more Democratic candidates than Republican, but they still maintain their neutrality and shop around at each election period in order to back the candidate most favorable to their aims.]

Gompers' six goals provided the philosophical backing for the American labor movement. His insight into how a union should operate and what procedures it should take in negotiation insured that American union-ism would reject radicalism and long-run goals in favor of short-run objec-tives of better wages and working conditions.

The advent of unions was, of course, not greeted with enthusiasm by the employers. In fact, the employers hired spies to determine whether and when sentiment toward unions was increasing; they employed yellow-dog contracts, which required that a worker promise not to join a union: they fired employees suspected of union sympathies; and they used strikebreak-ers and the lockout technique extensively (in a lockout employers prohibit union people from entering their place of employment). State militia, armed scabs, court injunctions, and other means were also used to oppose unionism.

The early history of organized labor was filled with a great deal of violence. The legal aspects of organized labor also reflect a great deal of ambivalence toward labor unions. There are distinct phases that labor unions went through in legal history. From 1806 to 1842, the courts held that unions were automatically conspiracies in restraint of trade and were therefore illegal. Unions continued to exist during that period but in a semi-legal and secret condition. From 1842 to the 1930's, unions were legal, al-though many of their acts were deemed illegal. In the 1930's, labor legisla-tion in almost all cases strengthened labor's position. Just the opposite happened in the late 1940's and 1950's, when the legal statutes were almost all antilabor.

LABOR AND THE LAW   The first major piece of legislation that affected American labor favorably was the Clayton Antitrust Act of 1914. As we have seen in Chapter 9, the Sherman Antitrust Act forbade monopolizing and restraint of trade. In order to prevent widespread antiunion activity by management under the prohibitions outlined by the Sherman Act, the Clayton Act exempted unions from antitrust prosecution in most cases.

The rationale for exempting labor unions from antitrust consideration was that labor is not a commodity and, therefore, should not be judged in the same terms as the commerce for goods and services. The argument still persists today in discussions on the labor movement over whether labor unions constitute a monopoly and whether they should be treated as mo-nopolies by the courts.

The next significant piece of legislation was the Norris–LaGuardia Act passed in 1932. Under this act, the yellow-dog contracts were forbidden. Workers could not be coerced into promising not to join a union as a con-dition for employment.

Unions won the right to bargain collectively by the passage of the Na-tional Industrial Recovery Act in 1933. Although this act substantially strengthened the unions' power, the legal protection of collective bargain-ing created new problems.

The two antagonists, management and labor, were now on a more equal footing. If the disagreements between them on the price of labor, the hours of working, and the quantity of production could not be worked out, then, of course, a strike or lockout would ensue. In order to prevent massive and costly strikes, the National Labor Relations Board was instituted in 1935 under the terms of the Wagner Act.

The Wagner Act was probably the most significant piece of prolabor legislation passed in the 1930's. It defined very explicitly labor's rights and what labor could expect as a fair bargaining position, and it also established the National Labor Relations Board. This board protects the rights of labor guaranteed by the Wagner Act. It also acts as the protector of labor in organizing unions.

If a union organizer persuades some employees to join a labor union, such workers are protected by the National Labor Relations Board from being arbitrarily fired. If it is determined that an individual was fired for his involvement in labor activity, then the National Labor Relations Board compels the company to reinstate the worker and pay him all his back pay. The board also protects the workers' rights to free speech and assembly and the right to strike.

Obviously, the legislation in the 1930's was set up to substantially strengthen labor unions in their relations with management. After the Second World War, a substantial amount of antilabor sentiment began building up in the United States and resulted in a number of laws that curbed union powers.

The first such antilabor legislation was the Taft-Hartley Act, passed in 1947. This act forbade unfair practices by unions and required that unions give sixty days notice when desiring to modify or terminate a collective agreement. Furthermore, the Taft-Hartley Act provides that the government can request an eighty-day injunction in the event of a strike that seriously endangers the national welfare. Even though this injunction is rarely used, it is an important weapon and one that labor unions must take into consideration when planning a work stoppage against a major industry.

The Taft-Hartley Act also banned the closed shop (a shop that must employ only union members). With a closed shop, if the union does not permit new members to join the union, then the employer may not hire whomever he wants. With the union shop, the employer may hire whomever he wishes, but the new worker must join the union within a stipulated period of time.

The last part of the Taft-Hartley Act, the right-to-work law, has promoted controversy ever since its passage. Under the terms of the right-to-work law, states may pass laws that allow workers the option to join or not join a union in a particular shop. Thus, workers have the right to work without being forced to join a union. The right-to-work law, in effect, makes the union shop illegal.

Of course, as the right-to-work law substantially weakens labor's bargaining position, it is not favored by union people. Union supporters also claim that it allows an individual worker the benefits of union activity without compelling him to share the costs. Another argument against right-to-work laws is that unions are democratically instituted in shops after a secret ballot. If the majority of those working in a shop vote to join a union, it seems logical, from the union point of view, that the minority ought to go along with it. Those who favor right-to-work laws claim that such laws provide protection for an individual worker to do as he pleases and still maintain his employment.

Another act that was passed after the Second World War was the Landrum-Griffin Act of 1959. The principal point of this law was to force unions to follow democratic procedures in electing officials. It also required that they hold elections every three years and account, in some detail, for the funds that they had collected and dispensed. The Landrum-Griffin Act tightened the government's regulations and restrictions concerning unions. It made the unions accountable for their elections and the inflow and outgo of their funds.

The rash of antilabor legislation in the 1940's and 1950's reflects the view among many people that labor unions must be restricted because they hold such enormous economic and political power. As with big business, such power, even when not used, is threatening.

UNIONS AND FULL EMPLOYMENT   Lionel Robbins, the British economist we discussed in Chapter 1, proposed in the 1930's a classical solution to the downturn in the economy of western Europe and the United States. He said that since employment was off, one quick and simple way to bring employment back up again was for wage rates to adjust downward to soak up the unemployed. If one envisions the wage as determined by the supply and demand of labor, one way to increase the level of employment would be to allow equilibrium in the labor market to determine a new equilibrium wage at a lower level and thus provide for greater employment. Robbins' conclusion on why the economy did not move upward in an automatic fashion was that wage rates were not flexible downward; they were not flexible, he stated, largely because of union bargaining power in the economy. His logic has the ring of authenticity that one finds in so many arguments of the neoclassical school, and his solution is certainly reasonable, assuming a free market and flexible wage rates. But John Maynard Keynes, the architect of modern macroeconomic theory, disputed Robbins' prescription for the economy.

Keynes' emphasis was not on the automatic mechanisms of the neoclassical school, but on the level of aggregate demand. He approached the problem from a different vantage point than Robbins. He stated that even if wage rates were flexible downward and even if the more workers would be employed at a lower wage rate, the lower wage rate would decrease consumption expenditures and thereby push employment downward again. In the absence of increased investment, the total aggregate demand would go down. Robbins replied that if consumption went down, the slack would be taken up by increased investment due to lowered interest rates. Keynes' reply was that investment does not necessarily react automatically to a reduction in interest rates. Keynes formulated this idea as a liquidity trap: at a certain low level of interest, investment will not increase largely, because businessmen have poor expectations about the future. In other words, investment becomes insensitive to reductions in interest rates below a certain point.

Keynes' now-famous liquidity trap cast a new light on the way a modern economy operates in a downturn. The presence of institutional factors such as labor unions does make wage rates inflexible downward. But even if they were flexible, according to Keynes, in the absence of any increase in investment or government spending the economy would continue on a downturn.

The problem of the union demand for more wages is one that critics of unions have repeatedly emphasized. When Samuel Gompers was asked what unions wanted, he replied simply, "More." This is, of course, the impression that most people have of the unions and their wage policies: that they consistently ask for more and more wages, regardless of the situation in the economy. The factor that is often overlooked is productivity.

If productivity (the output per hour) increases from year to year, then wage rates may go up without sending prices up. If a man produces 5 percent more goods per year, his wage rate may go up 5 percent without causing an increase in cost for the employer.

There is no question that wages were the prime consideration in the early days of union bargaining. But increases in wages for the stronger unions have given way in recent years to more demands for economic security and a change in the relationship between the employer and the employee. The tactics that unions have employed in order to obtain their demands are centered around the collective bargaining technique.

Collective bargaining provides a peaceful method for a union to obtain its demands. Collective bargaining means that an individual does not have to bargain by himself for higher wages, shorter hours, and other fringe benefits, but that the workers submit their bargaining rights to a larger unit called a union. Workers elect bargaining committees to negotiate for them and vote on whether to accept the contract that the union negotiates or to strike. Thus, the workers have the last say in any package that a union obtains for them.

The bargaining part of collective bargaining implies and requires a great deal of game-playing by the participants. The unions frequently make an initial demand that is exorbitant. Management retaliates with a long explanation of how difficult it is to make a profit in an economy plagued by unions. Both sides try to get public opinion on their side in the early phases of the bargaining session. If the bargaining is unsuccessful, if the participants cannot reach an agreement, they have one of two alternatives short of a strike or lockout. They may submit their differences to a mediator, a disinterested third party who tries to resolve them, or they may submit the details of the bargaining to an arbitrator. To do this the parties must agree beforehand to accept the findings of the arbitrator. Arbitration is rare in collective bargaining contracts. Both management and labor prefer to settle their grievances privately, without submitting the decision to binding arbitration.

If all else fails, of course, the union calls a work stoppage or a strike. Although this is the technique that is most often identified with unions, strikes are rare when compared with the total work hours that the American economy produces. Even in 1937, a year of massive strikes, only .43 percent of working time was lost through strikes. In recent years, time lost through strikes has been less than .25 percent of total working time. But the fact that strike time represents such a small percentage of total working time does not diminish the negative attitude that many people have toward unions.

If strikes are so rare, why are they given so much public attention? Strikes are the trump card in labor's hand. They are the final weapon that labor may employ in their bargaining sessions. Consequently, they are more talked about than actually resorted to.

Attitudes Toward Unions and Work

One would expect that management would hold a different view of the objectives of the labor movement. Although ideas and attitudes toward unions have changed somewhat among the educated management group in the United States, there is a basic conflict of interests between management and labor. In some large industries, management and labor cooperate well together; this usually results in large wage increases that are, in turn, the company's declared reason for raising prices. But most managers of small businesses believe—at least they state that they believe—in competition. And since unions by nature inhibit competition based on reducing wages by holding down the supply of labor, one would expect that a group of people who espouse competition in all aspects of life would be against the idea of unions.

The management view, if it can be stated simply as procompetition, has more often than not been found to be inconsistent. Most people who believe in competition believe in it for the other person. As we have seen in our discussion of oligopoly in Chapter 6, in an industry characterized by large elements of uncertainty, price competition is considered to be ruinous and is avoided as far as possible.

John Kenneth Galbraith has proposed that big and powerful labor unions have grown up as a "countervailing power" to big and powerful firms. It is his view that since the market no longer works to regulate business, it is inevitable that large counteracting organizations such as strong labor unions would develop in the vacuum.

The nonunion segments of the public have their own biases toward unions. It is often stated that unions drive up prices. This idea must be analyzed with care. As we have mentioned earlier (see p. 235), in order to effectively determine whether unions have in fact been causing higher prices, one must look at productivity figures in line with increased labor costs. Management has often used the demands of labor unions as an excuse for increasing the cost of their products to the consumer, and price increases usually exceed the increased labor costs per unit of output.

The availability of increased educational facilities and greater affluence have produced a general apathy among young people toward labor unions. In recent years there has been increased discussion about new modes and life styles among younger people. Although the generation gap has always existed, there is increasing awareness that many people under thirty desire a different form of life style than their parents. To be sure, numbers of younger people are entering labor unions, primarily the sons and daughters of existing union members, but there is not the interest in unions as a political topic that there was in the 1930's. Most of the college graduates under thirty tend to believe, because of their optimism about the future, that they can make it in the world without the assistance of a strong bargaining unit. Therefore, in spite of the increased tendency toward unionization among public employees such as teachers, mailmen, and sanitation men, there is a general apathy on the part of younger, college-educated people in the subject of labor unions.

Part of the gap between economic classes is attributable to the fact that union members generally support unions and believe that without them they would never have achieved the economic status that they have. In general, most union members believe that in order to achieve economic gain and offset the negative aspects of dependency on employers, workers must stand together and force management to listen to their collective opinion.

It is important to note that by no means is union membership predominant in all blue-collar occupations. Less than 50 percent of those employed in such occupations in the United States are organized in unions, and many of these unions are not characterized by a great deal of bargaining strength. Thus, only a small percentage of workers are materially benefited by membership in a bargaining unit. Many workers, particularly dishwashers, domestic workers, agricultural laborers, maintenance men, and other people on the periphery of the skilled trades, are not unionized or if unionized, are not represented by effective units.

By no means is there a uniform opinion of labor unions. Emotions on both sides run strong, particularly when the admission of black members into unions is an issue.

Problems of Black Workers

Black workers have particular difficulty in obtaining union jobs. Many of the reasons why they have difficulty are based on racial or cultural factors, and others are based on nonracial or economic factors.

Although blacks in the United States constitute about 12 percent of the total population, they have far less participation in the unionized blue-collar jobs. Although the data are difficult to obtain, it is clear from studies by the U.S. Civil Rights Commission that blacks constitute small percentages, usually between 1 and 2 percent at maximum, of the total unionized labor force. Why are blacks so underrepresented in the unions? The first and most obvious answer is discrimination by unions and management. In this sense both employers and union management are reflecting the prevailing social attitudes that have characterized blacks as more "suited" for hot, dirty, and disagreeable unorganized jobs rather than the high-skilled union jobs. Unions may also fear a white backlash if large-scale numbers of blacks are recruited for apprentice programs. Since management needs the unions to supply their skilled labor, the prevailing discriminatory attitudes of the unions have often been passively backed by management. Even if top management is willing to hire on an equal opportunity basis, the black worker often finds an uncomfortable situation when he encounters lower level management.

While racial discrimination is no doubt a major factor in the exclusion of blacks from unions, there are other nonracial factors that contribute as well. Since unions attempt to keep the price of their labor high by controlling the supply of labor, it is natural that they will discriminate against someone. If there are only a limited numbers of jobs in, say, the construction industry, then of course the jobs will go to the sons of existing members if possible. Since blacks are historically unrepresented in unions, they have no one to sponsor them in their efforts to break into the higher-paying unionized jobs. The control of entry into the apprentice programs is the primary way that blacks are excluded on a continuing basis from unions.

The primary factor that has excluded blacks from unions has been the same force that has relegated them to inferior occupations. Historically, blacks have lacked economic and social power and have therefore had little wherewithal to force whites to allow them to enter their unions. The only time that blacks were able to enter the skilled trades with relative ease was under slavery, when the slave craftsmen were protected from hostile whites by the slave-owning class. After the emancipation of the slaves, blacks continued to have a high percentage of the jobs in stable industries. But they were systematically excluded from the newer crafts such as electrical work, sheet metal work, plumbing, and pipe fitting. All these cultural and historical factors have worked to keep blacks, even when admitted into unions, in inferior jobs. Furthermore, unions in the U.S. do not have a history of social concern for people in nonunionized employment.

Until recent years, few blacks have applied for apprentice programs, in spite of the publicity given them by the civil rights movement. Their reluctance to apply for positions in unions is understandable considering their historical exclusion. Moreover, many employment and school counselors have advised black youngsters not to try to obtain positions in exclusive unions. In addition to the reluctance of unions to allow blacks in and the lack of push from school and work counselors, there is also the very real problem of education.

The statistics clearly show that not only do a smaller percentage of black teenagers complete high school than whites, but also the black high schools in many cases offer significantly poorer training in mathematics and the sciences than do the white schools. Many of the apprentice programs, such as electrical, plumbing, and sheet metal, require a certain amount of mathematics, and since many black youngsters were bound to be lacking in these skills, they did not qualify for the beginning apprentice programs. To be sure, there is the problem of testing, that is, the fact that black youths sometimes are barred from apprentice programs by biased tests. Social scientists have known for years that the way questions are worded or the type of questions asked can systematically exclude groups of people who have had different cultural experiences than the tests imply. This has certainly been the case for young blacks. In recent years there have been programs to tutor black young people in order to help them obtain better scores on the admissions tests, both for apprentice programs and/or entrance into colleges and other institutions of higher education.

All the above factors—racial discrimination, cultural factors, and the education problem—have contributed in excluding blacks from unions. The main economic factor to remember is that unions are based on limiting the supply in order to keep the price of their labor up. As long as they are intent on limiting the supply, then the form that the limitation takes will almost always be toward those members of society considered to be outsiders. No matter what the content of the rhetoric, the economic reason for the exclusion of blacks is that with very few openings available in the skilled trades, someone must be excluded. In this case it is easier to exclude blacks, and a rationale has been built around this exclusion to explain away the economic fact of a contrived scarcity. Much the same difficulty, although in a different form, exists in the problems of women workers.

Problems of Women Workers

Women workers have also been excluded in large numbers, either by choice or by circumstances, from the labor force and the institutions of bargaining power, the unions. It has not always been that way, however. During the Second World War, with so many of the men in the armed forces, women occupied a central part in the industrial fabric of the United States economy. As Betty Friedan has pointed out, women workers were in great demand for factory jobs such as welding and riveting during the war. After the war, since there was a shortage of jobs, women were excluded from many of the positions they previously held. Not only have they been excluded, but as Ms. Friedan has pointed out, they have also been told that they were not suitable for jobs that they had held in an earlier period. As with black workers, women workers have been told that they are not capable of holding down the jobs they wish to pursue. Part of this problem has been the traditional role of women as the raisers of children.

There is revived interest, largely through the impetus of the Women's Liberation movement, in providing day care centers for children of working mothers; this may alleviate the problem that mothers have in arranging satisfactory care for their children. However, even more important than that is a change in the attitudes that the public must achieve in order to allow women workers to participate fully in the economy. Up to the present, certain jobs have been reserved exclusively for women, while other occupations have been withheld from them. Even if women are allowed in jobs that have previously been exclusively for males, they are still exploited by lower pay for the same work. In addition to the lower pay, many highly skilled women have been hired, on a part time basis, for jobs that neither pay well nor afford any degree of economic security.

From an economic point of view, resources, in this case people, should not be wasted. The exclusion of black and women workers from the economy costs us a great deal in terms of goods that we have foregone as a result of not using our resources to the fullest. The problem, and this is the same for both black and women workers, lies in the fact that there has been a shortage of jobs. This situation is due partly to improper monetary and fiscal policies that result in unemployment of resources. As long as there is a scarcity of jobs, there will always be someone excluded. In order to get black and women workers fully into the employment stream, there must be a full employment priority in the United States.

It is thought by many that the shortage of jobs is due to a rapidly ex-

panding technology. The advent and increased use of automated techniques of production are thought to be the cause of much of the scarcity of
jobs. Is automation a new problem? What are the economic and social consequences of automation? Should we pursue a policy of retarding technological change because it displaces workers?

Automation

In the language of engineers, automation is the transference of the control
functions of human beings to computers and servomechanisms. Very simply, it is the replacement of people with machines. The reasons for the replacement of people with machines are obvious. (1) It improves the technological efficiency of the plant; that is, it produces more output with less
input. (2) It provides an easy answer to the personnel problems that constantly face management. Given the choice, management would prefer machines to people. Machines, although they break down, do not strike. Machines, although they require continuous maintenance, do not call in sick.
Machines do not have to be retrained and do not cause the innumerable
personal problems that people do. Thus, the process of automation is very
logical from management's point of view. The people who are displaced by
the machines, however, have an entirely different viewpoint.

Automation is a continuous threat to job security, and job security is
one of the pivotal elements on which labor unions rest their bargaining.
Since unions are interested in the welfare of specific workers, they are primarily concerned with the short-run implications of automation; others are
interested in the long-term results of automation. Figure 10-1 shows the
decreasing proportion of blue-collar jobs to 1971.

Automation is not a new problem. The replacement of people with
machines has been going on at a rapid rate since the industrial revolution.
Simultaneously, the total number of jobs has with occasional interruptions
risen continuously. Thus, in our economy, even though it takes less people
per year to produce the same output, the rising output has increased the
available numbers of jobs. Automation is a two-fold operation. On the one
hand, it displaces people from jobs, but on the other hand, it increases the
effectiveness of production, providing goods at a cheaper rate and increasing the aggregate demand for the entire nation, which, in turn, increases
the number of jobs. The constant pressure of unions for shorter working
hours for everyone has also created more jobs.

The economist perceives the problem of automation as being part of a
larger complex of problems. Increasing aggregate demand is the key to full
employment of resources, including people. With the proper balance of
fiscal and monetary policy, a course of full employment with stable prices
should be a top priority item. But the emphasis on aggregate demand, al-

FIGURE 10-1.   Decreasing Proportion of Blue-Collar Jobs

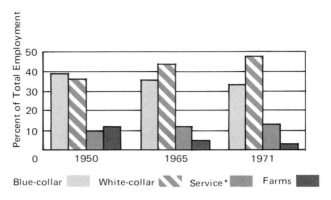

*Includes waiters, cooks, bartenders, policemen, firemen, private household workers, and so on.

Source: U.S. Department of Commerce, Statistical Abstract of the U.S., 1971. Washington, D.C.: Government Printing Office, 1971, p. 222.

though certainly appealing for economists, does not relieve the anxiety of those who may be displaced by changes in the combination of people and machines.

In recent years, strong unions have shifted their emphasis from increasing wage rates to a mix of increased wage rates and job security. Unions argue that the job belongs to the man, not to the company. If an employer replaces an individual with a machine, he should at least continue the worker in some auxiliary job related to the employee's former function. In recent years, the problem has been intensified by the complexity of new technological advances. At the beginning stages of the industrial revolution, it was possible to retrain craftsmen from hand methods of production to semiskilled, machine-oriented work. Now the transference of people to computer-oriented machines is difficult to make. The increased complexity of automation techniques has introduced a new group of specialists, those primarily concerned with computer operations, and has displaced many of the semiskilled workers who did the work previously.

Both unions and economists agree that one should not retard technological progress. The question is how rapidly it should proceed and what to do with the people that the progress displaces. The dignity of work and the feeling of importance is a commodity that is rare indeed and difficult if not impossible to purchase. We are proving more aware of the social and psychological effects of rapid technological change, and economic theory must take into account these changes and decide the optimum balance of goods, services, and means of producing them.

Summary

While Chapter 8 detailed the problems of economic stability and the resultant loss of many jobs, this chapter outlined why some people may not find work even if there are jobs available.

In some cases, people have banded together to form a bargaining unit called a union. In others, there have been discriminatory practices against black and women workers in order to keep them out of the labor force or to keep them at the lowest wages. In the case of unions, it has been a continuing battle by the workers to effectively counter the power of the owners, while black and women workers have had to battle a history of half-truths about their abilities.

While labor has had much legislation both in its favor and detrimental to its interests, the legal history of the labor rights of blacks and women has not been very long. Only in recent times has the legal system recognized their problems and taken some action to assist them.

Finally, Chapter 10 discussed a continuing problem—automation and its effects. Although debate has waned in recent years, the problem continues: how to incorporate technological advance with a concern for the displacement of the workers. In the absence of any effective, federally financed retraining policy, the problem will always be there. Again, it is an example of the solution being known but the absence of will preventing it from being realized.

QUESTIONS AND PROBLEMS

1 What are your opinions of Samuel Gompers' original goals for the labor movement? Do you think he was wise in his direction?

2 Would you join a union in your chosen profession if one was available? Why or why not?

3 Do you feel that automation is a threat to the worker? What would you do if the workers in your union were threatened with automation?

4 Explain the right-to-work law. Are you in favor of it?

5 The strongest unions seem to be in the strongest industries. Is this a coincidence? Give some reasons for this occurrence.

6 Some say that strikes benefit no one. If this is so, why do they occur?

7 Labor's demands have changed slightly in recent years. What is the nature of the change and why has it happened?

8 Why have black workers had so much difficulty in entering unions? Are their problems similar to those of women workers?

BIBLIOGRAPHY

KUHN, ALFRED, *Labor: Institutions and Economics.* 2nd ed. New York: Harcourt Brace Jovanovich, 1967.

MARSHALL., F. RAY, *The Negro and Organized Labor.* New York: Wiley, 1965.

MARSHALL, F. RAY, and BRIGGS, VERNON M., JR., *The Negro and Apprenticeship.* Baltimore: The Johns Hopkins Press, 1967.

SMUTS, ROBERT W., *Women and Work in America.* New York: Columbia University Press, 1959.

11

Poverty
and the Distribution
of Income

We shall soon with the help of God be in sight of the day
when poverty will be banished from this nation.
—Herbert Hoover, 1920

President Johnson's War on Poverty highlighted the dilemma that the richest nation in the world finds itself in. While there is overall affluence, the distribution of income in the United States is not very good. John Kenneth Galbraith has also pointed out the discrepancies between the study of production and the study of income distribution. In his now-famous work *The Affluent Society*, Galbraith stated that we have solved the problems of production—that is, we now can produce with massive efficiency and technological progress—but we have not yet solved the problem of who gets the product.

In this chapter we shall examine the facts of income distribution. The theory of income distribution was discussed in Chapter 7. How is it presently distributed? How has the distribution changed over time? Who is living in poverty, and how much would it cost to eradicate poverty? What are the causes of and cures for poverty?

The Pattern of Income Distribution

The empirical evidence we shall examine below indicates a wide discrepancy between those who have substantial incomes and those who are on the bottom rung of the economic ladder. The study of income distribution, although not a new factor in economic discussions, has taken a new tack in recent years. The neoclassical economists, whom we have discussed in Chapter 7, assumed that the income distribution was given; there was nothing that could or should be done to change it. In recent years it has become apparent, especially after the publication of books like *The Other America* by Michael Harrington and the screening of prominent TV pro-

245

grams such as the now-famous CBS Special "Hunger in America," that the income distribution in the United States should be studied for a possible clue as to how to increase the income of those on the lower end of the income spectrum.

Table 11-1 shows the distribution of income from 1947 to 1969. In spite of all the rhetoric about a trend toward more equal distribution, the pattern of distribution is about the same as it was in 1947. The figures in Table 11-1 exclude unrealized capital gains, capital gains that are not received in cash through the sale of capital assets. Thus, the inequality is greater than the statistics show. For upper-income families, capital gains constitute a sizeable share of their incomes.

TABLE 11-1   Distribution of Before-Tax Family Income

Family units rank	Percent of total income					
	1947	1950	1957	1960	1965	1969
Lowest tenth	1	1	1	1	1	1
Second tenth	3	3	3	3	3	3
Third tenth	4	5	4	5	5	5
Fourth tenth	6	6	6	7	6	6
Fifth tenth	7	8	8	8	8	8
Sixth tenth	9	9	9	9	9	9
Seventh tenth	10	11	11	11	11	11
Eighth tenth	12	13	13	13	13	12
Ninth tenth	15	15	16	16	16	16
Highest tenth	33	29	29	27	28	29

Source: U.S. Department of Commerce, Statistical Abstract of the United States: 1960. Washington, D.C.: Government Printing Office, 1960, p. 318; ibid., 1971, p. 317.

Also, family income does not give an idea of how many people there are in the family nor how many of them are working. Families with more dependents would have less income per person than families with fewer dependents.

The distribution of income among individuals without families is even more unequal than that among families. Table 11-2 shows the distribution of individual income for 1969.

The data we have seen above are often incorporated in a Lorenz curve, named after its inventor, M. O. Lorenz. A Lorenz curve is merely a graphical representation of the percentage of income received compared with the percentage of families receiving it. The income distribution figures for 1969 shown in Table 11-1 are presented as a Lorenz curve in Figure 11-1. The 45-degree line is drawn for reference and represents perfect income equality. The further the Lorenz curve is away from the 45-degree line, the greater the inequality. The Lorenz curve is useful in comparing different countries or in making income distribution comparisons over

TABLE 11-2   The Distribution
of Unrelated Individual
Income, 1969

Individual rank	Percent of total income
Poorest fifth	3.4
Second fifth	7.7
Middle fifth	13.7
Fourth fifth	24.3
Richest fifth	50.9
Richest 5%	21.0

Source: U.S. Department of Commerce,
Statistical Abstract of the United States:
1971. Washington, D.C.: Government
Printing Office, 1971, p. 317.

FIGURE 11-1.   A Lorenz Curve of Income Distribution, 1969

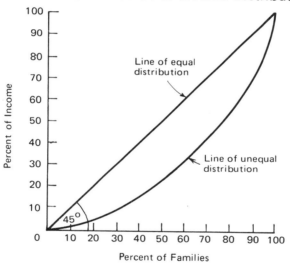

Source: Table 11-1.

time. Also, the effect of progressive taxes or transfer payments could be
shown on such a figure.

The raw figures given above tell us something about the composition
of our nation's income distribution. In order to be more precise about income, in the following section we will define poverty both as an economic
and as a social concept.

Defining Poverty

The official government definition of poverty for a nonfarm family of four is income below $3,968 per year in 1970. This concept is arrived at by considering the things that a family of four needs to buy to sustain itself at a minimum level. Those of you who have earned summer income or have discussed with your parents the problems of raising children know that an income of $3,968 is not very much. For example, it is estimated that for a family of four to live in a medium sized city at a moderate level required $10,664 in 1970. Thus, the minimum or poverty level is less than 40 percent of the moderate level for an individual trying to support himself and three dependents in an urban area. As most of the families living in poverty are concentrated in the cities, the $3,968 figure is certainly on the conservative side.

Defining poverty by an income level, although quantifiable and therefore easy to handle statistically, does not express the entire dimension of being poor. Some have argued that being poor includes a set of conditions that may be economic, physical, and social. To be poor in a modern day society of affluence means most likely that one lives in an urban area, has a large family, is either unemployed or underemployed, or is disabled or over sixty-five years of age. In many cases the same families remain in poverty for generations because children inherit the handicaps and hopelessness of their impoverished parents. Thus, the modern version of poverty is unlike that of the 1930's, which was a temporary condition caused largely by the depression in the American economy.

Being poor in our society unfortunately also means in many cases being without hope. This is the most tragic part, for individuals may adapt to shortages of income, but the hopelessness that the situation implies is a very difficult thing, indeed, to live with.

The dimensions of poverty in the United States are given below in Table 11-3. As the figures show, the percentage of all people who were below the poverty level decreased from 12.8 percent in 1968 to 12.6 percent in 1970. However, the total number of people below the poverty line increased by 133,000 from 1968 to 1970. From 1959 to 1970, the total number of people below the poverty line decreased by approximately 14 million; the percentages of poor in the total population went from 22.4 percent to 12.6. The reduction in poverty is an admirable record for the American economy. During the same period, 1959 to 1970, the number of poor whites decreased from 28 million to 17 million, a reduction from 18.1 percent to 9.9 percent. The reduction in the Negro and other race category was smaller, going from 11 million to 8 million, 56.2 percent to 32.1 percent, from 1959 to 1970. It is important to note that the figures in Table 11-3 are

TABLE 11-3 Persons Below Poverty Level by Race, Selected Years
(in thousands of persons)

Race	1959 Number	Per-cent	1965 Number	Per-cent	1968 Number	Per-cent	1970 Number	Per-cent
White	28,484	18.1	22,496	13.3	17,395	10.0	17,480	9.9
Negro and other races	11,006	56.2	10,689	47.1	7,994	33.5	8,042	32.1
Total	39,490	22.4	33,185	17.3	25,389	12.8	25,522	12.6

Source: U.S. Bureau of the Census, Current Population Reports, Series P-60, No. 77, "Poverty Increases by 1.2 Million in 1970." Washington, D.C.: U.S. Government Printing Office, 1970.

based on income levels figured in dollars of constant purchasing power; thus, the reduction is not due to an inflationary increase in incomes. The alarming thing, of course, is the record of the years 1969 and 1970. While we have been making great headway in reducing the number of people under the poverty level, we suffered a setback in 1970. This reverses the trend of the previous eleven years and adds a new note of discouragement to an otherwise encouraging set of figures.

The above figures were obtained by the Census Bureau by sampling, and there is some statistical error attached to each figure. Although the error is not of tremendous magnitude, it is still important to note that the figures should not be interpreted as significant down to the last digit.

There are several things to bear in mind in assessing the overall situation. For one, as we mentioned above, the official definition of poverty is $3,968 for a nonfarm family of four in a nonfarm occupation. This is hardly a sufficient income for a life free of economic insecurity, and it is ridiculously inadequate for an urban family. Even though the figures show the number of people in bare subsistence income families to be decreasing, one would certainly not say that the American population at the bottom end of the economic ladder has become affluent.

The Causes of Poverty

There is no question that one of the chief causes of poverty is a poor start in life. Horatio Alger optimism notwithstanding, there are very few individuals who can overcome an initial economic disadvantage. Starting life at the lower end of the economic ladder is analogous to a relay race. At the beginning of the second lap, everyone starts not anew, but with a handicap dependent on the speed of the runner of the first lap. Thus, an individual whose parents were not successful in the economic sphere by and large will be unsuccessful himself. One factor involved in this problem is that however widespread the supposed ability of everyone to attend school, educational opportunities are in fact limited to those from families in the middle- and upper-income brackets.

There are a number of reasons for this. It has been shown conclusively in studies on college admissions that individuals from lower-income groups score lower on the standard tests that are given to potential college students. Since college enrollments are limited, the colleges by and large take those students who have a higher probability of staying in college. The series of standard tests is meant to determine this. Thus, students from lower-income groups have greater difficulty in gaining access to higher education. This is especially true for black students. Family income is the variable that comes closest to predicting with accuracy whether a student will remain in college; low incomes are correlated with low achievement in college.

Since young people from poverty communities know that their chances of entering colleges are limited indeed, they quite naturally do not depend on higher education as a means of upward economic mobility. It has often been said that people from poverty communities are shortsighted in their goals. This may be true, particularly when one considers the experience that they have had.

The constant disappointment that confronts people from poverty communities militates against the optimism that is necessary for people to attain higher levels of income. Consider yourself as an example. It requires tremendous optimism and faith in the future of the economy to put aside four years of your earning capabilities and invest in yourself through higher education. If your experience had told you that you would be unsuccessful at this venture or that even if you were successful, the economic rewards would not compensate you for your costs, you would not be so willing to endure these college years.

Thus, it is probably correct to assume that individuals within poverty communities have shortsighted goals. But it is also correct to assume that these goals are well founded on their experience. They know from experience not only that they will probably not have a chance to attend college, but also that they will probably not get a very good job or be able to advance in their work.

Since people from poverty backgrounds are in many cases unskilled, and because they are in many cases discriminated against because of their race, they are usually the last ones hired and the first ones let go in a slowdown in the economy. The unemployment rates for black workers are much higher than the rates for their white counterparts. Not only are the unemployment rates higher, but the irregularity of many jobs and the unrewarding nature of the work combined with very low pay increases the likelihood of people changing jobs. All these factors contribute to keeping the poor poor and aggravate their feelings of helplessness and lack of economic power. Automation has taken the toll of many minority workers. We have already seen how labor unions have discriminated against black workers. The traditional means by which Americans have advanced themselves, by exerting market power over their labor services by means of a union, have oftentimes been closed to those in the poverty community, particularly black workers.

Scholars in recent years have paid particular attention to the psychological aspects with which the black worker approaches his employment. It has been said that if you control a man's mind, you do not have to tell him what to do, for he will react in predictable ways. Thus, the black male has been in effect "convinced" that his work output is inferior to that of his white counterpart, and in many cases he feels that he is not *able* to attain the economic levels of his white counterpart. The recent surge of black nationalism and black pride may change this psychological mind set to some degree. But there is no doubt, at this writing, that the black worker is at a serious disadvantage in entering the income and production stream.

The above factors all may be lumped together in a chain of events called a circular causation of poverty. Once an individual is in the poverty level, all the factors work against his getting out of it. If an individual has a low income, his chances of obtaining higher education are slim indeed; therefore, the chances of advancing by that route are in effect closed to him. It is also true that since his income is low, he cannot afford to set aside years for training in either a skill or a white-collar occupation. No matter what he does, he is largely confined to his present economic situation.

It has often been said by critics of those who are in the poverty community that they are unwilling to work and exert themselves in attaining jobs that will give them some economic security. Anthony Downs, in a statistical work entitled *Who Are the Urban Poor?* examined the numbers and reasons why people were in a poverty situation. He concluded that almost 90 percent of the individuals who were classified as being poor were so for the following reasons: (1) they were disabled; (2) they were children; (3) they were over sixty-five; (4) they were in households headed by females; and (5) the working male was not receiving a large enough wage to raise the family above the poverty category. Only a small percentage of those in poverty were classified as able to work but not employed. Even among this small percentage there were no doubt some whose skills did not meet those required for employment. Also, an individual with a history of cyclical employment becomes discouraged with the job opportunities and does not look as vigorously as he used to for fear of being disappointed.

Thus, it was concluded by Downs that although in many people's minds the most common cause of poverty is an unwillingness to work, this was actually a small factor indeed in the elements that contribute to a low income.

Certainly, as we have seen in Table 11-3, racial factors are an important indicator of who is in poverty. The figures from the Census Bureau revealed that while more whites are in poverty than blacks, a greater percentage of the black population is poor. Not only do blacks suffer a disadvantage in the income they earn, but even though they come to about 12 percent of the population, they control less than .5 percent of the nation's economic assets. In spite of their low economic status, blacks are required to pay taxes and serve in the armed forces on an equal basis with other Americans. In fact, their military participation is generally greater than the average, and black fatalities in Vietnam have come to about 16 percent of the total. Unemployment figures for black workers also run high. It is estimated that unemployment of black workers usually runs about twice the rate of white workers and is more severe in the cities, where it is estimated that 25 percent of black workers are unemployed.

Even if blacks and whites had similar low incomes, the black family is still at a disadvantage. Negro poverty is distinguished from white poverty by five factors. First, the income that both have, even if hypothetically identical, buys less for a poor black family than for a poor white family. It has been verified in many studies that the poor in urban areas, particularly black people, pay more for the same goods and services (especially rent) than middle-class whites do. Second, the blacks tend to be concentrated in areas of high unemployment and thus do not have the geographic access to the jobs. Third, blacks suffer more from changes in governmental programs such as urban renewal, aid to education, agricultural subsidies, manufacturing relocation, and minimum wages. For example, while urban renewal has been lauded by many as a means of clearing the slum areas from the cities, it has resulted, in many cases, in merely relocating blacks to other substandard dwellings. Urban renewal has concentrated on providing parking garages and high-rise, middle-class apartment dwellings, not on building housing for low-income people. And since black families have less mobility because of discriminatory factors, they are unable to relocate as easily in other parts of the city as the comparable white families. Fourth, black families do not benefit as much as white families from governmental transfer payments. Relatively few blacks receive old-age, survivors, and disability insurance. Black families also receive less than a proportionate share of aid to dependent children. Thus, the transfer payments that supposedly provide a floor of income for families with lower than acceptable incomes do not benefit black families much. Fifth, as we have mentioned above, discrimination and low incomes tend to restrict educational opportunities for blacks and consequently restrict them to the economic status that they are in.

The above factors work against families escaping from the poverty level. There are, however, some cures for poverty that have been discussed with increasing vigor in recent years. We shall examine them next.

The Cures for Poverty

Of all the cures for poverty, the one most frequently mentioned is more education. Education is usually thought of in the broadest sense, meaning higher educational opportunities for those youngsters academically inclined and retraining of workers who are, either by automation or cyclical unemployment, out of their jobs.

WHO GOES TO COLLEGE? In spite of the myth that exists in the United States that all those who are capable of going to college somehow end up in institutions of higher learning, the opposite is the case. Figures reveal that individuals from middle- and upper-income families are those who in most cases end up in college and complete the four-year program. Very few youngsters from poor families ever make it to institutions of higher learning and even when they do, their dropout rate is very high. Several factors account for this.

The student from a poor community, although convinced of the economic benefits of higher education, is not at all convinced that he should borrow large sums of money to be able to attend four years of college. Since there are limited numbers of outright grants, and these grants are in many cases restricted to those students who show high academic promise, the youngster with limited apparent promise receives, not a grant to pay for his education, but the opportunity to obtain a loan. Even though a loan may be an economic benefit to a hardheaded businessman, it is a scary proposition for a young person who is not convinced that he can make it through four years of higher education.

Figures released by the Health, Education and Welfare agencies show that in more than two-thirds of the cases, parents finance about 70 percent of their children's college expenses. This means that the family is the primary factor in supplying the wherewithal for a student to attend college. Since young people from poverty communities do not have this economic backing, they are left completely dependent on borrowing sizeable sums to complete their education.

In some cases, low-cost state universities have alleviated the problem. New York State and California have two of the most comprehensive college systems in the United States. Both have as goals the expectation that any resident of the state is free to matriculate at one of the colleges in the state. In fact, this is not the case.

Figures from the California system reveal that it is the middle- and upper-income students who end up at the colleges in the California system.

Since the tax base on which the colleges are financed tends to be regressive, this has resulted in a distribution of income from the less affluent population to the more affluent college students, quite the reverse of what the education programs are supposed to do.

In New York State, the college system has expanded tremendously in the last twelve years, but with the expansion of the State University, the pressure to get into the colleges has increased. Since there are no income quotas for admission to the colleges, those students with higher educational attainments are allowed into the low-cost State University, leaving behind those youngsters from poor families.

Thus, the educational opportunities for the poor are not as available as they may seem. Part of the reason is that enrollments are limited, and the more poorly prepared students are discriminated against. The children of the poor are more likely to have deficient educational backgrounds. But problems exist also on the other side of the education picture, in manpower training.

MANPOWER TRAINING   In recent years there has been a proliferation of programs designed to retrain workers who have skills that are becoming obsolete or do not pay a suitable wage. These manpower programs have largely been less than completely successful. Designed to train people in skills they do not have, the programs must, to be successful, have a student for a considerable length of time. The sad fact is that many workers with families to support cannot allocate a large block of time, with little or no income, to retrain themselves in a different skill. The workers with insufficient income tend to become discouraged with the program and drop out before they have attained the level of skill for which the program is designed. And in many cases, even when the workers have completed the manpower training program, there are no jobs waiting for them.

Even with well-designed manpower training programs, it is difficult for workers in the middle of their lives to pick up another skill. They do not have the flexibility that young people have and sometimes are embarrassed and discouraged by the process of relearning at a stage in their lives when they should be guaranteed steady employment.

The downturn in the economy in the early 1970's has resulted in a tremendous loss of jobs. Even skilled workers with many years of experience have had difficulty maintaining their previous levels of employment. There has been virtually no room in the economy for those workers who, even if completing a manpower training program, are embarking on a different career.

After the summer riots of 1964 and in line with President Johnson's War on Poverty, some businesses, notably the Ford Motor Company, announced that they had begun their own training programs to hire and train those that were called the hard-core unemployed. The program did not last long. The downturn in business in 1969–71 resulted in economic difficulties for the companies. They decided that they could not afford to keep workers on their payrolls when they were only learning and not contributing adequately to the revenue of the companies. One cannot entirely blame the businesses; after all, their chief concern is to make a profit. Some programs must be worked out to benefit corporations, either by tax incentives or by cash payments by the government to businesses to retrain workers and guarantee employment at the end of their training.

TRANSFER PAYMENTS   As we have learned from the discussion in Chapter 2 of national income, transfer payments are payments to individuals who are not engaging in a productive output in the economy. They are designed to accomplish a two-fold purpose. One is to tide an individual over a difficult downturn in his earning power. A second purpose of transfer payments is to act as an automatic stabilizer; they automatically provide a cushion of consumption under which the economy will not fall. Since the 1930's, there have been numerous transfer payments available to workers who have experienced downturns in their employment. The most common transfer payments have been unemployment compensation, welfare benefits, and some aspects of the social security program. Unemployment insurance, as the name implies, accrues only to those who have been employed. If an individual loses his job which he has held for a minimum number of weeks, he is eligible for unemployment payments. He is eligible for such payments only if he has worked, only after the time period has elapsed, and only if he is not subsequently employed. Unemployment payments are designed to be a temporary plug in the gap of income.

Welfare benefits encompass most of the programs that are funded by local governments to provide assistance for those who have limited incomes. Briefly stated, a welfare recipient must be below a certain income level, and in the case of aid to dependent children, the male head of the household must not be present. The welfare program has not been well received by the recipients, the government officials who administer it, or the general public that pays for it indirectly through taxes.

There are a number of criticisms of the prevailing welfare system. It has a paternalistic air about it, and it is often degrading. A person on welfare, especially in the program of aid to dependent children, is subjected to a series of investigations by a case worker to assure the agency that the requirements of welfare recipients still apply. Another problem is the cost of administration. Since the program is supposedly designed to help individuals, it requires an enormous administrative staff. The overhead costs of the welfare program eat up so much of the benefits that too little is left over to finance the individuals.

Further criticism of the welfare program is the fact that the benefits vary greatly from state to state. New York State, for example, has attracted numerous people from lower-income rural areas in the southern states where welfare benefits are lower. Among the reasons they have migrated to New York State is the fact that they feel they will be economically better off with the higher welfare payments that will accrue to them. Thus, the differences in welfare benefits have produced migration patterns that, although alleviating the problems of the rural southern states, has intensified the problems of the large northern cities.

President Nixon has proposed a plan to combine the welfare system with a job-mandated program. Under his proposal a family of four would receive a minimum allotment of $2,200. This allotment, however, would exclude the family from food stamps. Food stamps are a method of providing a family with greater purchasing power for food. A family pays a fraction of the total face value for stamps that can be used to purchase food. Nixon's proposal also requires that able-bodied welfare adults without school-age children sign up for employment or lose the welfare allotment. If there are no private jobs available for such able-bodied adults, they would move into public service jobs at a minimum of $1.20 per hour. Under this plan, the federal government would pay the first full year's costs of the worker's public service employment. The states would then pick up 25 percent of the second year's cost and 50 percent of the worker's salary the third year.

Whether Nixon's proposal is any different than previous welfare programs and whether it will work remain to be seen. From the figures given above, it does not appear that the recipient will be any better off monetarily under the new plan.

One of the difficulties in trying to eliminate poverty through a work incentive program has been the lack of day-care centers for children of working mothers. It is estimated that there are more than 11.6 million working mothers in the country today. More than 4 million of these have children under six years old. However, there is only room for 640,000 children in licensed day-care centers, and more than one-third of them are privately run. The problem is especially crucial for poverty people, even if the husband is able to work. If both husband and wife were able to work, the combined family income might be enough to get them above the lower edge of the poverty line. Of course, if the husband is either disabled or otherwise not around to contribute to the economic welfare of the family, then the question of day-care centers becomes even more crucial. A work incentive plan for people below the poverty line makes little sense without adequate day-care centers for the children involved.

Another solution to the welfare system is the negative income tax.

NEGATIVE INCOME TAX The negative income tax idea is usually attributed to Milton Friedman. Friedman's basic hypothesis is that the welfare system has not worked and that the negative income tax would be a viable alternative. The negative income tax, as the name implies, operates on the same principle as the income tax, except in reverse. It is predicated on the fact that if an individual does not reach a certain income in a given year, the government will pay money to him to make up the difference between his guaranteed income and the actual income he receives. The most common proposals seek to provide incentives to work and to earn money. Supposedly this could be accomplished by paying people a subsidy in order to bring their income up. Even if an individual worked, the family would be allowed to keep a percentage of the subsidy, thus increasing their income and encouraging work.

The taxation system, although progressive, does not benefit individuals on the lower end of the income scale. For example, if a father of three children makes $2,000 in a given year, he pays no income tax. He claims five deductions and a total deduction from his income tax of five times $675, or $3,375. Although he pays no income tax, he really does not benefit from the fact that his deductions outrun his income. If he made $3,375, he would still pay no income tax; thus the individual making $2,000 is penalized because he cannot take advantage of the tax rates.

The administration of the negative income tax would be far simpler than administering the present welfare system. Even more important is the fact that the negative income tax is predicated on the idea that the sole criterion for help is a lack of income. It avoids all of the complications that the welfare system has built in. For example, the negative income tax is applicable whether the father is home with his family or not.

Moreover, incentive plans can be built into the negative income tax. For example, if an individual earns more than the minimum guaranteed income, he would be allowed to keep a percentage of the extra amount that he earns. This would encourage people to obtain employment in order to increase their income. Under the welfare system, if an individual obtains employment and income, he suffers the loss of his welfare benefits. This discourages him, of course, from finding supplements to his welfare check.

All the cures of poverty that we have mentioned in this section, namely educational opportunities, manpower training, transfer payments, and the negative income tax will work only as long as the economy is rolling at a full employment level. If the economy dips below full employment, as it has in the most recent years, those individuals just above the poverty line slip a notch into the poverty area. Thus, a full employment economy is an absolute necessity if any inroads are to be made into the problem of people living in chronic poverty. A full employment economy will not solve all the problems, but it will absorb many of the individuals who are able to acquire a skill.

The argument over who is qualified to work becomes academic when the economy is running at a full employment clip. If businesses need more workers than are available, they will make efforts to train workers regardless of their qualifications. If they have very few jobs available, they of course become very selective in choosing individuals for the spots. Our nation has had a chronic shortage of jobs. We have examined the problem in terms of the qualifications of the individuals who are looking for the jobs. But this is not always the problem. The problem in many cases has been the sluggishness of our economy in not providing sufficient numbers of jobs for the people who can fill them.

As shown by President Nixon's message on welfare reform, our social system is permeated with the idea, for better or for worse, of work as a requirement for a subsistence level of income. But there have been demands at various times in our history for equality of income. Most economists do not feel that inequalities of income are necessarily bad in themselves; it depends on the gap between the haves and have-nots. Utopian demands for equal incomes are predicated on the idea that human motivation should not revolve around the necessity to have more material goods than one's neighbor. However admirable this idea may be, most social scientists concede that certain differences will be inevitable between individuals. What concerns those who are interested in providing adequate incomes for poor people is that the lower end, or the floor of incomes, be set at such a level to allow everyone a respectable level of living. Thus, if there were no one in poverty there still could be some people who make, by their own ingenuity and efforts, a large income. As long as those at the lower end of the economic ladder are provided with sufficient incomes to give their lives dignity, then the income gaps between people become less important. Moderate-income differentials may provide a necessary stimulus to high-level performance.

Summary

Of all the problems you will study in this book, none is more serious than poverty. This chapter outlined the blueprint of poverty—the unchanging pattern of income distribution. As we have seen, the lack of economic resources often means a lack of hope; the lack of hope often condemns yet another generation to poverty.

Poverty continues in spite of much apparent effort to alleviate it. While more students are attending college, the ones who succeed are generally not from poor families. While manpower training receives much publicity, there is no effective means of insuring attendance and often no jobs at the end of the training.

Transfer payments, such as unemployment insurance and welfare benefits, remain the most frequent cure for poverty. While every state has them, few people are satisfied with them. Those who receive transfer payments find them inadequate; those who pay them feel overburdened. The welfare system is top-heavy with administration, and the overhead costs are too great for the little effective aid it provides.

The negative income tax is the one bright hope in the struggle to abolish poverty. Cash grants to individuals based on their need seem to be the simplest and most effective way to eliminate poverty. Whether the country is willing to finance such a system to the amount required remains to be seen.

QUESTIONS AND PROBLEMS

1 Do you agree with John Kenneth Galbraith that we have solved our production problems but not our distribution problems?

2 Why is the median income used in income statistics?

3 Do the income figures in this chapter indicate that poverty is being eradicated? Do you agree that the definition of poverty should be based on an income figure? Why or why not?

4 What is the difference between income and wealth?

5 List some of the reasons why you are attending college. If you had to finance your entire education by borrowing, would you stay in college?

6 Why is black poverty different from white poverty?

7 Has there been an urban renewal project in your hometown? Has it been successful in increasing available housing?

8 List some of the reasons why manpower training programs have not been successful. What would you do to change this?

9 Do you favor a negative income tax? Why or why not?

BIBLIOGRAPHY

FRIEDMAN, MILTON, *Capitalism and Freedom*. Chicago: University of Chicago Press, 1962.

HARRINGTON, MICHAEL, *The Other America: Poverty in the United States*. New York: Macmillan, 1962.

MILLER, HERMAN P., ed., *Poverty American Style*. Belmont, Calif.: Wadsworth, 1966.

12

Urban
Problems

> Any city, however small, is in fact divided into two, one
> the city of the poor, the other of the rich; these are at
> war with one another.
>
> —*Plato*

Living in cities is often not pleasant. Indeed, for inner city residents in our largest cities it can be hazardous. Prevented from obtaining better housing elsewhere because of economic or social segregation, the inner city resident fights a daily battle to keep alive. Even when "slum clearance" projects are initiated, the results are not much different from the previous situation. For example, in a large slum clearance project in St. Louis the tenants of the new housing complex were asked to list their grievances. They complained of broken glass and trash, dangerous elevators, rats and cockroaches in the buildings, nonresidents urinating in the halls, constant violence and the threat of violence. These complaints were not of century-old buildings, even though they have similar problems, but of a project hailed by city planners and architects as a breakthrough in urban residences. The above complaints are all too common in many of our cities. Plagued by a shortage of housing and recreation areas, the cities have little revenue to solve these explosive problems.

This chapter will highlight some of the reasons why cities have fallen into such despair. The solutions all involve massive infusions of money, jobs, and imaginative social programs—not easy solutions for such difficult problems.

Migration, Urbanization, and Overcrowding

In order to know the sources of the problem, one has to know what the problem is. It can be stated simply: there are too many people in too small an area with too little housing, and too little financial resources to alleviate their situation. One has to look at urban areas as centers and locations of people. One can also view urban areas in terms of transportation systems, economic systems, social clusters of people, and political systems. But however appealing the systems approach, one comes back to the fact that urban areas involve people.

The figures for urban population growth reveal some startling developments. As Table 12-1 shows, the standard metropolitan statistical areas (the cities and suburbs) have grown at a 16.5 percent rate from 1960 to 1970. While there has been some growth in the central cities (6.4 percent), most of the increase in population has occurred in the suburbs (26.7 percent). The white population, moreover, has migrated out of the central cities, and the black population has moved in. Thus, the growth of the metropolitan areas can be attributed to blacks moving into the inner city and whites migrating to the suburbs.

As a further development, the urban population in the United States grew from less than 46 percent of the total population in 1910 to more than

TABLE 12-1   Population by Residence and Race 1960 to 1970

Residence and race	Population (in thousands) 1960	1970	Percent change 1960–1970
Total population:			
Standard metropolitan statistical areas	119,595	139,387	16.5
Central cities	59,964	63,816	6.4
Outside central cities	59,631	75,570	26.7
Nonmetropolitan areas	59,728	63,798	6.8
Total	179,323	203,184	13.3
White population:			
Standard metropolitan statistical areas	105,180	120,424	14.5
Central cities	49,440	48,796	−1.3
Outside central cities	55,741	71,628	28.5
Nonmetropolitan areas	53,652	57,189	6.6
Total	158,832	177,612	11.8
Negro population:			
Standard metropolitan statistical areas	12,710	16,786	32.1
Central cities	9,950	13,097	31.6
Outside central cities	2,760	3,689	33.7
Nonmetropolitan areas	6,083	5,887	− 3.2
Total	18,793	22,673	20.6

Source: U.S. Department of Commerce, Statistical Abstract of the United States: 1971. Washington, D.C.: Government Printing Office, 1971, p. 16.

70 percent in 1968. There were 85 million more people living in urban areas in 1968 than in 1910, while the nonurban population for the same time period had increased by only 20 million. If the increase were distributed among the fifty states on a more or less even basis, then the problem would not be as great as it is. The fact is, however, that in eighteen states more than 70 percent of the population lives in areas classified as urban. Furthermore, 40 percent of the urban population live in cities that have more than 100,000 people.

There are economic explanations for these figures. Since the cities are cultural and employment centers, we expect them to have large numbers of people. Remember the example of larger firms operating with greater and greater efficiency as they grow; similarly, cities can achieve economies of scale by being larger. The same police and fire departments, sanitation system, and other service departments could service a city of 100,000 almost as easily as it could one of 80,000. But also like large firms, cities may achieve diseconomies of scale; they may go beyond the point where the cost schedule is a minimum and may, in fact, be on the upward side of the average cost picture. Many cities are in this situation. They have, from both an economic and social point of view, too many people in too small a space for the resources that the city can command.

How have the cities grown? Have they increased in population merely as a result of the families living within cities producing more children? Or have they grown as a result of migration from rural to urban areas?

In the older urban areas of New York, Chicago, Detroit, Philadelphia, St. Louis, Baltimore, Cleveland, and Minneapolis, 75 percent of the growth for the period from 1960 to 1967 was accounted for by the excess of births over deaths. In the newer cities, such as the California cities, Houston, Dallas, Miami, Phoenix, and Atlanta, the increase in population is largely accounted for by a net migration of population into the cities. In addition, the older cities have in many cases experienced a migration of some residents outward. Why do people migrate? What compels people to move to or away from urban areas?

In the case of the newer cities, the migration patterns have obviously been accounted for by younger people moving to the urban areas in search of new and better jobs. It is most often younger people who move, largely because they have the social and economic flexibility to do so. In the older cities, the net migration outward is accounted for by families moving to suburban locations. Thus, in the older cities the jobs remain within the city while the people move outward. The reasons for the exodus of people from urban areas to the suburbs will be examined below. What remains in the older cities is a population of either very wealthy people who can afford the better living areas in the city or those on the lower end of the economic scale who cannot afford to move to the suburbs. The middle class in many cities has almost disappeared.

Equally important to the size of a city's population is the race, age, and ethnic distribution of people within the city. The figures for the decade 1950 to 1960 reveal rather dramatically the migration pattern of blacks and other races from southern to northern and western states. California, for example, received the greatest number of blacks and other minority groups (354,000), while Mississippi lost the greatest number of blacks and other minority groups (323,000).

The cities, particularly those in the northern and western states, are the net recipients of black citizens largely from rural areas in the south, while the older cities have been losing white middle-class citizens to the suburbs. One should not be surprised by this development. Many rural blacks have migrated to the northern and western cities in search of better job opportunities. As with all migration patterns, families and friends follow those who have already established themselves. Some of the clustering of black citizens in urban areas may be accounted for by the fact that people feel more comfortable with people from their own racial background. Of course, we must not overlook the fact that discriminatory factors largely prohibit blacks from living in many of the suburbs; thus, clustering by choice is not the only reason for the large migration of black people to specific areas within the city.

The migration patterns plus the lack of housing within the central cities have intensified the overcrowding of the cities. Overcrowding simply means too many people in too small an area. Due to the discriminatory housing patterns and the migratory patterns mentioned above, blacks and other migrants have been largely confined to geographic clusters within the cities. This has resulted in overcrowding in certain areas within the cities, but not in all areas. Since the inner city is composed largely of older multilevel dwellings, the only economic use of such dwellings is to carve out apartments, usually substandard, for people with large families.

Thus, the economic effect of attracting people to the cities and the subsequent migration of other people from the cities is a localized overcrowded condition. Congestion is exaggerated by the fact that those in the suburbs commute back to their work in the cities. The transportation systems are overcrowded with many people who are not residents of the city. The people from outside who travel to the commercial districts do not, in many cases, pay a fair share for the transportation systems that they use, the social facilities that they require, and the economic burden that they place on the city. The factors mentioned above all contribute to a decline in the central cities of the United States, not only in the level of services that they provide, but also in the amount of revenue available to improve the situation.

Decline of the Central Cities

THE PROBLEMS OF HOUSING   The substantial economic and social decline in the central cities is especially acute in the area of housing. The National Commission on Urban Problems has found that in the central cities of the largest metropolitan areas, 23 percent of the land area was a specifically defined poverty area. Within these poverty areas were located 76 percent of a city's substandard housing units, 54 percent of its overcrowded units, 45 percent of its vacant housing units, 41 percent of the units in structures over twenty years old, 44 percent of the renter-occupied units, but only 19 percent of the owner-occupied units in the central cities. The defined poverty areas furthermore accounted for 79 percent of all the central city housing units occupied by blacks and other nonwhites. Not only were the poverty areas found to be lacking in almost all factors of adequate housing, but they also were found to have a much higher housing density than comparable areas in other parts of the cities. For example, in 1960 the poverty areas had 3,071 housing units per square mile, or 64 percent more than the 1,874 per square mile average for the other parts of the cities. The poverty community tends to be located in a specific geographic area, one that is characterized by a large number of substandard dwellings and high housing density.

The evidence is shocking, compounded by the fact that it is a common belief among many people that the government has been actively promoting new city housing. One is surprised to find such a dismal record in providing basic housing for many of our citizens. What then, we ask, has been the purpose of the Federal Housing Administration? The Federal Housing Administration (FHA) has contributed to housing in the suburbs rather than in the cities. Under the terms of an FHA contract, a homeowner gets a lower rate of interest than he would under competitive conditions. The reason the rate is lower is that the government guarantees payment of the loan should the borrower default. The FHA loans have helped those who are buying homes in suburban areas, but has rarely if ever touched the housing shortage problem in the central cities. Since buyers need a substantial down payment to acquire a house, and since racial discrimination has prohibited many blacks, even when they can afford it, from buying in the suburbs, the FHA loans have, in fact, tended to exaggerate the problems rather than alleviate them.

Other programs such as urban renewal have not been successful in improving the situation either. Urban renewal is a joint venture of the cities and the federal government. An individual developer buys land in the city, demolishes the existing buildings, and erects either housing, parking garages, or commercial enterprises in their place. Much of the project development costs are paid for by the federal government, but the primary financing is provided by the private developer who buys the land, develops it, and then resells it. Since the private developer is naturally interested in making a profit and since most urban renewal agencies are excessively influenced by commercial interests, urban renewal projects have tended to reduce housing rather than to increase it, by tearing down unprofitable substandard housing and replacing it with commercial buildings. Urban renewal projects have made the problem of housing shortages worse rather than better and have forced many blacks to move into the remaining neighborhoods that were already overcrowded. When an urban renewal project does contain a housing provision, it provides for middle- or high-income housing, thereby eliminating many units for the people who need housing in the central cities.

A similar and related difficulty exists in the area of education.

THE PROBLEMS OF EDUCATION Education is a critical part of our nation's economic and social life. If individuals with low incomes could be assured an adequate education, they would enter the labor force at a later date with a higher earning capacity. Such is not the case, however, for most residents in the central cities. Studies have shown that 31 percent of the children who completed ninth grade in the big cities failed to receive their high school diplomas as against 24 percent nationally. At least 6 percent of the children who start fifth grade in the big cities never start tenth grade. The figures for unemployment bear out the importance of education. The rate of urban unemployment for male high school dropouts sixteen to twenty-one years of age is 15 percentage points higher than the rate for high school graduates.

The pattern of education is clear. Youngsters in the central cities, by and large, have less likelihood of completing high school and, therefore, much less chance of obtaining high paying jobs or higher education than their counterparts in the suburban areas. Why is the situation so bad in urban education? The answer is complex. In some cases, the facilities of urban educational institutions are much worse than those in the suburbs. But facilities alone do not make the difference. Much of the problem for the urban dwellers lies in the fact that they do not have complete control of their school systems. In addition, the teachers in many of the urban schools do not insist on educational standards that they would require in suburban schools.

In many cases the problems also are those of misplaced emphasis. In urban schools the emphasis is primarily on control rather than on learning. School administrators perceive their role as warden and policeman rather than as intellectual stimulator. Constantly afraid of social unrest, the urban school authorities react with an inordinate control system that does nothing for the intellectual purposes of the school.

One recent answer to the problems of urban schools has been the voucher system. Since all public schools are financed through taxation, the lack of private management and ownership leads to a lack of incentive for a school to improve its output, the educational product that it produces. The only pressure on a school system to improve is the collective pressure of the citizens whom the school affects. The voucher system now being tried would give the student's family a credit of money equal to the average per pupil cost and thus allow people to choose the school to which they want to send their children. The school chosen would receive the voucher for the specific amount of the per pupil cost, which it would then submit to the federal government to be paid.

The voucher system introduces an element of personal choice in the educational system. A student's family could be expected to shop around to find the school that best met his educational needs. Schools likewise could be expected to prove their educational value or suffer the consequences of no revenue.

Critics of the voucher system have argued that this would exaggerate the differences in schools. As soon as the schools with reputations for achievement were filled, the schools with the greatest number of problems would again be left with the smallest amount of revenue. The question that remains is whether a different arrangement between buyer and seller will improve the educational output of the school system. There is no doubt that improvement is needed. The solutions, however, are not easy.

In addition to the problems of housing and education, the difficulty of moving within the city via a transportation system is also important.

THE PROBLEMS OF TRANSPORTATION Problems of housing and education are interrelated with the problems of transportation. It is the transportation systems, primarily the development of roads and mass transportation, that have accelerated the growth of the suburbs and consequently the decline of the inner cities. Thus, a modern city in the United States finds itself in a peculiar dilemma: it is overloaded with people, while it is financially almost bankrupt.

The transportation problem involves not only the problem of getting people to and from the suburbs to their jobs, but also the problem of getting people within the city to their work. Since the automobile and other transportation systems have become so prominent in the last fifty years, the individual has been separated by a great geographic distance from his job. In addition to the obvious benefits of mobility, the automobile has created many new problems. The automobile as a means of urban transportation has contributed to congestion, both by using up available road space and by eating up scarce urban real estate for parking and storage. In addition, the automobile has interfered with pedestrian flow and has been primarily responsible for the increasing air pollution in major cities. The automobile has also largely been responsible for the scattering of residences and the dispersion of individuals from their business areas to their residential areas. The possible alternatives to this congestion caused by the automobile are the following: (1) public planners could hope for a diminishing rate of automobile purchases, thus relieving the congestion by private voluntary means; (2) they could develop more efficient mass transportation systems to provide an alternative for automobile travel; or (3) they could redesign the cities so that residential and business establishments were closer together, thereby ruling out long trips for workers. The first alternative is obviously impractical, since the projections for the number of automobiles sold is increasing every year. The second is possible and may be the alternative that most public planners will take. The third would be an ideal long-run solution, but the problems that it presents in the short run are enormous.

The problems created by automobiles have been aggravated by the reduction of rail passenger service. On a nationwide scale, there has been a change in the rail network system. In 1971 a new rail system called Amtrak was instituted. The system is a quasi-governmental agency; that is, it is privately run but it is backed and heavily regulated by the government. In effect, it makes the railroad system a public utility. Since the railroad system has a high ratio of fixed to variable costs, it has all the characteristics of a public utility. The new system has reduced the number of trains available on certain routes and has reduced passenger travel, thereby trying to make the remaining trains more efficient.

Urban transportation systems not only suffer from the problem of high fixed costs in relation to variable costs, but also from the problem of a bimodal load on the system. The bimodal load means that the system is heavily burdened with riders only at two times during the day. When the commuters are entering the city and when city residents are going to work, between the hours of 7 and 10 A.M., the transportation system is used to capacity; the same holds true again when people are returning home from 4 to 7 P.M. In between, the use of the system is far below capacity. We know from our previous analysis that high fixed costs mean that the system is accumulating costs regardless of the use. Thus, the bimodal peak usage exaggerates the problem that is present in the urban transit system.

Suburbanization, Zoning, and Transportation

Two factors that we have already mentioned in our discussion of the problems of the central cities are chiefly responsible for accelerating the growth of suburban areas surrounding our major cities. The increase in suburban housing in the decade from 1950 to 1960 through the work of developers and the Federal Housing Administration who provided cheap mortgages for individuals who could qualify offered a pleasing alternative to overcrowded city life. The massive program of road building, also in the 1950's, provided a means of transportation for those suburban dwellers who worked in the city. These two factors, in addition to the fear of violence generated by poverty and racism in the central cities, explain the growth of the suburbs in the 1950's and 1960's. The growth has proceeded so far that one sees around every major city in the United States a cluster of suburban areas all feeding on the cultural and economic life of the city.

Not only do the suburban areas act as a drain on the resources of the city, but they also strain the transportation systems to the limit. In addition, the suburbs do not provide available housing for very many lower-middle income people. This is largely because of the zoning laws that are stringently applied in areas surrounding our cities.

An extreme example is the wealthy northern New Jersey community of Far Hills. It has a ten-acre zoning requirement, meaning that no one-family house may be built on less than ten acres of land. This, of course, makes the cost of housing prohibitively high and effectively excludes most people of lower income who might wish to move there from the city. More commonly, as in Monmouth County, New Jersey, the land is zoned for at least one-acre housing plots. In addition, the local building codes in the county require at least 1200 feet of floor space, assuring that virtually every new home will cost more than $30,000. The resulting segregation of people by income brackets also creates problems in education.

Research reports on education have found that most students throughout the country attend primary and secondary schools that are largely segregated racially. What was always assumed to be the case in the South has also proved to be the case in the northern cities. Most of the suburbs surrounding the northern and western cities are primarily white, and therefore their schools have an overwhelming white population. Segregation is, of course, one of the reasons why the suburbs have been so attractive to many people who wish to avoid the problems of the cities.

The differences in real estate taxes between the cities and the suburbs have also accounted for some of the migration to suburbia. In most suburbs the real estate taxes are lower than the taxes on a comparable property in the city. Since the suburbs do not have, in many cases, sewers or large police forces, this lower level of services results in less of a burden to the public sector. Also in the suburbs, since the density tends to be less than in the urban areas, it costs less to lay roads, build schools, and otherwise make improvements in the existing structures. Consequently, the cities are at a double disadvantage. On the one hand, it costs them more to keep up roads, highways, educational services; and on the other hand, they are suffering a loss of income as a result of people moving away from the central city. As more buildings are abandoned in the central city and the cost of providing services goes up, the tax rate on the existing buildings must go up. Thus, the central cities are at a further disadvantage compared with the suburbs. It is a spiral that is difficult to break. As people and industries migrate from the central city, the increased tax burden on those that remain forces more people and industries to move out, and so on.

One solution to the differences between the level of services provided by the city and the suburbs that has been mentioned in recent years is a switch to a metropolitan government. The process of making a metropolitan government merely means erasing the boundaries between cities and surrounding counties and towns. This would eliminate the problem of city services that are used by both residents of the cities and the suburbs being paid for only by city residents. A metropolitan government would consist of one governmental unit for the whole metropolitan area so that all citizens in the area would be forced to pay a share of the costs of the city.

One advantage of the plan is that it relieves some of the financial problems of the city government by forcing those outside the city to pay for a share of the costs. Another advantage is that it simplifies the governmental structure and makes one unit out of many. The commensurate disadvantage is that it erases boundary lines that in many cases have been historically established and grew up to differentiate a cultural center from an outlying district. Another disadvantage is in terms of the political power structure. In many major cities, black citizens now comprise a substantial part of the voting electorate. With this comes a voice in the political processes. If a metropolitan government were instituted, the rising political power of the black citizens in the city would be diluted. But for the same reasons, the political power of the white suburbs would also decrease.

Seen from the eyes of the white suburbanite, metropolitan government has nothing to recommend it. He gets an increased tax burden as a result of the inefficiencies of the city. He also has to pay for things that he was getting for nothing before, and he loses political power.

A modified form of metropolitan government provides that the counties share with the cities, on a prorated basis, certain service functions. While still maintaining the separate governmental units, the system would allow a sharing of equipment and services to effect economies of scale. Instead of separate police, fire, and snow removal and road maintenance departments, there would be combined county departments paid for by the people in the county, whether in the city or the outlying districts.

A classic example of a metropolitan form of government is in metropolitan Toronto. There they have erased the boundary line between city and county and, in effect, have one governmental unit. Similar experiments have been tried in Duval County, Florida, where Jacksonville is situated.

Metropolitan government would be a stop-gap measure to gain time in the relief for cities. Another possibility is for the cities to receive revenue from the federal government. This would involve an economic transfer of resources collected by the federal government to the state and local governments. The concept is called revenue sharing.

Federal Revenue Sharing with State and Local Governments

There is no doubt that the cities need financial relief. While the costs of government on all levels have gone up, the costs of city governments have gone up the most. As we have mentioned above, it costs a city government much more to lay a comparable length of road, to educate pupils in the schools, and to otherwise provide the same services as county and other forms of government provide. The reason city government is so costly is the urban density.

From the Second World War through 1967, for example, local governments, including cities, increased their tax collections 499 percent, but city costs have climbed nearly 10 percent faster. Since 1967 there have been increased demands for unionization of police and firemen and for improvements in the school and transportation systems. In fact, it has been estimated that the deficit of city finances from 1967 to 1977 would be $262 billion. The National League of Cities has estimated this as the gap between what the cities need to spend and what they can expect to get in the form of revenue. The increase in costs that cities are facing combined with their inability to finance them is creating an impasse.

Cities are unable to finance themselves for two reasons. First, cities are subject to the state government, and the states have seen fit to limit the cities' taxing powers; this is due partly to the states not wanting the cities to take from the same tax sources the states depend on for their support. There is also, among state legislators, a distrust of cities and a lack of understanding of the cities' basic problems. Cities are limited in that they may raise taxes only by property taxes or, in some cases, sales taxes. State statutes determine how much property tax they may collect. The state limit is often a percentage of the assessed valuation of the total property of the city. Since a sales tax is a regressive tax and is not at all popular, it is used by cities as a last resort to raise more revenue. Because states set the fiscal standards that cities must meet, states must take some leadership in alleviating some of the bind that the cities find themselves in.

Another reason cities cannot finance themselves is that they often compete with other local government units in trying to attract businesses. They offer low-tax incentives to induce businesses to locate in their geographic region. While this may do something to attract business, it certainly does nothing to alleviate the financial problem of the city. In addition to a loss in revenue as a result of such tax abatement given by the city, those employees brought in by the business buy houses in the suburbs and use the services that the city must provide through tax revenue from other people. To be sure, businesses bring in people who spend money in local retail establishments. But the main source of revenue, the income tax, does not usually go to the cities but goes instead to the federal or state government.

There have been many aid formulas used in the past to alleviate the fiscal plight of the cities. Some of these are unconditional or block grants, conditional grants and aids, and federal grants and aids for specific programs to cities. The block grant-in-aid is a grant with no strings attached. A conditional grant requires the city to raise part of the money for a specific program. Federal government grants are also available to help the financing of schools, highways, and other services. All of these have been insufficient to meet the needs of the cities.

Not only have the cities been receiving a very small amount through grants and aids from the federal and state governments, but they have been receiving less than the suburbs. Thus, the cities are in a double bind; their costs are greater than the suburbs', and they are receiving less per capita in aid than the surrounding districts. One way out of this dilemma is for the federal government to share its revenues with the state and local governments. There are many advantages to this plan.

Since the federal government has as its main taxing power the income tax, its tax revenue rises more than the increase in gross national product. This is due to the progressive nature of the income tax. Therefore, as GNP rises, the federal government receives a windfall in terms of the revenues that the new GNP generates. As we have seen earlier, the cost of collecting the federal income tax is very low. For these reasons, it has been thought that the federal government could allocate part of its tax revenue to the cities and states. This would provide the cities with a dependable source of income that would grow yearly with the increases in GNP, thus alleviating the need for a heavy dependence on the property tax.

One criticism of federal revenue sharing has been that it would be very costly, since the tax revenue would have to go from people in the city to the federal government and then be rebated back to the city government itself. Is this criticism well founded? Even allowing for the increased governmental machinery that would be necessary to administer this program, most economists feel that it still would be a cheaper and more reliable source of revenue than the dependence on the property tax. Since the cost of collecting the income tax is so low, the total cost of sending part of the money back to the city governments would not be an insurmountable barrier for the plan.

Another disadvantage of federal revenue sharing is that the funds can come with no strings attached. Such grants allow local governments to continue along the same path that they have been traveling. If a local government is not solving the needs of the poor, one would not expect that with a federal government no-strings-attached grant the situation would become any better.

Another serious question about federal revenue sharing is whether the federal government has any revenue to share. Economists have used the term *fiscal drag* to describe a situation in which the federal government takes in more and more taxes each year as a result of the growth in GNP without putting money back into the economy. The idea is that if the increment each year is not put back into the economy the economy would slow up. One solution for fiscal drag is to take the increment and give it back to the states and cities to help solve their problems. Thus, federal revenue sharing would accomplish two goals: it would relieve the financial pressures that are on the cities and states; and it would provide a method of putting back funds into the economy to promote prosperity and growth. The only problem with the concept of fiscal drag is that the needs of the federal government have been increasing more rapidly than the revenue to support such needs. The tremendous increase in federal government spending largely due to the Vietnam war and an expansion of public welfare programs has thrown into serious question whether the federal government has any excess revenue to share with the states. Even with the end of the war in Vietnam, there is some question whether the military budget could be effectively pruned, since the generals and admirals have a long list of priorities that they consider to be essential and that have been postponed as a result of the war.

There is some question, then, as to whether federal revenue sharing would improve the plight of the cities. No doubt, if enough money could be effectively withdrawn from the federal till, some of the financial problems of the cities could be alleviated. However, there needs to be a general restructuring and rethinking of what cities are supposed to do, how well they are doing it, and what should be done to improve them. We have too long separated man's working function from where he lives. We have essentially envisioned the United States as being an open system, where resources were unlimited and problems would basically take care of themselves. No longer do we have such a luxury.

Summary

The problems we have studied so far (pollution, sporadic employment, poverty) all seem to fall heaviest on urban dwellers. The problems of facing a harsh economic system are compounded when one lives in overcrowded conditions.

We have seen in Chapter 11 and again in Chapter 12 how harsh these conditions can be. Inadequate housing, poor educational systems, and archaic transportation all contribute to make the urban dweller's life very difficult.

To add to these problems, there is a decreasing amount of tax revenues available to municipal governments. Businesses are moving to the suburbs. Middle-income individuals are also vacating the cities and moving to the surrounding areas.

The federal government has assisted this outward migration by the

Federal Housing Administration's policy of low-interest mortgages. While the affluent taxpayers have been moving out, they have been replaced by low-income, displaced, marginal farmers and farm workers. Thus, the cities are faced with the most difficult of problems without the resources to adequately solve them.

One solution to these problems is federal revenue sharing, by which the federal government would collect the revenue through its income tax system and distribute it to the states and cities. This could provide some relief to the hard-pressed urban areas.

QUESTIONS AND PROBLEMS

1   Discuss some of the sources of the problems that beset our cities.

2   Why do the cities not have the financial resources to solve their problems?

3   Mention some factors that have contributed to the growth of the suburbs. How has the federal government contributed?

4   Why are the cities overcrowded? What can be done about this?

5   Would you as an elementary or secondary school student have favored a voucher payment system for education? Why or why not?

6   Give some arguments in favor of strict zoning laws. Whom do such laws benefit?

7   Discuss some of the problems inherent in a revenue sharing plan. Should the federal government remit revenues directly to cities or go through state governments?

8   What do economists mean by the term *fiscal drag*? How does it apply to revenue sharing?

BIBLIOGRAPHY

Downs, Anthony, *Who Are the Urban Poor?* New York: Committee for Economic Development, 1968.

Haddad, William F., and Pugh, G. Douglas, eds., *Black Economic Development*. Englewood Cliffs: Prentice-Hall, 1969.

Leahy, William H., McKee, David L., and Dean, Robert D., eds., *Urban Economics*. New York: The Free Press, 1970.

Tabb, William K., *The Political Economy of the Black Ghetto*. New York: Norton, 1970.

13

Problems
of Population

One of the greatest national assets of Chile, perhaps the
greatest asset, is its high death rate.

—*William Vogt*

Is it true that the "population explosion" is the cause of most of our troubles? Is this the reason why we suffer increasingly from soil erosion, excessive depletion of our natural resources, pollution of our environment, and overcrowding? Will our souls and spirits sicken amidst a widening tangle of concrete highways, ever taller buildings that pierce the clouds, more and more dust and dirt that obscure the sun, and rising levels of noise that may drive us mad before we gain a respite through deafness? Will zero population growth cure these social ills, or at least prevent their becoming worse? An understanding of the problems of population will aid us in answering these questions.

World population has been growing at a rate that has become frightening. Even a constant rate of growth adds ever larger numbers of people each year as the population expands; a 2 percent annual increase with a population of 3.5 billion people means adding 70 million people each year, which is the rate at which world population is now increasing. This means the population will double in about thirty-six years.

Table 13-1 shows the trend of world population since 1650. Notice that the increase in population from 1950 to 1970 was almost as great as that from 1850 to 1950. The percentage increase in the last twenty years was almost half as great as the percentage increase during the previous century.

If we assume that the poor countries include all those in Africa, Latin America, and Asia excluding the U.S.S.R. and Japan, 71 percent of the people of the world, or 2.6 billion people, live in poor countries. At least two-thirds of them, or 1.7 billion people, are not getting enough to eat. If we then add in those in the richer countries who are hungry, it is safe to say that half the people of the world are suffering from varying degrees of malnutrition. The momentous questions troubling the world are these: *Why*

275

TABLE 13-1   World Population, 1650–1970

Year	Population (in millions)	Increase from previous date (in millions)	Percentage increase from previous date
1650	545		
1750	728	183	34
1850	1,171	443	61
1950	2,406	1,235	106
1970	3,632	1,226	51

Source: computed from United Nations, The Determinants and Consequences of Population Trends (New York, 1953), p. 11; and Monthly
Bulletin of Statistics, Vol. XXVI, No. 1 (January, 1972), p. VIII.

*are people poor? What is the relationship between overpopulation and
hunger? What can be done about these problems?*

We shall examine first some ideas concerning overpopulation, including those of Malthus and his modern followers, and consider to what extent
their ideas are valid. Then we shall offer criticisms of the Malthusian ideas.
Finally, we shall suggest other causes of poverty that the Malthusians tend
to neglect in concentrating on only one facet of a large and complicated
problem.

The Idea of Overpopulation

THOMAS ROBERT MALTHUS   Thomas Robert Malthus (1766–1834) was a
clergyman, a writer, and a professor of history and political economy at
the East India College in England. His famous book *An Essay on the Principle of Population*, which first appeared in 1798, established his enduring
fame; it went through six editions during twenty-eight years.

The basis for Malthus' overpopulation theory was the law of diminishing returns. Because the land area is fixed, adding workers in agriculture
may increase output but not in proportion to the increase in workers. That
is, if you double the number of workers on the land, you will less than double the output. Therefore, the more people there are, the less food per person will be produced.

Man, being an improvident creature, tends to multiply recklessly; population when unchecked doubles every twenty-five years. Food production
cannot possibly keep up with this rate. Malthus' "law of population" was
that population tends to increase geometrically, while means of subsistence
increase at best only arithmetically. That is, every twenty-five years population tends to increase at a rate represented by the series 1, 2, 4, 8, 16, 32,
and so forth, while the rate of increase for food is represented by the series

1, 2, 3, 4, 5, 6, and so on. He pointed to America (the India or China of his day with respect to rate of population growth) for proof of his propositions.

Malthus identified certain preventive checks to population growth—those that reduced the birth rate. The preventive check Malthus approved was moral restraint. People who could not afford children should either postpone marriage or never marry; conduct before marriage should be sexually continent. The preventive check Malthus disapproved of was vice, under which label he included prostitution and birth control, both of which reduced the birth rate.

Malthus also recognized certain positive checks to population—those that increased the death rate. These were famine, misery, plague, and war. They were elevated to the position of natural phenomena or laws, necessary evils required to limit the population. These positive checks represented punishments for people who had not practiced moral restraint. If the positive checks could somehow be overcome, people would face starvation as a rapidly growing population depended on a slowly growing food supply. In the sixth edition of his *Essay*, Malthus pictured the positive checks to population as follows:

> It is an evident truth that, whatever may be the rate of increase in the means of subsistence, the increase of population must be limited by it, at least after the food has once been divided into the smallest shares that will support life. All the children born, beyond what would be required to keep up the population to this level, must necessarily perish, unless room be made for them by the deaths of grown persons. . . . To act consistently, therefore, we should facilitate, instead of foolishly and vainly endeavouring to impede, the operations of nature in producing this mortality; and if we dread the too frequent visitation of the horrid form of famine, we should sedulously encourage the other forms of destruction, which we compel nature to use. Instead of recommending cleanliness to the poor, we should encourage contrary habits. In our towns we should make the streets narrower, crowd more people into the houses, and court the return of the plague. In the country, we should build our villages near stagnant pools, and particularly encourage settlements in all marshy and unwholesome situations. But above all, we should reprobate specific remedies for ravaging diseases; . . . If by these and similar means the annual mortality were increased . . . we might probably every one of us marry at the age of puberty, and yet few be absolutely starved.

According to Malthus, then, poverty and misery are the natural punishment for the "lower classes," which have failed to restrain their multiplication. From this view followed his highly significant policy conclusion: there must be no government relief for the poor. To give them aid would cause more children to survive, and thereby ultimately worsen the problem of hunger. This is the way he phrased it in the second edition of his *Essay* in 1803:

A man who is born into a world already possessed, if he cannot get subsistence from his parents on whom he has a just demand, and if the society do not want his labour, has no claim of *right* to the smallest portion of food, and, in fact, has no business to be where he is. At nature's mighty feast there is no vacant cover for him. She tells him to be gone, and will quickly execute her own orders, if he do not work upon the compassion of some of her guests. If these guests get up and make room for him, other intruders immediately appear demanding the same favour. . . . The order and harmony of the feast is disturbed, the plenty that before reigned is changed into scarcity.

Malthus withdrew the above statement from later editions of the *Essay*, but he offered a specific proposal concerning the poor laws in the sixth edition.

I have reflected much on the subject of the poor-laws, and hope therefore that I shall be excused in venturing to suggest a mode of their gradual abolition. . . . We are bound in justice and honour formally to disclaim the *right* of the poor to support.

To this end, I should propose a regulation to be made, declaring that no child born from any marriage, taking place after the expiration of a year from the date of the law, and no illegitimate child born two years from the same date, should ever be entitled to parish assistance. . . .

With regard to illegitimate children, after proper notice had been given, they should not be allowed to have any claim to parish assistance, but be left entirely to the support of private charity. If the parents desert their child, they ought to be made answerable for the crime. The infant is, comparatively speaking, of little value to society, as others will immediately supply its place.

Let us see now how this message inspired the modern followers of Malthus.

THE MODERN MALTHUSIANS   The modern followers of Malthus differ with him in that they advocate birth control. They agree that overpopulation is the major cause of poverty, and like Malthus, they tend to ignore other causes. The more moderate neo-Malthusians point to overpopulation as a major cause of hunger and conclude that hunger leads to social unrest and conflict. They admit that improvements in technology can buy time for the world, but the relentless growth of population must be halted eventually if it is not to lead to catastrophe. Long before the present concern about problems of our ecology became popular, the neo-Malthusians were warning us about pollution, congestion of people, and the depletion of natural resources.

The more extreme neo-Malthusians believe that wars are caused by overpopulation, and they help solve the problem by reducing the population to match the food supply. They assert that high death rates are a national asset in poor countries, and that we should not attempt to lower their death rates until the birth rates decline. Some consider drastic remedies for overpopulation, like mixing oral contraceptives in the drinking water of whole populations, throwing people off welfare if they have more than a certain number of children, or determining child-bearing quotas for people and punishing them if they exceed their quota. One ingenious economist suggested that poor people could supplement their incomes by selling their child-bearing quotas to the rich.

We shall cite here two of the vast array of extreme neo-Malthusian statements that have been made. The first was made by Harrison Brown in his *The Challenge of Man's Future* (New York: Viking, 1954, p. 221).

> A substantial fraction of humanity today is behaving . . . as if it were engaged in a contest to test nature's willingness to support humanity and, if it had its way, it would not rest content until the earth is covered completely and to a considerable depth with a writhing mass of human beings, much as a dead cow is covered with a pulsating mass of maggots.

The second example of doctrinaire neo-Malthusianism comes from the "Campaign to Check the Population Explosion" of New York City. This organization ran a full-page advertisement in the *New York Times* on July 19, 1968. The headline proclaimed, "HUNGRY NATIONS IMPERIL THE PEACE OF THE WORLD." The text of the advertisement read in part:

> Food shipments by the United States to hungry nations abroad, most of it on a give-away basis, have amounted to the gigantic sum of over $12 billion since Congress enacted the so-called Food for Peace Law in 1954.
>
> Although this program was an act of unparalleled humanity on the part of the American people, it was in our own interest. Congress recognized that the United States could not remain an island of prosperity in a sea of hunger and poverty indefinitely.
>
> However, there are now more hungry people in the world than there were in 1954. It would appear that we have been pouring food into a bottomless pit. . . .
>
> The answer is birth control. And if corrective measures are not taken here and now the resulting world-wide misery, strife, revolutions and wars will make our experience in Viet Nam appear minor by comparison.

Whether our "humanity was unparalleled" is open to some question. If we add up our net national product during the thirteen years between 1955 and 1967, we find that for every $550 or NNP, we gave away $1 for food distribution abroad.

The Validity of the Malthusian Ideas

It is true that we cannot go on increasing the world's population forever. A doubling every thirty-six years as is happening now would eventually leave us with literally standing room only. Sooner or later the rate of increase will have to slow down and ultimately cease. There is much disagreement about how many people could eventually be supported comfortably on this earth, and whether we are on the brink of disaster now or have been at any time from 1798, when Malthus first published his book, to the present. But it is impossible to conceive of the present rate of growth of population continuing for centuries.

There are other projections of growth to worry about also. The number of automobiles in the United States increased from 49 million in 1950 to 109 million in 1970. If we assume that the number of cars will double every 20 years, we will have 3.5 billion cars in 100 years; it will mean 950 cars for every mile of road in the whole country. That rate of growth will have to slow down and cease.

A second point on which we agree with the neo-Malthusians is that burgeoning population aggravates the problems of pollution and exhaustion of natural resources, and it lowers the quality of life. But we also recognize that the contamination of the environment in the United States is proceeding at a far faster rate than the increase of population. The multiplication of cars is a much greater danger than the multiplication of people. It has been found that from 1946 to 1968, the nation's population increased 48 percent. Yet various measurable pollutions, such as algae in Lake Erie, bacteria in New York harbor, and smog in many cities, increased by 200 to 1,000 percent. There is some relationship, however, between the number of people and the number of cars, the amount of power generated, the raw materials consumed, and the contaminants ejected into the environment. If people everywhere continue to aspire to our reckless and wasteful way of life, the effect could be devastating. We suspect that if others emulate us, there will be less for us. While we exhort the poor at home and abroad to have fewer children, we who are affluent might do our share to save the world by drastically cutting down on our extravagant consumption.

One can become a complete Malthusian at five in the afternoon on any workday in New York City. The automobile and passenger traffic during rush hours is phenomenal. It is discouraging to be part of the press of population on the highways, at the beaches, in the national and local parks, and in the overcrowded cities. Part of the congestion in the cities, however, can be attributed to the poor distribution of our population. New Jersey is our most densely populated state with 953 people per square mile of land area. Wyoming is the most sparsely populated (except for Alaska) with 3.4 people per square mile. Suppose communities of 50,000 people were constructed in Wyoming with good houses; adequate recreation, cultural, and educational facilities; and enough light manufacturing to provide employment. Would people from New Jersey or New York City be willing to move there? If the availability of water is considered to be a barrier to the growth of population, it is interesting to note that Cheyenne, Wyoming has more precipitation than Los Angeles, Denver, or Salt Lake City. We do not disperse our population to Wyoming because people will not move there without jobs, and factories will not be built there unless an adequate labor force is available. Coordinated planning could accomplish what will not happen by itself. And if the cost of manufacturing were a few percent higher in Wyoming than in New Jersey, the social benefits of a more evenly distributed population would more than compensate society for the increased costs of production.

Our third area of agreement with those who warn of overpopulation is in its effect on the economic development of the poor countries. The higher the birth rate, the more has to be spent on feeding, housing, educating, training, and looking after the health of the children. These increased expenditures on supporting consumers who are not yet producers will cut down the funds that can be saved and invested. Even as children grow up and enter the labor force, the limited capital and the increased labor supply will reduce the average output per worker below what it might be. If on the average you have one tractor for every 100 agricultural workers, your average output per worker will be less than if you had two tractors for every 100 workers. A high birth rate changes the labor-capital ratio at both ends, by increasing the labor and simultaneously reducing the capital. A reduction in the very high birth rates would speed up the process of economic development and raise the average per capita incomes. The nation's income would be divided among fewer people than would otherwise be the case, and there would be more income to divide.

Fourth, we agree with the neo-Malthusians on the necessity of birth control, and give them credit for pioneering in the struggle to legalize contraceptives. When the Western countries were in the process of lowering birth rates, people were sent to prison for advocating means to accomplish it. Now the idea of birth control is widely accepted and no longer suppressed by punitive legislation. In fact, governments are increasingly participating in advancing programs for family limitation.

We shall now present our criticisms of the Malthusian ideas. In doing so, we shall identify other causes of poverty than overpopulation.

Criticisms of the Malthusian Ideas

POPULATION DENSITY AND THE OPTIMUM POPULATION The Neo-Malthusians frequently create the impression that the poor countries of the world are teeming with hordes of people packed tightly together on the land. It may be interesting to compare population densities in different countries and areas; this is done in Table 13-2. We can see that some of the rich countries in western Europe and Japan have very dense populations, with far more people per square mile than in India, Pakistan, and China. Many of the poor countries in Africa and Latin America have very sparse populations. Can one say, for example, that Bolivia is overpopulated with ten people per square mile?

Of course, the quantity of land per person is not the only considera-

TABLE 13-2 Population Density in Selected Countries and Areas, 1969

Country or area	People per square mile	Country or area	People per square mile
WORLD	68	EUROPE EXCLUDING USSR	242
United States	57	Belgium	822
		Netherlands	819
USSR	29	United Kingdom	593
		Italy	460
Oceania	5	West Germany	245
		France	239
ASIA EXCLUDING USSR	190	AFRICA	29
Japan	720	Uganda	104
Ceylon	486	Kenya	47
India	426	South Africa	42
Pakistan	307	Liberia	26
Indonesia	203	Congo	18
China	200	Zambia	16
SOUTH AMERICA	27		
Ecuador	55		
Colombia	47		
Chile	34		
Brazil	29		
Argentina	23		
Bolivia	10		

Source: United States Department of Commerce, Bureau of the Census, Statistical Abstract of the United States: 1971. Washington, D.C.: Government Printing Office, 1971, pp. 794–96.

tion. What is the quality of the land? Ten people per square mile would overpopulate the Sahara Desert. But the productivity of land can be influenced by tree farming in hilly areas, irrigation, soil conservation, soilless agriculture, livestock farming, and other improvements made possible through science and technology. Nor should we consider each country's man-land ratio in isolation from the rest of the world. If a country is industrialized, it can export manufactured goods and import food. Hong Kong would probably be considered overpopulated with 10,000 people per square mile. It imports not only food, but also drinking water from China. Yet Hong Kong in 1968 had a per capita GNP of $710, compared to $100 for India and Pakistan.

The concept of optimum population was introduced in the late 1800's. It represented an advance over Malthusian thinking, for Malthus thought only in terms of overpopulation being hopelessly inevitable. If people have control over their numbers, they can decide on a population policy to give them the best and most satisfactory level of population. But what is best? Generally the optimum population is taken to be the population that will give the greatest output per person.

A sparse population can result in inefficiency. There are certain economic activities that enjoy "economies of scale," that grow more efficient up to some point as the scale of business grows. Among these activities are railroad transportation, publishing, education, television and radio broadcasting, and research.

The optimum population for any one country or area is a changing quantity. A country may be overpopulated for agricultural use, but as it industrializes there may be a shortage of people. The American colonists spoke about overpopulation on the East Coast in the eighteenth century, yet there were far fewer people there at that time than now. As new methods and types of production are introduced, the optimum changes.

Figure 13-1 presents a hypothetical case of optimum population density. Suppose an agricultural society is very sparsely popululated. The average income per person may be extremely low. Perhaps the total production is too small to justify building a railroad; therefore, farm families will have to be largely self-sufficient. If they have to make their own clothing, furniture, shoes, farm tools, and so on, their efficiency will be low.

As more and more farmers settle in the area, their incomes rise. Suppliers will go into business to sell them both consumer and capital goods. Transportation facilities will expand, and buyers of farm products will appear. Research on better methods of production will be more feasible if there is a market for a million bushels of wheat instead of a thousand. As population increases, there is a rising income per person; this is shown as increasing returns in the left portion of the lower curve in Figure 13-1.

If the population keeps increasing, soon there will be fewer acres per

FIGURE 13-1. A Hypothetical Case of Optimum Population

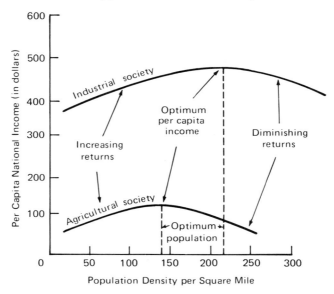

farmer. When the land is all occupied, increasing population will result in lower output per person; the law of diminishing returns sets in. Now the per capita income curve ceases to rise and begins to fall. The highest point of the curve represents the optimum population, with the highest output or income per person. At any less or any greater population per capita, income is lower.

The upper curve in Figure 13-1 shows the optimum population density after the same country industrializes. Now a greater population can be supported at higher levels of income. Industry makes agriculture more efficient as it supplies machinery, electricity, fertilizers, and insecticides to farmers. With the growth of population, there is a greater division of labor, greater efficiency in mass transportation, and lower per capita costs in providing education, recreation, television and radio, newspapers and books, and so on. But beyond a certain point, increasing the population density causes the per capita national income to decline; when that happens, we have gone beyond the point of optimum population.

The difficulty with the concept of optimum population is that we do not know how to locate it on a scale between under- and overpopulation. We can decide on extreme points on the scale. For example, the United States was underpopulated when the transcontinental railroad was completed in 1869, because there was not enough traffic to make the railroad efficient or profitable. But nobody can say what is the exact population density that will give the greatest output per capita. Besides, who is to say that greatest output per capita is the best or highest goal? People may have other values, and they may be willing to sacrifice some efficiency and productivity to achieve them.

THE GROWTH OF TECHNOLOGY   Malthus and his modern followers have ignored or underestimated the potentiality of increased food production. They have preached doom and disaster for almost two centuries. We are always on the verge of catastrophe, but we never quite get there in spite of the rapid growth of world population. Things are bad enough without making them seem worse than they are. Two population experts, for example, proclaimed that "the limits of human capability to produce food by conventional means have very nearly been reached" (Paul R. and Anne H. Ehrlich, *Population, Resources, Environment* [San Francisco: W. H. Freeman, 1970], p. 321).

Table 13-3 shows that we still have the potential for increased per capita food production. The increase in Far East production, from 1952 to 1970, has been impressive, and it results from the "green revolution." New varieties of crops have been developed that are increasing the harvests tremendously. Rice production in India grew from an average of 43,958,000 tons per year during the period 1952–56 to 70,039,000 tons in 1970. The increase in Pakistan during the same period was from 14,094,000 tons to 22,-015,000 tons. Wheat production in India went from an average of 8,709,000 tons during the period 1952–56 to 22,149,000 tons in 1970. During the same years, Pakistan's wheat production rose from 3,469,000 tons to 7,938,000 tons. World wheat and rice production expanded 52 percent from the period 1952–56 to 1970; corn rose 67 percent; and meat increased 62 percent.

Aside from conventional farming, there are many ways to increase food production. First, soilless farming, or hydroponics, can increase the output per acre eight to fifteen times compared with the best soil. Hydroponics requires cheap chemical nutrients for plants, electric power, water, and sunshine. Such farms are being operated commercially in Florida and elsewhere.

Second, algae farming could be used to produce livestock feed. Algae is twenty to forty times more efficient than crops in converting solar energy

TABLE 13-3   Index Numbers of Per Capita Food Production, 1963 = 100

						Area			
Year	World	Africa	North America	Latin America	Far East	Near East	Western Europe	Oceania	Eastern Europe and USSR
1952	90	94	99	96	88	88	80	91	78
1970	104	96	99	103	104	98	110	105	125

Source: United Nations, Statistical Yearbook, 1969. *New York: 1970, p. XXV; ibid., 1971, p. 20.*

into food, and it can be grown in sewage disposal and water purification plants.

Third, it is now feasible to produce high-protein animal feed from petroleum. British Petroleum brought a plant into production in 1970 that is producing 16,000 tons of protein per year. In mid-1971 France opened such a plant producing 22,000 tons of protein annually. By the end of 1971, Japan was producing more than 300,000 tons per year, and the U.S.S.R. has gone into production also.

Improvements in technology tend to offset the law of diminishing returns in conventional agriculture. They are also making vast new supplies of nutrients available from nonagricultural sources for animal feed and ultimately possibly for human consumption.

FALLING BIRTH RATES   The birth rate is much higher in the poor countries than in the rich, as shown in Table 13-4. The birth rate in the United States fell from 39.8 per 1,000 people in 1880 to 18.2 per 1,000 in 1970. Japan's fell from 34.3 in 1947 to 18.8 in 1970. Taiwan's was reduced from 45.2

TABLE 13-4   Birth Rates per 1,000 People, Selected Countries, 1970

Developed countries	Births per 1,000 people	Underdeveloped countries	Births per 1,000 people
Israel	26.8	U.S. Virgin Islands	49.5
New Zealand	22.1	Mexico	43.4
Australia	20.6	Algeria	40.9 (1968)
Japan	18.8	El Salvador	40.0
Netherlands	18.3	Guatemala	39.0
United States	18.2	Madagascar	38.6 (1969)
Canada	17.5 (1969)	Libya	37.9 (1968)
USSR	17.5	Dominican Republic	37.1 (1969)
Italy	16.8	Panama	37.1
France	16.7	Egypt	36.9 (1969)
Norway	16.6	Tunisia	36.2
Bulgaria	16.3	Jamaica	34.4
United Kingdom	16.2	Costa Rica	33.8
Czechoslovakia	15.8	Paraguay	33.4
Switzerland	15.8	Thailand	32.6 (1969)
Austria	15.2	Portuguese Guinea	30.2
Belgium	14.7	Guam	28.8
East Germany	13.9	Taiwan	28.1
Sweden	13.7	Lebanon	27.3
West Germany	13.3	Chile	26.6 (1968)

Sources: Monthly Bulletin of Statistics, Vol. XXVI, No. 7 (July 1972), pp. 6–7; Statistical Office of the United Nations, Department of Economic and Social Affairs, Demographic Yearbook, 1970. New York: 1971, pp. 619–27.

in 1953 to 28.1 in 1970. And the U.S.S.R.'s birth rate dropped from 24.9 in 1960 to 17.5 in 1970. Falling birth rates are significant because combined with increased food production they can ease the pressure of overpopulation.

Under what conditions do birth rates fall? There is strong evidence that the interdependent processes of urbanization, industrialization, rising incomes, increased education, and the rising status of women reduce the birth rate. In the United States in 1969, of all the women ever married who had completed their childbearing, every 1,000 farm women averaged 3,522 children, while nonfarm women had 2,549 per thousand. Urbanization by itself does not always lower the birth rate in all countries, although it frequently does. This is also true with education. The women in the United States who were married and had less than eight years of education had 3,523 children per 1,000 as of 1969. Those who completed four years of college or more had 1,996 per 1,000; if their birth rate prevailed for the whole country, our population would actually decline.

Why do birth rates fall as countries undergo economic development? We shall list six contributing factors.

1. Children are more of a burden in the city than on the farm. Farm children help support themselves by working at an early age. Living space and child care are more expensive in the city.

2. Childbearing does not interfere much with women's work on the farm, but it does interfere significantly with women holding jobs in the city.

3. The growing independence of women in more developed countries means that they have something to say about how many children they will have.

4. Impoverished people who are without hope for improving their situation will not try to restrict the birth rate; it seems futile to them to try to plan for the distant future. People who see before them the possibility of upward social mobility limit the number of children they have in order to get ahead. Those people who have already achieved a moderate degree of affluence try to preserve it by having fewer children. When they develop a wide range of interests and activities, they find that children interfere to some extent with their desired way of life.

5. Poverty and illiteracy interfere with the practice of birth control through lack of access to contraceptives.

6. People want children, among other reasons, to perpetuate their name and memory and to provide security in old age. When there is a decline in infant mortality and when the state provides social security, there is less incentive to have many children.

Thus, the neo-Malthusians emphasize the less workable sequence when they say that if poor people practice birth control they will be better off. The more relevant cause-and-effect relationship is that if people are better off they will practice more birth control.

The greatest weakness of the theory of overpopulation is its one-sidedness. It overemphasizes the population factor and neglects the other causes of poverty. This problem has many facets, and it will take a many-sided approach to overcome it. Birth control alone will not do the job. We therefore turn now to other causes of poverty that are especially applicable to the poor countries of Asia, Africa, and Latin America.

Other Causes of Poverty

WAR AND MILITARY SPENDING War, contrary to Malthus and some of his followers, is not caused by hunger and overpopulation; nor does it solve the problem of overpopulation. Instead, war is one of the greatest causes of hunger and poverty ever devised by man.

For every death during the First World War, $27,300 was spent by the belligerents on fighting the war and on the destruction of property. In the Second World War the cost was $64,500 per death. The Vietnam war cost $500,000 per fatality. Can anyone doubt that the world would have been better off with more people if the vast sums spent on war had been used for constructive purposes?

The world now spends $207 billion each year on armaments. As there are 2.6 billion people who live in the poor countries, this comes to $80 per person in those areas. This is equal to or greater than the per capita GNP in thirteen African countries, seven Asian countries, and one Latin American country in 1968. Military spending by the poor countries alone is more than twice as large as their total receipts of public and private foreign aid and investment.

In 1968 in the U.S., we had $3,319 invested per person in all our business buildings and producers' durable goods like machinery, trucks, railroad rolling stock, and so on. If all the military spending were made available to the poor countries to equip them as we are equipped with the same value of capital goods per person, this could be done in forty-three years. Perhaps this could be considered utopian, but let us at least admit that wars and military spending are far greater causes of poverty than high birth rates.

DISEASE Disease, instead of eliminating surplus population, is one of the major causes of poverty and hunger. Life expectancy at birth is below thirty years for males in some African countries and somewhat higher for females, compared with a life expectancy of over seventy years in some rich countries. Such a situation is tragic, both on a personal level and in an economic sense, in that many people are consumers without living long enough to contribute as much as they might to production.

In 1967 there were 150 million cases of malaria with 1 million deaths, most of them in the poor countries. Most people with this disease live on to be consumers, but they cannot produce when the disease strikes them; this usually occurs at the height of the agricultural season. In places where malaria has been curbed, as in Costa Rica and Pakistan, production increased significantly because people can do more work and because abandoned land has been brought back into cultivation.

Yaws is a disease that is widespread in Africa; it is not fatal, but it causes painful sores. If they break out on the soles of the feet, walking is impossible; if they appear on the palms of the hands, working is impossible. A 25-cent dose of penicillin can cure yaws and restore people to productive activities again.

LAND TENURE The concept of land tenure includes the relationships among people in agriculture and rural life, and the relationships between people and the land. It encompasses such matters as who owns the land, who extends credit to farmers and on what terms, how high the rents are, how the tax burden is distributed, who dominates the marketing process and what the marketing fees are, and which political groups are dominant in rural life. The conditions of land tenure lead to the conclusion that poverty and hunger are caused more by bad social conditions than they are by overpopulation.

Take, for example, the "green revolution" mentioned above as the program that is producing fantastic increases in the production of grain in the Far East. This program, paradoxically, is worsening the problem of hunger. In 1969, out of a total rural population of 434 million in India, 103 million owned no land at all, and another 185 million operated less than five acres per family. Taken together, these people represented 67 percent of the total rural population. An estimated 154 to 210 million of them live in abject poverty at a level of income of $21 per capita per year. The new very productive varieties of grain require expensive seeds, more fertilizer, more irrigation, and better farm machinery. It takes $1,000 to $1,200 to reequip a seven to ten acre holding to get the benefits of the green revolution. Farmers need cheap credit, but small farmers cannot get credit at all, or they borrow at usurious rates of interest of 36 percent per year or more. With the green revolution, land prices have risen three-, four-, or five-fold. Rents have risen from the traditional though illegal 50-50 division of the harvest to 70-30 in favor of the landlord. Landlords want to get rid of their tenants altogether, because they can make more money with the new technology by hiring labor that is overabundant and cheap. The tendency is for the cash tenants to become sharecroppers, the sharecroppers to become wage workers, and workers to lose their jobs as productivity rises. And to conclude this list of troubles, there is a lack of adequate demand for the increased output because of insufficient income of a substantial number of rural people. Hunger in India will not be averted by increased food production as long as there are no genuine and profound social changes.

The system of taxation is an example of what is not being done to overcome poverty in India. The central government of India has no taxes on agricultural property and income. The Indian constitution reserves to the states the power to tax the agricultural sector. The big landholders who have grown richer than ever in the green revolution in wheat are a major political force and major financial contributors to the ruling Congress Party. Therefore, only one of the eighteen states, Kerala, has enacted an agricultural tax.

Sharecropping, which is widespread in Asia and Latin America, is one of the worst systems of land tenure. Many agricultural improvements that are profitable for farm owners or cash tenants are unprofitable for share-croppers. Typically the sharecropper pays all the expenses of production and gives half the crop to the landlord. A farmer who owns his land or pays a fixed rent in cash would invest a dollar if he would expect to get back at least a dollar and a penny. But a sharecropper would invest a dollar only if the return on it was expected to be $2.02. If the sharecropper has to pay 25 cents interest on the dollar he borrows, he would have to get back $2.52 in order to make the investment worthwhile, because he would have to give the equivalent of $1.26 to the landlord—the dollar he borrowed and 25 cents interest to the moneylender—and he would be left with a penny to reward him. Sharecropping and usury result in backward farming methods, poverty, and hunger.

The World Bank has issued a considerable number of volumes analyzing the economic situation of different countries. Several of the volumes on Latin American countries describe the mistaken agricultural practices that prevail. The hillsides are tilled, and as they erode badly, the farmers toil and starve in an ever-worsening situation. The flat land in the valleys is grazed. Agronomists recommend a reversal of these practices. The hillsides should be grazed to a limited degree, and the valleys should be tilled. But their advice has not been taken. It is not a matter of education and information, but rather of who dominates society. The big land-grabbers took the best land in the valleys, and they forced the peasants to occupy the less fertile land on the hillsides. The big landowners found that grazing was more profitable than tillage, so they graze the land to the detriment of society.

The Peruvian situation of land tenure was typical of many of the poor countries. The 1961 agricultural census revealed that 83.3 percent of the individual farms were 12.5 acres or less each, and they included 6.1 percent of the privately held land. The farms of 250 acres and above made up 1.3 percent of the total number of farms, and they accounted for 83.3 percent of the land. In a predominantly agricultural country, this imposes poverty on the majority of the people.

It is significant to note that in the days of the Incas, before the Spanish conquest of Peru in 1533, more land was irrigated than at present. It is not known whether there were more people living in Peru then than now, but it is certainly known that they ate better then, due to a very different distribution system. Four hundred and forty years of Western influence, domination, and exploitation have added nothing to the welfare of the Peruvian Indians.

It should also be pointed out that those who eat meat and other livestock products deprive others of bread or rice or beans. An acre of grain will produce four or five times as many calories if consumed by humans than if the grain is fed to livestock and people eat the livestock products. In other words, producing livestock for food means you can feed only one-fourth or one-fifth as many people as you might. Meat does upgrade the diet because of its high protein content, but there is some basis for restricting meat production until all people in a country have their calorie requirements met.

WASTE OF THE ECONOMIC SURPLUS   Poor as the countries of Asia, Africa, and Latin America are, they do produce enough income to generate some significant saving and investment. The distribution of wealth is more unequal there than in the rich countries. Wealthy people use much of their wealth in ways that impede rather than promote economic development. From the point of view of the nation's requirements, they waste large sums of money in three basic ways. First, by lavish spending on domestic goods and services they divert resources from upgrading domestic diets, alleviating poverty, providing housing for slum dwellers, and expanding investment based on domestic resources. Second, by importing luxury consumer goods and services the rich use up foreign earnings that could be used to import some of the requirements for economic development. Third, the rich in the poor countries frequently invest wealth abroad, thereby depriving their own countries of the benefits of saving and investment. Of the many examples of the waste of the economic surplus, only four will be cited here.

First, an International Bank report on Cuba stated that in 1949, 12 percent of the gross national product was saved and 20 percent of that saving went abroad. Cubans were investing heavily in Miami real estate and in short-term securities in the United States. The rich people in the poor countries feel safer investing their money in the United States or depositing it in Swiss banks than they do leaving their money at home. This becomes a self-fulfilling prophesy. Sending the money abroad holds back economic development, intensifies poverty, increases social tensions, and endangers the security of the rich.

A second example was reported by an International Monetary Fund mission to Chile; they discovered that 27 percent of gross domestic investment was in luxury residential building during the period 1947–49.

Third, a committee of our House of Representatives reported that when the Agency for International Development (AID) made loans to finance imports of a country, the money was supposed to be spent on non-luxury commodities that were essential for the development of the borrowing country. But exceptions were permissible under the law. The exceptions comprised as much as 27 percent of Panama's imports financed by AID, 25 percent of Colombia's imports, and 75 percent of Mexico's imports. When asked specifically whether imports might have been for such items as Cadillacs or bulldozers, AID officials were unable to provide an answer. Brazil was importing racehorses, pearls, precious and semiprecious stones, alcoholic beverages, perfumes and cosmetics, arms and ammunition, record players and records. The suspicion was strong that these imports were financed with United States AID funds (House of Representatives, Report No. 1849, 90th Congress, 2nd Session, *U.S. AID Operations in Latin America Under the Alliance for Progress* [Washington, D.C.: Government Printing Office, 1968], pp. 17–19).

Finally, here is an example of the United States Department of Commerce glowing with enthusiasm over the possibilities of conspicuous consumption and waste in Africa:

> Prestige items in many cases outsell less expensive items in African countries—a leading brand of American dress shirts is a case in point. The medicine-man show sales technique was extremely effective in developing sales in our own country in the formative years and must not be overlooked in Africa (United States Department of Commerce, *A Special Report on Africa, Sales Frontier for U.S. Business,* [Washington, D.C.: Government Printing Office, 1963], p. 38).

This publication highlights the prospects of selling small refrigerators in Africa, and also room air-conditioners, canned and frozen foods, compact passenger cars, cosmetics, and other consumer goods.

Wealth and poverty are intertwined to perpetuate hunger. Overpopulation is peripheral to the major issues.

POVERTY BREEDS POVERTY   Poverty is one of the significant causes of poverty. It entraps whole countries in stagnation and hopelessness. If a country can break through the barriers to economic development, rising wealth feeds on itself and spirals upward. Greater wealth can result in increased saving and investment and a further expansion of wealth.

If the water in India's rivers were spread over the entire cultivated area, there would be three and a half feet of water for irrigation. India could then grow two crops each year over vast areas instead of one. But India is too poor to invest in this kind of a program that would go far toward eliminating poverty.

The Hwang Ho River, once called China's Sorrow, used to consist of 46 percent silt by weight. The soil loss in its whole drainage area was 10.7 tons per acre per year. Such terrible erosion can be and is being controlled by the present regime in China.

We are familiar in the United States with poverty breeding poverty. The poor are less educated, less well nourished, less adequately housed, and less healthy than the well-to-do. They cannot get good jobs, they cannot improve their strength and efficiency, and they pass these handicaps on to their children, to whom they cannot give the advantages of a good start in life. The handicaps arise even before birth. The newborn baby of a malnourished mother is likely to suffer physical and mental deficiencies.

These are social problems that can and must be solved. As John Milton said, "Accuse not Nature! she hath done her part; do thou but thine."

Summary

Malthus, using the law of diminishing returns and the improvidence of humanity, predicted that population would increase faster than the food supply. He thought that the birth rate would have to fall to prevent catastrophe. If that did not occur, then the inevitable consequence would be a rising death rate because of famine, misery, plague, and war. With world population now doubling every thirty-six years, the Malthusian warnings cannot be ignored.

Birth rates are, however, falling in the rich countries. Technology is expanding at an increasing rate, creating a potential for vast increases in the production of the necessities of life.

Many of the low-income countries are poor in spite of low population densities. Perhaps famine, misery, disease, and war, instead of being remedies for overpopulation, are causes of low productivity, the waste of resources, and hunger. Poverty itself can be a cause of poverty because it leads to stagnation and hopelessness, caused by cumulative defeats of efforts to bring about improvements. Poor systems of land tenure and the waste of economic surpluses that might be used productively but are not, are additional causes of poverty and hunger.

QUESTIONS AND PROBLEMS

1 Your authors speak of extravagant consumption by some of us. What consumption spending do you or your parents do that could be reduced or eliminated?

2 Automobiles are among the world's greatest polluters. What might be done to solve this problem?

3 Explain why certain economic activities are necessarily inefficient if they are pursued on a small scale.

4 Can you think of examples of other values or goals being more desirable than maximum efficiency and maximum output?

5   What is your opinion in the controversy over birth control? What is your solution to the population problem?

6   What do you think would be an optimum population for the United States? Why?

7   Look up the number of people engaged in agriculture in the United States in the past and now and the total farm output. How does this square with the law of diminishing returns?

8   To what extent is luxurious living by the rich in the poor countries necessary or defensible? To what extent should it be controlled, and how could it be done?

9   To what extent would a comprehensive drive to overcome poverty and hunger interfere with freedom, initiative, and independence of individuals?

10   Are all malnourished people poor? Are all poor people malnourished?

11   Do economists place too much emphasis on money and material things, and not enough on social, cultural, esthetic, and spiritual values?

12   If we adopted a policy of free and unrestricted immigration to the United States, what might be the consequences? Are you for or against such a policy? Explain your reasons.

13   This question is impossible to answer with a high degree of accuracy, but you can explore the literature and answer in terms of probabilities: How many people could live on this earth with a reasonably good standard of living?

BIBLIOGRAPHY

The Annals of the American Academy of Political and Social Science, "World Population," Vol. 369 (January 1967).

BROWN, LESTER R., *Seeds of Change: The Green Revolution and Development in the 1970's.* New York: Praeger, 1970.

DECASTRO, JOSUÉ, *The Geography of Hunger.* Boston: Little, Brown, 1952.

COCHRANE, WILLARD W., *The World Food Problem: A Guardedly Optimistic View.* New York: Thomas Y. Crowell, 1969.

EHRLICH, PAUL R., and ANNE H., *Population, Resources, Environment.* San Francisco: W. H. Freeman, 1970.

MEEK, RONALD L., ed., *Marx and Engels on Malthus.* New York: International Publishers, 1954.

OSER, JACOB, *Must Men Starve? The Malthusian Controversy.* London: Jonathan Cape, 1956.

SMITH, KENNETH, *The Malthusian Controversy.* London: Routledge and Kegan Paul, 1951.

TYDINGS, JOSEPH D., *Born to Starve.* New York: William Morrow, 1970.

UNITED NATIONS, *Demographic Yearbook.*

UNITED NATIONS, *The Determinants and Consequences of Population Trends.* New York: 1953.

UNITED NATIONS, *Monthly Bulletin of Statistics.*

WRONG, DENNIS H., *Population and Society,* 3rd ed. New York: Random House, 1967.

14

Problems
of
Agriculture

Blessed be agriculture! if one does not have too much of it.
—*Charles Dudley Warner*

Why should we devote a whole chapter to agriculture, which is a relatively declining sector in our economy? In 1790 about 90 percent of the labor force worked on farms; by 1972 this figure fell to 4 percent. From 1790 to 1920 the number of people living on farms kept rising until it reached 32 million, but by 1970 only 9.7 million people lived on farms. The number of farms declined from 6.5 million in 1920 to 2.9 million in 1970, while the average size rose from 147 acres to 387 acres.

There are many reasons for looking closely at the agricultural situation. First, our phenomenal increase in the efficiency of production can serve as a model for other countries in helping solve the problem of hunger, which was discussed in Chapter 13. Second, while in 1971 the disposable personal income of the farm population from farming was 3.6 percent of our total disposable income, our exports of farm products were 18 percent of the total; this bears significantly on the problems of international trade discussed in Chapter 15. Third, the poor countries, discussed in Chapter 16, can perhaps learn from us something about improving their own agricultural technology; this can generate an economic surplus for them that can be used for expanding investment and production in the nonfarm sector. Fourth, a larger percentage of people who live and work on farms are poor compared to the nonfarm population. Fifth, agriculture is important for the goods it supplies us; we spend 16 percent of our disposable personal income on food, and additional sums on nonfood items like cotton, wool, leather, and tobacco. Sixth, agriculture comes closest to the model of perfect competition, and we are thus provided with a case study to analyze that system.

We shall first apply to agriculture the demand and supply theory we covered in Chapter 5. Then we shall see why the farmers demand that the government should do something for agriculture; we shall also present an overview of two basic alternative government policies: price supports and income supports. Finally, the current farm programs will be presented and evaluated.

Demand, Supply, and Productivity

INELASTIC DEMAND The demand for farm products is quite inelastic. This means that the lower the prices, the less total revenue the farmer receives; the higher the prices, the more total revenue he receives. Various studies indicate that the elasticity of demand may average about .25. If this is true and if the price drops 10 percent, we will buy 2.5 percent more farm products; if the price rises 10 percent, we will buy 2.5 percent less.

There are three major reasons for the inelastic demand for farm products, especially for food. The first is that food is a basic necessity for which there are no substitutes. We satisfy our hunger before we spend much in other directions. That is why the poorer people are, the larger the percentage of their income they typically spend on food. Some people spend 50 percent or more of their income on food; such people live in poverty, or else they are unusually gluttonous.

The second reason for the inelastic demand for food is its rapidly diminishing marginal utility. If an affluent American family acquires a second car, its utility is fairly high. But if the same family doubled its food consumption from three meals per day to six, there would be a decline in total utility instead of an increase; marginal utility would be negative.

The third reason for inelastic demand is that the farmer gets only a small share of the dollar the consumer spends. The farmer get 40 cents for food, but for nonfood items he receives much less. To illustrate this idea, let us assume that the farmer gets 50 cents for the cotton that goes into a five dollar shirt, and any change in the price of cotton will result in an equal change in the price of the shirt. Assume further that the elasticity of demand for shirts at retail is 1; that is, if the price changes by 1 percent, the quantity demanded will change by 1 percent in the opposite direction.

Suppose the price of cotton goes down 10 percent; how much more cotton will be demanded for shirts? The cost of cotton going into the shirt will go down 10 percent of 50 cents, or 5 cents. The price of the shirt will go down 5 cents (1 percent of five dollars), and 1 percent more shirts will be bought. Therefore, 1 percent more cotton will be bought. The elasticity of demand for cotton is

$$\frac{\text{Percent change in quantity}}{\text{Percent change in price}} = \frac{1}{10} = .1$$

A 10 percent decrease in the price of cotton would result in a 1 percent increase in the quantity demanded.

The general principle discussed here can be stated as follows:

$$\frac{\text{Elasticity of}}{\text{demand at retail}} \times \frac{\text{Farmers' share of}}{\text{the consumer dollar}} = \frac{\text{Elasticity of demand}}{\text{at the farm level}}$$

In the above example, $1 \times .1 = .1$.

In the case of food, we know that the farmer gets 40 cents of each dollar spent by the consumer. Assuming that the elasticity of demand for food at retail is .5, then the elasticity of demand at the farm level is $.5 \times .4$, or .20.

The consequences to the farmers of inelastic demand will be considered further after we look at inelastic supply and increasing productivity in agriculture.

INELASTIC SUPPLY   The supply of farm products, like the demand, is quite inelastic. Output is fairly stable in the short run regardless of price. This is not true for any one product, but it is true for farm products as a whole. If the price of beans fell and remained low year after year while other prices remained stable, farmers would shift from the production of beans to the production of other crops. But if all prices fell, farmers would not reduce their output very much.

This is illustrated dramatically by the changes that occurred from 1929 to 1933 during the Great Depression. Farm product prices dropped an average of 63 percent, but production fell only 6 percent. In contrast, the prices of agricultural implements fell 6 percent, while their production fell 80 percent. This illustrates not only inelasticity of supply, but also the vulnerability of farmers to depressions in a laissez-faire economy. In such an economy they are caught in a squeeze of falling prices for farm products, while the prices of the things they buy fall far less.

Why do farmers not cut production drastically when demand decreases, as manufacturers do, and thereby avoid drastic reductions in prices? There are four important reasons for this inelasticity of supply.

First, each farmer, operating in a perfectly competitive market, can sell at the going market price all that he produces. He will not lower the price noticeably by maintaining production, nor will he raise the price if he reduces his output. This is shown in Figure 5-11 on page 112. It is in the interest of each farmer to have all the others cut back production to get higher prices, but he himself will make maximum profit if he maintains his output and sells it at a good price.

The second reason for inelastic supply is that most of the costs are already incurred by the time of harvest. If it costs $2.00 to produce a bushel of tomatoes and another 50 cents to harvest and market it, a farmer cannot hold out for $2.50 after he has produced the crop. To minimize his losses, he will sell the tomatoes for anything he can get over 50 cents a bushel.

The farmer cannot turn production off and on at short notice as the manufacturer can.

A third reason for inelastic supply is the high fixed costs in agriculture. If a farmer reduces his output, many of his costs will not be reduced at all. These fixed costs include interest and principal payments on the mortgage, property taxes, insurance premiums, and depreciation of machinery attributable to age. Even labor is largely an overhead cost, because 74 percent of the farm labor force are family workers and 26 percent are hired workers. One cannot gain anything by cutting back production and firing the members of the family. In contrast, manufacturers can cut back on variable costs like labor, raw materials, and electric power when they cut back production.

A fourth reason for inelastic supply is that farmers cannot hold their commodities off the market once they are produced. Most farm products are perishable unless processed further. Those that can be stored are also sold quickly (unless the government finances the storage) because farmers need the cash. Therefore they sell the goods regardless of price. In contrast, manufacturers and retailers can hold on to their goods until they get the price they want.

Increased productivity is the third factor, along with inelastic demand and supply, that has aggravated the farm problem.

INCREASING PRODUCTIVITY Taking 1967 as 100, total farm output rose from 44 in the period 1910–14 to 102 in 1970; crop production per acre increased from 57 to 102; and farm production per hour of work rose from 14 to 113. In 1820 each farm worker supplied 4.1 people with farm products. In 1920 he supplied 8.3 people. In 1970 he supplied 47.1 people.

It should be noted that this fantastic increase in productivity is not attained without some increases in off-the-farm efforts. Workers in industry who make machinery, petroleum products, and fertilizers are also helping agriculture become more productive. The use of mechanical power and machinery, again taking 1967 as 100, rose from 19 in the period 1910–14 to 103 in 1970; the input of fertilizer and lime went up from 7 to 113. Yet even if we consider farm output per unit of input, we find that taking 1967 as 100, it rose from 55 in the period 1910–14 to 99 in 1970.

It is interesting to note that government research, advice to farmers, and subsidies for conservation help increase farm productivity. While some government programs induce or compel farmers to restrict their acreage planted, other programs tell them how to produce more per acre. The government gets farmers to reduce production in areas of adequate rainfall; at the same time it offers large subsidies to irrigate farm land and increase production in arid regions.

Now we can examine the situation resulting from a combination of inelastic demand, inelastic supply, and increasing productivity. This is shown in Figure 14-1. The demand and supply at any one time are shown by the solid demand and supply curves. the price per unit of output is OA, OE units are produced, and the total revenue received by farmers is indicated by the rectangle OAHE.

FIGURE 14-1. The Long-Run Trend in Agriculture

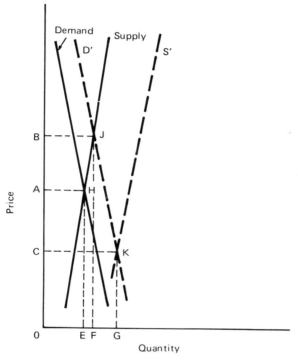

With the passage of time the demand for farm products increases because of the growth of both population and per capita income. The new demand is shown by the dashed demand curve. If the supply of farm products remained constant, the price would rise because of the inelastic demand and supply. The new price would be OB, the new quantity OF, and the new total revenue would increase to OBJF; thus farmers would be better off.

But increasing productivity in agriculture increases the supply to the dashed supply curve; farmers are willing to sell more than formerly at each price. The new price is then OC, the new quantity is OG, and the new total revenue is OCKG. Farmers now receive less money for a larger crop than formerly. This is the heart of the farm problem; this is why farmers urge the government to do something for them. We shall now look at the role of government in helping farmers.

Government Policy in Agriculture

WHY CANNOT FARMERS STICK TOGETHER? Farmers frequently blame themselves for their troubles. "If only we could stick together the way workers in unions and businessmen do, we could get our price." They look longingly at situation J in Figure 14-1, which is so much better than K. All they have to do is withhold part of the supply, and they will get more money for the smaller volume they sell. But farmers should not be so self-critical on this account, for they stick together about as well as any other group. It is the nature of their predicament that prevents them from solving their own problems, as the following example from the past will show.

Most of the Tokay grapes are grown around Lodi, California. In 1932 the growers got together and decided to hold out for at least a minimum price; they would sell all they could at that price, and the rest they would wihhold from the market. Growers of 85 percent of the grapes entered the agreement. But in four weeks the plan was abandoned, because the members of the agreement were supplying 50 percent of the grapes bought; the growers of 15 percent of the grapes, by staying out of the scheme, supplied the other 50 percent to the market.

The more successful and comprehensive the agreement is to withhold part of the supply, the greater the benefit to any "free rider" who sells all he has at the higher prices; he lets others sacrifice while he benefits to the maximum extent. This example involved a crop that was grown in only a small compact area. Imagine how difficult it would be to get together the producers of eggs in all fifty states, or the producers of potatoes or beans or hogs.

Unanimity is impossible where large numbers of people are involved. Because there are so few of them, oligopolists in business can do for themselves what farmers cannot do. If two or three or four firms dominate an industry, they know that price cutting will make them worse off. But if they curb production and maintain their prices, they will be better off.

In the case of labor, unanimity is never attained. But if 60 percent of the workers decide to strike, the other 40 percent must go along unwillingly for two reasons. First, it is difficult and expensive to run a plant with 40 percent of the labor force. Second, the 60 percent who wish to strike surround the plant and prevent the 40 percent from entering. The majority imposes its will on the minority.

Farmers cannot do that, as seen in several milk strikes that occurred in New York State over the years. If producers of 80 percent of the milk agree to hold out for a better price, the producers of the rest will ship their whole supply to market and profit from the sacrifices of the others. The majority cannot impose its will on the minority unless it patrols the highways and stops the milk trucks. This action brings out the police and all the force of the government to allow the nonstriking farmers' milk trucks to go through. The only recourse of the striking farmers is to take to the hills and shoot at the milk trucks that roll by; this has actually happened.

There are other reasons for farmers not being able to stick together, because there are many conflicting interests among them. Grain producers, for example, want high prices for their products, but livestock farmers who buy grain prefer low feed prices. New Jersey egg producers wanted high prices because it was expensive to ship feed in from the Midwest. Midwestern farmers could sell eggs to the big cities on the East Coast much cheaper, because shipping eggs costs far less than shipping the amount of grain required to produce the eggs near the market. Low prices benefited the midwestern poultrymen because they pushed most of the New Jersey chicken farmers out of production.

There is also a conflict of interest between large and small farmers, for example, on the problem of wage rates. Half the farmers hire no labor at all. Another 38 percent of the farmers hire very little labor. One percent of the farmers, the largest ones, pay 40 percent of the farm wages. In spite of farm employment being highly seasonal, farm wages averaged $1.85 per hour without room and board in June 1972 compared to $3.79 in manufacturing. Who was helped by low wages? The big farmers, who were the major employers. The small farmers were competing against cheap labor on the bigger and more efficient farms, and this depressed the prices of farm products and the incomes of the small farmers. If farm wages were twice as high, the small farmers would have fared much better. They did not realize this, for many of them absorbed the antilabor ideology of the big farmers and big business. This helped liquidate the small farmers; 55 percent of all farms disappeared betwen 1920 and 1970.

Because the farmers cannot help themselves as business and labor can, they look for government assistance. We need not think that the farmers are so ruggedly individualistic that government help has to be forced on them. Many of the federal farm programs for price supports and output restrictions since 1933 needed approval of two-thirds of the farmers involved in order to implement them. These programs were instituted for a limited number of years, and farmers were called on to vote repeatedly on acceptance or rejection of government restrictions. In almost all cases they approved.

Let us now examine the two major alternative programs for farmers— price supports and income supports.

THE THEORY OF PRICE SUPPORTS   If farm income is considered to be too low, the government can increase it with a price support program. The farmer is guaranteed a certain minimum price per unit of output. This creates an imbalance between the quantity demanded and the quantity supplied for two reasons. First, if the price is raised, people will buy less, although not very much less. Second, farmers will supply more, although not very much more, at a higher price. This is illustrated in Figure 5-16 on page 118. Overproduction of farm products does not mean that more is produced than people can use; it means more is produced than farmers can sell at the guaranteed price or some reasonably profitable price.

If the government provides a floor under prices, it has to be ready to implement this policy by inducing farmers to produce less, by buying up the surplus that cannot be sold at the guranteed price, and by storing, destroying, or diverting surpluses to lower-grade uses, like feeding potatoes to cattle.

FIGURE 14-2. Price Supports and the Cost to Consumers and Government

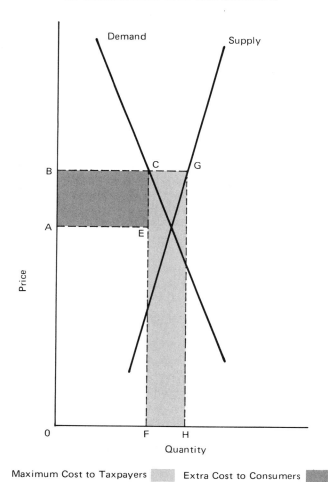

Figure 14-2 shows the price support situation and the possible cost to the government and the consumers. Under laissez faire the price would be OA per unit. If the price floor is set at OB, farmers will wish to produce the quantity OH. As only OF can be sold at that price, the government will have to buy up FH units, and the cost to the taxpayer will be price times quantity, or FCGH. The extra cost to consumers is the higher price they have to pay times the quantity they buy, or ABCE.

The government can reduce or eliminate the cost to the taxpayer by requiring that the farmers produce OF units. It can pay the farmers to produce less, or it can force them to produce less without paying them a subsidy, and it has used both methods. In either case the cost to the taxpayer is reduced.

It is significant to note that price supports benefit the farmers both at the expense of the consumers and the taxpayers. In recent years the federal government has spent about $5 billion annually to help farmers. Nonfarm consumers have paid about $4.5 billion more each year because of higher prices for farm products than they would have without federal price support programs. The total transfer from consumers and taxpayers to farmers of $9 billion to $10 billion annually is comparable to the total federal, state, and local cost of various public assistance (welfare) programs, including medicaid, which cost $12.8 billion in 1970.

The price support program helps mostly the big farmers, because they have the most to sell at the higher prices. Big farmers are also more highly specialized and grow only a few products. Small farmers are more diversified and are partly self-sufficient; they consume a larger percentage of their output than big farmers do. Therefore, the small farmers get price supports on a smaller percentage of their output than do the big farmers.

Price supports also benefit most those farmers with bumper crops, and it helps the least those whose output falters or fails. If your crop is half what it normally is, your benefits from price supports will be cut in half. But if you have an exceptionally large crop, your benefits will go up proportionally. For example, average corn production in Texas rose from thirty-two bushels per acre during 1962–66 to sixty-one bushels in 1970. In Florida during the same years production fell from thirty-nine to twenty-five bushels per acre. Obviously the corn growers in Florida needed more assistance than those of Texas, but the price support program for corn helped the Texas farmers with their large crops much more than the Florida farmers with short crops. The same thing occurs within states; those who are the most successful and affluent get the most from the government farm program.

THE THEORY OF INCOME SUPPORTS The income support program has been called the Brannan Plan after President Truman's Secretary of Agriculture, Charles F. Brannan, who proposed it in 1949. The basic idea is for the government to let prices find their own level in a free market, and then give the farmer a check for the difference between the market price and the guaranteed price. Thus, if the guarantee is 40 cents per dozen eggs, and the eggs are sold for 30 cents, the government gives the farmer 10 cents for each dozen eggs he sells.

The situation is shown in Figure 14-3. If the equilibrium price at E is considered unsatisfactory, the government guarantees the farmers a price of OA. Without any restrictions on output, farmers will produce OG units at that price. Consumers will buy that quantity only if the price is OC. Therefore the government will have to pay, if it is to meet its commitment to the farmers, a cash subsidy of CA per unit of output. The total expenditure by consumers for farm products will be OCFG, and the total government subsidy will be CABF.

FIGURE 14-3.   Income Supports and the Cost to Government

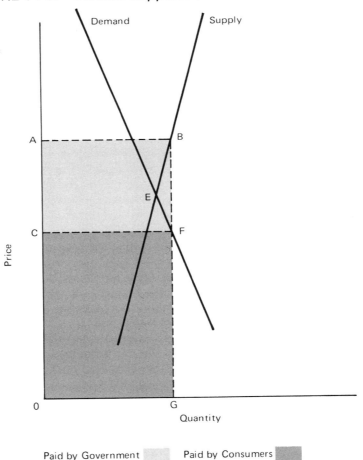

The income support program avoids the expensive storage of "surplus" farm products. Output does not have to be restricted, and part of the produce does not have to be destroyed or sold abroad cheaper than at home. This kind of policy would reconcile the interests of consumers and farmers. The former would get farm products at low prices. The latter would get their income raised through government subsidies instead of high prices in the marketplace. But the greatest burden would be thrown on the taxpayers; that is why the income support program was denounced and rejected.

Here you might object, saying, "Aren't we all both consumers and taxpayers? What difference does it make which group bears the burden?" It is true that we are all consumers and taxpayers, but our relative interests in these positions can vary greatly, as the following example will illustrate.

Suppose under the income support program food will be 10 percent cheaper and all federal taxes will be 2 percent higher than under the price support program. Suppose a family earning $8,000 a year spends $2,000 on food and $1,000 on federal taxes. It gains $200 on the lower cost of food, and it pays an extra $20 in taxes. This family, if it knew its own interests, would be enthusiastic about the income support program.

Suppose that Mr. Rockefeller has an income of $10,000,000 per year, and he pays $4,000,000 in federal taxes. As he does much entertaining and has many servants, he spends $200,000 a year on food. His benefit under the income support program would be a saving of 10 percent or $20,000 on his food bill. His cost would be an extra 2 percent in taxes or $80,000. He may well condemn this type of program.

In other words, the lower our incomes, the more our interests as consumers predominate over our interests as taxpayers. The richer we are, the more our interests as taxpayers predominate. It was the rich and powerful who had access to the news media and who maligned the income support program as being "socialistic," involving "government handouts," and being generally immoral.

The Current Farm Programs

MARKETING AGREEMENTS AND ORDERS   Marketing agreements and orders have been in effect since 1933. They provide a little-known but powerful means of keeping prices high by restricting the sale of farm products. They are widely used in the marketing of all kinds of fruits, vegetables, nuts, and milk. These regulations keep small sizes of fruits and vegetables off the market even though they are just as nutritious and palatable as the large sizes. This program may also limit the quantity of the large sizes and best grades that can be marketed. The milk marketing orders classify milk according to use and set minimum producer prices; the purpose is to raise the price of milk consumed in fluid form because of the inelastic demand.

Marketing agreements and orders are published in the government's

Federal Register. The following is what appeared there during July 1971. Earlier programs that continued to operate did not appear during that month, of course; only new, changed, or updated programs were published.

During July 1971, the shipments of lemons and Valencia oranges from Arizona and parts of California were limited to a certain number of carloads each week. Pears grown in California, limes from Florida, and peaches from Colorado had to be at least a certain minimum size in order to be marketed. Small potatoes could not be shipped from Colorado, Washington, Oregon, and Idaho unless they were destined for livestock feed, charity, canning, freezing, or other processing. All fresh cranberries had to be at least 13/32 of an inch in diameter in order to be sold. Dried prunes could not be shipped from California if there were more than 40 prunes per pound, and 28,000 tons of large prunes were sold as livestock feed during the 1970–71 marketing year to keep prices up. In the 1971–72 crop year, 40 percent of the California dried prunes were to be withheld from the market. The potential supply of celery grown in Florida during the 1971–72 marketing year was 8,541,000 crates, and the proposal was to permit 7,-887,375 crates to be marketed. Small and damaged peanuts were withheld from human consumption, and also those with more than a fixed moisture content. There were proposed restrictions on the marketing of dates and olives. These programs are costly to administer and increase the cost of living.

SIZE OF FARMS AND PRICE SUPPORT PAYMENTS The greater the output per farm, the greater the benefit under the price support program. This means that most of the payments go to the biggest farmers.

In 1971, 8.8 percent of the farms sold over $40,000 of farm products each; they accounted for 59.3 percent of the sales, and they received 34.5 percent of the direct government payments to farmers. The average payment per farm in this category was $4,289. At the lower end of the scale, 51.5 percent of the farms sold less than $5,000 each; they accounted for 5.1 percent of the sales, and they received 13.1 percent of the direct government payments. The average payment per farm in this group was $279. Beginning in 1971, large government payments were reduced. No grower could collect more than $55,000 on each of three crops—wheat, feed grains, and cotton—for a maximum of $165,000. But if a farmer were to divide up his farm legally among his family members, each person would be eligible to receive a $55,000 subsidy on each of three crops. This is known to have happened.

Sugar subsidy payments were not limited, however, and payments of over a million dollars per sugar grower continue to be made. Total sugar subsidies to United States producers are about $90 million per year, and the United States wholesale price of sugar was 11.8 cents a pound in July 1972 compared with 5.6 cents abroad. The public pays twice for our domestic sugar production, in high prices for sugar, and in cash subsidies to the producers. In 1969 the nine largest sugar producers in Louisiana (including the State Penitentiary, which got a subsidy of $50,985) collected a total of $945,296 in subsidies, while field workers in sugar were getting $1.53 per hour. In Florida twenty-three of the largest sugar producers received a total of $3,739,154, while workers were paid $2.04 per hour. In Hawaii the twenty-four biggest farmers were paid $9,404,248, and the workers received $3.08 per hour. In Puerto Rico seven large producers got $1,004,391 while the workers received $1.03 per hour, in spite of the fact that the cost of living is higher than in the United States. These are the kinds of "welfare" payments for rich farmers that are justified because of poverty in agriculture.

THE WOOL PROGRAM   President Eisenhower and the Congress adopted the income support program for wool even though he had called the Brannan Plan "moral bankruptcy" in his major campaign speech on farm matters in 1952. The previous price support program for wool was not working because our wool was moving into storage until we had accumulated 100 million pounds of unsold wool. Meanwhile we imported two-thirds of our needs in spite of the tariff.

In January 1972 under the income support system, the market price of wool was 63 cents per pound, and the support price was 72 cents. The farmers received the difference as a subsidy from the government. You might think that the authorities would ascertain how much wool each farmer sold and pay him 9 cents per pound. But that is not the way it was done. The program was given an additional twist in the direction of rewarding rich and successful farmers and penalizing the poor and unsuccessful. If the market price of 63 cents is increased 14.3 percent, it will yield the support price of 72 cents. The government does not assume that each farmer got the average market price and, therefore, should receive a 9-cent subsidy per pound. Instead, it ascertains not only how much wool each farmer sold, but what price he received. If a farmer has healthy sheep and good wool, is a good bargainer and attracts the big buyers because of the large volume of output, he might get 75 cents per pound. The government adds to that 14.3 percent as a subsidy, or 10.7 cents. If a farmer has sick sheep and poor wool, is an inefficient marketer, and produces a small output and has few buyers to choose from, he may get 50 cents a pound for his wool. His cash subsidy will be 14.3 percent of that, or a little over 7 cents per pound. Again we see that the more successful you are, the more you get from the government.

THE AGRICULTURAL ACT OF 1970   The government accepted the idea of income supports in the Agricultural Act of 1970. It did this only to a limited extent, and only for the major storable commodities, not for perishables as the original Brannan Plan proposed. The Agricultural Act of 1970 does away with specific acreage controls for individual crops. Farmers who want price or income supports are told to retire a fixed number of cropland acres from production.

Farmers are limited to a subsidy payment of $55,000 per person on each of three crops. There is no limit, however, on how much the government lends a farmer on his crop that is stored in order to raise the price. Nor is there any limit on the size of payment when the government buys a farmer's crop to implement price supports.

The wheat program provides that the price of wheat should be supported either by the government lending farmers money to keep the wheat in storage or by outright purchase. The minimum support price is $1.25 per bushel and the maximum is the parity price. The parity price is a very common term in agricultural and governmental circles. It is computed by a simple formula explained below.

Agriculture was considered to be in a good balance with the rest of the economy during the period preceding the First World War. The five years 1910–14 (August 1, 1909 to July 31, 1914) are therefore taken as the base years from which parity price is calculated. The aim is to give each unit of farm output the same purchasing power now as it had then. As a farmer once expressed it, if a bushel of wheat could buy a shirt before the First World War, it should be able to buy a shirt now. The average cost of all the things farmers bought during the period 1910–14, both for consumption and for productive purposes, is taken as 100. If the average price of these items doubled, then the price of wheat would have to double if it is to sell at parity price.

A guaranteed parity price does not mean that farm income will remain the same as in the base period. If a farmer produces many more bushels of wheat now than he did then, his income can rise. Parity price aims at stable purchasing power per unit of output rather than a fixed purchasing power for the farmer's total income.

Parity price supports based on the period 1910–14 introduced serious distortions in price relationships. For example, the efficiency of wheat production increased much more than the efficiency of producing livestock. Farmers would produce more and more wheat if they were guaranteed a parity price. At the same time consumer purchasing shifted away from wheat and bread to some extent and toward livestock products. This would tend to reduce further the price of wheat and increase the difficulty and cost of maintaining the price at parity. Actually by the end of the Second World War some commodities, such as beef cattle and lambs, were selling above parity, and numerous other farm products, including wheat, corn, potatoes, and citrus fruit, were selling below parity.

The government, therefore, modified the concept of parity price in 1948 by adjusting it to the price trends of the most recent decade. If the price of wheat tended to fall in recent years, its parity price would be lowered. If the price of meat tended to rise, its parity price would be raised. This revision affects parity prices for individual commodities, but it does not affect the level of parity prices as a whole for all agricultural products. Therefore our definition of parity price has to be modified; it means that a unit of farm product should have the same purchasing power as it did during 1910–14, but adjusted by recent price trends, up or down, of that commodity.

Taking 1910–14 as 100, farmers in May 1972 were paying an average of 428 for the things they bought; they were receiving 313 for the things they sold. That is, the cost of the goods they purchased rose 328 percent, and the price of their farm products rose 213 percent. The "parity ratio" gives the average purchasing power of farm products compared with the period 1910–14. It is calculated by dividing the prices received index by the prices paid index; in this example the parity ratio is

$$\frac{\text{prices received index}}{\text{prices paid index}} \quad \text{or} \quad \frac{313}{428} \quad \text{or 73.}$$

This means that in May 1972 a typical basket of farm products could buy 73 percent of what it would have bought in 1910–14.

Getting back to the provisions of the Agricultural Act of 1970, wheat is supported at between $1.25 per bushel and the parity price. Farmers may be required to keep up to 15 million acres idle in order to receive price supports. The government may even pay farmers for keeping more land idle than the mandatory acreage. The support price for wheat that goes into products used directly for human consumption, like flour, is at parity price; the wheat used as livestock feed or for export may be, and has been, below that. The processors of wheat for food have to pay 75 cents more per bushel than the basic government support price. Thus, some of the direct payments are borne by the consumers rather than the federal budget. If this does not bring that part of the wheat crop up to the parity price, government subsidies make up the difference. All farmers who are authorized to grow wheat share in the higher price of wheat used for food.

In the case of feed grains, the price of corn is supported at the level that encourages exports and prevents excessive stocks from accumulating. The minimum support price is $1 per bushel, and the maximum is 90 percent of parity. The prices of barley, oats, rye, and grain sorghums are similarly supported. The government makes income payments for corn to bring the total up to $1.35 per bushel or 70 percent of parity, whichever is higher, on half the output per farm. As a precondition for such price supports and subsidies, farmers may be required to keep part of their acreage idle. The government could pay them for diverting additional acreage away from productive use.

In the past, the price support program for cotton resulted in decreased exports and in decreased domestic use because of the rise of synthetic fibers. The Agricultural Act of 1970 sought to remedy this by allowing the price of cotton to fall and offering the farmers income payments. Price supports for cotton are to be low enough "to keep United States upland cotton competitive and to retain an adequate share of the world market for such cotton." It is interesting to note that most of the world's cotton is produced by countries that are too poor to subsidize their own farmers, and we are prepared to compete with them for our share of the world market even if we have to drive prices down to do it. The market price of cotton is supported at 90 percent of the world price during the two preceding years, but this can be lowered to maintain cotton sales at home and abroad. The government subsidy is added to the market price to guarantee the producers 35 cents per pound or 65 percent of parity, whichever is greater. Farmers may be required to set aside acreage for nonproductive use if they are to receive subsidy payments, and they may be paid for additional acreage set aside.

Under other laws the government limits the permissible production of rice, tobacco, sugar, peanuts, and extra-long staple cotton to keep prices high.

In view of the poverty and hunger at home, and even greater poverty and hunger abroad, our record of price supports, crop restriction, and the diversion and destruction of farm products is a sorry one indeed. It began with President Hoover in 1929 and reached unprecedented heights under Roosevelt. Every president since then, both Democratic and Republican, has continued these policies with minor modifications. In view of the poverty that exists, especially in agriculture, the distribution of government benefits mostly to the big, rich farmers is deplorable. Most neglected are over a million wage laborers on farms; they are among the lowest paid, most exploited workers in our labor force. The world certainly needs all the food that can be produced; and government aid should be for those who need it, not for the affluent.

Summary

Both the demand for and supply of farm products are inelastic. As the efficiency of production in agriculture is rising rapidly, the long-run tendency is for the prices of farm products to fall compared to prices of the things farmers buy. This trend is partly offset by rising population and rising per capita income, both of which increase the demand for farm products.

Farmers, operating under conditions that come close to the model of pure competition, have too little market power to improve their situation. They therefore have relied on the government to help them.

There have been two basic types of government programs to aid farmers. The first, relied on heavily in the 1930's and 1940's, was the price support and output restriction program. The aim was to give the farmer something approaching a parity price for his products. Parity price means that a unit of farm product should have the same purchasing power now as it had during the five years preceding the First World War. This type of program throws the greatest burden on consumers in the form of higher prices for farm products and greater expenditures on them because of the inelastic demand.

The income support program does not restrict the production and sale of farm products. The government pays the farmer the difference between the market price and some guaranteed price. This imposes the greatest burden on the taxpayers. In recent years this type of program has been used, along with some price supports and crop restriction, so that the United States could be competitive with other countries in selling wool, cotton, wheat, and feed grains.

Our government programs for helping farmers are geared to the volume of output. Therefore, they give most of the benefits to the biggest farmers. Beginning in 1971, the distribution of benefits was modified by limiting government payments to each farmer to $55,000 on each of three crops— wheat, feed grains, and cotton. In spite of this, most of the government benefits still go to the biggest farmers.

QUESTIONS AND PROBLEMS

1   Would farmers be better or worse off if tractors had never been invented?

2   If favorable weather increased the output of every farm 25 percent, would farmers be better or worse off?

3   If the government did nothing for farmers, is there a danger that farmers would cut production so much that most of us would be hungry?

4   How does the restriction of output and price supports square with the problem of world hunger discussed in Chapter 13?

5   Explain why high food prices are similar to a regressive tax.

6   Suppose a farmer invests $100,000 of his own money, and he has a net income of $10,000 per year. Is he doing well or poorly? Explain.

7   Farming has been highly mechanized with labor-saving machinery in spite of farm wage rates being about half of wage rates in manufacturing. Why has this happened, and what can or should be done about it?

8   Why do prices received by farmers fluctuate more than prices received by grocery stores?

9   The price of wheat averaged 87 cents during the period 1910–14. The index of prices paid by farmers, taking 1910–14 as 100, was 428 in May 1972. If the government were to support the price of wheat at 90 percent of parity, what would the support price be?

BIBLIOGRAPHY

Agricultural Situation (Monthly publication of the Statistical Reporting Service, U.S. Department of Agriculture).

CAULEY, TROY J., *Agriculture in an Industrial Economy: The Agrarian Crisis.* New York: Bookman Associates—Twayne Publishers, 1956.

HEADY, EARL O., *A Primer on Food, Agriculture, and Public Policy.* New York: Random House, 1967.

SCHULTZE, CHARLES L., *The Distribution of Farm Subsidies: Who Gets the Benefits?* Washington, D.C.: The Brookings Institution, 1971.

U.S. DEPARTMENT OF AGRICULTURE, *Agricultural Statistics, 1971.* Washington, D.C.: Government Printing Office, 1971.

U.S. DEPARTMENT OF AGRICULTURE, *1971 Changes in Farm Production and Efficiency, A Summary Report,* Statistical Bulletin No. 233. Washington, D.C., 1971.

U.S. DEPARTMENT OF AGRICULTURE, AGRICULTURAL STABILIZATION AND CONSERVATION SERVICE, *Compilation of Statutes Relating to Soil Conservation . . . ,* Agricultural Handbook No. 408. Washington, D.C.: Government Printing Office, 1971.

U.S. DEPARTMENT OF AGRICULTURE, ECONOMIC RESEARCH SERVICE, *Our 31,000 Largest Farms,* Agricultural Economic Report No. 175. Washington, D.C.: Government Printing Office, 1970.

15

Problems
of
International Trade

The gold standard is already a barbarous relic.
—John Maynard Keynes, 1923

International trade affects us all. We all consume some imported goods when we eat breakfast, for example, or buy pots, pans, and automobiles. Many of us work at producing things that are exported. When our government raises the price of gold, which it does not buy or sell, this seems far removed from our daily concerns; yet the result is that we export more goods because they become cheaper to foreigners, and we import less goods because their prices rise. When American tourists return to the United States from abroad, they learn that they can bring back less duty-free liquor and other goods than formerly; they suddenly feel the effect of the deficit in our balance of payments. This chapter will enhance our understanding of such matters.

Countries engage in international trade for three basic reasons. First, they buy abroad things they want but cannot produce at home. We, for example, import all our coffee, cocoa, tea, bananas, spices, silk, diamonds (both industrial and ornamental), natural rubber, and almost all our tin and nickel. We either cannot produce these things ourselves, or we could produce them only at prohibitive costs, as growing coffee and bananas in greenhouses.

A second major reason for international trade is that we thereby have a greater choice of goods. Some people prefer French wine or Japanese cameras or German automobiles or British textiles. These products may be cheaper or more expensive than the domestic equivalents; they may be better or worse in quality; or they may be so different as to make comparisons somewhat uncertain. But if consumer satisfaction is one of the goals of economics, that justifies international trade. Thus, we export our wheat and import Canadian wheat with a high gluten content to produce flour blends that consumers here prefer. We export tobacco and import types we cannot

315

grow. We export cotton and import long-fiber cotton from the United Arab Republic and short-fiber cotton from India for special purposes.

A third major reason for international trade is that we can buy goods abroad cheaper than at home. The international division of labor, like the domestic division of labor, increases efficiency and raises levels of living. For example, we can and do produce sugar, petroleum, iron ore, and textiles at home, but we also buy part of our supply abroad because it is cheaper.

In international trade the goods must ultimately be paid for in the currency of the producer. The British pound is more valuable than the United States dollar. But an American exporter would not get far if he earned pounds and tried to use them to pay his workers, or to buy supplies or pay taxes to our government. Therefore the problem of making international payments is also important in our analysis of the problems involved in international trade.

In this chapter we shall discuss first the basic theory of international trade. Then we shall analyze the balance of payments and what we mean when we say whether or not it is in equilibrium. We shall then review several types of protectionist measures and discuss their merits. Finally we shall consider the operations of two major international organizations.

The Theory of the International Division of Labor

THE THEORY OF ABSOLUTE ADVANTAGE International trade arises when one country can produce a commodity cheaper than another, and the second country can produce something else cheaper than the first. Both sides gain from such an international division of labor. Thus, we sell tractors to Brazil and buy coffee, or we exchange electric generators for bananas from Guatemala. This is called absolute advantage.

But how can we compare costs of production among different countries? Brazilian costs are given in cruzeiros, their currency, and our costs are in dollars. The exchange rate, the price of cruzeiros in dollars, will tell us how much coffee will cost us in dollars. The price of dollars in terms of cruzeiros will tell the Brazilians how much our tractors will cost them in their currency. But this method of comparing costs cannot be used to determine whether a country has an absolute advantage in trade or a comparative advantage, to be discussed below. In both cases people wish to buy foreign goods if they are cheaper.

In the late 1700's and early 1800's, the economists of the classical school used labor costs to compare the efficiency of production in different countries. This cost included both direct and indirect labor. They added the labor cost of actually making the final product, the labor cost that went into making the machinery and raw materials used, transportation cost, and so on. We can illustrate absolute advantage in this way: suppose producing a tractor costs us 10 days of labor, and it would cost Brazil 30. Suppose also that producing a ton of coffee would cost us 500 days of labor, and it would cost Brazil 50. Obviously we are more efficient at producing tractors, and Brazil is more efficient at producing coffee, and trade would be advantageous to both.

But what if one country is less efficient than another in producing everything? Should it protect itself from lower-cost foreign goods, or can it benefit from trade?

THE THEORY OF COMPARATIVE ADVANTAGE   The theory of comparative advantage tells us that if one country is more efficient than another in producing everything, it should specialize in producing those things in which its margin of efficiency is the greatest. The second country should produce those things in which its margin of disadvantage is the smallest. Only if one country is more efficient than another by the same percentage in the production of every good would there be no gain from the international division of labor. If one country is twice as efficient as another in producing everything, there will be no gain from trade. But if the first country is twice as efficient in producing one commodity and 50 percent more efficient in producing a second item, it should produce the first product for both countries, and the less efficient country should produce the second product for both countries.

Let us consider two areas and two commodities. One area can produce both commodities cheaper than the other, yet both can gain from the division of labor through free trade. In our first example we will consider labor cost rather than money cost to simplify the problem. Because the principle of comparative advantage applies within a country as well as between countries, we shall work out this theory on the basis of New York State and the state of Washington producing shoes and apples.

In Table 15-1 we assume that New York State can produce a pair of shoes with 4 hours of labor and a bushel of apples with 1 hour; Washington can produce a pair of shoes with 12 hours of labor and a bushel of apples with 2 hours. New York has an absolute advantage in both shoes and apples and a comparative advantage in shoes, because New York is three times as efficient as Washington in producing shoes, but only twice as efficient in apples.

TABLE 15-1   Comparative Advantage Within a Country Based on Labor Costs

	New York	Washington
Labor cost of a pair of shoes	4 hours	12 hours
Labor cost of a bushel of apples	1 hour	2 hours

318 Problems of the Nation's Economy

Washington has an absolute disadvantage in producing both shoes and apples, but it has a comparative advantage in apples. It is only a third as efficient as New York in shoes, but half as efficient in apples. Or to put it another way, shoes in Washington take three times as much labor to produce as in New York, while apples take only twice as much labor.

We assume that production can be expanded or reduced at constant cost per unit of output, that differences in cost between the two states persist, and that transportation costs are zero. New York should be willing to sell 1 pair of shoes for 4 or more bushels of apples, because the labor cost of 1 pair of shoes equals the labor cost of 4 bushels of apples in New York. Washington should be willing to offer 6 or fewer bushels of apples for a pair of shoes, because the labor cost of 6 bushels of apples equals the labor cost of 1 pair of shoes in Washington. Therefore, the limits of exchange are 4 to 6 bushels of apples for 1 pair of shoes.

Assume that the final terms of trade are 5 bushels of apples for 1 pair of shoes. What does each side gain from trade? If New York devotes 20 hours to producing its own shoes and apples, it can have 4 pair of shoes and 4 bushels of apples. Through specialization and trade, however, it can produce 5 pair of shoes in 20 hours, keep 4 pair, and exchange 1 pair for 5 bushels of apples. Its gain is 1 bushel of apples.

Washington can produce 1 pair of shoes and 4 bushels of apples in 20 hours. Or, alternatively, it can produce 10 bushels of apples, keep 5, and exchange 5 for a pair of shoes. Its gain is also a bushel of apples.

Our second example will deal with money costs and exchange rates, and it will illustrate one possible path toward international equilibrium. Assume two countries, the United States and Great Britain, and two commodities, cotton yarn and steel. Suppose, as shown in Table 15-2, that Great Britain can produce steel for £40 per ton and cotton yarn for £60 per ton and that the United States can produce steel for $100 per ton and yarn for $200 per ton. If the exchange rate is £1 for $4, British steel would cost us $160 while our own costs us $100; British yarn would cost us $240 while our own costs $200. As both our steel and yarn are cheaper than Britain's, we would refuse to buy either from her.

We can see that Great Britain would find that imported steel and yarn are cheaper than her own if the pound is worth $4. Our steel would cost her £25 compared to her own, which costs £40; our yarn would cost her £50 compared to her own, which costs £60.

The British will wish to acquire dollars to buy our goods, but we will not wish to buy pounds because we do not want the more expensive British goods. The price of the dollar will rise, and the price of the pound will fall. Suppose the exchange rate swings so dramatically as to leave the pound priced at $2.

We can see from Table 15-2 that at this new exchange rate we will want to import both steel and yarn from Britain. British steel will cost us

TABLE 15-2 Comparative Advantage Between Countries with Varying Exchange
Rates

	Cost of. Steel	Cost of Yarn	If £1 = $4		If £1 = $2		If £1 = $3	
			Cost of Steel	Cost of Yarn	Cost of Steel	Cost of Yarn	Cost of Steel	Cost of Yarn
United States	$100	$200	$100 or £25	$200 or £50	$100 or £50	$200 or £100	$100 or £33⅓	$200 or £66⅔
Great Britain	£40	£60	£40 or $160	£60 or $240	£40 or $80	£60 or $120	£40 or $120	£60 or $180

$80 a ton compared to our own, which costs $100; British yarn will cost us
$120 compared to our own, which costs $200. Britain, in contrast, will not
import our goods. Our steel would cost it £50 compared to its domestic
cost of £40; our yarn would cost £100 compared to its own, which costs
£60.

Our eagerness to buy pounds to pay for imports, and the British re-
fusal to buy dollars from us, will cause the price of the pound to rise and
that of the dollar to fall. Suppose the exchange rate becomes £1 = $3. We
can now see from Table 15-2 that British yarn costs us $180 per ton com-
pared to our domestic cost of $200; we therefore import yarn. Our yarn
would cost Britain £66⅔ compared to her domestic cost of £60; she will,
therefore, not buy yarn from us. British steel would cost us $120 compared
to our domestic cost of $100; therefore we do not import steel. Our steel
would cost Britain £33⅓ compared to its domestic cost of £40; therefore
Britain imports our steel. It is of mutual advantage for Britain to produce
yarn for both countries and for the United States to produce steel for both.

The principle of comparative advantage works all around us. Suppose
a dentist is twice as efficient as her secretary at typing and shorthand.
Should she do her own secretarial work? Not if she is ten or twenty times
as good at dentistry as her secretary is at dentistry. The principle of comparative advantage tells us that we do not have to be best in our field to
earn a living and make a contribution to the world's work. It will pay each
person, like each country, to work at that job where his comparative advantage is the greatest or his comparative disadvantage is the smallest. If I
am half as good as Henry Ford as a college teacher and one twentieth as
good at running the Ford Motor Company, he will not try to take my job.
Of course he never gave me a chance to compete for his job. And this
brings us to some of the limitations and qualifications that make the theory
of comparative advantage less than universally applicable.

THE LIMITATIONS OF THE THEORY OF COMPARATIVE ADVANTAGE The theory
of comparative advantage is a static principle based on the status quo of

the current situation. It does not consider the changes that are possible and necessary to redistribute the affluence that only a few enjoy for special reasons. This can be illustrated in the example of the dentist and the secretary given above. The latter might state his case like this:

> You have a comparative advantage in dentistry because your father once robbed a bank and got away with the loot. He could afford to educate you. My father, being honest and poor, could not send me to college. If I could have competed with you on an even basis, I would have had the comparative advantage in dentistry, and you would have been my secretary. As things stand now, you are rich enough to send your daughter to college, and she will follow in your footsteps and become a professional. I cannot afford to educate my son, and he will follow in my footsteps and become a secretary. I demand equal opportunity for my child so that the law of comparative advantage will be based on ability rather than on inherited affluence.

So it is with nations. Those countries that produce raw materials face serious disadvantages, but the principle of comparative advantage anchors them to their present pattern of production. If they can somehow wrench themselves out of their underdeveloped state, this principle can reassert itself on a higher level, with a division of labor among efficient industrialized countries of equal market power.

The theory of comparative advantage also assumes full employment. But suppose a country suffers from unemployment. If it costs $2.00 to produce a commodity and $1.90 to import it, comparative advantage tells us to buy it abroad. But suppose of the $2.00 domestic cost, $1.00 is for labor. By importing the commodity, labor will become unemployed. As workers are not left to starve to death, they will get half pay even if they do not work, or the equivalent of 50 cents per unit of output they might have produced. To the price of the imported item we must now add this 50 cent cost and so the item now costs more than the domestically produced item. This discrepancy is due to the social cost of the import being much higher than the private cost because of the unemployment it causes. Each item that is imported costs the buyer $1.90, and it costs society 50 cents for welfare benefits for the unemployed workers. As the country could make the commodity itself for $2.00 and thereby eliminate unemployment, it would be cheaper to make the good at home rather than import it.

There are two ways to handle this discrepancy. One method would be to produce the goods domestically and thus provide the goods and employment for less cost in the short run. In the long run, however, it may be better to import the goods and shift the workers, if possible, into enterprises that are more competitive. The latter method would also raise the income of the workers in the long run.

Another disadvantage of the first method is that if all countries suffer from unemployment, they cannot all increase employment by becoming more self-sufficient. They would simply reduce efficiency by curbing the international division of labor.

There are better ways for the rich, industrialized countries to reach full employment than through protectionism. If our textile industry declines because of imported textiles, we are likely to expand our exports of computers, because foreigners now earn more dollars to spend on our goods. Our economy is so diversified that we can easily shift production from those industries that have a comparative disadvantage to those that have a comparative advantage. Our real income will rise. If the unemployed textile workers cannot all find jobs in the computer industry, they could find jobs if the government followed the proper fiscal and monetary policies on a scale large enough to generate full employment.

The underdeveloped countries, in contrast, might be able to achieve fuller employment only through protectionism. Sudan, for example, earns 63 percent of its foreign exchange by the export of cotton. If it has unemployment, it might solve the problem by protecting its textile industry; it can then turn its own cotton into manufactured goods for sale within the country, even though its cost of production is higher than abroad. Why might a protectionist policy be good for Sudan and not for the United States? First, Sudan may have no feasible alternative employment. Second, Sudan may be too poor and underdeveloped to generate greater employment through monetary and fiscal policies. Third, other countries will probably buy the same amount of Sudan's cotton regardless of whether Sudan adopts protectionist or free trade policies; in contrast, the United States would export less if we were protectionist than if we increased our imports. Fourth, our increase of tariffs would be more likely to provoke increased tariffs abroad than would Sudan's. Therefore, comparative advantage can be permitted to operate more freely by a rich country than a poor one.

The Balance of Payments

DEBITS AND CREDITS The balance of payments is a record of all international transactions between the residents of a country and the residents of the rest of the world. It has debit and credit entries. In the United States balance of payments, a debit entry occurs when we make a payment to foreigners for whatever reason during the time period being considered. A credit is recorded when a foreigner makes a payment to us.

The following are debit items in our balance of payments. If we buy goods or services abroad, we have to pay foreigners for them. When we increase our checking accounts abroad, we are lending money to foreign bankers; as we hand them the money to hold for us, this is a debit. When we make foreign loans and investments, we are in effect handing money to foreigners, and these are debits. Even if a United States corporation sends machinery to its foreign subsidiary, this is a foreign investment, which is a debit. When we send gifts abroad, we are handing foreigners money or the equivalent in goods, and that is a debit. When we pay interest and dividends to foreign holders of our stocks, bonds, or bank accounts, these payments are debits.

Credits occur when foreigners hand us money for whatever reason. We receive payment when we export goods or services. If foreigners increase their bank balances in the United States, they are lending us the money, and this is a credit in our balance of payments. When foreigners buy our stocks or bonds, these are credits to us. When they pay us interest and dividends on our foreign investments, or when rich foreigners send gifts to poor relatives in the United States, these are credits in our balance of payments.

The debits and credits in a country's balance of payments are always equal (but as we shall see later, they are not always in equilibrium). The reason they are equal is that we use a double-entry system of international bookkeeping. Each transaction gives rise to both debit and credit entries, as the following examples will show.

Suppose we export 100 cases of whiskey to Great Britain, and we are paid £1,500 for them, or $3,600. The export of goods is a credit to us, but the debit arises when we increase our foreign checking account by that sum. If we use this money to buy 500 Bibles from Britain, the import of $3,600 worth of Bibles is a debit in our balance of payments. The credit arises when we draw funds from our foreign checking accounts to pay for our import of Bibles.

If we receive a $25 international money order from a rich British relative, the gift to us is a credit. Our debit of an equal amount arises when a British bank has reduced its checking account in the United States by $25 to make this payment. If we send a package of food abroad as a gift, the credit arises from our export of food, and the debit is the dollar value of our gift abroad. If a foreigner buys a United States government bond, the credit is the foreigner lending us money by buying our bond. The debit is our paying out dollars from foreign bank balances owned in our country.

If debits and credits are always equal, what do we mean by a deficit in the balance of payments? We shall prepare to answer this question by first looking at the United States balance of payments.

THE UNITED STATES BALANCE OF PAYMENTS Table 15-3 presents the United States balance of payments for 1971. It is the record of our transactions with the rest of the world.

Line 1 shows that in 1971 we imported more merchandise than we exported, by almost $3 billion. From 1893 through 1970, we always exported more than we imported, so that this represents a most unusual situation for

TABLE 15-3   United States Balance of Payments, 1971
(in millions of dollars)
(Details may not add to totals because of rounding.)

	Credits	Debits	Net Credits (+) or Debits (−)
I. *Current Account*			
1. Merchandise	42,769	45,648	− 2,879
2. Military transactions, net		2,854	− 2,854
3. Travel and transportation, net		2,246	− 2,246
4. Investment income	12,711	4,761	+ 7,950
5. Other services, net	728		+ 728
6. Remittances, pensions, and other transfers, net		1,459	− 1,459
7. U.S. government grants (excluding military)		2,014	− 2,014
8. Balance on current account			− 2,774
II. *Long-Term Capital Account*			
9. U.S. government capital flows and payments, net		2,382	− 2,382
10. Long-term private capital flows, net		4,128	− 4,128
11. Balance on current account and long-term capital			− 9,284
12. Other capital flows, net		1,812	− 1,812
13. Errors and unrecorded transactions, net		10,878	−10,878
14. Net liquidity balance			−21,973
III. *Balancing Items*			
15. U.S. outpayments of international reserves (such as our paying foreigners the short-term capital we owe them, or our increasing our reserve assets abroad)		8,333	− 8,333
16. U.S. receipts of international reserves (such as foreigners increasing their short-term capital in the U.S., or our withdrawing short-term capital from abroad)	30,306		+30,306
17. Overall balance			0

Source: Federal Reserve Bulletin, *Vol. 58, No. 6 (June 1972), p. A 74.*

us. As recently as the period 1965–69, our exports averaged almost $3 billion per year more than our imports. This dramatic change in merchandise trade stemmed from a slight growth in exports and a very sharp advance in imports; exports in 1971 were only about 2 percent higher than in 1970, while imports rose by nearly 15 percent. Because the average price of exports rose by 3 percent compared with 1970, there was a small reduction in the physical volume. Prices of imports rose 5 percent, which means that the physical volume of imports rose by about 9 percent.

In line 2 we see that our military spending abroad exceeded foreign military spending with us by about $3 billion. Our military spending abroad includes such items as renting barracks in Germany, buying food for our military personnel in southeast Asia, and buying explosives in Japan.

Line 3 indicates that we spend more in traveling abroad than foreigners spend traveling in the United States. In addition, other countries do more transporting of goods and passengers for us than we do for them. These items together left us with a deficit of over $2 billion in 1971. As this line gives us a *net* figure, it does not record the sums foreigners spent in the United States for these purposes.

Line 4 reveals one area of thriving foreign earnings for us. We earned $12.7 billion on our investments abroad, which is more than double the average in the period 1960–64. Foreigners earned $4.8 billion on their investments in the United States, which is exactly four times what they averaged during the period 1960–64.

In line 5 "other services" include such items as insurance, banking services, and film rentals. On balance we received $0.7 billion more than we paid out in this account.

Line 6 shows that we paid more in gifts, pensions, and similar items to foreign residents than we received from them.

In line 7 we see that our government made $2 billion of nonmilitary grants abroad in 1971.

Line 8 presents the overall balance on current account, which shows outpayments exceeding receipts by $2.8 billion.

In the long-term capital account of Table 15-3, line 9 shows that our government made loans abroad that exceeded repayments by $2.4 billion; the debit figure already has the credits subtracted.

Our private long-term capital outflow exceeded the inflow of foreign capital during 1971 by over $4 billion, as recorded in line 10. Not shown in the balance of payments, which records only one year's transactions, is the following fact: our long-term private investment abroad rose phenomenally, from $44.5 billion in 1960 to $116.0 billion in 1971. This helps explain our high investment income of line 4. Foreign long-term private investment in the United States rose from $18.4 billion in 1960 to $49.7 billion in 1971. In addition there were short-term capital investments in both directions that produced investment income. These short-term capital flows appear in the balancing items of Table 15-3, which explain how we meet our foreign obligations.

Line 11 presents a deficit of over $9 billion in the accumulated total credits and debits on current account and long-term capital.

Line 12 includes primarily short-term capital flows that are not balancing items because they were not undertaken specifically to meet our deficit.

The errors and unrecorded transactions of line 13 arise because the people who compile the balance of payments miss some of the information, and what they miss is entered into this category. For example, suppose you buy $920 worth of travelers checks, convert them in Great Britain into pounds, and spend $920 there as a tourist. The British banks that accept your checks cash them by collecting from United States—owned bank balances held in Great Britain. The balance of payments should include a debit of $920, which is your tourist expenditure; it should also include a credit of $920, which is a withdrawal from our checking accounts abroad, a short-term capital movement. But suppose you do not know that you spent exactly $920 in Great Britain, and you reply on a questionnaire from our government that you spent $900 there. Our withdrawal of funds from the British banks will still show a credit of $920, but tourist expenditures will be increased by only the amount of money you reported spending—$900. Therefore, $20 will be added to the debit item of "Errors and unrecorded transactions." There are many other situations, including the smuggling of goods into the country to avoid paying tariffs, that give rise to errors and unrecorded transactions. There are indications, however, that most of this item of almost $11 billion derives from unrecorded capital outflows in response to higher interest rates abroad or in anticipation of the devaluation of the dollar.

Our overall deficit in the balance of payments, as seen in line 14, was almost $22 billion in 1971. This deficit was financed by short-term capital movements. We reduced our checking accounts with the International Monetary Fund and in foreign banks, and foreigners increased their checking accounts and other short-term investments with us. These items appear as credits in line 16 to offset our deficit so that the overall balance shows neither a deficit nor a surplus; total debits and credits must always be equal.

We shall now look more closely at our deficit in the balance of payments.

Equilibrium and Disequilibrium
In the Balance of Payments

THE DEFICIT The deficit in the balance of payments for 1971 is shown in line 14 of Table 15-3 to be $22 billion. What does a deficit mean, if debits and credits are always exactly equal?

The current and long-term capital accounts in Table 15-3 cover all our international transactions that are undertaken for their own sake. We choose to engage in buying and selling goods and services, in buying foreign assets and selling ours to foreigners. Our government engages in buying and selling goods in its military programs, and it lends and grants military and economic aid abroad. When all these transactions are totaled, after all our commitments to make payments abroad are weighed against all our receipts from abroad, we end up owing $22 billion more than we receive. How do we pay these obligations?

An analogy is appropriate here between our international balance of payments and an individual's finances. An individual can spend more on consumption plus investment than he earns. He either draws on his savings, by reducing his checking and savings accounts, for example, or he goes into debt. So we can pay out abroad more than we receive by reducing our assets of foreign exchange or by increasing our liabilities to foreigners. Our deficit means that we are living beyond our means, and this cannot continue forever. It is not that we are too poor to live the way we do; it is that we do not earn enough foreign exchange. Ultimately we must pay for foreign goods, services, and investments in foreign currencies, and we are trying to spend more foreign currency than we earn. We can do this either by using up our reserves of foreign exchange, or by foreigners lending us the money to spend abroad.

Why do we have a deficit in our balance of payments? We cannot point to any one item as the cause, but some items are more influential than others. It is the total economic picture at home and abroad that produces our deficit. If, for example, we had lower taxes or lower wages or both, we would be more competitive in international markets. Of course wage cuts would make the cure worse than the disease. If Japan were not so competitive, our deficit would shrink. If our tourists stayed home, the deficit would be smaller. If we cut down our private investments abroad, the deficit would decline. Certainly our government's military spending abroad and its military and economic aid worsen the deficit.

Yet we cannot be certain to what extent each item affects the total balance of payments. Look at Table 15-3 again. In line 2 we see that our military spending abroad caused a net debit in that account of almost $3 billion. Can we conclude that if we eliminated our military adventures abroad, that by itself would reduce our deficit by an equal amount? Not at all. If we cut out military spending in Germany, Japan, or Vietnam, these countries would receive fewer dollars to buy our goods. Perhaps if we eliminated $3 billion of military spending abroad, foreigners might buy $2 billion less of our goods, and our deficit would decline by only $1 billion.

What can we do about our deficit? We can go along as we have been and live with it, as long as we have foreign exchange reserves to pay our bills and as long as foreigners are willing to lend us money on short term to pay for their goods. Or we could overcome our deficit by becoming more competitive in world markets. If, for example, our government drastically cut its bloated military budget, taxes could be lowered, and we could sell more abroad. We could accomplish the same thing by eliminating our social security system and ending payroll taxes. Eliminating paid vacations or cutting wages, as mentioned above, would lower our costs of production and reduce or eliminate the deficit.

Our deficit would disappear if we went over to a policy of freely fluctuating exchange rates. We shall discuss how this happens in the next section.

THE PROCESS OF ADJUSTMENT: FLUCTUATING EXCHANGE RATES   Most governments stabilize the exchange rates, permitting only minor fluctuations. If they allowed these rates to fluctuate freely or if they changed the rate, a deficit in the balance of payments could be eliminated. Let us see how this works.

The German mark was worth about 30 cents in mid-1972. Suppose the German producer prices the Mercedes Benz automobile at 20,000 marks; this will cost us $6,000. Suppose also that some Germans are interested in buying our whiskey, which we offer for $3.00 a fifth; this will cost Germany 10 marks. It will take 2,000 bottles of whiskey to pay for the car.

Suppose we are more eager to buy German cars than they are to buy our whiskey. When buyers of potatoes are more eager to buy at the going price than sellers are to sell, the price rises. Similarly, if we are more eager to buy marks than the Germans are to sell them to buy our goods, the price of the mark rises; the mark appreciates in value, and the dollar depreciates. Suppose the mark now costs 50 cents. There is no reason for domestic prices to change very much or very soon because of what happens in the foreign exchange market. The German car, which still costs 20,000 marks, will now cost us $10,000; our whiskey still costs $3.00, but it will cost Germany 6 marks at the new exchange rate instead of 10. It will now cost 3,333 bottles of whiskey instead of 2,000 to buy a car. We will want fewer cars at that price, but the Germans will buy more whiskey. Therefore, the deficit in the balance of payments will be reduced or eliminated. The depreciation of a country's currency stimulates exports by making them cheaper to foreigners, and it curbs imports by making them dearer in the country whose currency depreciated.

Why, then, do we not permit exchange rates to fluctuate freely and the dollar to depreciate? The first objection is that this will worsen our terms of trade. The terms of trade are the physical volume of goods we have to export to pay for a given physical volume of imports. The terms of trade worsen when we pay 3,333 fifths of whiskey for a car instead of 2,000. It represents a tightening of our belts, or the running of a discount sale. It is a drastic remedy that may be worse than the deficit.

A second objection to freely fluctuating exchange rates is that they create uncertainty and unexpected losses. Suppose you are an auto distributor and you signed a contract to buy 100 Mercedes Benzes at 20,000 marks each, to be delivered in four months and paid for in seven. You thought they would cost $6,000 each. You received the cars, sold them at $6,500, and congratulated yourself on making a good profit. But when the time came to pay for them, the mark went from 30 to 50 cents, and you found that you had lost a small fortune. Such fluctuations would discourage international trade. Therefore governments are reluctant to abandon the system of stable exchange rates.

A third objection to freely fluctuating exchange rates is that speculators could worsen fluctuations. If the gamblers in the foreign exchange market thought that the dollar would depreciate, they would offer to sell billions of dollars for future delivery. This would generate a panic flight from the dollar and force its depreciation. But if people are reasonably certain that the price of the dollar in terms of foreign currency will not be allowed to fall, they will be willing to hold dollars.

There is also something to be said in favor of freely fluctuating or flexible exchange rates. With flexible exchange rates, the foreign exchange market can adjust quickly to the supply of and demand for foreign exchange. This avoids the imbalances and discrepancies that arise under the system of fixed exchange rates. The old system used devaluation as a last resort to overcome the deficit in a country's balance of payments. A deficit country would generally be willing to devalue its currency because such a move would stimulate exports by making them cheaper in terms of foreign currency; devaluation would also reduce imports by making them more expensive at home. But would the surplus country be willing to have its currency appreciate in value? That would reduce exports and increase imports. There has been much more reluctance to appreciate currency than to devalue it.

Yet appreciation of some currencies may be just as necessary as devaluation of other currencies. Take, for example, the situation in 1971. The United States had a huge deficit in the balance of payments, and Germany and Japan had surpluses. If the United States devalued the dollar (which it did in December 1971 by raising the price of gold from $35 to $38 per ounce), that would hurt the competitive situation of other deficit countries. But if the mark and the yen were appreciated, that would help other deficit countries as well as us.

The virtue of freely fluctuating exchange rates is that some currencies can appreciate as readily as others move in the opposite direction. The adjustment is swift and automatic.

Basically the argument for flexible exchange rates relies on a free market to produce the best possible results. The proponents of fixed exchange rates still believe in a certain amount of government control to promote the best possible situation for a country in its international financial and trade relations.

THE PROCESS OF ADJUSTMENT: PRICE CHANGES   Price changes are another way to achieve equilibrium in international trade and payments. In the above example, our eagerness to buy German cars eventually raises their price in marks, and we buy fewer of them. The German reluctance to buy our whiskey lowers its dollar price, and they buy more. Thus equilibrium is restored.

What is wrong with this process of adjustment? Two things: it will not work, and even if it did, the cure would be objectionable. Prices today no longer move downward as they once did. And if they did, this would be associated with shrinking profit margins, reduced investment, and falling incomes. In addition, as the price of cars rose and the price of whiskey fell, our terms of trade would worsen, just as with the depreciation of the dollar and the appreciation of the mark. Reaching international equilibrium through price changes is too drastic and painful.

THE PROCESS OF ADJUSTMENT: INCOME CHANGES   The richer a country is, the more it imports both consumer goods and raw materials used for production. One example of this is the United States, which has twice the population of Pakistan and imports thirty-five times as much. The poorer a country is, the less it imports. This process can help reduce a deficit in the balance of payments.

Suppose each country normally spends 10 percent of its income on imports. Assume that formerly our balance of payments was in equilibrium, but now, for whatever reason, we import an extra $1 billion worth of goods from Germany. This may mean that we produce $1 billion less of our own goods, and employment and income fall. In subsequent rounds of spending, our income may fall by a total of $3 billion because of the multiplier (which was discussed in Chapter 3). We will therefore reduce imports by 10 percent of our reduction in income, or $300 million. Germany, meanwhile, by selling us an extra $1 billion worth of goods has an increased income of $1 billion on the first round of sales. Through the multiplier, her total income goes up $3 billion, and her imports go up 10 percent of that, or $300 million. Our deficit, which started out at $1 billion, is reduced to $400 million because of our reduced imports and Germany's increased imports from us through changes in income.

The role of income changes in producing international equilibrium was first explained by John Maynard Keynes in 1936. Frank W. Taussig, the great authority on international trade, wrote in 1927 that international equilibrium was reached quickly and smoothly, even before prices changed noticeably. "It must be confessed," he wrote, "that here we have phenomena not fully understood." Now, thanks to Keynes, we understand that income changes work in the same direction as price changes, and they reinforce them.

What is wrong with relying on income changes to produce

international equilibrium? In the above example, Germany would not object to rising income. But we would object to going through the wringer of falling income and depression to eliminate our deficit; it is better to live with the deficit. The next section will discuss how this can be accomplished.

CONTROLLED DISEQUILIBRIUM If a country wishes to avoid depreciation of its currency and falling prices and incomes, it can limit, overcome, or live with a deficit in the balance of payments through other means. It can curb the buying of foreign goods, services, and assets, limiting its purchases to what it can afford in terms of available foreign exchange. Thus, Great Britain during and for some time after the Second World War virtually prohibited her tourists from going to the United States, in spite of their wealth; the prospective, thwarted tourists were rich in pounds, but the country was poor in dollar assets. The United States has tried to curb our foreign investments and the amount of goods our tourists bring home. The emerging nations frequently restrict the luxury consumer goods that their rich residents can import; this is especially necessary to promote economic development.

Suppose a Mexican farmer wishes to import a $10,000 tractor from the United States, and a Mexican real estate speculator wants a $10,000 Cadillac. If the peso is worth 8 cents, each of these items will cost 125,000 pesos. With Mexicans eager to spend on imports more than they can earn through exports, they bid up the peso price of the dollar; that is, the peso falls. If the new value of the peso is 4 cents, the peso price of the tractor and automobile will double to 250,000 pesos. At this cost, the farmer would decide that buying the tractor is no longer profitable, but the rich man can still afford the Cadillac. Therefore he buys the dollars to pay for his luxury import. He has worsened the terms of trade for Mexico, and he has diverted resources from production to consumption. This is harmful to the nation, and the government may well rule that the import of tractors will be permitted, but not Cadillacs. In this case, laissez faire does not serve the interests of the nation.

By maintaining its currency at an overvalued rate in comparison with foreign currencies, a country prevents its imports from becoming more expensive and its exports from becoming cheaper. It then has to limit imports to what it can afford to pay for. By rationing foreign exchange, a government forces a balance of payments equilibrium by restricting imports to the value of exports.

Instead of devaluing the dollar as we did in December 1971, what else might we have done to overcome the deficit in our balance of payments? We might have stopped bombing Indochina and cut our military forces elsewhere. We could have taxed tourists heavily if they go abroad, and we might have prohibited additional foreign investment. We could have eliminated all military and economic aid to foreign countries. We could have raised our tariffs to curb imports, although this would violate our international commitments. We could have curbed domestic inflation and lowered the taxes on business in order to make our goods more competitive at home and abroad. All of these and other measures would reduce the debits or increase the credits in our balance of payments, thereby reducing or eliminating the deficit.

Protectionism Versus Free Trade

Tariffs are taxes added on to the cost of imported goods. They are designed to help high-cost producers to survive in competition with low-cost foreign goods. There are many arguments against tariffs, and a few in their favor.

INVALID ARGUMENTS FOR TARIFFS A totally invalid defense of tariffs is the idea that we should keep our money at home. This appears in the old saying, "If we buy foreign goods, we get the goods but foreigners get the money; if we buy our own goods, we have both the goods and the money." If this statement were true, it would be a wonderful world—for us. We could print and export $10,000 bills by the bushel, and we could import goods by the shipload. But foreigners are not fools; they can print their own money, too. If they accept our money, it is only to buy our goods, services, or securities. Actually our money seldom leaves the country when we buy foreign goods. We pay for goods with dollar checking accounts. The foreign exporter who receives these checks sells the dollars to his bank, and the bank sells the dollars to the foreign importers. Thus, in effect, The American importer pays dollars to the American exporter through the banking system, and the foreign exporter receives payment in his currency from the foreign importer.

In 1970, of our total imports of $59.3 billion of goods and services, we exported $787 million of gold to meet our foreign obligations. This is one dollar out of every seventy-five we spent abroad.

A second invalid argument for tariffs is that we must use them to protect our high wages; free trade will undermine our wage levels because of cheap foreign labor. This implies that free trade tends to equalize the incomes of the trading partners. But that is not the case. Trade may be of mutual benefit, but it does not equalize incomes. You can engage in free trade with the Rockefellers at the Standard Oil pumps, and your income will not become more equal to theirs. High real wages result from efficiency of production and the economic power of labor, and these will not disappear under free trade. The principle of comparative advantage would result in our producing those things in which our advantage is greatest or our disadvantage is smallest. Our high wage rates are consistent with low labor costs per unit of output if our productivity is high.

A third fallacious argument for tariffs is that they protect employment in an area or industry for the good of the country. If the textile industry goes under, it is bad for workers and investors in that industry. But from the point of view of the nation as a whole, as foreigners earn more dollars, they will buy more from us. It is possible for the foreigners to buy our securities, but generally they buy our goods and services with the dollars they earn. If they spend the dollars on our goods and services, we will lose employment in our relatively inefficient industries, and we will gain employment in our more competitive industries. Protecting an industry that cannot compete with foreign rivals can protect a community and a particular group of people involved in that industry, but it does not serve the interests of the nation as a whole. It should be noted that this argument applies only to the United States and other rich, developed nations.

A fourth false argument for tariffs is the so-called "scientific tariff." If foreigners can produce an item at 10 percent less cost than ours, we should impose an 11 percent tariff to equalize the cost of production. Then competition will somehow be fair. This undermines one of the major reasons for international trade, which is buying goods abroad cheaper than at home.

POSSIBLE VALID ARGUMENTS FOR TARIFFS   Tariffs might be used to curb imports and generate more employment at home. If all countries suffered from unemployment and all raised tariffs, they would not all be better off. As each country imported less, it would also export less. But if one country had a higher rate of unemployment than the others, if it had a deficit in its balance of payments, and if the others agreed not to retaliate, then higher tariffs could increase employment. This could also be accomplished in other ways, such as devaluing the currency or initiating a government public works program.

A second possible defense of tariffs is that they improve the terms of trade. We saw in Figure 5-12 on page 114 that a tax on a commodity under certain conditions will mean higher prices for the buyer and lower prices for the seller. If the foreign exporter gets less for his goods because of the tariff, the terms of trade move against him and in favor of the importing country. This will work only if foreign governments do not raise their tariffs also. Improved terms of trade can work for the side that raises the tariffs, but it cannot work for both sides simultaneously.

A third argument for tariffs that has some validity is the "infant industry" claim. A new industry is likely to be inefficient for two reasons. First, the industry may lack adequate capital, skilled workers, experienced management, and adequately trained scientists and technicians; it takes time to nurture new firms and industries to peak efficiency. The second reason for a new industry being inefficient is based on the economy of scale. The smaller an industry is, the less efficient it may be; as it grows larger, the efficiency increases and the unit cost of production falls. For either reason or both, a new industry may require protection for a limited number of years until it grows in size, gains experience, and becomes more efficient and competitive. Many of the leading industries in Great Britain, the United States, Germany, and Japan received government protection and support until they could stand on their own in competition with the rest of the world.

The fourth and best argument for tariffs is that they aid the economic development of emerging nations. The nascent industries in emerging nations can be crushed in competition with the same industries in rich countries; or they can be crushed by deliberate policies like price wars. But in time they can grow in size and efficiency and can become competitive. Therefore, in order to overcome the handicaps of poverty and the disadvantages of producing only raw materials, the emerging nations will have to restrict imports. This is a necessary but not sufficient condition to grow economically, and tariffs are one way to curb imports that could be produced at home, or to curb luxury imports. When a certain amount of economic development is attained, the principle of comparative advantage will reassert itself on a higher and more dynamic level that is more equitable to the poor countries.

It is frequently argued that governments might make the wrong decisions, protect the wrong industries, and thereby misallocate resources. Inefficient industries will, therefore, depend forever on protection. It should be pointed out that entrepreneurs operating under laissez faire frequently make wrong decisions; the high rate of bankruptcy attests to this. Their losses represent the misallocation of resources that is detrimental to society. There is no reason why a government's decision on which industries to protect should necessarily be worse than decisions arrived at privately.

ADMINISTRATIVE PROTECTIONISM AND QUOTAS Administrative protectionism is also called indirect protectionism or the invisible tariff. It is a way of enforcing import regulations and assessing tariffs that increase the protectionism of existing laws without actually raising the tariff rates. It raises the cost of importing goods and increases the uncertainty about what the tariff payment will finally be. Complex customs laws require customs brokers and customs lawyers employed by importers to facilitate their business with the government officials and the courts. The appraised value of goods and therefore the applicable tariff can be a controversial matter subject to prolonged litigation. A backlog of over 400,000 cases pending before the United States Customs Court means that three to twelve years elapse before cases are settled.

The classification of imported goods can be changed to raise the tariff. Ping pong balls were once classified as toys, and they were assessed a 10 percent duty. When the customs officials learned that some toy manufacturers used the balls to shoot out of toy guns, they were reclassified as ammunition, and the tariff rose to 95 percent of their value.

Little steel balls usable in ball point pens before 1951 were classified as ball bearings, and the tariff was 35 cents per 1,000. Then the balls were reclassified as parts of fountain pens, and the applicable tariff was 61 dollars per 1,000; this was thirty times their domestic cost of production.

A case settled in 1970 involved the import of four-way flasher switches for automobiles. The importer claimed that the article was a visual signaling apparatus, which called for a tariff of 8.5 percent. The customs officials ruled that the item was an electrical switch, and the tariff was 17.5 percent; this was sustained by the Customs Court.

In another 1970 case, the importer of rubber knives in rubber sheaths claimed that they were practical joke articles, and the tariff should be 20 percent. The customs officials classified them as toys with a 35 percent tariff. The Customs Court decided that if the rubber knife were realistic enough to cause fear or alarm, it would be a trick or joke article. But as it was not realistic, it was a toy and the higher tariff applied.

Our imports are normally valued at their price loaded on the ship in the foreign port. But in the cases of certain chemicals, rubber-soled footwear, canned clams, and low-value, knit wool gloves, the value is the American selling price (ASP) charged by domestic producers. This doubles the duties that normally would be collected.

Imported distilled spirits that are under 100 proof are assumed to be 100 proof if they are bottled abroad. The total overpayment of tax and tariff on 86 proof liquor is $1.71 per gallon. This moves the bottling of bulk imports to the United States.

Quantitative quotas are an additional device to restrict imports. They place limits on the quantity of goods that are admitted each year. This is even more protective than tariffs. With tariffs, if people want the goods badly enough, they can import them if they are willing to pay the duty. With quotas, there are absolute limits to imports regardless of the urgency of the want or the need for the good.

We have quotas on the import of wheat and wheat products, cotton and cotton waste, textiles, milk and cream, butter and butter substitutes, cheese, chocolate, ice cream, live cattle, beef, fish, sugar, potatoes, whiskbrooms and other brooms, coffee, peanuts, crude petroleum and petroleum products, and stainless steel cutlery. On imports from the Philippines, we have quotas on buttons, cigars, coconut oil, cordage, and tobacco.

Some countries have entered into agreements to drop all tariff barriers among them. We shall now examine one such organization.

International Organizations
and International Trade

THE COMMON MARKET The original European Economic Community, better known as the Common Market, included France, Germany, Italy, Belgium, the Netherlands, and Luxembourg. Three additional countries were admitted on January 1, 1973: Great Britain, Denmark, and Ireland. Six other European countries are due to have free trade with the Common Market in industrial products by 1977: Austria, Finland, Iceland, Portugal, Sweden, and Switzerland.

The full members of the Common Market have free trade among themselves and a common tariff against imported goods. They also have the free and unrestricted movement of goods, capital, and labor across national boundaries.

The Common Market can result in "trade creation" and an increase in efficiency, or in "trade diversion" with a reduction in efficiency, depending on the circumstances. We shall give an example of each.

Suppose France protected its industry producing typewriters with a 25 percent tariff. After she joins the Common Market, internal tariffs are eliminated, and Italy, a more efficient producer, sells France all the typewriters she wants. This is trade creation, and it lowers the cost of goods. Whenever the most efficient producer is within the common market area, the elimination of tariffs increases efficiency. This type of growth of international trade is probably the greatest advantage of the European Common Market.

Trade diversion is seen in this example. Suppose Italy had no tariff on imported tractors, and she bought all she needed from the United States, the most efficient producer. After Italy joins the Common Market, the tariff on tractors becomes the average of the six members' tariffs. Suppose it is 20 percent. If Germany's tractors cost 10 percent more to produce than those of the United States, Germany will capture the Italian market, because American tractors pay a 20 percent tariff but those from Germany pay nothing. This is trade diversion from a more efficient to a less efficient producer. Whenever the most efficient producer is outside the common market, the creation of a common market may lower the efficiency of production on a world scale.

The average rate of tariffs on manufactured and semimanufactured goods imported into the Common Market is about the same as ours—a little over 8 percent of the value of goods imported. But the tariffs on agricultural products are much higher, averaging 33 percent of the value of imports. High support prices for farm products within the Common Market provide a strong incentive to increase production. This not only displaces potential imports, but also generates surpluses which are exported in competition with nonmembers of the Common Market. The Common Market subsidizes the exports of their farm products, and sometimes the subsidies are greater than the world market prices. In early 1970, for example, the world price for soft wheat was around $50 per ton, and the Common Market subsidy was $57 per ton.

In 1958, in the first year of the Common Market, trade among the six members accounted for about 30 percent of total imports and about 30 percent of total exports. By 1970, intra–Common Market trade accounted for 48 percent of total imports and 49 percent of total exports by the members.

The agricultural policy of the Common Market was brought into full effect for basic commodities in 1966. Imports of such commodities from the United States fell 47 percent from 1966 to 1969, and then rose slightly in the period 1969–71.

Our workers are being hurt as our goods have some difficulty climbing over the tariff wall that surrounds the Common Market. But our big corporations have looked after their own interests very well by building plants within the market area; thus, they can enjoy free trade in the nine nations. This is seen in our trend of investment since the Common Market was organized in 1958. At the end of 1957, 6.7 percent of our total direct private foreign investment was in the six Common Market countries, and 42.5 percent went to Asia, Africa, and Latin America. From the beginning of 1958 to the end of 1970, the percentage of our capital going to the Common Market almost tripled to 19.0 percent; the percentage going to the poor countries was reduced drastically to 24.7 percent. The Common Market has thus given a twist to our foreign investment that is detrimental to the emerging nations. Both the curbing of our exports to the Common Market and the expansion of our investments there worsen the deficit in our balance of payments.

The Common Market is a rich men's club that has divided Africa, because the former colonies get special access to the Common Market, and other African states are denied these privileges. The organization also limits the social and economic policies of member countries. Great Britain, for example, will not be permitted to subsidize farmers directly to keep the prices of farm products low. Nor will she be allowed to buy cheap food abroad, because the farmers in the Common Market are protected by tariffs and high prices. Britain's cost of living is going up because she is changing her policies to qualify for membership. Subsidies to labor in the form of free or cheap housing or other benefits are supervised and curbed by the Common Market. This is to prevent one member country from getting a competitive advantage over the others by enjoying lower cash wages and, therefore, lower costs of production, along with higher fringe benefits provided by the government. Tax policy on business is limited by the need of each country to remain highly competitive with the others.

THE INTERNATIONAL MONETARY FUND The International Monetary Fund (IMF), an agency of the United Nations, was organized during the Second World War. It promotes stable exchange rates and freely convertible currencies for current account transactions. This means that if a British resident wishes to buy goods from the United States, he is reasonably certain that the pound will be priced at or near $2.59 and that he will be allowed to exchange pounds for dollars to pay for the goods. These, at least, are the goals, although they are not always achieved. Exchange rates are altered occasionally, and exchange controls sometimes are in effect even for current account transactions. The IMF also lends foreign currencies to countries that find themselves in *temporary* balance-of-payments difficulties.

The most interesting recent development involving the IMF has been the creation of Special Drawing Rights (SDRs) beginning in 1970. This system has also been referred to as "paper gold." It represents credit creation to augment the international means of payment.

Until 1970 the major international reserves that were used for payments among countries consisted of gold, British sterling, and United States dollars. Gold costs time, effort, and money to produce; its production has not kept pace with growing world trade; and much of it is used in space technology, in industry, in the arts, and in making jewelry. And if countries are to build up their dollar and sterling reserves, this means that the United States and Great Britain have to run deficits in their balances of payments. Deficits make people nervous, and they arise from a lag in exports compared to imports, which is bad for business. Therefore, SDRs were created to supplement existing reserves. This represents pure credit creation on an international scale. The IMF can now do what the commercial banking system has been doing all along, as seen in Chapter 4: it simply credits SDR sums to the accounts of the member countries, and they can make payments to each other by handing over SDR balances carried on the books of the IMF. It makes a lot more sense than digging gold out of the ground and then burying it again in some well-guarded vault.

In 1970, $3.5 billion were created and distributed, and in each of the next two years an additional $3 billion per year were added to the world's supply of reserves. Proposals were made that the poor countries should get all the SDRs as they were created. If this had been done, the gift would have cost the rich countries absolutely nothing except the benefits foregone. As the poor countries would spend these reserves, the money would very soon be distributed among the rich countries. Altruism being a minor motive in international relations, however, the rich countries took most of the SDRs for themselves. The twenty-one rich members of the IMF have 27.0 percent of the population of all the member nations, 81.3 percent of the GNP, and they got 68.3 percent of the SDRs. The poor countries in the IMF have 73.0 percent of the population, 18.7 percent of the GNP, and they got 31.7 percent of the SDRs. In the 1972 distribution of SDRs, the rich countries' share rose to 70.3 percent of the total.

Summary

The theory of absolute advantage tells us that if one country can produce a commodity cheaper than a second country, and the second can produce a different commodity cheaper than the first, it is mutually advantageous for them to trade.

But what if the first country can produce both commodities cheaper than the second? The theory of comparative advantage tells us that the more efficient country should export that commodity for which its margin of efficiency is greatest; it should import the commodity for which its margin of efficiency is smallest. This theory, however, is based on the existing situation; the process of economic development can alter a country's list of commodities in which it has a comparative advantage.

In this chapter we analyzed the construction and the significance of a country's balance of payments. This is a record of all the international transactions between the residents of a country and the residents of the rest of the world. Debits represent payments to foreign residents, and credits are receipts from foreign residents.

While total debits are always equal to total credits, a country's balance of payments can show a deficit. This means that if we consider all the transactions undertaken for their own sake, total outpayments or debits exceed total inpayments or credits. The difference is made up by movements of short-term capital, or gold where such payments are permitted.

The deficit is caused by a country trying to spend abroad more than it earns abroad. It can be cured by devaluation of the domestic currency, thereby making imports dearer to residents and exports cheaper to foreigners; by cutting costs and prices at home to become more competitive in world markets; by reducing incomes, which will result in fewer imports; or by restricting imports through higher tariffs, rationing foreign exchange, taxing tourists who go abroad, and so on.

The invalid arguments for tariffs that we considered are that they keep our money at home; that they prevent our high wage rates from being undermined by importing products made by cheap foreign labor; that they protect employment in an area or industry for the good of the country as a whole; and that scientific tariffs equalize the cost of producing foreign and domestic goods.

Tariff arguments that may have some validity are that they increase employment at home if other countries do not retaliate by raising their tariffs; that they improve the terms of trade so that a given volume of exports exchanges for a greater volume of imports than before the tariff was enacted; that they protect infant industries that need a chance to grow; and that they promote economic development in the emerging nations.

There are other restrictions on free trade besides tariffs. Administrative protectionism involves the enforcing of import regulations in such a way as to increase both the cost and the uncertainty of importing goods. Quantitative quotas limit the quantity of goods that can be imported each year. Common markets introduce free trade among their members, but they maintain tariff barriers against outsiders.

The International Monetary Fund is a United Nations agency that seeks to promote more and freer trade. Its goals are stable exchange rates and freely convertible currencies for current account transactions. One of its recent achievements was the creation of international means of payment called Special Drawing Rights.

We have touched at several points on the problems of the poor countries. In the final chapter we shall consider their situation in greater detail.

QUESTIONS AND PROBLEMS

1   Are there any other arguments you can think of, in addition to those given in this chapter, for or against protection?

2   How has our tariff policy evolved from 1790 to today?

3   Was there any conflict over tariff policy before the Civil War between the agrarian South and the industrial North?

4   Can the underdeveloped areas learn anything from our tariff history that is applicable to them?

5   Present your own example of a two-country, two-commodity model to illustrate the theory of comparative advantage. What are the limits of the terms of trade, and what is each country's gain from trade?

6   What would happen if each state and community in the United States could set up protective tariffs, or if each could persuade its residents to "Buy home products and keep our money at home"?

7   Why has gold production not kept pace with growing world trade?

8   Look up the meaning of the common term *favorable balance of trade*. Why is it called favorable? Why is this a misleading concept?

9   Suppose you are a tourist in Great Britain. You convert a personal check for $259 into £100, and you spend the money. The British bank sends the check to the United States for collection. What are the appropriate debit and credit entries in the United States balance of payments?

10   Our balance of payments is a record of the transactions between residents of the United States and residents of the rest of the world. Suppose you are a tourist in Great Britain, and you decide to live there permanently. Now you cash a $259 check for £100. What are the appropriate debit and credit entries in the United States balance of payments?

11   Should our textile industry be protected from cheap foreign imports?

12   Should our domestic camera manufacturers be protected from (a) better cameras coming from abroad at lower prices? (b) shoddier cameras coming from abroad at lower prices?

13   If we raised the price of gold to $50 an ounce and no other government took any action, what effect would this have on the deficit in our balance of payments?

14   What would happen if we announced that in three months we would raise the price of gold to $50 an ounce?

BIBLIOGRAPHY

BALDWIN, ROBERT E., *Nontariff Distortions of International Trade*. Washington, D.C.: The Brookings Institution, 1970.

COMMITTEE FOR ECONOMIC DEVELOPMENT, *The United States and the European Community: Policies for a Changing World Economy*. New York, 1971.

INTERNATIONAL MONETARY FUND, *Balance of Payments Yearbook*.

INTERNATIONAL MONETARY FUND, *International Financial Statistics* (Monthly publication).

KREININ, MORDECHAI E., *International Economics, a Policy Approach*. New York: Harcourt Brace Jovanovich, 1971.

SNIDER, DELBERT A., *Introduction to International Economics*, 5th ed. Homewood, Ill.: Richard D. Irwin, 1971.

UNITED NATIONS, *Yearbook of International Trade Statistics*.

16

Problems
of
Emerging Nations

Where Plenty smiles, alas! she smiles for few,
And those who taste not, yet behold her store,
Are as the slaves that dig the golden ore.
The wealth around them makes them doubly poor.
—*George Crabbe*

Robert S. McNamara is a brilliant executive who is a dominant personality in our computerized society; he is a master of both machines and people. When he was second in command at the Ford Motor Company, he was successful at promoting profitable operations for the company. When he was secretary of defense under President Lyndon Johnson, he directed the devastation of Indochina, although his optimism about winning the war was mistaken. When he became President of the International Bank for Reconstruction and Development and its sister institutions, he evolved into an ardent advocate of economic development for the poor countries, and he did outstanding work at that assignment.

McNamara delivered a speech at the Third United Nations Conference on Trade and Development in Santiago, Chile on April 14, 1972. This speech, largely neglected in the newspapers in the United States, tells us why the problems of emerging nations are so tragically significant. McNamara made the following points about the poor countries.

Children under five account for only 20 percent of the population, but for more than 60 percent of the deaths.

Two-thirds of the children who have escaped death will live on, restricted in their growth by malnutrition that can stunt both bodies and minds.

There are 100 million more adult illiterates than there were twenty years ago.

Death and disease are rampant, education and employment are scarce, squalor and stagnation are common, and opportunity and the realization of personal potential are drastically limited.

Economic growth in poor countries, in the early stages, is likely to penalize the poorest segment of society relative to the more affluent sectors unless specific action is taken to prevent such an effect.

The developed countries agreed that their governments should give development assistance to the poor countries that would reach .7 percent of the rich countries' GNP by 1975. Yet such aid from the United States fell from .5 percent of its GNP in the early 1960's to .31 percent in 1970, and it is likely to fall further to around .24 percent by 1975.

During the 1960's, the total GNP of the world increased by $1,100 billion. But 80 percent of the increase went to countries whose per capita incomes already average over $1,000, and that contain only 25 percent of the world's population. Only 6 percent of the increase went to countries whose per capita incomes average $200 or less, and that contain 60 percent of the world's people.

The wealthier nations could well afford to leave more of their markets open to agricultural imports from developing countries. They could also lower the tariffs on manufactured goods coming from the poor countries. In fact, the levels of tariffs on imports of manufactured goods from rich and poor trading partners, respectively, average out in the United States to 7 and 12 percent.

McNamara's views emphasize the problems of poverty and the need for economic development in most of Asia, Africa, and Central and South America.

Economic development has been of prime concern to economists only since the Second World War. Now interest centers largely on the problems of the poor countries in their efforts to get ahead. Literature on the subject has itself become a major growth industry—in the rich countries; we are most generous with our advice.

Why has concern with this problem suddenly developed? Was economic development not important before the Second World War? Was there not terrible poverty in Asia, Africa, and Latin America that might have been alleviated by economic development? There are several significant reasons for the earlier neglect of this problem and the tremendous emphasis on it in recent decades.

First, for a century or more before the Second World War, economic theorists were predisposed toward laissez faire, equilibrium, and harmony of interests. As it was assumed that the government was to do nothing about the economy, the emphasis in the study of economics was on how the economy worked rather than on what to do to make it work better. An analysis of equilibrium to show how it worked automatically was more important than studying the process of change and how to influence it. In this the best of all possible worlds, it was assumed that development would simply happen based on the self-seeking motivation of individuals to save, invest, and pursue maximum profit. But now more and more people believe that economic development can be promoted or retarded, depending on the policies adopted, and government looms large in this process. If something can be done about development, we must understand the process and what influences it.

A second reason for the burgeoning interest in economic development is the political independence won by most of the poor countries since the Second World War. When they were colonies nobody listened to them. As independent countries and members of the United Nations, their aspirations are being heard, and their influence is greater than it once was. Before independence they were mainly passive recipients of the byproducts of whatever kind of "progress" the dominating countries thrust on them. Now they have some voice in selecting the kind of development they hope to achieve. In addition, their votes in the United Nations have won them a considerable measure of attention from the great powers that formerly could ignore their wishes with impunity.

Third, the rich countries can profit from the economic development of the poor. Richer people make better customers. As poor countries develop, they provide more and more opportunities for investment, more raw materials desired by the rich countries, and better markets. The rich countries can unload surplus goods on them, especially agricultural and military goods in the case of the United States. They can promote their own shipping. We should note here that economic aid allows the taxpayers in the rich countries to pay for the exports of their businessmen and farmers to the poor countries. The same situation exists as did in the relationship between parent countries and colonies in earlier times; the costs to the rich countries are socialized, and the profits are private.

Finally, the rich countries have become interested in the economic development of the poor because of the Cold War. The United States and our allies are rivals of Soviet Russia and China for leadership of and alliances with the poor countries.

What do we mean by economic development? Although this term is sometimes used interchangeably with economic growth, there is a distinction between them. Economic growth may be defined as increasing total output, which can occur with no increased efficiency or rising standard of living. Growth can result from increased population, increased capital investments, longer hours of work, or a larger proportion of the population working, as when women, young people, and old people enter the labor force instead of remaining at home, in school, or in retirement. If the total hours worked in a society double but total output goes up only 50 per cent, there is growth even though efficiency has declined. Growth may even be associated with falling standards of living if population grows faster than output.

Economic development may be defined as rising output per hour worked or increasing efficiency in production. It is not necessarily associated with rising standards of living. If most of the benefits of increasing productivity go to the rich, the poor may become worse off for two reasons. First, their situation may actually deteriorate if they lose their livelihoods as artisans and small farmers. Second, even if their level of living does not decline, they feel poorer by comparison as the rich grow richer. This was expressed by the poet George Crabbe in the quote that appears at the beginning of this chapter.

We shall first describe some of the typical characteristics of emerging nations, contrasting them with rich countries. Then we shall present the ideas of some outstanding theorists of economic development. Their ideas differ widely and cover the field in considerable breadth and depth.

Some Characteristics of Emerging Nations

LOW PER CAPITA INCOME   *Emerging nations* is a polite term for poor nations. Some of them are not yet emerging toward anything, but they hope to emerge and develop. It is a better term than the once-popular *backward nations,* which implied contempt of the West toward the countries they dominated.

Table 16-1 contrasts the wealth and poverty of selected countries. A word of caution is necessary in interpreting this table. We should not conclude that the people in the United States are sixteen to fifty times as well off as those in the poor countries. The figures are overstated in the rich countries because our prices are likely to be higher, and therefore money income is not necessarily an accurate measure of real income. In addition, our income is raised by vast expenditures on armaments, transportation to and from work, police forces, pollution control, advertising, and so on; these increase our incomes, but they may represent deductions from our apparently high average income.

In contrast, many of the people in the poor countries do things for themselves outside the market economy, such as growing their own food or making their own clothes; much of this kind of activity is not counted in GNP, and their incomes appear lower than they actually are.

In Table 16-1 we see ten countries whose *average* per capita GNP was under $100 in 1969. In the United States they would die of starvation with such an income; but in the poor countries they do survive, although with undernourished, deprived, and shortened lives.

Yet, even though the poor countries' incomes will go farther than ours dollar for dollar, the differences in the total real incomes per capita are still fantastically large. The outstanding characteristic of the underdeveloped countries is that they are poor.

HEAVY DEPENDENCE ON PRODUCTION AND EXPORT OF RAW MATERIALS   A large number of the emerging nations are heavily dependent on the exports

TABLE 16-1   Per Capita Gross National Product for Selected Countries, 1969
(in dollars)

Rich Countries	Per Capita GNP	Poor Countries	Per Capita GNP
United States	4,240	Brazil	270
Kuwait	3,320	Ecuador	240
Sweden	2,920	Paraguay	240
Switzerland	2,700	Bolivia	160
Canada	2,650	Kenya	130
France	2,460	India	110
Denmark	2,310	Pakistan	110
Australia	2,300	Sudan	110
West Germany	2,190	Uganda	110
Norway	2,160	Indonesia	100
Belgium	2,010	Afghanistan	Less than 100
United Kingdom	1,890	Burma	" " "
The Netherlands	1,760	China	" " "
East Germany	1,570	Ethiopia	" " "
Israel	1,570	Haiti	" " "
Japan	1,430	Malawi	" " "
Puerto Rico	1,410	Nigeria	" " "
Italy	1,400	Tanzania	" " "
Czechoslovakia	1,370	Vietnam (North)	" " "
USSR	1,110	Zaïre	" " "

Source: "World Bank Atlas, Population, Per Capita Production and Growth Rates," Finance and Development, Vol. 9, No. 1 (March 1972), pp. 48–60.

of one or two raw materials. In Table 16-2 we see thirty-seven countries listed, each of which in 1970 depended on the export of one raw material for more than half the value of its total exports. Each of the sixteen countries listed in Table 16-3 depended on the export of two raw materials for more than half its exports. Most of the other underdeveloped countries were also exporters mainly of raw materials, with a somewhat more varied assortment of commodities.

There is another indicator that shows how heavily dependent the poor countries are on the export of raw materials. We find that in 1970 the exports of food, fuel, and raw materials from the developed areas accounted for 23 percent of their total exports; these same kinds of goods amounted to 77 percent of the exports of the developing areas.

Aside from exports, the domestic patterns of production show that the people of the poor countries are much more heavily dependent on agriculture than in the rich countries. Although the statistics are fragmentary and incomplete, we find that in the 1960's, 92 percent of the people in Malawi worked in agriculture, as did 90 percent in Ethiopia, 84 percent in Zaïre, 70 percent in India, and 55 percent in Paraguay.

TABLE 16-2   Countries Whose Export of One Raw Material Made Up More Than 50 Percent of the Value of Total Exports, 1970

Country	Export	Percent of value of total exports
Kuwait	petroleum	almost 100.0
Saudi Arabia	petroleum	almost 100.0
Libya	petroleum	99.5
Zambia	copper	95.3
Mauritania	iron ore	95.1
The Gambia	peanut products	95.0
Iraq	petroleum	93.7
Mauritius	sugar	91.2
Venezuela	petroleum	90.2
Iran	petroleum	88.7
Surinam*	aluminum (bauxite and alumina)	85.0
Burundi	coffee	84.4
Trinidad and Tobago	petroleum	77.3
Vietnam	rubber	77.2
Chile	copper	75.8 (1969)
Yemen	petroleum	74.0
Chad	cotton	70.7
Ghana	cacao	68.0
Zaïre	copper	67.1
Jamaica	aluminum (bauxite and alumina)	66.3
Algeria	petroleum	66.0
Sierra Leone	diamonds	61.7
Sudan	cotton	61.3
Colombia	coffee	60.8
Ethiopia	coffee	59.3
Nigeria	petroleum	57.5
Uganda	coffee	57.1
Rwanda	coffee	57.0
Niger	peanuts	56.1
Panama	bananas	55.9
Ceylon	tea	55.1
Somalia	live animals	53.2
People's Republic of the Congo	wood	53.0
Dominican Republic	sugar	51.9
Guyana	aluminum (bauxite and alumina)	51.3
Ecuador	bananas	50.9
Burma	rice	50.1

* International Monetary Fund statistic.
Source: International Financial Statistics, various 1972 issues.

TABLE 16-3   Countries Whose Export of Two Raw Materials Made Up More Than 50 Percent of the Value of Total Exports, 1970

Country	Exports	Percent of value of total exports
Uruguay	wool and meat	69.2
Gabon	petroleum and wood	68.3
Togo	cacao and phosphates	66.3
Indonesia	petroleum and rubber	65.7
Central African Republic	diamonds and cotton	63.1
Costa Rica	bananas and coffee	60.5
El Salvador	coffee and cotton	59.7
Honduras	bananas and coffee	59.3
Senegal	peanuts and oil, and phosphates	55.9
Malawi	tobacco and tea	55.4
Egypt	cotton and rice	54.9
Peru	fishmeal and copper	53.9
Haiti	coffee and bauxite	53.7
Ivory Coast	coffee and cacao	53.7
Malaysia	rubber and tin	53.0
Bolivia	tin and antimony	50.7

Source: International Financial Statistics, *various 1972 issues.*

In the rich countries generally less than a quarter of the population depends on agriculture for a living. Even for rich countries that depend heavily on agricultural exports, the percentage of the labor force in agriculture is small. For Canada it was 11 percent in the 1960's, for Australia 12 percent, and for Denmark 24 percent. It is under 15 percent for many countries, including the United Kingdom, the United States, Belgium, West Germany, the Netherlands, and Switzerland.

Why is poverty associated with the production and export of agricultural and other raw materials? Why does not the demand for such goods expand enough to result in significant growth of production and sales at remunerative prices? There are six major reasons to explain why the demand for raw materials does not grow in proportion to the growth of income over the years.

First, if people's incomes are low, they spend a large portion of it on food. As their incomes rise, the *percentage* they spend on food falls. This means that the demand for farm products does not expand very much. And if a country seeks to grow by expanding its agriculture at a higher rate than the demand increases, the gross receipts of farmers are likely to decline.

Second, as countries grow rich they tend to shift from light industries such as textiles, shoes, and canning, to heavy industries such as engineering, chemicals, nuclear energy, and computers. As they grow still richer they shift more to the service industries such as medical, educational, and recreational services. These shifts reduce the relative importance of raw materials. With the increase of income, the demand for raw materials does not increase in proportion.

A third explanation of the lag in the growth of demand for raw materials lies in the agricultural protectionism of the rich countries; this can be seen in the protection of agriculture in the United States and the greater protection for farmers in the European Common Market.

Fourth, as countries grow rich they become more efficient in producing raw materials. This makes it increasingly difficult for the poor countries to compete with them in that sphere.

Fifth, substantial economies have been achieved in the industrial uses of raw materials. Examples are electrolytic tin plating instead of dipping sheets of iron in molten tin, and the systematic recovery and reprocessing of metals and paper.

Sixth, the industrial countries have increasingly tended to displace natural raw materials with synthetics. This has occurred with nitrates, rubber, plastics, textile fibers, sisal, leather, diamonds, and many other products.

With all these forces working against the producers of raw materials, the poor countries will have to industrialize if they wish to enjoy rising incomes.

LOW ENERGY CONSUMPTION AND LOW SOCIAL OVERHEAD CAPITAL   The rich countries consume much more energy per inhabitant than the poor countries. This is seen in Table 16-4. North America, for example, uses 35 times

TABLE 16-4   Energy Consumption in Coal Equivalent, 1970
(in pounds per person)

Area	Energy consumed
World	4,156
North America	24,077
USSR	9,779
Oceania	8,868
Europe, except eastern Europe	8,325
Central America	2,462
Middle East	1,705
South America	1,553
China	1,157
Asia except Middle East and China	1,056
Africa	686

Source: Computed from Statistical Office of the United Nations, Department of Economic and Social Affairs, Statistical Yearbook, 1971. New York: 1972, pp. 336–39.

as much energy per capita as Africa, and Europe uses five times as much as South America.

There is no direct cause-and-effect relationship between energy consumption and income. The relationship is more a reciprocal circular one. If a country has more mechanical power, it grows richer; those countries that depend mostly on hand labor are poor. If people are richer, they use more energy to heat larger homes to higher temperatures or to cool them in hot weather or climates. Energy consumption thus is both a cause of and a consequence of wealth. It also depends partly on climate; people in cold countries use more fuel for home heating than those in warm countries. With increasing wealth there can be more wasteful uses of energy, as when rich people heat their swimming pools, use air conditioners lavishly, and drive high-powered cars. But the fact remains that energy consumption reflects mechanization and industrialization, and to that extent it rises as incomes rise. High energy output is a necessary but not sufficient requirement for economic development.

The production of electricity—one of the more important types of energy—is a key requirement for economic development. It is an example of social overhead capital, a type of investment that is necessary to promote development but is unprofitable in the narrow accounting sense. Therefore, government has to provide it, for private enterprise will not. This relates to our discussion of private and social costs and benefits on page 223. There we saw that for certain types of investments, the private costs are high while most of the benefits accrue to society rather than to the entrepreneur; consequently, the government has to finance and operate such enterprises.

We can classify social overhead capital into two categories: those that are temporarily unprofitable for the private entrepreneur but can be expected to become profitable as development proceeds, and those that never generate enough profit to pay for themselves in the narrow accounting sense. The first type is illustrated by electricity. If there is not enough electricity, industry may not arise or expand; yet power plants are not built, because there is not enough industry to use the power. This impasse can be overcome by the government, which builds a power plant that is temporarily unprofitable, but will become profitable in the future as more and more industries demand more and more electric power. The same situation holds true for railroads, irrigation works, and telephone and telegraph systems.

Examples of social overhead capital investments that are necessary but unprofitable even in the long run for the private entrepreneur are schools, highways, medical facilities, some research projects, flood control, soil conservation, afforestation, and so on.

Therefore, one of the characteristics of emerging nations is that they have too little investment in social overhead capital, and they are too poor to expand such investment rapidly. Agricultural communities can, however, mobilize their surplus labor to construct social overhead capital like irrigation canals, wells, schools, roads, health clinics, sanitary facilities, and so on; these necessary projects will not be accomplished by private enterprise.

OTHER CHARACTERISTICS OF EMERGING NATIONS Birth rates in the poor countries are very much higher than in the rich, as indicated in Table 13-4 on page 286. As we saw in Chapter 13, high birth rates may handicap the drive toward economic development. But poverty helps cause high birth rates; with affluence these rates tend to fall sharply. We may therefore have an interdependence in the inverse relationship between birth rates and economic development.

People in the rich countries have far more education and a higher rate of literacy than people in the poor countries do. Although the statistics on illiteracy rates are fragmentary and incomplete, the available contrasts are clear. Most rich countries have illiteracy rates below 10 percent of the population. Most poor countries have rates that vary from 50 to 97 percent.

Here a word of caution is essential. A close relationship between literacy and high income does not prove a cause-and-effect relationship. It means merely that these factors occur together. Perhaps rich countries can afford more education, and the literacy results from high incomes rather than causes them. Certainly if we could teach most of the people of a poor country to read and write within three months, they would not automatically become rich. There are other requirements that must be met to increase a country's income. But education helps if countries seek wealth through developing modern industry, science, technology, and commerce. Rising literacy and rising incomes are interdependent and cumulative.

As a final overview of the process of economic development we present Table 16-5, which was developed by Hollis B. Chenery. The table shows that fundamental structural changes occur with growth and affect the rate of growth. There is in fact an interaction, a cumulative change: as resources are reallocated to new uses, economic growth occurs; as growth proceeds, resources have to be reallocated to new uses.

We see in Table 16-5 that as countries grow richer, the percentages of income or output saved and invested (lines 1 and 2) grow larger; the amounts saved and invested grow even larger than the percentages because of the growing absolute level of per capita income. The percentage of income collected in taxes (line 3) grows at first with rising income, and then it seems to level off. The percentage of school-age children in school (line 4) and the adult literacy rate (line 5) rise.

In the second part of Table 16-5, output composition, the share of production accounted for by primary products, or raw materials (line 6), falls as output rises. The amount of raw materials produced rises, however, with rising income; this can be checked by multiplying the primary share of gross domestic product by the per capita GNP in every column.

The industry share of gross domestic product (line 7) rises sharply as

TABLE 16-5 Variations in Economic Structure with Level of Development, 100 Countries, 1950–65

	GNP per capita (in 1964 U.S. dollars)				
	100	200	400	800	2000
I. Accumulation					
1. Gross national saving as percentage of GNP	12.0	14.8	17.6	20.5	24.6
2. Gross domestic investment as percentage of GDP *	15.1	18.2	20.8	23.0	25.4
3. Tax revenue as percentage of national income	12.7	16.7	21.8	28.0	28.0
4. School enrollment ratio	36.2	52.6	66.9	78.9	91.4
5. Adult literacy rate	36.5	55.2	71.5	85.4	93.0
II. Output Composition					
6. Primary † share of GDP	46.4	36.0	26.7	18.6	9.8
7. Industry share of GDP	13.5	19.6	25.5	31.4	38.9
8. Service share of GDP	34.6	37.9	39.9	40.5	39.3
9. Utilities share of GDP	5.7	7.0	8.3	9.7	11.7
III. Population and Labor Force					
10. Primary labor as percentage of total labor force	68.1	58.7	43.6	28.6	8.3
11. Industrial labor as percentage of total labor force	9.6	16.6	23.4	30.7	40.1
12. Utilities and service labor as percentage of total	22.3	26.7	31.7	39.2	51.6
13. Urban population as percentage of total population	20.0	33.8	45.5	55.3	65.1
14. Birth rate per 1,000 people	41.8	36.6	31.1	25.3	17.1
IV. Trade					
15. Exports of goods and services as percentage of GDP	13.2	16.3	19.1	21.8	24.8
16. Imports of goods and services as percentage of GDP	18.7	20.6	22.3	23.8	25.5
17. Primary exports as percentage of total exports	78	68	56	46	33
18. Primary imports as percentage of total imports	18	25	28	30	30

* Gross domestic product
† Primary production is production of raw materials, mostly agricultural.
Source: Finance and Development, Vol. 8, No. 3 (September 1971), p. 19.

countries grow richer, and the service and utilities shares (lines 8 and 9) rise more slowly.

In the third section of the table, the percentage of the labor force producing raw materials (line 10) falls sharply as average income rises. The percentages of the labor force in industry and utilities (lines 11 and 12) rise, as does the percentage of the population living in cities (line 13); urbanization is an important part of the process of economic development. Birth rates (line 14) fall as countries grow richer.

Finally, the last part of Table 16-5 tells us that as countries grow rich, both exports and imports of goods and services (lines 15 and 16) increase as a percentage of output. While the exports of raw materials (line 17) as a percentage of total exports falls, the amount rises. We can see this operating in the United States over the years. In 1860 we exported raw materials worth $229 million, and they made up 72 percent of all our exports of merchandise. In 1960 we exported $4.2 billion worth of raw materials, but they made up only 21 percent of our exports.

Finally, in the last line of Table 16-5 we see that as per capita income rises, the imports of primary products rise as a percentage of total imports, but they finally cease rising at the highest level of income.

Theories of Economic Development

SCHUMPETER: THE ROLE OF THE ENTREPRENEUR Joseph A. Schumpeter (1883–1950) believed that the entrepreneur is the key figure, the prime mover, in economic development. He is not necessarily the capitalist (although he may assume that role also), who provides the capital for investment; therefore, he is not the risk-taker. He is the innovator, the man who does things in new and better ways. The entrepreneur is not an inventor, but he puts the inventions to work. He spurs economic development in five possible ways. First, he introduces a new good, that is, one with which consumers are not yet familiar, like the automobile; or he introduces a variation of a familiar good, like toys made out of plastic materials instead of wood or metal. Second, the entrepreneur introduces a new method of production or a new way of handling a commodity commercially; an example would be the basic oxygen process for making steel, which was much more efficient than the old methods and required large new investments to modernize the old steel mills. Third, the entrepreneur opens new markets, like selling refrigerators in Africa and transistor radios throughout the underdeveloped world. Fourth, he opens new sources of supply of raw materials, such as the oil fields in the Middle East. Fifth, he reorganizes industry, such as creating a monopoly or breaking up a monopoly to make room for himself. An outstanding example of the first case was the creation of the United States Steel Corporation in 1901 by combining many large and small steel companies. An example of the breaking up of a monopoly was the decline of the railroad with the rise of trucking for carrying freight, and buses and airplanes for passengers. The entrepreneurs are the driving force behind economic development.

According to Schumpeter, not all heads of business enterprises are entrepreneurs. Most of them do perfunctory work, like assigning people to their tasks, supervising them, and maintaining discipline. Such business leaders are in a rut, and they work out of habit; they do what is familiar, routine, and tested by experience. Only a few are daring enough to experiment with new ideas. The lure is profits. If the entrepreneur is successful, he will receive profits; but a host of imitators follow where he pioneered, and under the force of competition profits soon disappear, to reappear elsewhere under new and different prioneering successes. As Schumpeter says,

[Profit] slips from the entrepreneur's grasp as soon as the entrepreneurial function is performed. It attaches to the creation of new things, to the realisation of the future value system. It is at the same time the child and the victim of development. Without development there is no profit, without profit no development. For the capitalist system it must be added further that without profit there would be no accumulation of wealth (*The Theory of Economic Development* [New York: Oxford University Press, 1961], pp. 153–54).

Schumpeter was writing only about capitalistic economic development. Although he was devoted to capitalism and its institutions, he was detached enough to recognize that his analysis was not based on any value judgment about the virtues of the entrepreneurial system.

It may, therefore, not be superfluous to point out that our analysis of the rôle of the entrepreneur does not involve any "glorification" of the type, as some readers of the first edition of this book seemed to think. We do hold that entrepreneurs *have* an economic function as distinguished from, say, robbers. But we neither style every entrepreneur a genius or a benefactor to humanity, nor do we wish to express any opinion about the comparative merits of the social organisation in which he plays his rôle, or about the question whether what he does could not be effected more cheaply or efficiently in other ways (*The Theory of Economic Development*, p. 90).

Others have drawn from Schumpeter the conclusions that he wished to avoid. They glorified the entrepreneur, saying that without him economic development would lag. According to them, a major reason for underdevelopment is that the poor countries have been unable to produce enough qualified entrepreneurs.

To illustrate these fallacious arguments, we shall quote from a prominent theorist on economic development:

Let us say one word about the relationship of the Schumpeter theory to the problems of underdeveloped areas. Tautological though the theory may be, there can be little doubt of its relevance. The lack of adequate entrepreneurship is one of the most frequently cited obstacles to take-off in such countries. . . . Schumpeter's theory also raises doubts about the possibilities of successful development in countries which *start* with a climate inimical to entrepreneurship, as is the case in many of the underdeveloped countries. . . . It may be possible for the entrepreneurial function to be performed by government agencies instead of by private individuals, but the Schumpeter theory would throw some doubt on this possibility (Benjamin Higgins, *Economic Development: Principles, Problems, and Policies*, 2nd ed. [New York: W. W. Norton, 1968], p. 105).

To demonstrate how development can proceed without the profit-seeking entrepreneur, it is interesting to note that in both a planned East German economy and a "free" West German economy, industrial production increased 53 percent from 1963 to 1970. During the same period industrial production increased 75 percent in the U.S.S.R. and 39 percent in the United States.

Entrepreneurship among the indigenous people in the colonies was frequently thwarted by the dominant powers. Poverty and lack of education kept people from seizing business opportunities when they appeared. Thus, in 1954 the British in Kenya spent £5 on every African child in school and £84 on every European child. Until 1950 the British prohibited the Africans from growing coffee, and after that the Africans—but not the Europeans—had to get a license for doing so. Africans were not permitted to sell tea for cash, even on the local market, and were thereby kept in a barter economy. African growers of maize received less for their product from the Kenya Maize Marketing Board than did European farmers. African traders were restricted to back-country rural areas, and they were severely limited in the credit they were allowed, even if the lenders were willing to extend credit to them; therefore, they had to buy at retail in order to sell at retail. Africans were not permitted to engage in manufacturing without a license, and licenses were not granted if the government decided that increased competition was "uneconomic."

Indigenous entrepreneurship is sometimes stifled by foreign businessmen even now in independent countries. The representative of a giant foreign firm in Peru thought it was perfectly proper for each foreign businessman in Peru to give his business of insuring, shipping, advertising, and selling on commission to his fellow nationals rather than to Peruvians.

Schumpeter's theory of economic development is probably less relevant to the poor countries now than it was to the rise and evolution of entrepreneurial societies in the West.

BARAN: THE MARXIST ANALYSIS Paul A. Baran (1909–64) believed that economic development depends on the class struggle. Society has to be transformed, and as always, certain classes and groups obstruct basic change, while others advance it. Today we have proof, said Baran, that an economy based on comprehensive economic planning can function and grow without the benefits of private enterprise. The dominant interests in the advanced capitalist countries are inimical to economic development in the poor countries because the latter are indispensable as the hinterlands of capitalism, supplying it with cheap raw materials, profits, and investment outlets.

In addition to the interrelated political problems of class struggle and imperialism, the underdeveloped countries must consider the problem of the economic surplus. A country's *actual* economic surplus is identical with current saving or accumulation; it is the difference between society's current output and its current consumption. A country's *potential* economic surplus is the difference between the output that could be produced in a given natural and technological environment and what might be regarded as essential consumption. According to Baran, the actual surplus is less than the potential because of (1) excess consumption by the rich and middle classes; (2) output lost to society because of unproductive workers—advertisers, tax-evasion specialists, makers of armaments, and so forth; (3) output lost because of the irrational and wasteful organization of the existing productive apparatus; and (4) output lost because of unemployment caused by the anarchy of capitalist production and the lack of effective demand.

Potential economic surplus can become *planned* economic surplus in a comprehensive socialist society. A socialist community guided by reason and science can use its resources to expand investment and production most efficiently, while at the same time pursuing a scientific policy of conservation of human and natural resources. The guiding force is not profit maximization, but a rational plan reflecting society's preferred balance of current and future consumption.

According to Baran, the rate and direction of economic development in a country at a given time depend on the size of the economic surplus and how it is used. The surpluses drawn from countries such as India by the dominant powers could have gone far in promoting economic development if they had been invested in the countries that produced them. The present problems in the poor countries are that the actual economic surpluses are much smaller than the potential surpluses, and much of the surplus is wasted in lavish consumption rather than used to promote development. This surplus, while small in *absolute* terms, is a large *share* of total output—as large as, if not larger than, in advanced capitalist countries. It must be invested under government planning for maximum impact.

Baran offered several observations on problems of development. A land reform that merely breaks up large estates is inadvisable because it will simply increase the peasantry's consumption and because small inefficient holdings will keep production down; large-scale farming is required for economic development. The increase of Western assets in the underdeveloped part of the world is only partly due to capital exports in the strict sense of the term; it is primarily the result of the reinvestment abroad of some of the economic surpluses secured abroad. Businesses are established by foreign corporations in poor countries to facilitate exploitation by foreign merchant capitalism. Some native merchants emerge within the orbit of foreign capital, and they use their influence to perpetuate the status quo. Native industrialists and feudal landowners also oppose change, and thus foreign exploitation is continued while popular movements for social and national liberation are suppressed—at least temporarily. But ultimately the property of foreign and domestic capitalists and landowners must be expropriated. Economic development will then proceed simultaneously by industrialization and the improvement of agriculture.

Baran's analysis neglects certain key issues that have not been honestly faced by most of the present rulers of the communist countries. First, how can a national economic plan follow the desires and needs of society rather than the whims of the governing elite? Second, why have economic difficulties continued to plague the development process in the communist countries, such as the lag in sugar production in Cuba? Third, how can the centralization of economic decisions and organization be made to serve a broadening political democracy? Finally, is the distribution of income as equitable as it might be, or are more equal incomes incompatible with incentives to produce? These are some of the unsolved problems of Marxist societies.

NURKSE: BALANCED DEVELOPMENT   Ragnar Nurkse (1907–59) proposed that the dichotomy between demand and supply is applicable to the accumulation of capital. Capital formation is not entirely a matter of the supply of capital or saving, although this is the more important part of the problem. There may be a snag on the demand side as well. The inducement to invest is limited by the size of the market, and the size of the market is limited by poverty.

Countries are poor because they are poor; it is a vicious circle. The supply of capital is governed by the ability and willingness to save; the demand is governed by the incentives to invest. A circular relationship exists on both sides of the problem of capital formation in the poverty-ridden areas of the world. On the supply side, the lack of capital results in low productivity, low income, and low saving. On the demand side, low productivity results in low incomes, low buying power, and, therefore, low inducement to invest.

Nurkse argued that if poor countries are to advance, they must rely increasingly on industrialization instead of primarily on the production and export of raw materials. Manufactured goods could be produced for export to the rich industrial countries, or for sale at home, although Nurkse said that exports to the rich industrial countries offer little hope of success.

We can appreciate this gloomy conclusion of Nurkse's when we look at the trade policies of the rich nations, for they frequently discriminate against the poor. Tariffs and taxes on tropical agricultural products such as coffee, tea, and cocoa in European countries are revenue-raising measures at the expense of the emerging nations. (See Figure 5-13 on page 115, which shows that under certain conditions a tax on a commodity will fall on the producer.) Agricultural production both in Europe and the United States often works to the great disadvantage of underdeveloped countries; the protection of domestic sugar beet production is an outstanding example. The developed countries also protect their manufacturing industries. The more processing is involved in the production of a good, the higher the tariffs. To illustrate this tendency, we shall give three examples of

United States tariff rates as of 1972; these are the lowest rates applicable under our international agreements.

The poor countries produce 38 percent of the world's supply of iron ore. There are no tariffs on our imports of iron ore, pig and cast iron, and iron or steel waste or scrap. Bars of wrought iron pay a tariff of $10 per ton to $10 plus 2 percent of their value. Forgings and bars of iron and steel pay 6 to 9.5 percent of their value. Cast iron pipes pay 10 to 12 percent. Thumb tacks pay $32 per ton, steel wool pays $40 per ton plus 6 percent, and common straight pins pay 20 percent. Ball and roller bearings pay 7 percent of their value to $40 a ton plus 9 percent.

All of the world's natural rubber is produced in the poor countries. We admit crude and scrap natural rubber without duty. As of 1972, auto and bicycle tires pay 4 to 5 percent of their value. Rubber bathing caps pay 6 percent, and rubber gloves pay 5 to 35 percent. Rubber toys and balls pay 7.5 to 17.5 percent. In case an emerging nation would produce rubber combs and sell them to us, we have singled that out for especially prohibitive tariffs. If the comb is worth 3 cents or less, the duty is .2 cents and 5 percent of its value; if the comb is worth more than 3 cents, the duty is .7 cents and 12 percent.

The poor countries produce 62 percent of the world's output of cotton. We impose no duty on cotton and cotton waste, although we limit the quantities that may enter the country. As of 1972, cotton yarn pays 3.4 percent of its value to 3.6 cents per pound and 13 percent duty. Cotton cloth not fancy, figured, bleached, or colored pays 5.9 percent; if bleached, 7.8 percent; if colored, 9.7 percent; if fancy, figured, and colored, 11.2 percent. Cotton handkerchiefs not hemmed, fancy, figured, or colored pay 17.5 percent; if hemmed, 25 percent; if fancy, figured, or colored and hemmed, 25 percent. Cotton gloves pay 25 percent. Cotton shirts, blouses, dresses, and underwear pay 35 to 42.5 percent of their value.

Many other examples exist of protection for our processing of raw materials. All our economic aid to the poor countries is minor compared with the benefits they could receive if we did not try to prevent them from manufacturing goods and selling them to us.

The rich countries generally give equal treatment to all countries, rich and poor, in their trade policies. That is, if the United States has a tariff on the imports of a manufactured product, the same rate of tariff will apply to the imports from Germany and India. As an Indian official pointed out, "Equality of treatment is equitable only among equals."

The poor countries have long pleaded for tariff preferences for a limited number of years to enable them to attract capital and promote industry. They ask that tariffs on goods imported by rich nations should apply to goods originating in other rich areas but should not be imposed on goods coming from emerging countries. The European Common Market has suggested a few steps in this direction, but other countries are temporizing, insisting on many exceptions to this principle. The United States, for example, objects to tariff preferences for textiles, shoes, petroleum products, and certain agricultural commodities.

Now we can begin to understand why Nurkse saw little hope of the emerging nations greatly expanding their export of manufactured goods to the rich, industrial nations. Increasing the sale of manufactured goods at home requires a simultaneous advance in domestic agriculture for two reasons: farmers have to supply food to sustain the expanding industrial labor force, and farmers have to be able to buy the increasing flow of products from industry.

There has to be a similar balance development within the industrial sector. By itself a single industry cannot create sufficient demand for its own output. If you put up a shoe factory in a country where the people are too poor to buy shoes, perhaps your employees could afford them, but that would not justify building the plant. The same is true with a shirt factory, a hand-tool factory, a bedding factory, a factory making household utensils, and so on. Each business, considered by itself, would be unprofitable. But if all were built together, the workers in all would have higher incomes than formerly and could buy the output of each plant. Balanced expansion can accelerate the overall rate of growth of output. Once the vicious circle of stagnation is broken, the circular relationships tend toward cumulative advance.

In underdeveloped countries, Nurkse believed, the forces that could defeat the grip of economic stagnation must be deliberately organized through some central direction or collective enterprise. The actual investing could be undertaken by private enterprise, although the state might enforce compulsory saving and then coordinate investment. The deficiency of demand arises only in the private sector of the economy. For the economy as a whole there is, of course, no deficiency in the demand for capital. A shoe factory, for example, may not sell its output if people are too poor to buy shoes. But a government can have an unlimited demand for schools, hospitals, power plants, railroads, and so on. Therefore, most underdeveloped countries will need a combination of private and government action in saving and investment. Each country must work out its own combination according to its particular needs and opportunities.

It should be added that the difficulty of Nurkse's approach is that balanced development requires large amounts of capital that the poor countries have difficulty acquiring. Furthermore, exporting the surplus of efficient plants that cannot sell their whole output at home would permit unbalanced development.

MYRDAL: CRITIC OF THE STATUS QUO   Gunnar Myrdal (born 1898) believes that standard economic theory does not explain the reality of underdevelopment and the need for development. He argues that ever since Adam

Smith's time, economists have been justifying the status quo. The unrealistic assumptions that conceal their ideology are harmony of interests, equilibrium, laissez faire, and free trade. With these they explain away the large and growing international inequality.

The interests of the rich and the poor countries are not necessarily harmonious, according to Myrdal. Economic theorists assume, for example, that capital movements counteract international inequalities. Labor is abundant and cheap in the poor countries, and scarce and dear in the rich; capital is scarce and dear in the poor countries, and abundant and cheap in the rich. Therefore, labor will migrate from the poor to the rich countries, and capital will move from the rich to the poor. But it does not work that way. Immigration has been restricted by the rich countries, and capital does not rush to the poor countries even though rates of return are high.

Myrdal asserts that the harmony of interests is a basic predilection of economic theory, and it is a comforting thought for those who have drawn a lucky number in life's lottery. This doctrine identifies "what is" with "what ought to be." Conservative economic ideology has concluded, for example, that inequality of income serves both rich and poor because it leads to greater saving and investment, and ultimately to higher incomes for all. Myrdal denies this, saying that inequality is an obstacle to development. The rich in the poor countries squander their incomes on conspicuous consumption, conspicuous investment such as fancy office buildings, and in capital being sent out of the country. The poor need more consumption to improve their nutrition, health, housing, and education. Such consumption will enable people to be more productive. Therefore, consumption becomes, not an alternative to investment and economic development as standard theory says, but a means to promote development.

Myrdal further criticizes the standard concept that the economy in all its aspects tends toward stable equilibrium. On the contrary, he states, there is cumulative growth and cumulative stagnation unless something is done to narrow the income gap. He uses the following example to illustrate this idea: a factory burns down and is not rebuilt in the same community. As workers lose their jobs, incomes and the demand for goods decline. Unemployment spreads and the city's economy spirals downward. Businesses move out and young people leave. As incomes shrink and the average age of the population increases, tax rates have to be raised. Public services deteriorate, bus lines shrink, the community becomes less attractive, and the stagnation feeds on itself to make things worse until something happens or something is done to halt and reverse the process.

This cumulative process also works if the initial change is for the better. The decision, for instance, to locate an industry in a particular community gives a spur to its general development. Employment expands, incomes rise, local businesses flourish, and labor and capital are attracted from outside to exploit the expanding opportunities. Local tax rates fall, and the amount and quality of public services increase.

Thus, the play of market forces normally tends to increase rather than to decrease the inequalities between regions. Stable equilibrium is illusory. The American myth, says Myrdal, is based on an upward spiral: "Nothing succeeds like success." But, he adds, the reverse is also true: "Nothing fails like failure." The Bible gives a perfect expression to this folk wisdom: "For unto every one that hath shall be given, and he shall have abundance: but from him that hath not shall be taken away even that which he hath" (Matthew 25:29).

Standard economic theory is predisposed toward laissez faire; consequently, inequalities of income in the poor countries are great and are growing greater. The rich countries have diverged considerably from laissez faire to ameliorate social conditions, but this has not happened in the poor countries. The latter cannot afford egalitarian and welfare policies. They do, however, need more national economic planning to give an upward push to economic development. Government in the emerging nations will have to take over many functions that in most developed countries are left to private business. It must plan to increase investment, raise productivity in agriculture, improve the levels of health, education, and training of working people, and so on.

The free-trade doctrine that is so deeply embedded in orthodox economic theory serves the rich countries but not the poor, according to Myrdal. Established industries will impede not only the new industries of the emerging nations, but also the old industries and handicrafts. This process can be seen in the hampering of industrial growth of underdeveloped areas within countries, as in southern Italy and the southern states of the United States. Under free trade and laissez faire, poor countries and regions remain agricultural and poor, while the rich grow richer. The producers of raw materials employ mostly unskilled labor; they face inelastic demand in the export markets; and the demand does not increase much. Price fluctuations of raw materials are excessive. In the rich countries, any increase in efficiency in producing manufactured goods tends to increase the incomes of the producers. Improvements in the efficiency of production of raw materials in the poor countries tends to reduce prices, passing the benefits on to the rich. The free-trade doctrine is incompatible with the need to mobilize scarce foreign exchange for high-priority uses to serve the goals of development. For example, the import of luxury consumer goods has to be restricted to permit more imports of capital goods.

Protectionism, says Myrdal, is necessary for the emerging countries to industrialize. Many manufacturing industries are thwarted in their growth or prevented from ever coming into existence because of the small size of the domestic market. Local industries can be given their chance by protecting them against foreign competition. Moreover, every new industrial enterprise benefits the economy as a whole, although this benefit does not enter into the calculation of profit. Yet the country that uses protectionism to promote development must be judicious in protecting only those industries with which it has the greatest chances of success. In the long run, according to Myrdal, a dynamic theory of comparative advantage can and should operate within the framework of state economic planning for development.

Myrdal claims that the underdeveloped countries need tough, radical reforms. They must break up inegalitarian and rigid economic and social stratification. Not much has come out of all the talk about land and tenancy reforms. Even when legislated, they have mostly been mini-reforms or an outright sham. Recommendations for land reform from Western developed countries are now dying down. The discussion by their experts and officials are increasingly centered only on technological improvements. Thus, the developed countries are now strengthening the powerful vested interests that have been delaying or stopping land reform in the underdeveloped countries.

The poor countries need to promote industrialization that will give impetus to agricultural development. They need additional investment in labor-intensive village projects, such as the construction of roads, bridges, irrigation canals, soil conservation terraces, warehouses, drainage ditches, wells and water tanks, afforestation, and pasture improvement. They also need consumer projects, such as construction of school buildings, dispensaries, village privies, and gutters. They have to clean their wells and kill their rats. These presuppose collective organization and action, says Myrdal.

The poor countries should gear some of their industrialization toward meeting other requirements of agriculture. They should expand the production of fertilizers, pesticides, agricultural machinery, and other agricultural implements.

The underdeveloped countries should avoid going into debt to foreigners. Their total external debts rose from $10 billion in 1950 to $40 billion in 1965. Annual payments of interest and amortization over the same period rose from $0.8 billion to $3.6 billion. In the middle 1950's, less than 4 percent of their exports had to be used for debt service payments. By 1965 the proportion had risen to 9 percent. (By the end of 1969 their external debts rose to $53 billion, annual payments rose to $5.2 billion, and 11 percent of their exports was used for servicing their debts.) Poor countries should rely more on mobilizing their own resources for economic development rather than depend on foreign loans.

The emerging nations, especially in Latin America, should get more of their direct private investments from countries that are smaller and farther away than the United States. Other governments will be less tempted and less able to use political or military strength to defend the interests of their investing concerns. Dispersed in this way, the foreign investments would cause less fear of intrusion on the independence of an underdeveloped country where investments are made. For the same reasons, more of the direct investments should be carried out by firms that are not as large as most of those from the United States that are now involved in foreign investments.

Education, says Myrdal, is a very important factor in the development process. In most former colonies, education has not changed much from the earlier colonial pattern. The colonial governments neglected popular education while building up an educated elite who were taught to become "deskmen" and to avoid soiling their hands. This policy helped preserve the barrier between an entrenched upper class and the masses of people. Importance was placed on passing examinations and acquiring status, while practical training for life and work was ignored. What is required is the liquidation of illiteracy, the extension of adult education, the expansion of technical, vocational, and professional training, and especially a policy of increasing the number and qualifications of trained teachers.

Myrdal also advocates the spread of birth control among the masses of people. Corruption must be stamped out and stricter social responsibility enforced. Taxation of income and wealth has to be reformed and enforced. Economic and political power has to be shifted from the ruling elite toward the lower strata of society.

Summary

Most countries in Asia, Africa, and Latin America are poor; Australia and New Zealand and most countries in Europe and North America are rich.

The poor countries generally rely heavily on the production and export of raw materials. They produce and use little energy per person. Birth rates are high, education and literacy are low, saving is low both in percentages of income and in absolute amounts. The poor countries also have low investment in social overhead capital—projects that are necessary and useful, but are unprofitable in the narrow accounting sense, such as schools, medical facilities, flood control, and soil conservation. Other projects are likely to be unprofitable in the early stages of development, but they may become profitable later on, such as railroads, irrigation works, and telephone and telegraph systems.

Why are so many countries poor? There have been many theories to explain it. Some say that countries remain poor when they do not produce enough qualified entrepreneurs to promote business enterprises. Marxists claim that the economic surplus is wasted by the rich and by the irrational organization of the system of private enterprise; this surplus could be used for better purposes to increase production. Ragnar Nurkse emphasized the vicious circle of poverty, which means that countries are poor because they are trapped and thwarted by poverty. He also thought that balanced development on a broad front would create a domestic market for the increased output by raising incomes simultaneously with increased output. Gunnar Myrdal, as a critic of the *status quo*, denied that there is necessarily a harmony of interests between the rich and the poor countries; nor did he believe that the economy tends toward stable equilibrium or that the differences in income between rich and poor countries will tend to disappear under free markets and free trade. He urged the poor countries to undertake tough, radical reforms if they want to move toward economic development.

This completes our analysis of some major economic problems. You can now go forth and find additional problems. A much more exciting, and more difficult, task is to seek solutions.

QUESTIONS AND PROBLEMS

1   Should the United States have a foreign aid program? Why or why not?

2   What is meant by *imperialism?* Do you agree with the concept?

3   Most of the former colonies gained their independence during the two decades following the end of the Second World War. Do you think their poverty and underdevelopment can still be blamed on colonialism and imperialism?

4   Suppose you were asked to draw up a plan for the economic development of a poor country. What would you look at, and what kinds of recommendations might you suggest?

5   Why is it considered to be a disadvantage for a country to rely heavily on the export of raw materials?

6   Why cannot the emerging nations follow the path the rich countries took in promoting economic development?

7   The rate of earnings on investment in the poor countries is much higher than in the rich; why does our capital flow mostly toward the latter?

8   Is industrialization essential for economic development, or can agriculture provide the basis for it?

9   Why are incomes in agriculture generally lower than incomes in industry?

10   Look at the courses offered at your college or university. Which of them would be appropriate for schools in emerging nations? Which courses are not offered at your school but would be appropriate for schools in emerging nations?

11   Are there any disadvantages in economic growth and development?

12 What principles and ideas have you learned in standard economic theory that may not be appropriate for underdeveloped countries?

13 What are the obstacles to economic development in the poor countries?

BIBLIOGRAPHY

BARAN, PAUL A., *The Political Economy of Growth*. New York: Monthly Review Press, 1957.

FRANK, ANDRE GUNDAR, *Latin America: Underdevelopment or Revolution*. New York: Monthly Review Press, 1969.

MEIER, GERALD M., ed., *Leading Issues in Development Economics*. New York: Oxford University Press, 1964.

MYRDAL, GUNNAR, *The Challenge of World Poverty*. New York: Pantheon, 1970.

———, *Rich Lands and Poor*. New York: Harper & Row, 1957.

NURKSE, RAGNAR, *Problems of Capital Formation in Underdeveloped Countries and Patterns of Trade and Development*. New York: Oxford University Press, 1967.

OSER, JACOB, *Promoting Economic Development, with Illustrations from Kenya*. Evanston, Ill.: Northwestern University Press, 1967.

RHODES, ROBERT I., ed., *Imperialism and Underdevelopment: A Reader*. New York: Monthly Review Press, 1970.

SCHUMPETER, JOSEPH A., *The Theory of Economic Development*. New York: Oxford University Press, 1961. (Originally published in German in 1911.)

SINGER, H. W., *International Development: Growth and Change*. New York: McGraw-Hill, 1964.

INDEX

INDEX

Italic page numbers refer to tables and figures.

competitive firm, 131; and monopoly, 136; and oligopoly, *134;* and prices, 123; and production decisions, 103
Profits: definition of, 158, 171; and economic development of poor countries, 343; and inflation, 181–82; and investment decisions, 60, 78–79; and monopoly, 136; and production decisions, 59, 212; of public utilities, 219–20; and role of entrepreneur, 352–53; sources of, 158–60; and total costs, 100–01; and urban rent, 151
Progressive income taxes, 183–85 (*see also* Income taxes); as automatic stabilizer, 199
Progress and Poverty (George), 160
Property taxes: advantages and disadvantages, 185; and price of land, 152
Proportional tax, 183
Prosperity, 53
Protectionism (*see also* Tariffs): administrative, 333–34; and economic development, 360–61; and employment, 321; vs. free trade, 331–34
Psychological effects of poverty, 249
Public opinion: and regulation of utilities, 219–20; of unions, 237
Public policy (*see also* Fiscal policy; Monetary policy; Stabilization policy): and balance of payments equilibrium, 326–27, 330–31; in depressions, 50; and gold standard, 65; and normative vs. positive economists, 8; restriction of agricultural output, 115–16; and simultaneous inflation and unemployment, 56–59, 182–83
Public utilities: and borrowing, 191; government regulation of, 204, 216–20, 227; profits on investment in, 159
Purchasing power, and money, 64–65
Pure food and drug laws, 203

Quality of goods and services, and national income accounting, 23
Quality of life, and national income accounting, 224–25

Quantity theory of money, and equation of exchange, 80–81
Quotas on imports, 215, 334

Race: persons below poverty level by, 248, *249;* and poverty, 250–52; and residence, *262,* 263
Radical economics, 7, 9
Rail network system, 268
Rationing, and prices, 119
Raw material producers, 344–48, 356–58; and comparative advantage theory, 320; with exports of one raw material comprising more than 50 percent of total exports, *346;* with exports of two raw materials comprising more than 50 percent of total exports, *347*
Raw materials, processing of, 357
Real estate taxes, urban and suburban, 269–70
Real income, and inflation, 181
Recessions: and inflation, 197; of 1970–71, 182–83; and tax cuts, 191–92
Regressiveness in taxation, 184
Relatively elastic demand, 111, *112*
Relatively inelastic demand, *110*
Rent (*see also* Rent theory): arising from intensive cultivation, *150;* increases in, 289; and single tax theory, 160–61, 171
Rent theory (*see also* Rent): and definition of rent, 147–48; and law of diminishing returns and intensive cultivation, 149–51; and price of land, 151–52; and rent arising from extensive cultivation, *148, 149;* and urban rent, 151
Residential home construction, during Great Depression, 179
Resource allocation: and advertising, 141; in market economy, 121–22; and microeconomics compared with macroeconomics, 6–7; and military spending, 28
Retail business, waste and inefficiency in, 122
Retirement benefits, and saving, 39
Revenue sharing. *See* Federal revenue sharing
Ricardo, David, 147
Right-to-work laws, 233–34